MANAGEMENT CHALLENGES IN
CANADIAN FEDERAL CORRECTIONS

MANAGEMENT CHALLENGES IN CANADIAN FEDERAL CORRECTIONS

Margaret Jackson, Sherry A. Mumford,
and Monica Jobe-Armstrong

SIMON FRASER UNIVERSITY
PUBLICATIONS

MANAGEMENT CHALLENGES IN CANADIAN FEDERAL CORRECTIONS
Copyright © 2009 by SFU Publications

Library and Archives Canada Cataloguing in Publication

Jackson, Margaret, 1942-
    Management challenges in Canadian federal corrections / Margaret Jackson, Sherry A. Mumford, and Monica Jobe-Armstrong.

Includes bibliographical references.
ISBN 978-0-86941-300-5

1. Corrections--Canada--Administration--Textbooks.
2. Correctional Service Canada--Management--Textbooks.
I. Margaret Jackson II. Mumford, Sherry Anne III. Jobe-Armstrong, Monica.

HV9506.J32 2008   365.068   C2008-906785-1

Printed in Canada by Hignell Book Printing
Cover design by Greg Holoboff
Book Design and Typesetting by Robert D. MacNevin

Simon Fraser University Publications
1300 West Mall Centre
8888 University Drive
Burnaby, British Columbia v5A 1s6
Canada

FSC

Mixed Sources
Product group from well-managed forests, controlled sources and recycled wood or fibre

Cert no. SW-COC-003438
www.fsc.org
© 1996 Forest Stewardship Council

SFU PUBLICATIONS

Contents

Preface

I did not originally set out to write a book. I was fortunate enough to be invited to lunch by Dr. Margaret Jackson to discuss renewing material for a Criminology course that had been offered through Simon Fraser University. I count that as one of my luckiest days. It allowed me to venture down a path filled with opportunities and challenges in terms of the new lessons it offered and the interesting people I had the privilege to meet. This was not a journey I could do on my own, so I was again quite fortunate that my colleague Monica was able to commit the tremendous time needed to writing some of the chapters of this book and that she has a great love of the endless possibilities associated with the production of a book of this type.

After many discussions with Margaret where she offered her encouragement and insight, it became clear to me that this book needed to become a living account of what transpires in the Correctional Service of Canada (CSC) through the eyes of those involved with the daily operations of such facilities. Certainly, there was an abundance of material and great pieces of work that we could draw upon to put together what we hoped would be a clear, concise account of how decisions are made at the level of the CSC administrator. But it was the desire to have something truly dynamic that inspired me to suggest we interview as many CSC administrators as we could, selecting them from sites across Canada. That would add a certain breath of fresh air to the more abstract information we would provide in the book.

Arranging the interviews, however, presented quite a challenge to us both in terms of settling on dates and times and on contacting various people. But we forged on with questions and tape recorders in hand, and managed to capture some excellent perspectives and, in some cases, quite profound messages, which we hope to have incorporated into this book. This provided the extraordinary interplay between the written expectations of CSC and the living reality of the various administrators' roles reflected in those interviews, which ultimately affects front line staff and inmates/offenders alike.

This book is a document that should provide you with an opportunity to learn from the writings of scholars, legislators, and law makers, while tempering those written words with the spoken words of individuals whose role it is to apply them in their everyday work lives. It presents an opportunity to look at commonalities among administrators and agreement about the written word, but it also provides evidence of some real struggles and disagreements between that which is said to be true (the written word) and the application of that "truth" in real life situations. It is with this in mind that we encourage and challenge you to venture forth, read the book, and use it to help form your ideas and knowledge around the operation of corrections in Canada. We hope it will engender you to ask questions, challenge perceptions, and ultimately help to shape your own views on the nature and notion of incarceration in Canada.

— *Sherry Mumford*

This book began as an idea about how to teach corrections at a university level; it has grown, tree-like, to its present form. As described above by Sherry, its seed evolved in discussions with her while she was teaching an upper level online course on the administration of prisons for which I became responsible. We thought that the administration of prisons was a reasonably dry subject taken on its own and that many theory books about this subject did not engage students enough, likely because these books relied mostly on facts and figures plus long excerpts from legislation, law and other such material. In revising the online course, the idea of including the voice of actual CSC administrators emerged. The course would combine interviews with administrative staff with theory. It was also viewed as a great idea for a new format to teach advanced students about decision making in the management of CSC. It combined, after all, two major channels of learning: the first a necessary basis in theory, law, codes of ethics, and comparative models of prison management, the other was very close to praxis; students could learn from the purposeful and meaningful interaction of experienced staff with each other and with prison populations.

The course was successful, and the next step emerged quickly. Through discussions with SFU Publications, it became clear that the concept seemed ready-made for a textbook. The thorny problem we confronted was how to format the approach is a way that allowed theory and abstraction to come together understandably with the living quality of speech and the dynamic context of immediate problems and immediate perception. We worked through a number of layouts. After testing a number of possible alternatives, the result of our efforts is the following textbook. It has been organized around the major areas of decision making and management in Canada's federal prisons and its goal is to teach students about management decision making, and to do so dynamically. Interleaved with material about ethics, levels and principles of management, policy, human and financial resources, prison populations, and programming, you will find responses and discussions by wardens, deputy wardens, prison psychologists, health personnel and correctional officers. The usual approach is to reduce this experience to abstraction. In this text another direction is taken: narrative and theory are meaningfully meshed.

Through much perseverance and hard work, Sherry and Monica have managed to get these two very different genres to come together successfully. This cross-genre approach has been worked out in each chapter, and the hope is that the guidelines and histories of Canada's Federal prison system lift off the page and demonstrate how these work in the life of the staff who must put guidelines and regulations into practice and who, of all those in CSC, should know most about these institutions work.

We hope you can learn from these two streams of knowledge, and we welcome any commentary you may have on this most satisfying project.

— *Margaret Jackson*

Acknowledgements

The authors would like to express their gratitude to the Correctional Service of Canada administrators who participated in the interviews, which formed the foundation for and provided much of the information recorded in the various chapters. We would also like to acknowledge the ongoing support of Harold Golden, CSC former Regional Administrator of Correctional Programming, who assisted us in making contact with the various interviewees, clarifying some of the roles of the administrators and providing some critical feedback on portions of the manuscript. Finally, we want to acknowledge the great assistance that Dr. John Whatley, Director, Simon Fraser University Publications, has provided throughout the process.

Much appreciation to my mom, and to my kids—Todd, Brandi, Serene, and Jared—for their patience and support throughout this project, and to Paul for technical support. — *Sherry Mumford*

To my wonderful husband Jason, and my children Sara and Jack, thank you for your love, encouragement, and support. — *Monica Jobe-Armstrong*

MANAGEMENT CHALLENGES IN
CANADIAN FEDERAL CORRECTIONS

1 Introduction to Management Challenges in Canadian Federal Corrections

This book is written in a way that illustrates or emphasizes the practical issues associated with federal correctional administration and practice in Canada. It incorporates current abstract material with interview information or narratives provided by various agents of administrative practice within Correctional Service of Canada (CSC) to whom we are very grateful. Transcripts of the interviews are set off from the body text using double indents and are presented intact with no alterations to the grammar or use of various jargons by the interviewees. Within each chapter a unique number is assigned to each anonymized administrator and a heading set in bold text.

This book assumes that you have some basic knowledge of Criminology, the criminal justice system, and perhaps Correctional Service of Canada as a subsystem of the criminal justice system. Therefore, you will not find, for example, extensive theoretical or philosophical explanations underpinning the area of correctional administration and practice, nor an extensive explanation of the historical origins of correctional practice that can be found elsewhere. Likewise, only a brief overview of the criminal justice system will be presented. In order to get the maximum benefit from the abstract information in each chapter and the narratives, it is useful to approach the material through the skills of critical thinking or reasoning. Using critical thinking and analysis, the reader should assess the two sets of materials presented in each chapter. By comparing and contrasting this information, the reader could for instance begin to form an opinion about the applicability and merits of both the narratives and the abstract material. In other words, it is important to be able to make the connection between the abstract material and the experiential narratives presented in each chapter. Following many of the administrators' comments, questions are included to promote critical thinking and reasoning and provide a connection between what the administrators say and the abstract material.

The Social Contract and Social Control

John Stuart Mill (1859), in *On Liberty*, said,

> Though society is not founded on a contract, and though no good purpose is answered by inventing a contract in order to deduce social obligations from it, everyone who receives the protection of society owes a return for the benefit and the fact of living in society renders it indispensable that each should be bound to observe a certain line of conduct towards the rest. (p. 141)

Mill was referring to the concept of the *social contract*, best known from arguments developed by Jean-Jacques Rousseau in the eighteenth century. Rousseau held that there is an implicit understanding that being part of a society also means there is a responsibility or expectation that people will behave appropriately in relation to other members of a society. Pollock-Byrne (1989) has noted that all people living in a society have implicitly assented to this "contract" that restrains individual liberty in return for the safety and the advantages a group can provide. Therefore, as members of society, people have not only agreed to abide by the rules inherent in the social contract but also to accept the application of punishments, when the rules are broken.

In this way, the social contract can be said to provide the rationale for punishment. However, it also relies on a social consensus, which, some argue, may exist more in theory than in reality. Since members of the same society supposedly share the same goals and beliefs, the social contract presumably permits society to punish or correct those who offend against it. In reality, though, there are always individuals who regard themselves as disenfranchised and see no advantage in sacrificing their liberties for the good of society. It is often such individuals who commit crimes and end up in the correctional system.

In addition to a social contract, which provides the basis for social control and punishment, there is a more recent concept that is often referred to as the *moral contract*. According to Ekstedt and Jackson (1996), this contract exists between society and those individuals who through election or appointment, have the responsibility "... outside of the context of positive law" (p. 243) to maintain social order. In other words, the moral contract "... seeks to conserve and preserve the status quo by protecting the interests of all people in their interactions with each other" (p. 243). It is also concerned with the expectation of the boundaries within which any governing agency must operate when carrying out its practices.

Breaking the social contract often results in what society and the law define as a "crime." What is a crime? According to Griffiths and Cunningham (2003), "it is an act committed or omitted in violation of a law forbidding or commanding it and for which punishment is imposed upon conviction" (p. 16). Why do people commit crimes or end up in prison? Here is what one CSC interviewee had to say:

Administrator 1: Although there may be some offenders who came from a disadvantaged life or broken home, our theory of criminal behaviour points out that for every one who became an offender, there are ten more who didn't. Our position is that people make choices, and in most cases they know right from wrong and they make those choices because the positive payoff seems to exceed the negative consequences. CSC spends a little less time on family of origin issues and a little more time on conscious choices, responsibilities, and accountability. It is a little bit like the difference between cognitive behavioural interventions, which we believe in, and I say, without being disrespectful, the notion of 12 step programs, which leave room for the offender to feel incapacitated. That is, he is not capable on his own of changing, that there is a power bigger than he is and he needs to turn this problem over to somebody else. I mean, there are certain times or situations in life, or addictions, for example, for that kind of thinking, but in my view you have to be very careful about alleviating or removing responsibility from people.

Cognitive behavioural focus is about making choices, and offenders are where they are because of that; they can also affect the consequences that arise from that and a person can make a difference in their own lives. They do not have to depend on someone else. They can lean on somebody else for support and garner support from a variety of sources, but in the end, they are the ones who have to make the decisions. It is a tough message, but one that we will not be straying from in corrections, for a long time. We do acknowledge that some of these guys came from dysfunctional backgrounds and experienced abuse. However, we prefer to look at where they are now and ask how they will change what they have become and how they will become somebody different, as opposed to focusing on what was their experience and how they got here. We are not as concerned about why they got here as we are about how they are going to move on from here. You always hear stories about offenders who get out of jail, then commit a crime in order to get back into jail because its winter and they have no place to go, no food to eat, and no means to support themselves, and it's a tremendously sad reality. For some offenders, they are so dysfunctional and so incapacitated that that is their salvation.

Although Administrator 1 suggests that family of origin and family history play a role in how or why offenders commit crimes, the suggestion here is that corrections puts more emphasis on the offenders' choices in life, and their ability to take control and make changes. If you were this administrator, how would your belief around "choice and changes" influence the rehabilitation of the offender who is "so dysfunctional and so incapacitated" that incarceration becomes their salvation?

The Canadian Criminal Justice System

The Canadian criminal justice system is basically composed of the police, courts, and the correctional system (both provincial and federal), and is considered part of governmental operations. However, there are volunteer and non-profit agencies that provide time and assistance to support the overall criminal justice system.

The role of the police is often complex and officers require the ability to multi-task. They have a primary responsibility to respond to crime and to engage in crime prevention activities. In other words, the basic mission of the police is to prevent crime and disorder. Therefore, the test of police effectiveness or efficiency is the absence of crime and disorder, and so it is based on crime rate levels and clearance rates. One of the important facets of police work is the laying of information when an individual is suspected of committing a crime at a certain location at a specified time, although many factors must be taken into consideration in determining what actually happened. This laying of information may include the use of police discretion in some cases.

In Canada, there are both provincial and federal court systems. According to Griffiths and Cunningham (2003), "... courts are responsible for determining the guilt or innocence of accused persons and for imposing an appropriate sentence on those who are convicted" (p. 136). In doing so, the courts must also guarantee that the individual's Charter rights are being respected. If the accused is found guilty and the disposition includes incarceration, the offender may be sentenced to either a provincial or a federal institution, based on the two-year rule.

The *Canadian Constitution Act* of 1867 (formerly *British North America Act*) gives the federal government jurisdiction over penitentiaries, and the provincial government's jurisdiction over prisons. Generally speaking, what separates the two jurisdictions is the two-year rule, which specifies that adult offenders sentenced up to two years less a day, are sent to provincial prisons or jails, while adult offenders sentenced to two years or more, are sent to federal penitentiaries or to the federal correctional system. In some cases, provincial governments have made agreements with the federal government so that offenders from both jurisdictions reside in one institution. For example, up until early 2004, Burnaby Correctional Centre for Women (BCCW) was an institution where both federally and provincially sentenced women resided.

The present form of the Correctional Service of Canada (the federal corrections system) was created in 1978 through an amalgamation of the National Parole Service and the Canadian Penitentiary Service. It is comprised of five regions: the Atlantic region, covering the four Maritime provinces; the Québec region; the Ontario region covering as far as Thunder Bay and including Nunavut Territory; the Prairie region, including Manitoba, Saskatchewan, Alberta, the Northwest Territories and the area west of Thunder Bay, Ontario; and the Pacific region, including British Columbia and the Yukon. According to Sections 3 and 5 of the *Corrections and Conditional Release Act* (CCRA) (1992):

3. The purpose of the federal correctional system is to contribute to the maintenance of a just, peaceful, and safe society by,

    a) carrying out sentences imposed by courts through the safe and humane custody and supervision of offenders; and
    b) assisting in the rehabilitation of offenders and their reintegration into the community as law-abiding citizens through the provision of programs in penitentiaries and in the community.

5. There shall continue to be a correctional service in and for Canada, to be known as the Correctional Service of Canada, which shall be responsible for,

    a) the care and custody of inmates;
    b) the provision of programs that contribute to the rehabilitation of offenders and to their successful reintegration into the community;
    c) the preparation of inmates for release;
    d) parole, statutory release supervision, and long-term supervision of offenders; and
    e) maintaining a program of public education about the operations of the Service. (http://laws.justice.gc.ca/en/C-44.6/39663.html)

The Purpose of Corrections

> **Administrator 2:** It has been said that the measure of a civilization is the manner in which they treat their criminal population and that is relatively true.

One of the most important and highly debated questions in corrections concerns the purpose of corrections in the first place. In Canada, for example, is the purpose or focus of corrections *public safety, offender rehabilitation, or offender punishment*? Pollock-Byrne (1989) describes corrections as a "schizophrenic system paying homage to several masters, including the principles of retribution, reform, incapacitation, deterrence, and rehabilitation." She further asks whether treatment and punishment can occur at the same time under the same roof. Are correctional officials paying lip service to a treatment ethic while continuing to do the same things they have always done? Although the criminal justice system seems to be subject to political influences, often the result of public pressure—for example, a return by some segments of society to a more hardened opinion of criminals—the correctional administrators who were interviewed seem pretty clear about what the purpose of corrections in Canada is. The CSC administrators have identified the following themes as important to the goals of corrections: *protecting the public; changing behaviour; reintegration; rehabilitation; carrying out the punishment prescribed through the sentencing or incarceration of offenders;* and *perhaps moving into the realm of providing some prevention in an effort to educate young people about the realities of incarceration.* Here is what they had to say:

> **Administrator 3:** Correcting ... correcting. I'm not into vengeance. Correcting. No bigger, no smaller.

> **Administrator 4:** Protection of the public, pure and simple. I mean for the length of time that they are in. We have some fellows here that may never leave here and we are protecting the public by keeping them in here. That's the easiest job to do. The other job is to change their behaviour, change their attitudes, things like that. You do that through correctional programming. Very difficult. Very difficult given that the people that we see, they were in trouble in grade seven, they had problems in school, dysfunctional families, problems with their families, abuse of substances. May have done some time, may have been involved in group homes. By the time we get them sometimes we use the slang term "the last chance." A lot of emotional damage and behavioural issues by the time they get here.

Administrator 5: It is pretty simple from my perspective. We are here for the protection of society, the protection of the public, and we are here to administer the direction of the courts or the sentence of the courts. We are here to rehabilitate our inmates, which is done through the administration of programming, good dynamic security, interactions, work programs, release type of programs, so that the inmate can be eventually released back into the community. Therefore, the punishment mandate, which is part of the old model, is delivered through the sentencing from the courts and our focus is on preparing the inmate for reintegration back into society.

We do not want to send that individual back into the community with the same violent tendencies he/she may have had that brought them into contact with the criminal justice system in the first place. Reintegration is the focus and time may be the barrier. Many of these inmates are being sent to jail for pretty minor offences, and with the two-year rule, the Judge may or may not sentence them to two years plus a day, for example, and if they are sent to federal institutions there is the good possibility that they can take advantage of effective programming. I am sure there are hundreds of other jurisdictions that are faced with this as well. It is unfortunate, and I do not know what the solution is. However, it is a reality. Guys come in and sometimes they leave even worse off, most often because there is no programming available. Others may come as the most violent people in our society and when they leave, they are able to successfully live and function within society because they have had the opportunity to take advantage of programs in the federal system.

While the protection of the public was an important theme in the responses from some administrators, others highlighted the importance of rehabilitation of the offender for successful reintegration back into society. Although the overall goal is public protection, there are differing ways to achieve this goal.

Administrator 6: Definitely rehabilitation. Incarceration is the punishment and what they do during incarceration is our job. We have basically two choices: we can ignore them and they can go out into the community at two- thirds of their sentences, probably more dangerous than when they came in. Or, we can work with them, and that is the philosophy that we take on from intake where we do a very thorough assessment—it can take anywhere from seventy to ninety days depending on the length of their sentence—develop proper programs that are all researched and accredited and see that they are matched to the programs, and we determine the most appropriate placement for them, whether it is maximum, medium, or minimum security. Then we prepare them for release to the community where they are continuously supervised and programmed in the community, right through to Warrant Expiry. The support networks that we have in place are great, although there is always room for improvement.

Administrator 7: There is no doubt that rehabilitation is the primary focus. However, in the next few years I hope to see corrections move more into the preventive stage. We already do many presentations in school have a lot of university Criminology students come through facilities we hold some open houses for the communities to come and see our facilities and I think we need to continue with the public education, public awareness of what it is and what we do. The saddest thing is to see the young offender facilities fill up … I would hate to see us adopt the "lock them up and throw away the key" mentality, because most of those people will eventually come out of the system. If it is a brutal system, then they learn brutality, and that is what has happened to too many of our guys before they even get to us. They have learned brutality. They have learned that you behave in a certain way. Therefore, what happens when they live in this environment and they foster this throughout their formative years? Many of our people come in around the age of twenty to twenty-one years of age and they stay until they are around twenty-eight, twenty-nine years old, and then they are out. Those are very formative years, to learn. We need to make sure that what they are learning will be helpful to them.

Administrator 7 raises an interesting point around a possible role for corrections in providing public prevention and awareness activities related to crime, the criminal, and corrections. Others may argue that this is extending the role of corrections beyond their primary mandate. What would be some of the arguments for and against a prevention role for corrections?

Administrator 8: I've been in corrections a long time. My beliefs are the same as the mission statement. It is through the slow, gradual reintegration process that you best protect society. That's what it is all about.

Administrator 9: To me, I think we were very fortunate to have a commissioner like Ole Ingstrup to come on board when he did. I was in corrections at the time. I can remember being a parole officer on the street and there was talk about us getting guns and us getting handcuffs and going towards the U.S. model. And he came from a different continent and a different country and a different view and led us in that way. That was back in 1988–89 that the mission statement came out. It has gone through a number of different ministers, different leaders of political backgrounds and twelve years later we have some reduction in crime, we have some reduction in recidivism. So is it doing what it's supposed to be doing? I believe it is.

Administrator 10: Rehabilitation for sure. Yeah, yeah.

While the theme surrounding rehabilitation is frequent, administrators are quick to point out the importance of the mission statement in reinforcing the purpose of corrections. Furthermore, there is some discussion about avoiding the more punitive correctional role as exemplified by some countries such as the United States. Reintegration is another important theme in light of the recognition that in this county it would be rare for someone to spend their entire natural life within prison. Reintegration is seen as important in preparing both the offender and the community for their eventual and inevitable release from prison.

Administrator 11: The main purpose of corrections is to ensure and protect the rights of society and ensuring that when we have the offender in our care we do everything possible to ensure that he creates, poses, a lesser risk when he returns to the community.

Administrator 12: So, the parole officers basically drive the case and the program deliverers that are in the RACP's (regional administrator of correctional programs) domain, make sure the programs they get meet the prescribed standards. And we are responsible to see that they get their programs at the most appropriate times in their sentence and it's all basically mapped out and achieved.

Administrator 13: It has to be rehabilitation. We do not live in a society or system now, whereby someone goes to prison for life. I can count on my fingers how many inmates I know that are in here for life. The bulk or majority of our offenders get out, and it is our responsibility to ensure public safety by saying that yes, they are getting out. However, these are the things we have done with him and he has done for himself, and these are the things we think he needs in place in the community in order to be safe. When we start talking about things like cutting parole so there is no parole or no pre-release or anything like that—we are just going to keep them until they spend their whole sentence in jail—that guy will walk out with absolutely no support systems in the community. People sometimes have a hard time understanding that. We would much rather see a guy come out on a gradual release, perhaps into a halfway house for awhile, where they are still monitored, still have the ability to take programming and then gradually out that way, rather than have a guy serve all the way to the end of their sentence and then get released. We have absolutely no control over them when they reach their Warrant Expiry; that is it. Our job is to make sure we prepare the person as well as we can, for release and it is the communities' part to prepare themselves for the release as well.

Administrator 14: Punishment is a bit of a harsh word. Justice might be a better word, and then when you get into talking about justice you can talk about traditional justice or restorative justice, which is a fascinating concept and a lot different from what most people's view of what justice should be. Without doubt, correctional systems—and the Canadian correctional system is no different—has a number of responsibilities. One is certainly to protect society, which means to incarcerate and to hold offenders until the end of their sentence or until someone deems it appropriate for them to be released. This is very much, in my view, a punishment. If all you do is punish, the research is very clear that in fact, punishment in and of itself, results in increased levels of recidivism-as much as a seven percent increase, research suggests.

Any correctional system which punishes only, which exists in some environments we spoke about previously, the result is a prison population which doesn't change and which ultimately ends up in the community doing more of what they always did. I think that the proper goal of any correctional system should not just be incarceration or punishment, or protection of society through incarceration, but you need to look at the more longer term benefits of some kind of behavioural change, and hence the notion of rehabilitation or reintegration. Both of these are critical elements of what we do. I also think that you could probably look at our mission statement and pull out about four major themes, one of which is respecting the rule of law. In other words, it is our role as a prison system to abide by the law and to honour legislation.

It is also apparent in discussions with some administrators that there is a belief that prisons house society's outcasts, individuals who have been written off and whose needs may not have been appropriately responded to by other agents of government. In other words, many individuals who end up in prison have never had their basic needs met—food, shelter, education and health care—all of these are, however, provided within the prison setting. Sadly, it would seem that some individuals have had to give up their freedom in order to receive the kind of care that most of us may take for granted.

Administrator 15: Our paramount role is the protection of society, so that is an important purpose of corrections, but protection of society can be achieved in a number of ways. One way is by simply locking people up. Another is by making long-term changes—rehabilitation. A third theme of our mission is helping offenders become law-abiding citizens through reintegration. And the fourth is providing a safe, secure, and humane environment for offenders while they are incarcerated. That is also a role of corrections, and an important one. Safe, secure, and humane are different terms from, for example, pleasant, luxurious, and recreational. I think it is important to draw that distinction because there are often comments or debates from people about the prison environment and you really only have to walk through a prison to recognize that it is not a fun place to be. Despite the grounds and the natural, open environment in some of our facilities like William Head or Ferndale, in my view that is superficial stuff. The real issue is the eight by ten cell that you live in for sixteen hours a day, sometimes longer on some days, depending on what is going on. Certainly for large chunks of your life. The fact is that you have limited access to your family and your loved ones and you never get to go to a baseball game, to a movie, or to a restaurant. You lose a lot of freedom by virtue of being behind bars.

Yes, we do provide three meals a day and proper health care and so on, and some people argue that the general public does not always have access to that. I am not sure you can answer all of the problems of the world by comparing real life society with life in a prison. The fact is that there is an obligation in law to provide certain things for offenders including three meals a day or at least adequate food, proper health care. The fact that these guys committed crimes does not mean they are no longer entitled to be treated for their illnesses. Nor are they not entitled to be educated and in fact, the more that you continue to take those things away from them the more likely it is that they will return to society even more dysfunctional than they were before. It is a very hard thing for most people to accept. Sometimes even I struggle with it when you see families that cannot afford proper medical care or medical insurance, their kids are suffering or cannot afford to eat particularly well, and you see these offenders eating relatively well. It is a difficult reality and not one that I would ever want to make light of, but I am not convinced that anything we do in the prison environment creates a luxurious reality or life for offenders. We try to make it safe, dignified, but we do not spend a lot of money on things that are not a part of the basic needs package and those are things that are required by law and certainly in my view of a humane civilization.

Administrator 16: The bottom line is that if I had to summarize everything that I think corrections is all about, it would be to alter behaviour through the changing of values, attitudes, and beliefs. Everything else—the humanity, dignity, safety, security, and the protection of society—is all linked into that single objective. In doing that, you get into the whole area of restorative justice because you build up a sense of empathy and the whole idea of people wanting to return to people, that which they took from them in the first place. In a way, this may be a somewhat idealistic way to think but in a nutshell, that is what I think corrections is and in fact, the term "corrections" is a very good one for that because it suggests that we are trying to correct behaviour. We cannot go back in time to correct those events. We can only correct the behaviour that got them here now and that may inevitably get them here again in the future.

If anything, I would argue that it is the government who fails to take care of the general public or citizen adequately, more so than the government or the correctional services, which gives too much to offenders. I do not think that offenders' lives are particularly wonderful. I do think that for some people in society it is very sad that they live the way that they do. My preference would be to see the standard of living in society raised rather than the standard in prisons lowered because lowering the prison standard is only another indication of our failure as a society and only breeds discontent and dysfunction—anger, hatred, hostility, resentment—in the jail. I don't think it serves anyone's best interest. If you treat people like animals then they will behave like animals.

Section 3 of the *Corrections and Conditional Release Act* (CCRA) speaks to the purpose of corrections as incorporating public safety, incarceration, and rehabilitation/reintegration of offenders. Variations of these themes also appear in the interviews given by Administrators 3 to 16. In examining their views on the purpose of corrections, are there some themes that stand out more than others? Are there different planning and practice implications associated with different themes?

Some members of the public hold the view that offenders are often afforded luxuries to which others within the general public may not have access. Administrators 14, 15, and 16 have commented on this public sentiment and made reference to the fact that such safety, security, and humane treatment, including the provision of basic needs, is in fact mandated by law. As a correctional administrator, what would be your response to the concerns raised by some members of the public and what evidence would you use to support your response?

Conclusion

This chapter has provided you with a brief glimpse into the overall criminal justice system and highlighted what some CSC administrators believe to be the purpose of the Correctional Service of Canada. Corrections is viewed and continues to view itself as the tail end of the criminal justice system— the place where individuals whose status and circumstances have been determined by the decisions of others reside. However, corrections is also a social, political, and bureaucratic enterprise, one that has as its functions the carrying out of the sentences of the court, ensuring public safety, and working with the offender to ensure a timely and as far as possible, a successful reintegration experience into the community. This often poses complex challenges and difficult decisions for administrators and other managers within correctional institutions. The following chapters will discuss some of these challenges in greater detail, primarily through the presentation of views expressed by the Correctional Service of Canada administrators.

Study Questions

1. Based on the discussion by CSC administrators, what do you think the purpose of corrections is? Be prepared to defend your answer.
2. In your own words, what do you understand the quote by Mill to mean?
3. What are the differences between the *social contract* and the *moral contract*?
4. Why are they important for society to have?
5. Briefly name and describe the different components of the criminal justice system.
6. How does the rehabilitation of offenders benefit society?

Bibliography

* Items with asterisks are also suggested readings for the chapter.

Corrections and Conditional Release Act (1992). http://laws.justice.gc.ca/en/C-44.6/index.html

*Ekstedt, J. and Jackson, M. (1996). *The Keepers and the Kept: Introduction to Corrections in Canada*. Toronto, Ont.: ITP Nelson.

*Griffiths, C. T. and Cunningham, A. H. (2003). *Canadian Criminal Justice: A Primer*. Scarborough, Ont.: Nelson Thomson.

*Mill, J. S. (1859). *On Liberty*. London, England: Penguin Books.

Pollock-Byrne, J. (1989). *Ethics in Crime and Justice: Dilemmas and Decisions*. Calif.: Brooks/Cole.

Suggested Readings

Corrections in the 21st Century. Glencoe McGraw Hill. http://www.glencoe.com/ps/corrections/chapresources/

Jackson, M. (2002). *Justice Behind the Walls: Human Rights in Canadian Prisons*. Vancouver: Douglas & McIntyre.

2   Ethical Issues in Correctional Decision Making

This chapter explores the frequently debated topic of ethics and how ethics applies to certain circumstances or even certain professional practices, such as those in corrections. As Ekstedt and Jackson (1996) have stated, "in correctional practice, the application of ethics involves correctional workers clarifying both their personal values and the values articulated by the correctional institution or system" (p. 242). In Chapter 2 we delve into ethical cultures, codes of ethics, and codes of conduct, and touch on a number of specific ethical issues, including staffing, injection drug use, harm reduction, security issues, and victim rights, which are discussed further in later chapters.

Ethics, Morals, and Values

According to Almond (1998), the prerequisite of ethical reasoning includes free will and the possibility of altruism. Moreover, the basis of morality is comprised of principles, rights, obligations, and the role of intuition and virtues. Concrete moral problems normally involve serious debates about such contentious issues as life and death, human relationships, war and violence, equality and justice, and the relationship towards animals and nature. But, do morality and ethics, words that are interchanged daily in conversations, mean the same things?

Some authors (Barry, 1985; Sherman, 1981) have defined ethics as the study and analysis of what constitutes good or bad conduct or behaviour; whereas, morals and morality refer to what is judged as good conduct or behaviour (and immorality as bad conduct or behaviour). Ekstedt and Jackson (1996) define ethics as "the application of moral values or principles to decisions in public or private life" (p. 242). Still others use the word morality when they discuss the total person or the sum of the person's private actions or behaviours in every sphere of life and thus often describe a person as being "moral" or "immoral."

On the other hand, the word ethics is used to describe certain types of behaviour, usually related to a profession, which are often specified in a code of ethics. Frequently, discussions of morality end up describing concepts related to sin or religion, whereas ethics is often restricted to or identified with an analysis of behaviour relevant to certain professions (Pollock-Byrne, 1989, p. 5, 31).

The concept of "values" is also related to morals and ethics. Values refer to the desirability, worth or importance of an action, and judgements of worth often parallel moral judgments of goodness and what is right. Individual values form value systems, whether they are at the level of the "individual person" or at an organizational level such as that of the Correctional Service of Canada. Therefore, organizations or individuals usually give priority to the things they consider important in life and engage in behaviour that is generally consistent with their values. Discussions about values often focus on making a choice or passing a judgement. For example, if university students are presented with an opportunity to cheat on an exam, they face competing or conflicting values: the value of academic success and the value of honesty. The choice they make may depend on their particular value system. However, we often live our lives without taking a close look at the value system that influences our behaviour.

Frequently, a relationship exists between values and morals inasmuch as one's values may dictate one's moral beliefs. For instance, those who value marriage may consider involvement in adulterous behaviour as immoral, as the majority of people in western societies do. An explicit value system is a part of every ethical system and typically, most ethical systems incorporate the values of life, respect for the person or individual, and the survival of society. Therefore, when behaviour is consistent with moral values or principles, an individual is said to be acting "ethically" or in an "ethical" manner (Ekstedt and Jackson, 1996, p. 242).

Most writers agree that morals and ethics refer to behaviours and not beliefs. Furthermore, they refer to human behaviours as opposed to animal behaviours. This position is based on the premise that of all the members of the animal kingdom, only humans have the capacity to be "good," and "bad," both of which involves a voluntary, rational decision and subsequent action (Pollock-Byrne, 1989). In this view, human behaviours stem from free will and free action. However, the presupposition that intent and free will are accompanied by voluntary control over behaviour may not be correct, as it does not take into consideration that some actions are caused by life circumstances and are not voluntary at all. For example, some argue that those individuals from disadvantaged or impoverished backgrounds with criminal role models cannot help their subsequent involvement in a criminal lifestyle. Therefore, it is necessary to examine the relative freedom of choice for all groups. Those groups considered incapable of being morally culpable have generally been the insane and the young. But, even our views about who should be able to decide rationally what is good or bad is challenged when we face, for example, individuals with alcohol and drug addictions. Do these individuals have an illness that renders them morally inculpable? Or, are they individuals characterized by a moral weakness or some form of personality defect? When we examine the question of rationality and responsibility, we are also constantly dealing with debates about when, or at what stage, a child can be said to have reached the "age of reason." Certainly, current Canadian legislation governing issues around youth criminality and justice is a prime example of just such a debate. Consequently, we frequently face conflicting or competing values, which results in the possibility of an "ethical bind," (p. 242) which occurs "only if one is required to act" (p. 242) in a situation (Ekstedt and Jackson 1996). This can often be a challenge faced by CSC administrators and front line staff when competing individual and organizational values require some type of response or action, which results in ethical binds.

Finally, morals and laws may be parallel to one another because in a general sense they deal with individual behaviours. What is illegal or legal may be confused with what is right or wrong. However, our laws do not provide comprehensive definitions of moral behaviour. For example, although laws governing specific types of sexual behaviour define their legality, people may view the same behaviours as either moral or immoral. Some of the most serious ethical dilemmas arise when the moral and the legal appear to conflict. For instance, both moral and ethical arguments are associated with abortion. In some cases, ethics may be compared to regulations or standards because they are similar in the ways that they deal with behaviour specific to a profession or an occupation. Regulations, frequently imposed by outside bodies, often address ethical considerations. According to Pollock-Byrne (1989), "... often regulations and rules for behaviours seem to expand in inverse relation to the practiced ethics of a particular profession or organization" (p. 7). In other words, when problems arise in terms of individuals remaining consistent in ethical behaviours, an attempt is made to bring people back in line, "... with formulation or expansion of rules" (p. 7). The most successful ethical standards in terms of directing professional practice seem to be those that are consistent with and supported by an organizational ideal.

Ethical Cultures within Organizations such as CSC

Research supports the view that the ethical standards of an organization affect staff job satisfaction, commitment to the organization, turnover, and levels of stress. As mentioned elsewhere in this book, the organizational response to unethical work practices is often to introduce more rigid and inflexible procedures, and their introduction can result in the perpetuation of the very behaviours they seek to deter. Furthermore, there is a strong relationship between the perceived ethical standards of managers and administrators and the job satisfaction of their staff. Organizational ethical standards affect organizational commitment, which can be described as an individual's psychological bond to the organization, including a sense of job involvement, loyalty, and belief in the values of the organization. However, ethical stress is an ongoing and expensive problem for the public sector and it generally occurs when an individual's ethical standards are different (be they higher or lower) than those of either the organization or co-workers. Situations where such stress is likely to occur include those where:

- rules are often bent or broken
- distrust is prevalent
- promotions and rewards are not based on merit
- management does not emphasize excellence, efficiency, quality, and teamwork

Some of the situations that lead to ethical stress among the staff at CSC are discussed later on in the section which discusses interviewees' responses to staffing issues. Ethical stress or an unethical work force is self-perpetuating. Those with ethical standards that conflict with the organization may choose to leave the organization. Nonetheless, there seems to be little that managers and administrators can do to change individuals' personal moral beliefs, values, and ethics. What they need to do is understand and change the factors specific to the organization that have been found to contribute to unethical decision-making in the first place. In other words, they must positively influence the ethical culture of the workplace. Some of the factors that have been found to influence ethical beliefs and decision making in organizations include:

- peer group influence
- leadership and management influence
- clearly stated missions and values of how the vision will be made a reality
- consistently applied rewards and sanctions
- features of the organization itself
- corporatization or privatization
- ethics training which looks at actual ethical and unethical practices in the organization

- codes of ethics, which should reinforce the shared set of beliefs that arise from the vision and mission.

Codes of Ethics and Codes of Conduct

The existence of codes of ethics and of procedures, rules, and defined roles are related to greater perceived ethical behaviours in organizations. Restricting decision making to the top ranks affects the perceived ethical behaviour in some, but not all, organizations. Acceptance of authority and a strong enforcement of rules and regulations do not seem to have an effect on the perceived ethical behaviour in any organization. In part, CSC has addressed this top-down decision-making process through the introduction of participatory management, which attempts to move away from the traditional style. As Ekstedt and Jackson (1996) have stated, the traditional style of management is akin to the "command" style of decision making, whereas participatory management involves more of a consensus approach (pp. 76–77).

Codes of ethics establish guiding principles for appropriate behaviour that are more like value statements, making broad aspirational guidelines rather than prescriptive statements. In contrast to codes of ethics that are guidelines, codes of practice or conduct are generally quite prescriptive, often specifying to staff the dos and don'ts of their respective practice. Therefore, codes of conduct are essentially seen as prescribing behaviour according to the "letter of the law" or in terms of black and white. Codes of ethics, on the other hand, allow staff with differing ways of seeing things to come forward to discuss the "grey" areas. Because codes of ethics are basically conservative, they usually identify the parameters of conduct within which accountability is structured and grievances are resolved. Ekstedt and Jackson (1996) have stated that "one of the purposes of a code of ethics is to satisfy the public that the agency or profession is keeping faith with the moral contract" (p. 243). They believe the moral contract focuses on public expectations about the boundaries that any governing agency must operate within when carrying out its practices.

In December of 2005 CSC created the Values and Ethics Branch, which focuses on the implementation of key elements of the CSC Ethics Strategy. In addition to this, the Values and Ethics Branch has a variety of potential functions, not the least of which is to develop more of an understanding of the ethical dilemmas faced by both the organization and its staff. In an effort to create a stronger values-based workplace, planning is underway to create a work environment that ensures values and ethics are more fully incorporated into decision-making practices and are understood by employees at all levels within CSC. These plans include:

- Values and Ethics Unit: integrate existing programs such as internal disclosure under one umbrella to provide strategic direction for a co-ordinated ethics program in CSC
- National Values and Ethics Program: implement program and collect baseline data to establish targets for future improvement
- National Informal Conflict Management Systems (ICMS): develop and implement the system
- Strengthened Independent Audit Function: further enhance the independence and effectiveness of the Audit Committee by increasing the number of external members.

The proposed Values and Ethics Branch, which required $900,000 for the 2006/07 operational budget, is depicted in Figure 2.1.

Figure 2.1. Structure of proposed Values and Ethics Branch

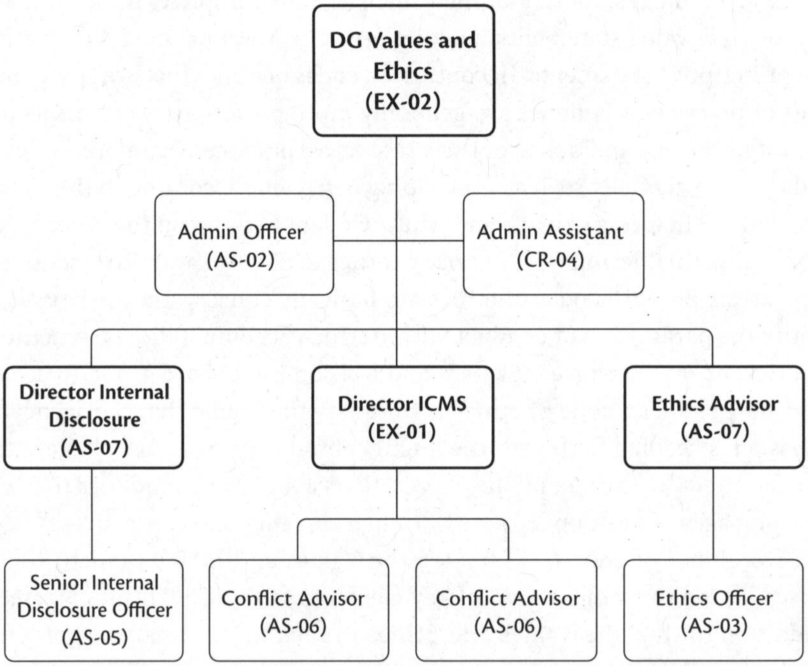

Source: Report on Governance Structures for Values and Ethics. Correctional Service of Canada.

Upon receiving a disclosure the Values and Ethics Branch will assess the inquiry and consider whether or not there is a need to refer it to another organization within CSC. For example, harassment complaints will be referred to human resource management for investigation and remedy. Issues related to inappropriate conduct, etc., would be subject to administrative investigations by CSC, and, depending on the nature of the case, may be examined by the Values and Ethics Branch itself.

CSC differentiates between compliance-based behaviour and ethically-based behaviour and the expectations that come with each. Compliance-based behaviour is often governed by external laws, is considered to be compulsory behaviour and the goal is to prevent staff from acting in an unlawful manner. Ethically-based behaviour often refers to the discretionary behaviour and decisions made by staff; ethically-based programs encourage an independent critique of the decision-making process. According to CSC, "(i)n supporting employees, values-based programs try to create a safe zone for employees to discuss ethical issues and introduce ethical concerns into decision-making." Through the implementation of values-based ethics program, CSC hopes to increase staff commitment to the organization, ensure that staff integrity remains intact, and assist or support staff in the delivery and receipt of "bad news."

Correctional Service of Canada has a booklet entitled *Standards of Professional Conduct*, which was designed in part to provide direction for staff dealing with difficult or ethical decisions. It states:

> The primary emphasis of the Standards of Professional Conduct is on promoting ethical behaviour consistent with the mission. It recognizes that Corrections is a complex field, which frequently presents an employee with difficult practical and ethical decisions. The principles set out in the Standards of Professional Conduct are intended to guide staff in situations where the right course of action may not always be clear.

Staff who fail to abide by these standards, including actions where they fail to report illegal acts or acts of harassment, are subject to disciplinary action under CSC's Code of Discipline if they are caught (For more information on the Standards, check CSC Commissioners Directives 060 Code of Discipline).

In correctional work, using a reasonable degree of individual discretion is expected, especially for those officers and other professionals working on the front lines, which provide the greatest potential for ethical binds to occur. Moreover, it is very important to recognize that because their liberty is reduced, inmates are extremely vulnerable to unethical conduct on the part of correctional officers and treatment staff. Professional ethics exist to guide individual decision makers in their use of discretion and include the importance of integrity, and respect for and protection of individual rights.

Public service *values* do not always involve a choice between right and wrong. For example, the choice could be whether or not to pursue a career in public service. However, in public service *ethics*, the issue of the potential for wrong-doing, legal or not, is front and centre. Ethical issues, therefore, are by their nature issues of conscience where one option is arguably wrong, or at least more wrong, than the other. Tait (1996) referred to public service as a special calling. It is not for everyone, and environments such as CSC may be especially challenging. Those who devote themselves to it may find meaning and satisfaction they could not find elsewhere. However, the rewards are not material; they are moral and psychological, perhaps even spiritual. They are the intangible rewards that proceed from the sense of devoting one's life to the service of the country, to the affairs of the state, to public purposes great or small, and to the public good. But the rewards of being in the public service, like those of other professions, come at a price. The price is submission to very high standards of professional conduct, public scrutiny and accountability, learning to hold a public trust, and to put public interests and safety ahead of self. It also requires respecting the authority of the law and of democratic will. The values of public service can be seen as both its price and its reward.

If we have reason to pay more attention to the tasks of leadership, we also have reason to expect much of it. It is through leadership and example, above all, that values have force in daily life and become part of the real conduct of a community. Leadership values come not only from the top, but from the middle and lower levels of public servants, who show public service values in their daily work and lives, and sometimes ask themselves whether these same values (and indeed moral values) are shared by the higher levels of the Service.

In a U.S. study by Stohr, Hemmens, Marsh, Barrier and Palhegyi (2000), researchers were attempting to develop an instrument to measure the presence of ethics in correctional staff. What they concluded was that correctional workers had a healthy sense of distrust, which assisted them in carrying out the core functions of the institution, that is, the safety and security of the facility. Within many correctional institutions in the U.S., there still exists a power base that comes from a hierarchical structure where the power is concentrated among the top echelons of the organization. However, informal mechanisms exist to regulate the power differential through the actions of middle management and their staff. It is accomplished through the efforts to professionalize the workforce and, to a large degree, through the existence of subcultural influences within the organization itself, not unlike the case in some Canadian institutions.

As in Canada, correctional work in the U.S. is characterized by discretional decision-making, which is often used in situations that are relatively minor in nature, hidden from top management and supported or at least sanctioned by the organizational subculture (Stohr et al., 2000; Ekstedt and Jackson, 1996;

Pollock-Byrne, 1989). Therefore, ethics training as well as a strong ethics code help prevent abuses in the workplace. For instance, in correctional work organizational subcultures have sets of norms or expected behaviours. These may include, for example, a prohibition against reporting wrongdoing, the protection of members, extensive discretion, power and authority invested in officers, and the ability to use force in dealing with inmates. Often, standards of ethical practices in correctional institutions or definitions of "doing the right thing" include references to such behaviours as not hitting or otherwise assaulting inmates and the duty to protect and treat others fairly, including those inmates often looked upon with disdain because of the nature of the offences they have committed. In addition, there is a belief that all staff members have important knowledge to contribute to the organization and, in fact, that inmates themselves often have important insights into the operation of the organization, which are found to be consistent with the presence of other ethical behaviours. Furthermore, the ability to break with the organizational subcultures and take the initiative to report on inappropriate or unacceptable behaviours is also associated with ethical behaviours.

In Canada and the U.S., managers and correctional officers agree that some behaviours and issues such as legal behaviours, following rules and procedures, maintaining social distance from inmates and having a duty to both the inmates and the public are integral parts of their professionalism. Some correctional staff also believe that outsiders have limited understanding of correctional work, although that view may be more closely associated with subcultural values within the organization. In the U.S. study, Stohr and colleagues (2000) also found the greater the belief that the use of abusive or offensive behaviour towards inmates was inappropriate, the greater the presence of other ethical behaviours. However, what these researchers concluded was that although there was an assumption that certain ethical questions or questions relying on "doing the right thing" would yield the same response, it was not always true, leading to the conclusion that responses to these "no-brainers" were not always as clear or certain as was previously assumed. Below are some of the ethical issues that were identified and discussed by CSC administrators and managers.

Ethical Issues for Correctional Staff and Correctional Organizations

Staffing Issues
According to some interviewees, one of the ethical concerns involves staff issues versus high CSC and public expectations. They often identify negative issues concerning staff. Some staff lack values, integrity, or even knowledge or

respect for the law. Others are not knowledgeable about CSC policies or use poor judgment when dealing with situations. Here are some comments made by interviewees about ethically challenging issues:

Administrator 1: In terms of public perception or expectations, one of the challenges of CSC is to try to create an understanding of who we are within our own community and that is something, for whatever reason, we have not managed to achieve at the level that we would like. We know we are respected around the world as having probably one of the best correctional systems anywhere and we are more successful with respect to our programming than almost any jurisdiction. There is high level of cynicism in the population at large about corrections, and the fact that people think we are "molley-coddling" offenders. This issue is raised regularly, so it creates an atmosphere where there is a lot of prodding by Canadians and often by our own staff. One of the challenges as an administrator is to keep your staff "up" when they go home and talk to their friends and people around them in their community who are saying we are not doing an exemplary job when we think we are. We are not excellent but we are certainly as good as we can be given the technology, and we are trying to learn on an ongoing basis so we can become better at our jobs. That is not widely accepted in the population at large, and so sometimes staff question themselves that they are doing the right thing and sometimes staff will deny where they are working.

This is very, very sad, because if we are professionals who believe in what we are doing then we should be out telling everybody about it. But when our own politicians do not seem to support us and do not seem to appreciate the success that we are having, it becomes very demoralizing for all levels of staff.

Furthermore, *the issue of values among staff* is also somewhat disturbing to me. For example, the fact that when there is recruitment for officers, some of the scenarios that are given are supposed to identify values that would not be consistent with humane treatment of offenders. However, this does not always show up because it is easy from reading the scenarios to figure out what types of responses you would be required to make in order to make the passing grade. A process more like the one that recruits have to undergo with the Vancouver Police Department would serve our needs better. They use a type of lie detector tester and ask a series of questions which are then asked again, two or three days down the road in a different way, a different manner. These responses would then be measured again and compared to the original ones. It saddens me to see some of the recruits, for example, who are getting through and have their own control issues and are operating often with a high testosterone level, for example pushing offenders' buttons, which makes it not only unsafe for other offenders and staff, but makes it unsafe for the public. In terms of the female recruits, I do see that from time to time and it does seem to be an issue for some women who I suspect may have come from some pretty awful life experiences with men in their background, and this may be a way or a vehicle for them to get even. However, I want to make it very clear, however, that I strongly support the presence of female staff at all levels of our organization. They have had a profoundly positive effect in creating a more humane and caring and normalized environment.

The continuing theme of political involvement and influence as factors in determining correctional policy is further reiterated in Administrator 2's comments. The issue of political involvement can raise interesting and often heated debates among scholars and researchers alike. Perhaps there would be more acceptance of political decisions that were based on well-researched concepts. But, at least one administrator suggests that emotional influence often plays a bigger role.

Administrator 2: The situation where I have seen our ethics tried more often than anything is in that *less-than-political involvement.* I mean, that happens and it is happening more, but it generally happens when you have a government in power for a long time. At least in corrections, because it is a dog's breakfast, it is a no man's land for a politician. One of the greatest politicians that we had in my thirty years of corrections was Andy Scott. I loved listening to what he was saying; I thought he was very sincere about it. He might just have been the biggest con that I encountered but he got out there and engaged people. I was so impressed with him, and neither before nor since have I seen anybody come close to him. So, that kind of political involvement, bring it on! But bowing to the lobbyists and that kind of stuff—hogwash. The best example of that for me is when a government administrator bowed to whatever pressures there were and made a unilateral decision that all lifers would now spend a minimum of X number of years in maximum security institutions. That's not right. That goes against everything we know. But we allowed that thing to happen. I think that is the most ethical problem we have to face ... and I can see more of that coming down the road. Political involvement should only occur into what we know to be correct. Listening to them, certainly. Holding up our correctional research to those things, certainly. But making a decision on an emotional platform, that to me is ethically wrong. The same way I think it is ethically wrong to take a job so it can get you to your next job.

Organizations such as CSC employ thousands of individuals. Such individuals are in the public spotlight in terms of their attitudes, behaviours, and decisions, and within the organization itself there is also a strong expectation that employees will strictly follow the Code of Conduct. There is a belief that individuals who accept the responsibility of working for CSC will exhibit loyalty and dedication to their respective positions. However, this is not always the case.

Administrator 3: We have always been accountable to the Canadian public and perhaps more so over the last year. There have been some new forces coming into play—pictures being released to the press, Michael Harris' book, and things of that nature. I do not think we have necessarily always been fairly treated. Overall the Service has integrity, has belief in what it is trying to do. But the Service is also made up of human beings who may have other agendas. So perhaps we can further try to work out some of the tools that we have for approving staff into the Service, ensuring that their values and beliefs are similar to what we are looking for to fit with our mission and our mandate and take action on those that do not. However, we need a few more tools. It is not that easy to dismiss staff. Do we need further definition, further emphasis on our Code of Conduct, perhaps? Maybe that should be a mandatory element and expanded upon. What is it, to be a public servant?

Administrator 4: I work for the Correctional Service of Canada. However, I cannot forget that I also work for the public. That is my part and I think we should put more emphasis on that, with every department. We are representatives, our boss is the public, and that is to whom we are accountable for our behaviours and our actions. We need to be modelling societal values too. We need to emphasize the role of the public servant perhaps. We are the biggest public servant employer in this county and there is not a whole lot to compare to. So, the role of the public servant could probably be elevated because it is not necessarily an easy role either, but who are we actually working for? We are working for the public, but what we are trying to do is to create a safe environment for the public and that includes our site as well. Comments that we make, words that we say, will they enhance what we are trying to do in terms of public safety?

Other areas that present ethical issues in terms of staffing involve *the dilemma of doing one's job versus building a career to move up politically.*

I think the most significant ethical question in my mind that we have been faced with in the last twenty years has been people taking care of their correctional career, not their correctional job. That would probably be the thing that I've found most difficult. You go to work in corrections, for whatever reason you got here but now you are here. Do you do the job that you are paid to do or do you look at your next career move, so that you can have more influence in correctional policy or so that you can make more money? There has been too much of this, in my view. People moving up—not because they wanted to influence—I'm a missionary, I'm sure of it. I'm sure with another turn I could have had a cloth on. So for me, I place the value on doing the job, and then for one reason or another moving on and doing a job, doing the best I could with the job. Not making decisions on what would be most politically advantageous to me. Or taking on the projects that are politically advantageous. But it happens all the time.

It seems, then, that some of the issues confronting staff involve public misconceptions, which are sometimes fuelled by political and media reports, and demoralize some staff. The whole issue of involvement by politicians is also raised by the CSC interviewees, as is the question of values among staff. In other words, do they bring a set of values to the job site that is consistent with the tough work they must do? In addition, one interviewee raises the question of whether the choice to be working in the correctional field has more to do with taking care of a future correctional career, rather than looking after the current correctional job and how it might affect the quality of work being done.

Given the various ethical and moral dilemmas described by Administrators 1 to 4, what is the value in CSC having the Standards of Professional Conduct and Codes of Ethics? How might an individual's morals, ethics, and values interact with Section 3 of the CCRA as discussed in Chapter 1? Administrator 1 suggests that one answer to the dilemma of hiring inappropriate staff is to require a more stringent recruitment process for potential employees, such as the one used by the Vancouver Police Department. What are your views on this?

Conflicting Goals of the Public Versus CSC Versus Legislation

In identifying some conflicting goals, CSC interviewees agreed that one of the most prevailing themes relates to which mandate or goal should be followed when dealing with offenders. In other words, is it the public's goal of increased incarceration, or CSC's goal of offender reintegration? Included in this mix, of course, is the whole issue of sentence disposition as defined by the legislation. Here is what the interviewees had to say:

Administrator 5: For some managers there is the issue of the *balance between meeting their budgets and delivering services.* That is a big ethical issue in my view. As an example, when we were going through our exercise last week identifying what we could look at to cut, one of the Unit Managers stated that it's to the point where when they order things such as toilet paper, it's really right down to the crunch. The manager was saying it's amazing the impact of not being able to get a couple of rolls of toilet paper to the inmates in Unit Three. Because we don't have the money to have the stuff on the shelves, this was the example that manager used, or because we don't have the money to have the plumber on staff, we have to bring somebody in. So we have an inmate who is in segregation, and they are there with their plugged flush for a little bit longer than they would normally have, and the impact of that is so great at the institutional level it is amazing. It can cost more money in the long run because we have the inmate flipping out, breaking up other stuff because he didn't get his flush fixed within a reasonable amount of time. And as crazy as it sounds, that's the reality. The guy that was here before me said it is amazing the impact that a plugged flush will have in Unit Three at the Atlantic institution.

So that's one of the issues and I think it comes from some ... I don't know if it is mismanagement over the years, you know, because the government has had the money to buy the things and then we've had money left over so we've used that for other stuff but that's a major issue. If we cut this, what kind of impact is it going to have over here? We're going to save one hundred thousand dollars over here but we are going to spend one million dollars fixing the institution over here. Sometimes that's not always easy to demonstrate.

Administrator 6: *Public opinion re increased incarceration versus CSC goal of reintegration versus sentence disposition is another issue.* I think it is one of the main ethical issues inasmuch as we look at our belief in rehabilitation and by way of public pressure and stuff, are we going to be swayed away from that belief? I think that is something that we measure every day. We have a mission document that was done in 1986 which clearly outlines the principles and visions of the Correctional Service of Canada. If you study those values and ethics kinds of issues, you find that values can change over time. Do the staff that we have working now, really espouse the mission document of 1986, or is it time for us to review it again and perhaps revamp it? Those are things that are not spoken about, but I think these are things, in any organization that we have to keep looking at.

Administrator 6 raises a good question. Should organizational mission statements, including that of CSC, be reviewed on a regular basis? In today's current climate, if public sentiment were to influence the revision of the CSC mission statement, what changes might you expect to the wording?

Administrator 7: Ethically, I think we also have to look at what do we mean when we say that we are going to isolate a person off from the rest of the population? Ethically, what does that mean to us? When we have ethical issues around long-term supervision, what does that mean? An offender has finished his sentence, but the court has imposed a ten-year long-term supervision on that person. What does that mean to us? How do we balance that with our belief that people have to work toward rehabilitation and a guy just doesn't want to do that and he is going to be coming out into the community. Those are the kinds of issues that I think are facing our staff every day and they are really difficult sometimes, to have to work through.

Administrator 8: We are continually trying to develop more partnerships with communities and involve communities more within our facilities for example, by way of recruiting volunteers. We have developed some partnerships with universities for example, because the reality is offenders are citizens of a community and will be returning to their communities somewhere. Corrections doesn't have the luxury of choosing their own clients; we get who we get. The more that we can create orderly transitions and clarify the terms of ownership of the problems, the more likely it is we will have successes. All too often, these people have existed in an environment for twenty-five or thirty-five years, where all of the various social systems have failed in terms of assisting these guys to lead socially acceptable lives, and we get them for often a fairly short period of time and we are expected to achieve perfection. Even though I believe we do a good job, often we do not have enough time. We have to release people whether we want to or not. For example, those who we know are still dangerous have to be released if their sentences are expiring, and many times we can predict who will reoffend and who will not, but there is nothing we can do about it because we don't control who exits the door unless they are out on a conditional release. So it is a very frustrating reality for people because often the faces that are associated with serious crimes in the communities are often the faces we would very much like to keep. But we have no choice but to release them because they are finished and sometimes we have to release them on Statutory Release because they don't meet the detention criteria either.

However, we don't want to detain them either, because if they get out of detention at Warrant Expiry, there is no supervision. Often it is much less risky to release them at Statutory Release because at least they will have the supervision and control as they move out into the community, knowing full well that some of these people will probably get reinvolved in criminal activities. But the reality right now is that if we have a determinate sentencing structure, that's just something you have to live with. It's a systemic reality and to be critical of corrections because of the fact that some of the people, when they get out, may commit a crime, it is not necessarily a reasonable portrayal of what we achieve.

There is tremendous pressure placed on CSC staff to release offenders to the community by their day and full parole eligibility date as opposed to releasing them on their statutory release dates. As you know, full parole eligibility is normally set at one third of the offender's sentence. Sometimes it can be set by the judge at one-half for extremely violent situations, but normally it is one-third. Then day parole eligibility is set for six months prior to full parole eligibility date or six months into the sentence, whichever is longer. So for an offender serving two years, full parole eligibility would be at eight months—day parole date if you subtract it from the full parole date, would mean eligibility would be at two months—however, by the rule mentioned previously, it would actually be six months because it has to be a minimum of six months. The point here, is that despite the short sentences we are seeing from the Courts now—roughly thirty-three of all offenders entering the system now are serving exactly two years, and eighty percent of all offenders entering the system in the Pacific Region are serving less than four years—the pressure is immense to address the risks and the needs of these offenders within very short time frames. The fact is that despite the short sentences, these guys are coming to us with extensive criminal histories and entrenched antisocial values, which require significant program interventions. To get those interventions done prior to day parole or full parole date is next to impossible in many cases. So on the one hand, you have this tremendous pressure internally to start programming. It's not intended to create pressure but it is pressure on parole officers, case managers, programming staff, and our managers as well to move offenders through programming and the system at such a rate that they can then be released into the community at the earliest possible time. Of course safety of the public should be and remains our paramount consideration, so this creates an ethical dilemma.

Thus, the conflict lies in the reality that several offenders have led criminal-istic life styles for many years, and along with this comes entrenched and often antisocial behaviours. On the other hand, success is measured by the ability of offenders to complete programs, even in the face of time limitations posed by shorter sentences.

Administrator 8: What should be our primary focus: meeting the meas-urement criteria—the criteria by which we are measured for success, that is—is reintegration a success based on the degree to which we get the offender out by the day and full parole eligibility date? Or, on the other hand, we have this tremendous responsibility to protect society and should we make sure that offenders receive all of the programming they require, prior to release? Therefore, we have the pressures to release them by day parole and we have pressures to give them all sorts of programming that could take them well beyond their day or full parole dates and closer to their statutory release dates and yet we know this is going to be chalked up as a failure. This is because the Correctional Investigator and others assess CSC on the basis of what percentage of offenders are incarcerated beyond their day and full parole eligibility dates. In his latest report, he criticized CSC because there were a significant percentage of offenders who are incarcerated or kept in custody—and not at the lowest level of security—well beyond their day and full parole eligibility dates. So the ethical dilemma is to what degree do we allow ourselves to be influenced by the pressures to release by day and full parole eligibility dates in order to get a good report card and yet balance that against our mandate to protect society. Obviously, in my view, we should always err on the side of protec-tion of society, which means we will always look bad to those people who measure us against such criteria as the percentage of the population who are released by day and full parole eligibility dates. It is a dilemma, it is a frustration, and I believe that it is something that we need to educate the assessors in rather than to change anything that we are currently [doing], because the fact is, in order to address risk and need we have to provide the appropriate interventions, and those interventions take time. Because the courts are giving out shorter sentences and we are standing by our position that inmates require the appropriate programming before they can get released, there is a greater percentage of offenders remaining in custody beyond their day and full parole eligibility dates. Therefore, the Correctional Investigator and a number of other agencies and organiza-tions are saying that CSC is failing in its reintegration agenda because we are not getting people out by the dates that they are entitled to be out.

Therein lies the rub, because the day parole eligibility date and full parole eligibility date are exactly that—eligibility dates. They are not rights or guarantees of release. If everything is done, if they have done everything that they have been asked to and their risk is now manageable in a community environment, then they are *eligible for consideration;* it isn't our decision. It is the parole board's decision.

The statutory release date is the one that we have no choice in, so as an offender approaches his statutory release, now we are in a situation where we definitely have to start thinking, what is the best strategy to program for this individual before he gets released, *because he is going out.* So with say three months left to go until the S.R., there is no point in saying he needs a nine-month violent offender program. At that point we are better off to give him, say, a three-month Anger and Emotions Management program, because at least that will give him some skills to deal with his violent cycle or his aggression cycle. Therefore, he may be able to substitute some constructive behaviours for the criminal behaviours that he's used in the past. Under those circumstances we are more than prepared to alter the original Correctional Plan or the original program plan and for example, cancel the nine-month program and give him the three-month program because it is better than nothing. And again, this follows along the lines of a harm reduction concept that if we are going to release him to the community anyways, let's at least release him with some skills so that he has a chance of not reoffending. Whereas if it is a day parole or full parole eligibility date, we are not prepared to compromise the program plan at all because it is the offender's responsibility and our responsibility to ensure that there is a reduction in risk to the degree possible and we *don't have* to release them on those dates.

Whether criminality is the responsibility of the community, the family, or the offender is a question that has often been debated. CSC has a mandated responsibility for the rehabilitation of offenders, but what is the community's responsibility, if any, in this process? What are some of the conflicts between public expectations, CSC mandate to rehabilitate offenders prior to their release back into the community, and the realities of this process as discussed by Administrator 8? Other interesting points raised by Administrator 8 centre on the ethical dilemma that sometimes arises when CSC is faced with following the legislation in ensuring offenders are ready for release by their specified eligibility dates versus the issue of public safety—that is, reintegration versus rehabilitation. Are there ways to make these two important concepts more compatible?

Administrator 9: *Program refusal issue or the resistance to programming* is another issue related to the previous issue regarding the releasing of sex offenders. Many offenders are held beyond their day and full parole eligibility date, not just because of the programming issues discussed previously, i.e., requiring enough time to finish the program(s) before they are released, but also because of their own refusal to participate. This is the dilemma; when we are funded for programming, from Treasury Board or from National Headquarters, we are funded on an estimated twenty-five percent refusal rate on average, across the board for programming. In other words, our funding is predicated on a twenty-five percent of the offenders, needing programming who will not take it. Therefore, we get seventy-five percent of our need funded with the assumption that twenty-five percent will never take the program because they will refuse. If we say that in the Pacific Region, four hundred offenders need a specific program, we will be funded for three hundred of those offenders to take that program. Although this funding model has been around for a long while, it still represents relatively current thinking. When you go to Treasury Board to ask for money, the first thing they ask is what your level of need is. And when you tell them, they want to know how many of those inmates will actually participate—so to be honest with the Treasury Board we tell them we have a twenty-five percent refusal rate across sex, violence, and all of these programs combined. Therefore, they tell us we will be funded at that rate because historically we have been unable to get that other twenty-five percent into treatment.

Now consider the previous dilemma, which was that programming often takes offenders past their day and full parole eligibility date and the pressure is on us to release them by those dates. If an offender refuses to take a program, then the longer he refuses, the longer the delay until he is released. Potentially, if he refuses right up until statutory release, then he is released without having taken any programming but having served the full legal requirement of the sentence and then representing the highest possible risk to society. Refusers, in my view, often represent the most dangerous of the offender population, although some guys may refuse because they know what they did was wrong and they know how to correct it. They do not necessarily need anyone to help them and will leave and go and change their lives on their own. However, this does not happen a lot. Most people need some help. Nevertheless, a few guys will achieve that. A vast majority of them are refusing because they continue to be committed to an antisocial criminal lifestyle, criminal attitudes, values, and beliefs. These guys when they get out are going to be your recidivists, the people who are going to commit new crimes and the people who are going to be a threat to society.

So the inclination or common sense approach would be to go after this refusal group and try to change their minds, try to get them to be willing to take these programs, because if they don't, they represent the highest risk, and if they do we may actually reduce their risk to the point where we are really contributing to the safety of society. However, the dilemma then becomes if you were to reduce your refusal rate to fifteen percent what happens to your funding base? Your funding base is at seventy-five percent of your need, but if you suddenly have people to the tune of eighty-five percent of your need base willing to take the programming, then you end up with a ten percent gap between your program capacity and your program need. You end up with more and longer wait-lists and more people incarcerated beyond day and full parole eligibility date, and you exacerbate the problem to the point where now you have huge numbers of offenders, literally hundreds of offenders who are going to be delayed. Not only are they delayed, but also they are willing/wanting to take the programs, telling us that they are convinced now that they should take the programs and now we cannot provide it. *So the more we work to overcome program resistance, by overcoming the refusal issue, the more of a backlog and wait-list and a negative assessment we create for ourselves and the tougher it is to manage the programming agenda.*

Therefore, a dilemma certainly exists for the time being. What we might be able to do at some time is that if we do get this eighty-five percent level of participation or willingness and we do have this excessive backlog we could perhaps go to Treasury Board and say we have introduced tools like *motivational interviewing, motivational enhancement programs, treatment readiness programming,* to encourage more offenders to participate. We could argue that our refusal rate is now only fifteen percent or ten percent and we need a larger funding base and Treasury Board may respond to that. However, it is in the transition between current and new thinking, that the dilemma will be felt. In my view, the ethical dilemma is should we or should we not pursue the *refusers* and work toward motivating them to become involved in programming. On the one hand, from a strict safety and risk reduction principle you would have to say yes, that you should be challenging/encouraging those guys. On the other hand, from a budget management perspective and performance assessment perspective, you might just say that if they do not want to participate, then fine. Chances are you are not going to be successful in motivating them anyways, and you can rationalize this by saying let's put the money into those guys who are really motivated and really want to do well. Funding versus principles; it is an interesting dilemma. For me personally, there is no question what the answer is: you do the right thing from a public safety perspective. For other people the right thing may be living within their budget. You cannot extend yourself beyond your budget, and if seventy-five percent is your funding level, then you should be providing for that level of need.

Administrator 9 raises an important point. In looking at program participation rates and drop out rates, should this be examined strictly from a safety and risk reduction perspective or from a budget management and performance assessment perspective? One could argue that each perspective presents its own set of ethical dilemmas.

Administrator 10: Another ethical issue is around sex offenders and whether they should be released into the community even if it seems premature. Ethically, of course, there is always that discussion around sex offenders and should they be released into the community when we clearly know that they have not released their need or desire to sexually offend. And I think it comes back to the philosophy of what does reintegration mean. We're providing them with a support network to reduce their chances of harming society, so by not doing that, we are releasing them without that kind of support network. That's always an ethical toss-up because we know if we release them at Warrant Expiry Date without a support network his chances of recidivating are extremely high, whereas if we release him earlier we can implement the support network with that offender. We are not saying that he will never commit crimes again, but at least we have provided him with some contacts. He may go to seek support and inevitably they have to be released, which is stipulated in the legislation. This legislation is there to say that conditional release or early release is there for a reason—it provides an opportunity for supervision and support. And that's what we are always balancing.

Administrator 11: Where we are moving to in corrections is to really engage the community—to get back to having them involved and to help to create some understanding that these are our neighbours. Whether you are looking at it in a macro or micro level, they are still part of our community. Sex offenders right now present the most contentious issues in terms of harming society, and what we are trying to do right now is to build on that. We have what we call the *Circles of Support* groups, and we currently contract with them now and really try to engage those types of interventions to work with these sex offenders on release, because they are going out into the community, and how we do that can be effective or ineffective. The more opportunities we have to engage those types of groups or individuals or agencies into that mix the safer society is going to be. We have to look at the ethical issue and yet balance our mandate and protection of society in the bigger picture.

Administrator 9 has raised some interesting ethical questions to add to the preceding narratives regarding the timely release of offenders versus the need to complete programs. In echoing the question raised by this administrator, should CSC pursue the refusers of the programs and work towards motivating them to participate or not? What might some of the costs and benefits be?

While many of the interviewees have thought about conditional releases and the importance that programming plays in achieving some success with offenders' post-release, the issue of refusers has been raised. Coupled with the refusal rate is another issue: the requirement to argue one's case to the Treasury Board to obtain sufficient funding to provide the programming necessary for offenders who will one day be released. Both of these factors have a considerable impact on CSC's ability to meet its goals for successful reintegration of the offender once the release date and sentence requirements have been met.

CSC, Injection Drug Users, and Harm Reduction

Within corrections, another contentious issue is drug use, and in particular, injection drug use among offenders. This complex issue involves the use of drugs, the methods of using them (i.e., by injection), and the prevention of the spread of communicable diseases such as HIV and hepatitis. Some CSC interviewees commented:

Administrator 12: Harm reduction presents a moral and ethical dilemma and is a contentious issue in society generally, but within the corrections system, with offenders, probably even more so. This is particularly so because much of the harm reduction we talk about in the prison environment is related to addictions—opiate addictions in particular—as well as the use of condoms and the use of bleach and those type of things. Obviously, these are issues that some people in society take offence to because they consider harm reduction in general, and especially for offenders, a nurturing of the addictive behaviour or the dangerous high-risk behaviour. As you know, CSC has not adopted a needle exchange program because they feel that this is taking the harm reduction concept a bit too far for a prison environment. Nevertheless, certainly in many countries, and in many cities in many countries, there are needle exchange programs. For example, we have them here in Vancouver. Therefore, a pure harm reduction approach would certainly incorporate that kind of initiative, but certainly, CSC has not undertaken to move that far. That in and of itself represents an ethical issue for us because on the one hand, for example, needle exchange is a significant tool in the fight against spread of communicable disease such as Hepatitis C and HIV/AIDS, and we choose not to utilize it. In other words, we have chosen to adopt our own version of harm reduction based on what will be palatable in terms of public reaction, politicians' reactions, the House of Commons, and so on. In my view, this is an issue that CSC has to address. If we support a harm reduction model, we should embrace it totally in the same manner that the community does or we shouldn't be in the business of harm reduction at all because I am not sure that we should distinguish between levels of harm reduction.

Administrator 13: One of the other ethical dilemmas involved in this of course is that here, offenders are being treated with methadone and other harm reduction techniques when many citizens in society are not able to access those kinds of services for a variety of reasons or are not receiving assistance in order to access these services. So clearly the dilemma that exists in society also exists in corrections, although to a heightened degree because of the nature of the population we are dealing with. And of course there are citizens who would argue that they have limited access to methadone because they are required to pay for it, although once they reach the threshold of somewhere around six hundred to eight hundred dollars, they would normally be covered by PharmaCare. So at some time during the year they are also being supported. But the difference I think is whether a person is classified as "inmate" as opposed to an "offender," inmate meaning incarcerated in a Correctional Service of Canada facility and offender meaning either operating out of the community on a day or full parole or statutory release and/or residing in a residential centre which is connected with the community rather than CSC itself. That's the distinction between inmate and offender. For inmates, CSC has from a legal mandate perspective the responsibility to care for the health of inmates under its jurisdictions, so there is a law that requires us to provide those services. Whereas for offenders, the law does not require us to, and in fact, requires the offender and the community to take on some of those responsibilities. So even our offenders, when they re-enter the communities, even if they are on parole, are required to contribute to their own health requirements to the degree that they can. If the inmate has absolutely no source of funds social assistance will support them, or if their medical card has not come through yet, for example, they may be subsidized for a period of time, but only up until they have a source of income and then the responsibility is turned over to them. So there are many ethical dilemmas associated with harm reduction, including needle exchanges and methadone maintenance in the prisons, medical care and issues related to Hepatitis C and other communicable diseases.

To further complicate this situation, the argument as to who is responsible for an offender's health care has not been satisfactorily settled. Many community organizations responsible for public health care believe that the offender is still technically serving part of their sentence, albeit outside of the prison setting, and is, therefore, still the responsibility of CSC. CSC states that once the inmate has been released into the community, and still has some obligations to serve out the rest of their sentence, the offender/community are responsible for providing health care.

Administrator 14: The whole issue of infectious diseases is still a problem in jail—the sharing of needles by inmates, etc. We have taken some baby steps thus far in addressing these problems and have consulted with people who operate needle exchanges on the outside because they see it from all angles. People will probably be surprised to hear this from the area of security, but I support the needle exchange. This is because when I was an IPSO, every time correctional officers would seize needles from inmates they turned them over to me. I was like the contraband control officer and saw many of the homemade needles that they made from pen barrels, rubber soles from their running shoes to make the plungers, they use nails and they find all types of horrid devices to use for the needles—just the most disgusting things that you have ever seen and these are often shared. Therefore, I think there are positives to having a needle exchange, and it can work to our advantage as well. Before handing out needles, we would know who is using the drugs and we would know that we would lower the risk of staff being infected with dirty needles. Some of the inmates are lazy, and in some institutions like Kent, for example, if there is not always someone responsible to make sure that bleach is available, the program will fail, and of course it already has to some degree. With a needle exchange, however, the onus is on the inmate to bring back the dirty needle in exchange for a new one and this will be a more effective program, thereby lowering the rates of infections among injection drug users.

I think methadone use is another ethical issue. It is not that I do not like the idea of using methadone; it is the way it is being managed or monitored that bothers me.

Administrator 15: There are, to be sure, issues, and methadone is another example of a highly contentious issue—the notion of replacing one addictive drug with another addictive drug and are we really doing anyone any good? By "we," and I mean those of us who believe in harm reduction; it is by far a better option, because despite the fact that it is an addictive drug and it's almost as difficult to wean oneself off of methadone as it is to wean oneself off of heroin, the fact is that one can lead a somewhat normal life ... enjoy one's family, drive a car, find a job, go to church, play sports, and do all of the things that "normal" people do. Without methadone and using opiates they are incapacitated, and become tax absorbers rather than tax providers. In my view, and in the view of corrections, at least to some degree, harm reduction remains a viable option in the prison environment.

In terms of accessing the methadone maintenance program, in the past, Phase One of the methadone program was introduced, and only those offenders who were on methadone in the community prior to coming into a correctional institution, could get onto the methadone program inside. The idea was that CSC would continue with a program that the individual had been involved in prior to incarceration. The second situation in which methadone could be accessed was the "exceptional circumstances" phase, and that was brought in to address emergency or crisis situations when the health of the offender was being jeopardized by his continuing addiction and by failing to intervene with the methadone program could seriously impair the individual's long term health and possibly endanger their life. In addition, another criterion for accessing methadone under the exceptional circumstances phase was that all other interventions or attempts to overcome the addiction, such as programming or counselling, have failed. So in this phase of the methadone program, offenders had to demonstrate all three of these criteria: programming/counselling had failed, the health of the offender was continually being jeopardized, and that there was a crisis situation from a medical perspective in terms of this man's health/survival. If we could establish those three things then we could get this individual on methadone even if he had never been on it before. The third phase of the methadone maintenance program provided an opportunity for any offender with a serious addiction problem to develop a case through his parole officer for involvement in the methadone program regardless of whether he had ever been on it before and regardless whether he fully meets the criteria of being in crisis.

Although the use of harm reduction strategies has been commonplace throughout the delivery of a variety of health services (e.g., preventative vaccinations), it has created some heated debates when included in a discussion of those individuals with drug addictions. The controversy has been particularly noticeable when examining drug addiction within CSC. We have heard from some administrators who support the idea of harm reduction as a necessary service that should be available to inmates/offenders, and they have spoken briefly of the benefits of adopting this framework. However, front line staff have not always supported this. What might some of the objections be to implementing a full-scale harm reduction program for CSC? Would the adoption of a harm reduction program be consistent with the mission statement and the responsibilities of CSC as articulated in the CCRA?

On the one hand, it would seem that CSC has established a unique program to assist offenders who would benefit from being on the methadone maintenance program. This program not only identifies criminogenic needs and offers some solutions for severe drug cravings and withdrawal symptoms through the stabilization of drug using offenders, but also offers the offender the opportunity to participate in programming and to lead a more normal life once they are released (see CSC Commissioner's Directive 800–1). However, as some of the CSC interviewees stated, the issue of the transmission of communicable diseases within the CSC population is a large one, and embracing and fully applying harm reduction along with some of the more controversial harm reduction strategies has not met with a unified response.

Offender Management and Security Issues

The appropriate use of force when faced with security matters is another issue that CSC administrators struggle with, as the following interviews outline:

Administrator 16: An issue of interest to me is that of security issues, and this might fit into being an ethical issue regarding *the use of more humane methods of restraining equipment for disruptive inmates.* We have been looking at various forms or different levels of force because right now we have restraining equipment, which is based on the level of threat or force. So right now for levels of force that are threatening, we have gas and batons, and then we go right up to firearms. Therefore, in the event that gas or batons are not successful in controlling the situation, the only level of force you can go to is firearms. What we have been trying to look at is other levels of force that are non-lethal, or, should I say, not completely non-lethal, but less lethal. Therefore, we have looked at things like a "shock sock" for example. Instead of going and hitting someone with a baton and inflicting permanent damage, for example, because if you do hit someone with a baton you can break a bone, fracture the skull if they did manage to get hit on the head, etc., you can use an alternative to the levels of force that we have. This is one such device, which of course is much softer and less lethal that will knock a person over, but will not inflict any permanent damage. Nevertheless, people have been generally scared to look at this type of technology because there have been some deaths in the U.S. where they use this type of stuff. Therefore, although some might argue that this technology is still lethal, the response is that this is true. However, it is much less lethal than the other levels of force we employ currently. For example, the use of batons can be lethal, using gas can also be lethal if you release it on someone, who, for example, may have a heart or breathing condition; they can die from that. Therefore, we are saying that this is an alternative and is less likely to inflict permanent damage.

The other thing that we looked at is the use of *"Tasers."* These are being used everywhere in police agencies across the world and they are the preferred thing to use. Therefore, a disruptive person, or a person who is violent, threatening, or maybe holding weapon, before the only alternative for a police officer was to maybe have to shoot a person. Therefore, someone is coming at you with a knife and you had possibly had to shoot him or her … so you either have killed him or her, or possibly seriously injured him or her. However, with the tasers, you can still keep that safe distance between yourself and the perpetrator, but when you use it, I guarantee you will knock them down, but there will not be any long lasting effects. Tasers completely disable the person and allow the officers to get in and subdue them or restrain them right away without any threat.

Corrections for some reason will not look at the taser. Well, what I should say is that we did look at it and were going to run it in a pilot project back east. But senior management had heard that they put out around fifty thousand volts of power. However, it's not the volts that hurt you; it's the amps that hurt you, and these devices have around thirteen amps, and these devices are actually powered by a nine volt battery. But what people have a tendency to hear is that it has fifty thousand volts and they then assume you will electrocute someone if you tase them. The taser does not influence or affect the rhythm of the heart; it interrupts the impulses or the messages between the brain and the muscles and the person becomes limp or falls to the ground. So right now, we only have batons or firearms, nothing in between. There are other alternatives out there, in my view, which are more humane.

Some important issues have been raised by this administrator; for example, the need to have available less lethal forms of restraint or control when the need arises to use them. Recently, the use of tasers has garnered some media attention. In view of what you might have read or heard about tasers and Administrator 16's view of tasers, what is your position on CSC's use of them as a more humane alternative to current methods of restraint and control? What might some of the ethical dilemmas be in using or not using tasers on disruptive inmates?

Although there are several technological advances in the field of security equipment, not everyone is in agreement about which device is appropriate to use in CSC security practices. Perhaps part of the reason has to do with the cost of such devices. However, other confounding issues revolve around the possible lethality of using such equipment as tasers on offenders who pose a threat to staff and other offenders.

Victims' Rights in Influencing Correctional Decisions

Another issue raised by CSC administrators in the context of ethical dilemmas is the involvement of victims in the affairs of CSC and its relationship with offenders. As Administrator 17 states, how far do we go in allowing victims' input into the criminal justice process in terms of trials, sentencing options, and eventual conditional releases? There have been several recent cases where victims of crime have criticized the criminal justice system for what they believe is lenient treatment of those individuals charged and/or convicted of a crime.

Administrator 17: Victims—how far do we go? I believe that victim rights are good for the entire criminal justice system. But how far do we—how far do we have that influence decision-making. I think it should influence decision-making and I, quite often when I am talking to inmates, when we are talking about their case, I refer to their victim. I ask them "have you thought about your victim? Do you know what they are doing now?" That type of thing. You can't forget the victim. We are going to have to make decisions; hopefully ethics will control that process but that's a separate area.

Administrator 18: Victims' rights—balancing victims into our work as previously mentioned, and we are making great gains ... but again, the balance of "should he be released" because of the victims or not ... I would like to use a different approach, which is, let's include the victim in the release strategy. One needs to understand that he is going into the community, so let's get everyone involved to the level they want to get involved or volunteer to be involved.

Can you identify any ethical dilemmas that may arise as a result of having victims of crime involved in the decision making process around the offender's release strategy?

Conclusion

Making the distinction between morals and ethics, as previously discussed, is not always easy. Morality has been described in terms of behaviours, which are generally characterized in terms of being either good or bad. Ethics is most often associated with professional behaviours and provides a set of standards against which we can measure our decisions. Many organizations have established codes of ethics, codes of conduct, and codes of professional practice to guide the actions of employer and employee alike. These are often based on principles aimed at placing the public interest before all others.

However, within most organizations, such as CSC, the potential for ethical binds occurs—that is, the "contradiction or conflict between what is expected and what is perceived to be right." The solution to these conflicts appears to include negotiation and compromise, achieving a balance on both sides. However, in those cases where no reasonable solution can be reached, individuals and organizations may part company, or a tear in the fabric of the organization itself may result. Some of the ethical dilemmas faced by CSC as an organization and some of the management and staff issues provide excellent examples of such ethical binds and philosophical inquiries. In some of these cases, there have been some workable solutions developed, while others continue to challenge the morals, ethics, and values of those involved.

Research has shown that a poor ethical culture in an organization can contribute to workplace stress. There also exists a strong relationship between perceived ethical standards of organizations and management and staff job satisfaction. Greater job satisfaction results in higher morale, greater cooperation, less staff turn-over, less conflict, greater efficiency, and better overall functioning of the organization. Employees want to belong to something they can believe in and a sense of high corporate or organizational ethical values appears to be one of those things they can believe in.

On the whole, the Public Service of Canada has a high standard of ethical behaviour. However, ethics need attention on an ongoing basis in corrections as well as other public institutions and among other professionals. This need has not arisen because the public service is experiencing major problems, but rather because ethical values are so important in the daily lives of public servants, and pressures on them raise new or deeper ethical issues, such as the public interest over personal career interests in a time of downsizing. Every day, in myriad ways, public servants make decisions and take actions that affect the lives and interests of all Canadians. They handle private and confidential information, provide help and service, manage and account for public funds, and answer calls from people at risk. Because public servants hold such a significant public trust, ethical values must necessarily have a heightened importance for them.

Study Questions

1. Discuss the differences between the concepts of ethics, values, and morals.
2. Pick one of the ethical binds discussed by CSC administrators and discuss the ethical decision making a person employed by CSC may face when dealing with this issue. In reading the CSC Standards of Professional Conduct, can you identify a situation faced by a CSC employee that might conflict with the ethical standards dictated by the Standards of Professional Conduct?
3. Discuss and give some examples of how ethical stress develops within an organization. What can an organization do to remedy this?
4. In terms of decision-making practices, describe what is meant by "discretional" decision-making. What is meant by "compulsory" decision-making? Give examples to support your discussion.
5. This chapter discusses some of the ethical issues as recounted by CSC administrators. What are their concerns regarding staff issues versus high CSC and public expectations?
6. What is an ethical subculture? Can you give examples of places where they might exist?

Bibliography

* Items with asterisks are also suggested readings for the chapter.

*Almond, B. (1998). *Exploring Ethics. A Traveller's Tale*. Oxford: Blackwell Publisher.
Barry, V. (1985). *Applying ethics: A text with readings*. Belmont, Calif: Wadsworth.
Correctional Service of Canada. *Recommendations of the Coroners Inquest into the Death of Robert Gentles*. http://www.csc-scc.gc.ca/text/pblct/gentles/38_e.shtml

*Correctional Service of Canada. Report on Governance Structures for Values and Ethics. 7.0 Correctional Service of Canada (CSC). http://www.hrma-agrh.gc.ca/veo-bve/publications/rgs-rsg07_e.asp

*Ekstedt, J. W. and Jackson, M. A. (1996). The ethics of correctional practice. In, *The Keepers and the Kept: Introduction to Corrections in Canada.* (p. 240–255). Toronto: ITP Nelson.

*Pollock-Byrne, J. (1989). *Ethics in Crime and Justice: Dilemmas and Decisions.* Calif.: Brooks/Cole.

Sherman, L. (1981). *The teaching of ethics in criminology and criminal justice.* Washington, D.C.: Joint Commission on Criminology and Criminal Justice Education and Standards, LEAA.

Stohr, M., Hemmens, C., Marsh, R., Barrier, G. and Palhegyi, D. (2000). Can't scale this? The ethical parameters of Correctional work. *Prison Journal,* 80(1), 56–79.

A Strong Foundation: Report of the Task Force on Public Service Values and Ethics. (1996) John C. Tait, Chair. Ottawa: Canadian Centre for Management Development. http://www.ccmd-ccg.gc.ca/Research/publications/pdfs/tait.pdf

Suggested Readings

Erwin, R.E. (Winter/Spring 1993). Loyalties and why loyalty should be ignored. *Criminal Justice Ethics,* 12(1), 36–42.

Independent Commission Against Corruption; Code of Conduct and Ethics. http://www.icac.nsw.gov.au/pub/public/pub2_21q.pdf

Jones, J. and Carlson, D. (2001). *Reputable Conduct: Ethical Issues in Policing and Corrections, 2nd ed.* Upper Saddle River, NJ: Prentice Hall.

Robinson, D. (1992). Commitment, attitudes, career aspirations and work stress: The experience of correctional staff. *Forum on Corrections Research,* 4(1).

Souryal, S. and McKay, B. (Summer/Fall 1996). Personal loyalty to superiors in public service. *Criminal Justice Ethics,* 15(2), 44–63.

3 Correctional Service of Canada – The Organization

This chapter explores the organization of the Correctional Service of Canada and its three levels of management: national, regional, and institutional/district parole offices. The national office focuses on planning, approving, evaluating, monitoring, and auditing the planning and policy development for the Service. The task of regional headquarters is to implement CSC policy, programs, services, and activities in the facilities and community offices within the region. Finally, the institutional and community centres in each region are responsible for operationalizing the policies and programs. Although the Correctional Investigator and the National Parole Board are independent of the CSC, both affect its work and act as partners in various capacities; therefore, we include their roles in this chapter. Lastly, some basic facts about corrections are detailed.

The *Corrections and Conditional Release Act* (Section 5) established that the Correctional Service of Canada shall be responsible for the following:

a) The care and custody of inmates;
b) the provision of programs that contribute to the rehabilitation of offenders and to their successful reintegration into the community;
c) the preparation of inmates for release;
d) parole, statutory release supervision, and long-term supervision of offenders; and
e) maintaining a program of public education about the operations of the Service.

The commissioner of corrections is appointed by the governor in council. This individual is responsible for the regulation and management of the Service. The commissioner reports to the Minister of Public Safety Canada.

National Management Level

The commissioner is based at National Headquarters in Ottawa and works with a support group that includes a senior deputy commissioner, a deputy commissioner for women, five regional deputy commissioners, seven assistant commissioners who each head a CSC sector, an executive director, a general counsel, and a chief audit executive for CORCAN. Together they plan, approve, evaluate, monitor, and audit the planning and policy development for the Service. The specific responsibilities for each position are described on the CSC website, as below:

> The *senior deputy commissioner* is accountable to the commissioner. The senior deputy commissioner's main role is to support the commissioner, focus on the management of strategic issues and act as the commissioner when required.

> The *deputy commissioner for women* is responsible for the development and oversight of programs for women offenders.

> The five *regional deputy commissioners* are responsible for the management of CSC operations within their respective regions, implementation of correctional policy, and leadership in providing advice on criminal justice system matters.

> The *assistant commissioners* are responsible for the management of CSC operations within their respective sectors, implementation of correctional policy, and leadership in providing advice on criminal justice system matters.

CSC Sectors

> The *Women Offender Sector* is responsible for effective policy and program development, implementation, and ongoing program delivery for federally sentenced women.

> The *Correctional Operations and Programs Sector* is responsible for the integrity of community and institutional operations across CSC and for improving the delivery of safe corrections.

The *Policy and Research Sector* is responsible for strategic planning and strategic policy. It also responds to offender redress and human rights issues, requests for access to information and privacy, and issues raised by the correctional investigator.

The *Performance Assurance Sector* assesses, measures, analyzes and evaluates operational performance in CSC.

The *Corporate Services Sector* is responsible for informatics and technological support, technical services, finance and material management.

The *Human Resource Management Sector* serves as a focal point for the resolution of administrative and human resource activities and providing interpretations of policies, directives and guidelines.

The *Health Services Sector* is responsible for the quality and integrity of health services provided to federal offenders in institutional and in some community settings across CSC. This includes health care delivery such as assessment, diagnosis, treatment, health education, disease prevention, harm reduction, monitoring, surveillance and follow-up care. The sector is also responsible for effective health policy, as well as program development and implementation that will contribute to offenders' rehabilitation and successful reintegration into the community.

The *Public Affairs and Parliamentary Relations (PAPR) Sector* is the focal point for CSC's communications, citizen engagement and outreach services. The work of the sector is aligned with the Service's mandate to contribute to the public safety of all Canadians.

CORCAN is a special operating agency of CSC responsible for aiding in the safe reintegration of offenders into Canadian society. CORCAN provides employment and training opportunities to offenders incarcerated in federal penitentiaries and, for brief periods of time, to offenders after they are released into the community.

The *executive director* is responsible for coordinating, preparing and vetting matters related to the preparation of correspondence to the commissioner, the Minister's Office, members of parliament and legislative assemblies. The director also transmits and interprets

policy and political issues and coordinates or prepares briefing documents for the Minister.

The *chief audit executive* is responsible for the effective management of
the internal audit function designed to assess and improve the effectiveness of risk management, control and governance processes within CSC.

The *General Counsel* is responsible for the resolution of legal issues,
and the interpretation of policies, directives, and guidelines. (Correctional Service of Canada, 2008)

Figure 3.1. Executive Committee of the Correctional Service of Canada

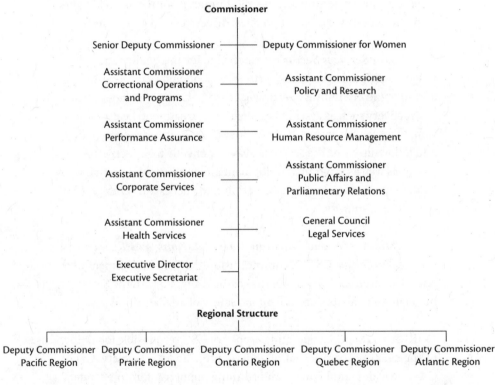

Source: CSC Website *How We Operate* 2008

Regional Management Level

Regional headquarters are the delivery arms of the Correctional Service of
Canada, tasked with implementing CSC policy, programs, services, and activ-
ities in the facilities and community offices within the region. The Correctional
Service of Canada is divided into five regional headquarters: Atlantic, Québec,
Ontario, Prairies, and Pacific regions.

These regional offices support the regional deputy commissioners at National Headquarters who are responsible for the administration of institutions in their respective regions.

Figure 3.2. The Five Regions of CSC

Pacific Region serving British Columbia, and Yukon Territory. (Abbotsford)

Prairie Region serving Alberta, Saskatchewan, Manitoba, Ontario West of Thunder Bay, and the Northwest Territories. (Saskatoon)

Ontario Region serving Ontario as far west as Thunder Bay, and Nunavut Territory. (Kingston)

Québec Region serving Québec. (Laval)

Atlantic Region serving New Brunswick, Nova Scotia, Prince Edward Island, and Newfoundland & Labrador. (Moncton)

(Correctional Service of Canada 2007)

In each region, there is an assistant deputy commissioner who reports to the deputy commissioner. He or she heads a regional administrative structure that has regional administrators for the core groups of operation: Security, Aboriginal Issues, Programs, Health Care, Human Resources, Reintegration, and Chaplaincy. They report to the assistant deputy commissioner and the chiefs in each section report to them.

In the following sections, correctional administrators describe some of the positions at regional headquarters:

Security

Administrator 1: In general, we are responsible for anything in relation to the security across the region. So we're the policy experts in those areas and our major areas of responsibility are things like search and seizure, use of force, and we actually participate in the use of force review in addition to sort of being the policy experts. It starts at the sites and they do a review there. There is a requirement that pre-planned use of force must be videotaped and there is a whole bunch of documentation that goes along with that. So the sites review that and they send it here. We review it and we send it on to National Headquarters and the Correctional Investigator and they do the same thing. They review the same package to ensure compliance with policy.

Contingency plans—we ensure that they are updated on an annual basis at all the sites—the community and the institutional ones. We also do a quality control check on them to ensure that everything is in them that should be there and with September 11th there have been some changes and we will be seeing more changes with that.

Urinalysis—we have a urinalysis program under the CCRA. Again, that is one of our major areas of responsibility. We receive the budget for that as well so as part of that we send some of the money to the community because they use it to pay the collectors because normally it is a contractor, not CSC staff, who do it in the community. In the institution it is not a contractor, it is CSC staff who do it, so there is no additional funds in that way. There is a whole bunch of operational issues with it. The budget that we keep, they send their invoices here because it is a national contract and we ensure the invoices for the actual analysis of the sample is paid.

I would have to say that those are the major areas of responsibility. Some of the other things, like, we often get questioned about escorts, the number of correctional officers required in escorts. We attend the correctional officer training program for the issues that relate to us. So those ones that we talked about. So things like that come up sort of. Any enhanced reliability checks for the region, that people have a criminal record, comes to our office so we sort of ... we prepare the memo for our deputy commissioner's signature to the field and they explore it a little further and do an assessment as to whether we should grant enhanced reliability for that person. Then it comes back to us and our deputy commissioner makes a decision on whether it will be granted or not. We are responsible for the cancellation or withdrawal of those as well.

So those are, like, the major issues that sort of we deal with every day. So we are not just setting the policy; we are involved in the application of it as well. We conduct security reviews on various items. For example, when a warden changes, we'll do a change of command audit of all the security functions. So that would include searching, principal entrance things, use of force, staff, that same type of thing. So we are making sure that everything is in order before the new person takes over.

We do security reviews in the community and the institution. We have gone to do a few in the parole office, those types of things. We usually do those once a year but it varies. We've done—in fact in the last six months, this is fairly new—we've done a number of threat of risk assessments on various items. We went to an institution and did a threat risk assessment on the requirement of a correctional officer in the kitchen because there are inmates working in the kitchen. I went to a women's facility, and we did a threat risk assessment there on the requirement for a second primary worker to do the rounds on evenings and back shift. So that is something else that we participated in.

Administrator 2: I am responsible for the security position here at head-quarters, and our main function at Regional Headquarters is to ensure that all of the security functions, security programs and policies in the region are being adhered to and are being followed. This involves not only the corrections staff, but also the institutions themselves. As a management team within institutions, they are responsible for seeing that the policies are being followed. Therefore, when we go in and audit security functions within a site, we are actually auditing the entire institution and I would go back, report to deputy warden or the warden, and identify any deficiencies in adherence to the policies.

One of the things that really take up a lot of our time is *the monitoring of use of force*, and all staff are required to fill out reports following such use of force. So, for example, the cabinet in my office is full of such reports from institutions for such use of force, which is a common occurrence. Therefore, my staff here receive such reports even if the inmate is not taking the initiative. So if in the report it was found that the officer used excessive force, I would identify that as a deficiency to my supervisor who is the assistant deputy commissioner and those deficiencies are then stipulated in a prepared memorandum and the warden can take certain actions. It is a very tight and restricted policy. When you have eight hundred to nine hundred correctional officers in this region at any given time, if they are not up to date or up to speed on the policy, it can create quite a problem. Therefore, our primary function is to make sure that in this region all of the policies, procedures and standing orders with respect to security are followed.

Both Administrators 1 and 2 comment on the time-consuming nature of monitoring use of force. The Commissioner's Directive on Use of Force (567–1) states that each incident involving use of force must be reported accurately and subsequently reviewed at the institutional, regional, and national levels. For pre-planned use of force or potential use of force incidents, videotape recordings must be made. As Administrator 2 states, the use of force policy is very tight and restricted, and a large amount of time is spent and documentation generated following each use of force incident. Why do you think all use of force incidents undergo such rigorous review? Can you think of both positive and negative impacts of having such a tight and restrictive policy?

Personnel

In terms of human resources, or the management of personnel, one CSC Administrator explained:

Administrator 3: Personnel are comprised of five major areas and I oversee four of these. The fifth area is training and this is overseen by the Director of the Staff College.

Number one: *staffing*—recruitment outside and within appointments, with the exception of correctional officers which come through the Staff College. Nurses and psych staff are handled by the Regional Health Centre.

Number two: *responsibilities for Classification*—organization structure, classification of jobs, provide feedback to supervisors and employees and are responsible for the construction of job descriptions.

Number three: *HR management*—the "softer side," such as employment equity, performance appraisals, succession planning, and overseeing the responsibilities related to official language requirements. The Federal Department must provide some level in other languages—i.e., French/English—must arrange testing to verify level of expertise, establish rules and responsibility re bilingual positions, and this is an administrative function.

Number four: *Staff Relations and Compensation*—oversees things like the relationships with the union; disciplinary issues in the sense that I provide advice/guidance, is provided to managers with respect to individual employee situations and whether there should be a verbal, written, financial penalty or a suspension or even a termination; grievances; union strike issues—designations and exclusions for example. On the compensation side, the paying of staff, advice/guidance re discretionary benefits; advice re retirement options and benefits.

Reintegration

The concept of reintegration of offenders is the primary goal of CSC. Almost from the moment an inmate begins his or her sentence, reintegration planning takes place to ensure that they are as prepared as possible. Through various testing, assessments, and programming, inmates are geared toward their release back into the community

Administrator 4: We work very closely with National Headquarters when it comes to the monitoring and reintegration of offenders. Reintegration is ... basically our mandate in the CSC is to provide offenders with safe and timely release into the community. That means once they are brought to us from the court system, we take them into our Reception Centre, we do what is known as an intake assessment and we develop a Correctional Plan. We go through a variety of testing, look at the results of other assessments—for example, we look at a number of psychological testing, educational assessments, substance use assessments, vocational testing— and all of that information is analysed. We interview the offender and we assign that offender to a security classification where he can continue with programming. As you know, we have a variety of programming available for offenders. So basically, my responsibility is to monitor each step of that process, as the offender goes into the institution and takes his programs. We prepare him for release, whether it is to transfer him to lower security, or release him to the community. We prepare documentation for the parole board and they make the decision. What I am doing is overseeing from the deputy commissioner perspective, whether or not all of that has been done according to our policies. We would be preparing documentation or strategies for our region to specify where we need to improve or what we are doing well, and share those practices across the country.

I have a number of staff that work here in this department. Our portfolios that we are mainly responsible for here, while I say reintegration specifically, we are also looking at victims issues, we look at work release, we prepare for the deputy commissioner work release programs that extend beyond sixty days ... it's warden's authority under sixty days and the deputy commissioner after that. We also are the coordinators for inter-regional transfers within the region. We also look at population management, we manage that portfolio here as well. International transfers is something we have a role in and work directly with NHQ on this—statutory release, detention etc. all of the portfolios that pertain to reintegration we have a play in monitoring, developing strategies, and where we are doing good work, we share that. So it really is a big department.

Operations

In terms of the operation of CSC, one administrator noted the extent of responsibility attributed to the assistant deputy commissioner of operations:

> **Administrator 5:** I am in the position of assistant deputy commissioner of operations. We look after the institutions and the parole districts. We provide a lot of guidance, leadership, budgeting, and funding, and a lot of—not really the hands on kinds of administration for the institutions and parole districts, but more we provide a lot of leadership to the wardens and the district directors. That is what we do regionally. The wardens and the district directors report functionally up to me—as I mentioned, this position has responsibility for the operational side of things. So if they have any difficulty with the running of the institutions, any security policies, reintegration policies, case management, parole decisions, those sorts of things—getting people ready for the streets is the sorts of things we do. Reintegration is really the fore of it. Safety is also part of our mandate with respect to both the security of the inmates and the staff. I am directly linked to the running of the eight institutions and parole districts here, so anything like that the deputy wardens will report to me on the running of these areas. We are having some difficulty writing the segregation policy. We do a lot of policy interpretation for example, accommodation planning, and population management—how do we move offenders from here to there and also within specific security divisions and levels within the institutions. We provide a lot of the logistical infrastructure for them to move around and operate in. Therefore, it keeps us busy, but the public is very happy when we are successful.

Correctional Programs

In terms of programming responsibilities, much of the reintegration agenda is reflected in functions such as programming, management, and budgeting responsibilities.

> **Administrator 6:** My role is that I represent the region for all the correctional programs that our national organization develops, like the program for substance abuse, program for sex offenders, living skills, family violence, all those programs. I am the administrator that makes sure the appropriate funds, appropriate standards are maintained in the programs

in both the institution and the community for the offender population. I manage the budget for that and I provide functional supervision to the assistant warden of correctional programs to ensure that the offender needs are appropriately identified and that we have enough resources to meet those needs. I allocate the budgets to the different institutions and communities for specific programs based on offender needs.

Administrator 7: My reporting accountability as the regional administrator of correctional programming (RACP) is directly to the assistant deputy commissioner of correctional operations (ADCCO) who is the 2-IC (second in command) directly-reporting to the deputy commissioner. Then reporting to me here at Regional Headquarters, I have a series of project managers as well as a couple of clerical staff who support, the entire cluster. Reporting to the project managers are the quality assurance staff and program delivery staff. In my cluster or division we have fifty-eight-point-five staff, including myself. Most of the R.A.s have six to eight people reporting here at the regional level and the difference for me is that we have clustered the program delivery function. Instead of having program officers reporting to managers at the site, they report here, deliver at the sites, and the sites provide the day-to-day support. Therefore, the roles are a little bit reversed and that is why my group is larger, and we have done that largely because program delivery is a very specialized area and the people delivering the program need to have expert leadership and supervision. This is provided by my project managers here at Regional Headquarters who are experts in such areas as substance abuse, living skills, family violence, and so on. That is the biggest difference between my shop and that of other R.A.s. They have their teams here at Regional Headquarters as well; they just do not have their teams in the field. Although if you talk to the R.A. of Informatics, his setup is identical to mine—he has a team here in RHQ and a team out in the field, again because of the specialization associated with his division. So to summarize, there is the ADCCO, there is my level, there are project managers and there are field delivery staff.

In addition to the reporting structure consisting of the ADDCO, now ADC 10, regional administrators, project managers and field delivery staff, which often makes up the bulk of a cluster or division and brings "team management" responsibilities, there are also other specific duties involved in correctional programming including resource allocation and management, data collection, and evaluation, as described by Administrator 8.

Administrator 8: Functional—in our context, corrections—means something other than "line" related, so we talk about functional authority as being responsibility for a particular area without having line authority; in other words, we offer consultative and supportive services but we don't have direct control in terms of giving direction to the staff in that area. Line authority is the opposite, then. It's direct supervisory control. I am sure that is a fairly common situation in all organizations. My primary function is to develop and oversee the programming agenda in CSC, and that includes a whole variety of things from development, to program implementation, to monitoring programs for quality assurance. In evaluating programs there are resource management issues related to programming—identification of resources, the management of those resources, and the allocation of those resources. There are responsibilities for our program delivery staff, and in my area there are about forty such staff at the delivery level, and then we have functional responsibility for another one hundred staff or so in the field in the areas of social programs or core activities, program coordination at the sites, and to some degree program delivery at the sites for staff who deliver program, at various sites but do not report directly to my shop.

The social programs area or core activities area or the whole social development area includes recreation, arts and crafts, social and cultural development, and to some degree visits and correspondence. The primary programming areas that CSC are involved with includes substance abuse, academic and vocational education, living skills programs, violence, sex, family violence, special needs groups, unique offender populations, and so on. You could of course break each of those areas down; for example, for education we deal with learning disabilities, English as a second language, adult basic education, GED to some degree, which also has a variety of sub-categories.

So to get back to function, it's to oversee programming capacity in terms of management, program delivery, and to contribute to the reintegration agenda. Although I am unable to show you a copy of the newer analysis of our cluster operation, I do have the older one here. We call it a cluster operation because we've basically clustered or centralized program delivery services under the RACP, and so the program delivery staff at all of the sites report here, but they operate out of the various individual sites. So part of our function, then, is to manage contracts and to conduct needs analysis, to do program planning, program implementation, quality assurance, provide functional management or guidance/advice to the field and to senior managers throughout the region, making training available to staff is an important one also—not only the staff who are involved in program delivery, but also the staff who are involved in the management of programs. Part of our role is to also conduct staffing or hiring initiatives to bring new people into the organization. We also maintain statistics and databases around the work that we do. That's important, being able to report on those.

As described by Administrators 5, 6, 7, and 8, Regional Headquarters are responsible for implementing CSC policy, programs, services, and activities in the facilities and community offices within the region. The responsibilities and functions of these positions are numerous and vast. Can you see the potential benefits and pitfalls of having these positions at a regional level as opposed to at a national or operational level?

Operational Management Level
Each region consists of

> correctional facilities classified as maximum, medium, and min-
> imum security, women's facilities, district offices, parole offices, and
> community correctional centres. These facilities are responsible for
> the delivery of programs, secure housing, the safe reintegration of
> offenders by implementing both national and regional policies and
> programs, and for participating in the formulation of corporate policy
> and plans and ensuring their appropriate implementation. (Treasury
> Board of Canada Secretariat, 2003)

Correctional Facilities
Roles and Responsibilities
On September 4, 2007 a new institutional management structure was implemented. Interim guidelines (Guidelines 005–1) were developed to define the
roles and responsibilities of the new institutional management structure and
are as follows:

Warden
In correctional institutions (see Appendix B for a list of all institutions in
Canada), the wardens are in charge of all aspects of the prisons' operations, as
described by one of the correctional administrators interviewed:

Administrator 9: My role as warden is obviously the overall administration of the institution in terms of what our mission is and the reintegration.
So the gradual integration to the community for the individuals that are

here and to ensure that the daily operations of administrating a sentence is done in accordance with the rule of law, in accordance with our own policies and regulations and other covenants that control and that we are administratively bound. The Canadian Public Service—the rules that regulate us. So the overall assurance that's required.

Deputy Warden

The deputy warden is the next most senior position and is in charge of all operations and interventions in the institution. The deputy warden is responsible for program management, offender activities, case management, operations management, spiritual services, and everything that involves security intelligence in the institution.

Assistant Wardens

In larger institutions, several assistant warden positions may exist as described below. In smaller institutions where these positions do not exist, the responsibilities outlined are assigned to the deputy warden.

Assistant Warden, Operations (AWO) or Manager, Operations (MO)

The individual in this position holds responsibility for such areas as managing institutional operations, proposing local policies involving institutional routine, offender movement and counts, management of discipline and search plans, reviewing and updating the contingency plan, coordinating the Emergency Response Team, and preparing Post and Standing Orders. This individual also supervises the correctional managers.

Assistant Warden, Interventions (AWI)

This person is responsible for managing all professional correctional interventions in the institution (e.g., case management, human, financial, and material resources related to programs, education). The AWI is also the link to correctional authorities in the community, the Citizens' Advisory Committee, and volunteer groups.

Managers
Correctional Manager (CM)

The correctional manager is responsible for the daily operations in the institution—operational planning, financial management, staffing and personnel management, and decisions affecting offenders, e.g., visits, segregation, inmate movement—as well as supervising a group of correctional officers (I and II).

Manager, Assessment and Intervention (MAI)

The manager, assessment and intervention is responsible for the administration of case management and sentence management duties in the institution and supervises parole officers and case management activities.

Manager, Programs (MP)

This individual is responsible for managing programs and social activities for offenders.

Manager, Intensive Intervention Strategy (MIIS)

The manager, intensive intervention strategy is responsible for the implementation and management of the National Intensive Intervention Strategy in an institution for federally sentenced women and a functional responsibility for a multidisciplinary team.

Figure 3.3. Model of New Institutional Management Structure (2007)

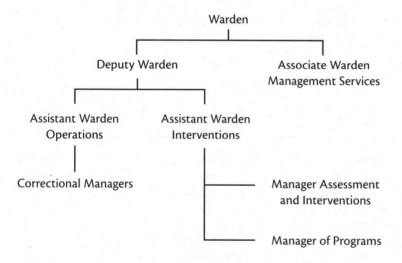

Previous Institutional Management Models

Prior to the implementation of the new institutional management structure on September 4, 2007, the two- and three-headed models of institutional administration were the most commonly implemented models. A brief summary of these models is included here for comparison purposes. Interviews with key informants occurred before September 4, 2007. Therefore, their comments reflect their experiences with the two-headed model.

In 1986 a report released by CSC and authored by Terry Sawatsky (then a deputy commissioner with CSC) outlined problems associated with the existing model of institutional administration. The results of the Sawatsky report led to the emergence of the two-headed model and the three-headed model of institutional administration. In British Columbia, the Matsqui, Mountain, and Kent facilities adopted the three-headed model, while other institutions in B.C. retained the two-headed model. However, according to Ekstedt and Jackson (1996), all sites eventually adopted the two-headed model (p. 100).

Figure 3.4. Models of Institutional Administration

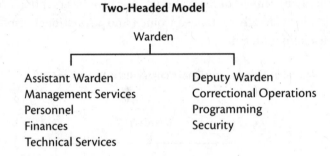

Two-Headed Model

Warden

Assistant Warden
Management Services
Personnel
Finances
Technical Services

Deputy Warden
Correctional Operations
Programming
Security

Three-Headed Model

Warden

Assistant Warden
Management Services
Chiefs of Personnel
Finances
Technical Services

Deputy Warden
Correctional Operations
Coordinators of:
• Security
• Case Management
• Unit Management
• Chaplaincy
• Psychology

Assistant Warden
Programming

Source: Ekstedt and Jackson, 1996, p. 100.

A warden described the reporting structure of an institution in greater detail:

Administrator 10: It's a two-headed model. I'll use that term. Directly under me is an assistant—in other institutions we would call them an assistant warden management services; here it is known as a team leader of Management Services and I have a deputy warden. The organizational chart goes down from there. So under the Management Services—she is responsible for the engineering and maintenance of the institutional plant itself—she has the chief of engineering and maintenance. She has the chief of Material Management for all our contracting needs, whether it is to have the road plowed, parking lots plowed, to electrical contracts, to all the contracts that may provide services here. Part of the philosophy of the regional facilities and also Creating Choices was to bring the community in. So we have a number of different contracts out there. So they are responsible for all the contracting processes whether it is on-site psychologists or contracting for delivery of programs or elder services, native liaison services, all of that. So all of those contracts are under Management Services.

The women living in the houses are also responsible for food preparation of their own [so] we maintain the food stores area. So each week the women do up their grocery list. They all receive a *per diem*. They combine that money together to create the groceries for the following week. So we have people employed in stores and as well for clothing, which is issued by the institution. So there is that side. That's all material. It's the functioning— the daily functioning of the institution. The institutional canteen, that sort of thing. Any electrical work, all the construction that's been going on. So that takes care of that side of the house.

Under the deputy warden, that's where the majority of the positions do fall under. She's responsible for psychology, for health care, for our correctional operations staff, our program staff. That would be out of the one hundred employees, probably seventy-five would fall under that. Under programs, she has a program coordinator. Right now we don't have a chief of health care. The deputy warden oversees it all. They work under a team setup—self directed work team setup. Psychologists—we have two psychologists. Again, we are small and there are fewer numbers so our hierarchy is probably flatter. We are not administratively heavy.

We also have two team leaders for correctional operations which would be known as unit managers in the other institutions. I'll use both terms. One is for the general population assigned to that, a team leader and the other team leader is for the structured living environment and the secure unit. So those are two other middle managers and they supervise as well the managers. They are middle managers as well but are correctional supervisors which, we call here reintegration operations supervisors. There are six of those and one is associated with the secure unit, so a total of seven. So they are here every twenty-four hours when other managers aren't.

That's pretty much our structure. We have about twenty contractors that come in on a regular basis. Our teachers are under contract. We have a person that delivers our Positive Directions—our canine program. So they are here on a regular basis. Another core program is Survivors of Abuse and Trauma, and she is an outside contractor. We have E. Fry [Elizabeth Fry Society] come in. We have volunteers come in. We have Circles of Support that start here for women going out into the community. So under our contract, a chaplain that comes in. She has a whole contingent of around two hundred volunteers. They may come in once a year or may be regular visitors. We also have our elders coming in, and Native liaison. It all falls still under the deputy warden's overall coordination through the program coordinator.

Executive Director, Regional Treatment Centre

The executive director of the Regional Treatment Centre has the responsibility to deliver programming to those inmates who have a variety of mental health issues from Axis 1—serious and persistent mental illness—to brain injury cases, as well as quite a few developmentally delayed individuals including those who may be identified as having brain dysfunctions. This mandate is carried out in many ways, including the delivery of intensive programs for sex offenders and VPP—violence prevention programs. The management structure of the Regional Treatment Centre is described below:

Administrator 11: As for the management structure, what we are doing right now is that we are moving away from the historical management structure, which was a hierarchical structure by profession, i.e., all of the psychologists reported to a psychologist, all of the nurses reported to a senior nurse, to a system which is more interdisciplinary than multidisciplinary in its approach because we still want each profession to focus on its particular skill set but to work and problem solve as a team. So what we are doing is setting up six clinical team leaders, three in our Rehabilitation Unit and three in our psychiatric hospital and each of them will have a number of nurses, a senior nurse, occupational therapists, psychologists, recreational therapists, etc., and each of these team leaders will have a particular group, such as the acute mentally ill, people who are moving along and are not in their active phase of managing medications and that kind of stuff, managing mental illness, and then we will have a team for the Behavioural Management Unit that I mentioned before. We will have one for geriatrics and those kinds of issues, as well as a group for the brain injury group and for the marginal group and those kinds of people. The correctional staff will also be working with the clinical team leaders. The clinical team leaders will report to a unit director, and in the case of the psychiatric hospital, it will be a psychiatrist, and she will have an associate director who is a unit manager—or an operational manager who will take care of the day-to-day things, whereas the psychiatrist will be in charge of the clinical issues, and we'll have a similar structure in the Rehabilitation Unit and the unit directors will report to the executive director. It's the first kind of organizational model of its kind in Canada, so we hope that it will work, and in viewing the research literature in terms of program management models, this approach has one of the highest probabilities of succeeding. It certainly will break down the historical separation of various disciplines working in a sort of isolation from one another. We've been using a multidisciplinary structure to some degree, but haven't had the management structure that really supports this, so we're quite excited about this new approach.

We think with our ... facility and with what our mandate is and what we are trying to do, what with the new Reception Centre at the ... facility and the medical hospital for the Region and so combining those five units together, the program unit which will be for violent and sex offenders as well as putting into this unit our other intensive programs such as intensive substance abuse, our intensive family violence program, and our Aboriginal intensive violence program "In Search of Your Warrior," allowing all of our intensive programs to be flexible and in one facility. We will have a lot of capacity to work with the program delivery people in terms of clinical supervision and that sort of thing. And it also provides for an environment that is conducive to change because one of the biggest things from my perspective in terms of success is not what happens during the program, but what happens in the other twenty hours of the day. If you do not have an environment that is conducive to change, i.e., values, programming, support through expectations of reasonableness and where there is no role playing, where you are not required to posture or be involved in impression management. One of the things that is so interesting about our facility is that people who come from Kent—and there they are sworn enemies to anybody who's a sex offender—once they get to our facility and their next door neighbour in the next cell is often a sex offender, but here they do very, very well. They tend to act out continuously in maximum, and then they get to our place where they don't need to show that they're somebody so they have to deal with their own reality and have to change their own reality.

I remember one of the guys who had served many, many years and was known as a hard case inmate by staff across Canada, who came here and said this was the worst facility he had ever been in, much worse than the Special Handling Unit, because here not only did he have to learn to live with other offenders that he didn't particularly like, but he had to learn to live with himself, and this was even more difficult because he had to real- ize what kind of person he had been all of his life, what kind of damage he had done and how he had hurt other people. He said it was quite difficult for him to face and more difficult than any other place he had been in, but notwithstanding, the guy was dramatically different when he left our facility. So I certainly think we met our mandate in terms of challenging him—getting him to look at himself and his offences and the underlying factors that he needed to address in terms of how his life script was written. So you learn to manage your risk, not necessarily reduce your risk.

As this CSC administrator has noted, the success of the Regional Treatment Centre has a lot to do with its ability to form strong teams among various disciplines and employees. In addition to this, reasonable expectations as well as an environment and a set of values that are conducive to or encouraging of change, are only some of the important and necessary components for the Regional Treatment Centre to operate in a successful manner.

At the time of these interviews, CSC used the unit management organiza- tional structure within its institutions; that is, the older two- or three -headed model. With this structure, the physical environment and teams of staff were organized in such a way as to promote more meaningful interaction between staff and inmates by creating smaller, semi-autonomous units with a consistent team of staff working with the same group of inmates. How do the comments by the administrators on roles and responsibilities within institutions reflect or dispute this previous approach?

Community Corrections Staff

Very few offenders sentenced in Canada serve their entire sentence in prison. Almost all eventually return to the community and experience has shown that they are more likely to succeed if they are supervised and supported when they are first making the transition from the institution to the community. The com- munity corrections staff of the Correctional Service of Canada do carry out this supervision. While under supervision, offenders must adhere to conditions set out upon their release.

The parole officers are responsible for supervising offenders in the commun- ity, ensuring that the offender is following his or her Correctional Plan, and to use risk factors to assess and manage the offender's level of risk. Parole officers can take administrative measures if the offender has breached, or seem likely to breach their parole conditions. In supporting offenders so they can follow their correctional plans, parole officers will link them with community agencies that can help them secure housing, seek employment, receive counselling, and so on. In some parole offices, parole officers also deliver programs for offenders in areas such as substance abuse, anger management, and sexual offending.

On the community side, parole officers report to a parole supervisor who reports to the district supervisor. He or she, in turn, reports to the deputy commissioner of the region. The responsibilities of the community service were described by one correctional administrator:

> **Administrator 12:** We are a community service. Within CSC there is the two—there is the institutional and the community side of the business. There are also regional offices and national offices. We are a community part of the organization, and we are responsible for those offenders released from an institution on some conditional type of release—and that could be either federal or provincial offenders—through the parole process. There are a few things that we get involved in that are outside of that—offenders who have reached their warrant expiry but that still require some form of assistance.

An individual can be released from a correctional facility under different types of releases:

- Temporary release
    - Escorted temporary absence
    - Unescorted temporary absence
    - Work release
- Conditional release
    - Day parole or work release
    - Full parole
- Statutory release
- Release on expiry of sentence

Although often used interchangeably, individuals released on day parole to a halfway house run by a community organization or those who are released on full parole are referred to as *offenders*, while those released on work release and still reside within a corrections facility are referred to as *inmates*.

The Correctional Investigator

The Office of the Correctional Investigator was established under the CCRA. The correctional investigator is appointed by the Governor in Council for a term not exceeding five years, though he or she can be reappointed for a further term. Section 167(1) of the CCRA details the function of the correctional investigator:

> 167. (1) It is the function of the Correctional Investigator to conduct investigations into the problems of offenders related to decisions, recommendations, acts or omissions of the Commissioner or any person under the control and management of, or performing services for or on behalf of, the Commissioner that affect offenders either individually or as a group. (http://www.laws.justice.gc.ca/en/C-44.6/40242.html)

The primary purpose of this office is to "investigate and bring resolution to individual offenders' complaints … as well as review and make recommendations on the Correctional Service's policies and procedures associated with the areas of individual complaints to ensure that systematic areas of concern are identified and appropriately addressed" (Correctional Investigator Canada, 2002). The correctional investigator does not investigate problems relating to the National Parole Board, a provincial correctional facility, the Provincial Parole Board, or a provincial officer. Investigations are initiated at the request of the minister, after receiving a complaint by or on behalf of an offender or by the correctional investigator on his own initiative. In carrying out an investigation, the correctional investigator holds broad powers to collect information or documents, inspect premises, and summon individuals to testify under oath. Upon the investigation's completion, the correctional investigator informs the commissioner of his or her findings and may also make recommendations and give reasons for them, although the commissioner is not legally bound to act on the findings or recommendations of the correctional investigator. If the correctional investigator determines that no reasonable action has been taken after a reasonable amount of time has passed, the correctional investigator relays to the minister the same findings and recommendations given to the commissioner.

The correctional investigator reports annually to the minister on the activities of the Office of the Correctional Investigator. In addition to the annual report, the correctional investigator can make a special report to the minister at any other time if he or she deems the issue to be too urgent or important to wait for the next annual report.

The National Parole Board

Although it is independent of the Correctional Service of Canada, the National Parole Board works in close partnership with the CSC within the Ministry of Public Safety Canada. The National Parole Board has offices in the Atlantic,

Québec, Ontario, Prairies, and Pacific regions, as well as a national office in Ottawa. The national office is home to the Appeal Division, Corporate Services, Policy, Planning and Operations, Legal Services, Performance Measurement, and Clemency and Pardons Division.

According to the regulations of the CCRA, the National Parole Board consists of not more than 45 full-time members and some part-time members. The members are recommended by the minister and appointed by the Governor in Council for periods not to exceed 10 years for full-time members and three years for part-time members. As stated in Section 105 of the CCRA, members appointed to the Board "shall be sufficiently diverse in their backgrounds to be able to collectively represent community values and views in the work of the Board and to inform the community with respect to unescorted temporary absence, parole and statutory release." In September 2006, the National Parole Board was comprised of 73 Board members—41 full-time and 32 part-time—as well as 350 employees with an annual budget of $43.1 million.

The purpose and responsibility of the Board is as follows:

> The Board is an independent administrative tribunal that has exclusive authority under the *Corrections and Conditional Release Act* to grant, deny, cancel, terminate or revoke day parole and full parole. The NPB may also order certain offenders to be held in prison until the end of their sentence. This is called detention during the period of statutory release. In addition, the Board makes conditional release decisions for offenders in provinces and territories that do not have their own parole boards. (National Parole Board, 2003)

Only Ontario and Québec currently maintain their own parole boards that have authority to grant release to offenders serving their sentences in provincial institutions. British Columbia's Board of Parole was eliminated on April 1, 2007.

In making decisions on the cases brought before them, the National Parole Board follows their policies, and in order to access risk it also receives information from other sources, including judges, the Correctional Service of Canada, police, victims, the offender, psychiatrists, prosecutors, etc. Most decisions are made after a hearing with the offender, but some decisions are reached after a file review (National Parole Board, 2003). If the inmate is granted a release the CSC supervises the offender in the community and reports any changes in the offender's case or level of risk to the Board.

Under the *Criminal Records Act* and the *Criminal Code of Canada*, the Parole Board is also responsible for "making decisions to grant, deny and revoke pardons" (National Parole Board, 2003). A pardon is "a formal attempt to remove the stigma of a criminal record for people who, having been convicted of an offence, have satisfied the sentence and remained crime free" (National Parole Board, 2003). In addition, through the Royal Prerogative of Mercy, the National Parole Board makes recommendations for the exercise of clemency.

Some Basic Facts about the Correctional Population

The following basic facts about the correctional population come from the Correctional Service of Canada's website (Table 3.1):

Table 3.1. Inmate Population Classification, according to Security Level as of April 11, 2004

Security Level	Men	%	Women	%	Aboriginal			
					Men	%	Women	%
Maximum	1,737	14	36	9	367	17	13	12
Medium	7,359	61	170	45	1,397	64	58	54
Minimum	2,226	18	140	37	318	15	27	25
Not yet classified	712	6	33	9	111	5	10	9
Total	12,034	100	379	100	2,193	100	108	100

Inmates are assessed at the start of their sentences to determine the risk they pose to the public and to the security of the institution, staff, inmates, and themselves. Their security level and risk is reviewed throughout the sentence and can change over time.

Table 3.2. Total Number of Admissions in 2003–2004

Men	7,308
Aboriginal Men	1,317
Women	386
Aboriginal Women	106
Total	7,694

Table 3.3. Profile of Inmate Population on April 11, 2004

	Men		Women		Aboriginal			
	Number 12,034	%	Number 379	%	Number of Men 2,193	%	Number of Women 108	%
Age 20 to 39	7,243	60	263	69	1,543	68	88	81
Serving a first penitentiary sentence	7,796	65	316	83	1,411	64	90	83
Length of sentence								
Under three years	2,746	23	140	37	530	24	33	31
Three to under six years	3,422	28	117	31	662	30	32	30
Six to under ten years	1,679	14	39	10	319	15	16	15
Ten years or more	1,477	12	15	4	220	10	10	9
Life or indeterminate	2,710	23	68	18	462	21	17	16
Offence								
Murder – first degree	693	6	16	4	106	5	1	1
Murder – second degree	1,648	14	50	13	292	13	14	13
Schedule I (excluding sexual offences)	5,837	49	214	56	1,154	53	81	75
Schedule I (sexual offences)	1,814	15	9	2	442	20	3	3
Schedule II (drugs)	1,466	12	74	20	117	5	14	13
Non-scheduled (non-violent)	1,828	15	44	12	260	12	6	6

Note: Individuals could appear in more than one category. Source: Correctional Service of Canada, 2005c

Following sentencing by a court, offenders enter a federal penitentiary for the first time on a warrant of committal or through an international transfer. They may also return to the penitentiary during their sentence if their conditional release is revoked by the National Parole Board for the commission of a new offence or for a breach of a condition of their release, or if suspended by their community parole office even if the NPB does not revoke.

Aboriginal people represent approximately 16% of the federal offender population but only about 3% of the general population in Canada. The proportion of Aboriginal people (both men and women) is greater (18.5%) in penitentiaries than under supervision in the community (12.7%). In 2003–2004, 28% of women and 18% of men incarcerated in federal institutions were Aboriginal. In addition, in the 2007–2008 Estimates *Report on Plans and Priorities*, the Correctional Service of Canada outlined a number of changes to the offender population profile that have occurred between 1997 and 2005 that are presenting significant security and reintegration challenges. These changes include:

- More extensive histories of involvement with the court system—roughly nine out of ten offenders now have previous criminal convictions;
- more extensive histories of violence and violent offences, with far more assessed as violence-prone, hostile, impulsive, and aggressive on admission;
- an increase of more than 100% in the proportion of offenders who are classified as maximum security on admission—another of the progressive difficulties facing CSC. Thirteen percent are now classified at this level on admission;
- an increase of 33% in the proportion of offenders with gang and/ or organized crime affiliations—one in six men and one in ten women offenders now have known affiliations;
- an increase of 14% in the proportion of offenders serving sentences for homicide—it now stands at more than one in four male offenders;
- an increase of 71% in the percentage of male offenders and 100% increase in women offenders identified at admission as having very serious mental health problems—12% of male and 26% of women offenders are now so identified;
- an increasing prevalence of learning disabilities as well as offenders with low functioning capacities;

- an increasing over-representation of Aboriginal offenders—19% of the institutional population is now of Aboriginal ancestry, while less than 3% of the Canadian population is Aboriginal;
- an increasing prevalence of substance abuse—about four out of five offenders now arrive at a federal institution with a serious substance abuse problem, with one out of two having committed their crime under the influence of drugs, alcohol, or other intoxicants;
- an increasing rate of infectious diseases—inmates now have a seven to ten times higher rate of HIV than the general Canadian population, and approximately a 30 times higher rate of Hepatitis C. (Correctional Service of Canada, 2007)

In addition, the CSC has noted a trend towards shorter sentences, resulting in an increase of 62% in the proportion of male offender admissions serving a sentence of less than three years.

Conclusion

The three management levels of the Correctional Service of Canada—national, regional and operational—were detailed in this chapter. The focus of management shifts from planning and policy development to implementation as one moves from the national level to the regional level to the operational level. Independent from but closely involved with the CSC is the correctional investigator and the National Parole Board. This chapter also summarized some basic statistics about the correctional population, which lead to interesting observations and bear consequences in the areas of programming and reintegration.

Study Questions

1. Discuss the role of the National Parole Board and how it relates to the Correctional Service of Canada.
2. In terms of the current federal inmate profile, discuss what impact this might have on program planning in the penitentiaries.
3. What are the positive and negative impacts of establishing the new institutional management structure and abandoning the two-headed model?

Bibliography

* Items with asterisks are also suggested readings for the chapter.

*Correctional Service of Canada (1991). *Our Story: Organizational Renewal in Federal Corrections*. Ottawa: Canadian Centre for Management Development.

Correctional Investigator Canada (2002). *The Correctional Investigator Canada*. http://www.oci-bec.gc.ca/index_e.asp

Correctional Service of Canada (2005). *Basic Facts About Federal Corrections*. http://www.csc-scc.gc.ca/text/pblct/basicfacts/BasicFacts_e.shtml

Correctional Service of Canada (2006). *Parole and Community Corrections*. http://www.csc-scc.gc.ca/text/faits/facts03_e.shtml

Correctional Service of Canada (2007). *2007-2008 Estimates: Report on Plans and Priorities*. http://www.tbs-sct.gc.ca/rpp/0708/csc-scc/csc-scc_e.pdf

Correctional Service of Canada (2007a). *How We Operate*. http://www.csc-scc.gc.ca/text/organi/organe04_e.shtml

Correctional Service of Canada (2008). *How We Operate*. http://www.csc-scc.gc.ca/text/organi/operat-eng.shtml

Ekstedt, J. W. and Jackson, M. A. (1996). Offender programs. In, *The Keepers and the Kept: Introduction to Corrections in Canada*. (p. 86–121). Toronto: ITP Nelson.

Government of Canada (1992). *Corrections and Conditional Release Act*. http://laws.justice.gc.ca/en/C-44.6/index.html

National Parole Board (2003). *Overview of National Parole Board Website*. Government of Canada. http://www.npb-cnlc.gc.ca/about/overw_e.htm

Treasury Board of Canada Secretariat (2003). *Correctional Service of Canada Organization. Info Source Depository Services Program*. Government of Canada

Suggested Readings

Correctional Investigator (2002). *Annual Report of the Correctional Investigator*. Ottawa: Public Works and Government Services Canada. http://www.oci-bec.gc.ca/reports/AR200102_e.asp

National Parole Board (2002). *National Parole Board Policy Manual, 1(6)*. http://www.npb-cnlc.gc.ca/infocntr/policym/polman_e.htm

4 Principles of Management and Administration

Until the 1950s, organizations were relatively stable entities. Then the business world became more interested in finding ways to make their organizations more effective and efficient. Theories using terms such as *learning organizations, organizational development, change management, transition management,* and *new public management* began to emerge, and despite their differing labels the principles behind them are very similar. Slowly, these principles began to influence not only private organizations, but public ones as well. This chapter will look at the pillars that "good" organizations are built on and the extent to which the Correctional Service of Canada has been successful in implementing them.

Theories of Organizational Development

French and Stewart have defined *organizational development* as "a model designed for planned, systematic, and ongoing problem and action-oriented processes that focus on both technical and human improvement within the organization. This long-term approach needs management support and is based on sound management theory and practice" (2001, p. 1). Senge (1990) described *the learning organization* as a place where "people continually expand their capacity to create the results they truly desire, where new and expansive patterns of thinking are nurtured, where collective aspiration is set free, and where people are continually learning how to learn together" (p. 3). Bridges (1991) discussed the difference between *change and transition management*. The *Oxford English Reference Dictionary* (1996) defines change as: "the act or an instance of making or becoming different" (p. 243) and transition as: "a passing or change from one place, state, condition, etc., to another" (p. 1,530) Bridges (1991) described change as a process that is external and situational, as opposed to transition, which is internal and psychological. In order for transition to be successful, the people involved need to let go of inadequate ways of thinking and acting so they can internalize a new mission based on new ways of thinking and acting. Trust and a shared vision are key to letting go and internalizing a new mission. Bridges (1991) believed that "the key to capitalizing on change lies in understanding and utilizing the cycle of challenge and response ... challenge and response is the key to success in a time of rapid and far reaching changes" (p. 82). Tupper (2001) defined new *public management* as "a complex set of ideas about the political, economic and organizational bases of modern society. It prescribes flexible organizations that seek business efficiency and greater responsiveness to citizen interests" (p. 142).

By the mid-1980s, the new attitude within corrections had created a ripe environment for organizational development (Fleisher, 1996). Duguid (1993) stated that by that time, correctional staff "were increasingly discontented with being merely humane keepers, passive providers of opportunity" (p. 5). In Canada, this discontent led to a major reorganization of the CSC in the late 1980s, well described in the following excerpt from *Our Story: Organizational Renewal in Federal Corrections* (1991):

> The business of federal Corrections is widely regarded as one of drama and suffering. It is also one that touches at the very core of two of our society's most fundamental values: human freedom and public safety. Consequently, the Correctional Service of Canada must frequently respond to political and public demands for assurance that we are doing what is needed.
>
> Given this situation, it seems that it would be difficult for us, the managers and employees of the Correctional Service of Canada, to do any more than to simply cope or to focus the bulk of our energy on just administering the prison system. Indeed, it appears that it would be easy for us to fall into the trap of believing that our fundamental object is to "stay out of trouble."
>
> Yet for many of us, simply staying out of trouble is not enough. We really want to do the best job we possibly can. We want to do good Corrections—to serve our Minister (the Solicitor General of Canada), the government, and the people of Canada well. It is evident to us that we have to do more than just administer the prison system. We believe that we have to take the initiative to define what good Corrections is and to chart a course to make sure that good Corrections is what we do. The predominance of this sentiment among a significant number of us prompted us to develop a clearly stated and highly

integrated set of goals for the Correctional Service of Canada. This
set of goals became our Mission Document (p. 3).

Pillars of Successful Organizations

AIM

To begin a major reorganization, an organization first has to establish AIM—in
what direction is it going to go? (Ingstrup, 2002) In order to answer this question, we can stipulate three target areas: Mission and Values, Leadership, and
Accountability.

Mission and Values

To establish aim, an organization needs to be clear about its mission and its
operating values. The importance of a clearly articulated and communicated
vision to focus on organizational change is clearly emphasized in the change
management literature (Shepherdson, 1995). A mission is "the ultimate goal—
the direction for a never-ending journey of improvements" (Ingstrup, 2002, p. 3).

Our Story (1991) describes the purpose of developing a mission statement
for the CSC:

> The purpose of a mission is to lead. We wanted a declaration that
> would not simply describe what federal Corrections is but rather
> what it should strive to become in the future. Such a declaration had
> to define the very reasons for our organization's existence and, most
> importantly, our ambitions—our ultimate organizational objectives.
> Furthermore, we wanted to clearly articulate the most important
> overall strategies required to achieve our ultimate objectives. At the
> same time we had to "bite the bullet" on the realities of the social
> institution that we manage. To us, then, a mission statement was to
> be a vision for the future, a blueprint for development, change and
> improvement....
>
> The Mission Statement is about people—their potential and our
> role in tapping that potential. It moves from the individual to the
> organizational to the wider collectives of Canadian society, the justice
> system, and national and international Corrections. It recognizes
> the past, but moves towards the future. It grounds the Service in its
> wider world (pp. 46, 50).

Since its development in 1989, the Mission Statement of the CSC has had
only minor revisions and it now reads as follows:

The Correctional Service of Canada (CSC), as part of the criminal justice system and respecting the rule of law, contributes to public safety by actively encouraging and assisting offenders to become law-abiding citizens, while exercising reasonable, safe, secure and humane control.

The words "and respecting the rule of law" were added to the original statement in 1996.

As CSC developed its mission statement, they also developed core values that guide their work:

Core Value 1
We respect the dignity of individuals, the rights of all members of society, and the potential for human growth and development.

Core Value 2
We recognize that the offender has the potential to live as a law-abiding citizen.

Core Value 3
We believe that our strength and our major resource in achieving our objectives is our staff and that human relationships are the cornerstone of our endeavour.

Core Value 4
We believe that the sharing of ideas, knowledge, values and experience, nationally and internationally, is essential to the achievement of our mission.

Core Value 5
We believe in managing the Service with openness and integrity and we are accountable to the Minister of Public Safety Canada. (CSC, 1991, p. 2)

In interviews with correctional personnel, it was very apparent that the mission statement and core values are not just words on paper—they are the "words to work by." Both were prominently displayed in lobbies of correctional institutions and on the office walls of wardens and policy makers. Interviewees discussed the intricacies of the mission statement and core values with ease, attesting to the strength of both in the day-to-day operations of the CSC:

Administrator 1: We talk about them all the time as a senior management team when we are forced to make decisions, and I use it—the mission in particular—guiding me in terms of making decisions about sending inmates to segregation, or sending them to another institution, or things like transfers and temporary absences. They intertwine all the different activities that we are involved with.

Administrator 2: The mission statement … we had a change in the mission statement and it was in direct relation to the Arbour Inquiry. So did it change the way we do our business? I hope it did, improved what we did, and made us more accountable for ensuring we are applying the rule of law in all of our policies. Our duty to act fairly is another one. We have that duty to act fairly. We are responsible to the public and we are responsible to adhere to Canadian law and policies.

Administrator 3: One of the primary elements of the mission statement is the whole notion of helping offenders to reintegrate back into the community, so obviously, being involved in programming, we feel that we are at the heart or core of what corrections is all about, or certainly what the mission is all about. Nobody works in programs without believing in the capacity of pretty much all offenders, to change, and become law abiding citizens which is very much consistent with our mission. In the program area, the people are totally committed to the mission, and demonstrate that every day in terms of the work they do in the classrooms and at RHQ. You simply couldn't do this work and not believe in what you are doing. So for us, I think the mission statement is integrated automatically; it is tougher in some other areas where people are doing, for example, security work, as it is more difficult for security officers to integrate the mission into their day-to-day regimes. They have more of a custody and control responsibility so it would be easy for them to focus on that aspect of their job instead of perhaps the reintegration aspect. For us, however, that certainly is not an issue.

Bridges (1991) stated that a transition is internal and psychological, and in order for transitions to be successful people in an organization need to internalize a new mission based on new ways of thinking and acting. In addition, Tupper (2001) stated that new public management is business efficient and has a greater responsiveness to citizens' interests. How does the mission statement of the CSC reflect these characteristics of an organization that has undergone transition? Can you find examples of these characteristics in the above comments by administrators?

Leadership

Also key to developing aim is effective leadership. The leaders in learning organizations are different from leaders of the past. Today's leaders need a combination of interpersonal and analytical skills (Stoyko, 2001). Ingstrup (2002) outlined the key elements of leadership as "the ability to listen, a desire to involve others and the skill required to delegate without abdicating responsibility" (p. 4). Some research calls leaders taking an organization through a major reorganization "change masters." Kanter defined change masters as the people "with the ideas that move beyond the organization's established practice, ideas they can form into visions ... the concepts and visions that drive change must be both inspiring and realistic" (as cited in Shepherdson, 1995, p. 11).

The motivation for organizational change and CSC's own change master came with the appointment of Ole Ingstrup as the commissioner of corrections. One correctional administrator saw his arrival as the catalyst for reform within the CSC:

> **Administrator 4:** I think we were very fortunate to have a commissioner like Ole Ingstrup to come on board when he did. I was in corrections at the time. I can remember being a parole officer on the street and there was talk about us getting guns and us getting handcuffs and going towards the U.S. model. He came from a different continent and a different country and a different view and led us in that way. That was back in 1988–89 that the mission statement came out. It has gone through a number of different ministers, different leaders of political backgrounds, and twelve years later we have some reduction in crime, we have some reduction in recidivism. So is it doing what it's supposed to be doing? I believe it is.

In *Reflections of a Canadian Prison Warden*, Ron Wiebe (2000) commented on the impact Ole Ingstrup had:

> The era we have now moved into I would call that of *professionalization*, in which the organization has become much more professional and organized around corporate models. It begins with the initial appointment of Ole Ingstrup as commissioner in 1988. He had a vision of a much more organized, professional organization based on a clear set of values and principles, and of policies realigned so that they are consistent with our values. After four years as commissioner,

he served for about four years in other government appointments, then returned in 1996. He [was] an extremely demanding commissioner, with very high performance expectations. He suffer[ed] fools very poorly, and [was] not a person you can manipulate or sway to drop his agenda. He has brought an era where research is valued, and where corporate structures are tools that are designed to be effective, as opposed to something slavishly followed (pp. 19, 20).

Martin (1999) differentiated between an act of leadership and an act of management: "In general, acts of leadership are those activities necessary to define the destination of the organization (i.e., the bigger picture), while acts of management are those necessary for making the trip a reality (i.e., determining what compass points by which to steer)" (p. 1). Martin adds that although individuals may possess both leadership and management skills, those with good management skills tend to be promoted into leadership positions.

Ingstrup (2002) says that "leaders must demonstrate a commitment to their employees and in all they do be consistent with the mission and values; also there must be consistency among the leaders of an organization and perhaps most importantly—there must be absolute consistency between the leaders' words and deeds" (p. 4). There are a number of different levels of leaders within CSC. Unit supervisors are leaders for teams of correctional officers, wardens are leaders of institutions, regional managers are leaders of regional teams, and so forth. A couple of the interviewees commented on leadership:

Administrator 5: To me, it seems perhaps the most important single variable in success in corrections is to … to borrow a theological term, incarnate values in your life, and that's what I see as my responsibility as a leader—to live in such a way in terms of the way I work within the facility that people unequivocally know my commitment to the mission that we are about and the success of our enterprise, and that while we don't have to be happy with what our offenders did, we have to recognize them to be in every sense human, requiring dignity, respect, and acknowledgement if we expect them to change, and we do also expect them to change.

Administrator 6: I think we have a wonderful, wonderful mission statement that contains what we are trying to do and how we should be trying to do that. I just think it's great. I think there is some wonderful, wonderful wisdom in that book. Now, me as a human being, sometimes I don't have the ability to do it to the level that, in my view, is inherent, or implicit in the document. Like one of the kinds of things, I remember when I read it thinking my God, this is the mother of them all, is lead by example.

How do the administrators' comments above fit with Ole Ingstrup's definition of a leader and the key elements of leadership?

Accountability

Lastly, to establish aim an organization must have accountability. Belanger and colleagues stated that "at its essence, the process of accountability is really about identifying key results (openness), measuring performance (demonstrating competence), and reporting to the public and parliament on performance compared to the original key results identified (integrity)" (2001, p. 18). Ingstrup says that "good Corrections cannot be achieved and certainly not be sustained, without the ability on the part of the organization to clearly explain how and to what extent the organization is making progress relative to both its mission and values" (2002, p. 4).

The key to accountability is the ability to correct and manipulate the correct information in order to accurately measure the organization's progress. In its 2002 Performance Report, the Correctional Service of Canada reported on its initiative to improve the management of information within its organization:

> CSC and its partners require accurate, timely information about offenders to fulfill their mandates. This information must be managed effectively, so that it is adequately protected, accurate, and available to those who need it when they need it. The management of this resource is an important function for CSC.

> 2001/2002 was the second year of an initiative to improve the management of information within CSC and to ensure full compliance with information management policies. More than 250,000 offender files were reviewed and inventoried. One hundred-thirty thousand file volumes were disposed of in accordance with National Archive authorities, and more than 550 staff received additional training in records management.

> OMS, the Offender Management System, is a vital source of information to CSC and other partners in the criminal justice system. OMS currently serves nearly 9,000 users. A renewal project is underway, having received Preliminary Project Approval in March 2001.

CSC is a partner in the federal Integrated Justice Initiative, which will lead to the Canada Public Safety Information Network (CPSIN) to link federal and provincial organisations. The renewal of OMS will be an important component of CPSIN (pp. 21, 22).

Interviewees described the tools available to them within CSC to increase accountability including performance appraisals, training standards, various reintegration tools that measure escorted temporary absences, among others.

Administrator 7: Performance measures are a primary tool of most managers today. If they want to get work done then they set up performance measures and provide feedback to staff in terms of their performance.

There are national performance measures and regional performance measures and we set up local, our own performance measures. We may not use the exact same system but we can generate reports with some of the systems we use locally.

Our performance measures are expanding all the time. We have weekly meetings—what's called our reintegration meeting—and I chair that. Our managers are there, others—the supervisor of psychology, the supervisor of case management—and we discuss a number of issues. Segregation cases are all reviewed there, performance measures, and I might pick a couple that I think need more attention and highlight them, and the deputy warden may pick another group, and so on. Like I say, it is very fluid and ever evolving.

A lot of managers find them distasteful. A lot of managers find them dehumanizing and it fits a certain management style. One of my styles is to put performance results out there and let people do their own evaluations. That's how I work. If I see a deficiency in a certain area, I want to do better in that area. It's a new style and some managers are finding it difficult to adapt to that.

Administrator 8: We have performance measures and it's really taken off in the last number of years. We have a department at Regional Headquarters—performance assurance. We have a system called RADAR [Reports of Automated Data Applied to Reintegration] where I can look at individual units, I can look at individual parole officers, I can look at individual correctional officers, to see if they are doing their work. We had—maybe I'll do it this way. Performance evaluation reports. That's the annual report where I sit down with you and I go over your performance in terms of the objectives that were established the previous year and so on. Traditionally, it was difficult for managers to get them done on a timely basis and some people hadn't had one done for three years. We decided as a region to be in one hundred percent compliance. In other words, all employees would have an up-to-date completed performance evaluation report. That was due last September. The first thing you do is create a report that shows how many are done and which ones aren't done and then you pound away at people, reminding them that this is an important process and that it is part of their evaluation. And it goes back to the adage that what gets measured gets done. And we were successful as a region. We achieved the objective of one hundred percent compliance. All employees in the ... region everywhere have performance evaluation reports. A massive assault in terms of energy, so on and so forth. We did that for two reasons, in my perspective. It's a good show that we value employees' contribution. Secondly, it demonstrated to managers again that one hundred percent compliance is the norm.

That's the real side effect that the whole performance assurance and the measuring of results and so on what it has produced—the term one hundred percent compliance is overused and everybody refers to it and that is what the expectation is. I mean, we are not there yet in terms of performance, but that is what the expectation is.

Although employee performance appraisals are necessary for the operation of any organization, measurements are important in ensuring that the unit or facility is complying with the standards, standing orders, and legislation which govern the operation of correctional facilities.

Administrator 9: They have just completed a number of tools that will be self measuring tools—self monitoring tools—for wardens to have at their disposal, that the staff can conduct to ensure our own compliance in things like segregation, which is obviously a huge one. Compliance in things measuring from various reintegration components, UTAs (Unescorted Temporary Absences), ETAs (Escorted Temporary Absences), day paroles, waivers, postponements, withdrawals—all of that under the reintegration umbrella. Then there is all our policy compliance. Training standards is another. Are we completing things like performance evaluations? Are we meeting the standards for training? Under reintegration there is a huge number there. Are we releasing, at what point in their sentence are we releasing people? Is it at the earliest opportunity? Is it at the day parole opportunity?

We have, at our regional headquarters, a performance assurance division and nationally we also have one. We also, each warden and manager here, has access to a system called RADAR which allows me to do all sorts of different profiles, manipulations of information off our offender management system, which tells me where we are at. We also have the Correctional Investigator who comes in on a regular basis. They are also using some of our RADAR information to identify to us our compliance, to explain discrepancies, or looking for systemic issues that they may find.

It's another management system. The more you are familiar with it the easier it is to get the information. I'm a power user. I like to know what is happening here. Are we moving our agenda forward in the way that we should be? Are we compliant with things like reports—are they due on time? We have those time frames, and just from an overall management if not, what are the reasons, were the staff talked to, how do we correct it, or how do we explain it?

Likewise, it is important for CSC to be able to have readily available tools which help to monitor inmate trends, movement, progress, and characteristics.

Administrator 10: At the Regional Management Committee, which is usually once a month, they all choose what they call waves. So they can see this happening or because a lot of things are not just to identify, well this is late. It is to say that look, in two months time you've got all these guys or all these individuals are coming up for statutory release. Is there, within that pocket, individuals who may have gone out, done well, who we revoked, as an example, for smoking dope? Are there windows there? Perhaps we should be looking at those individuals for prerelease day parole. Are all these guys coming up that are two months from SR, are they going to stay medium? Maybe there is some of those that can be minimum. So you start looking at that. So we look at those kinds of waves coming up.

We also look at what we can do better. What our status is to date. So that gives us, the regional folks, which is coming back to National Headquarters too, these are some of the areas that we should be monitoring a bit more closely or we are seeing trends in this regard. What does it mean to your site? Go back and take a look at that.

And we have different mechanisms in place here too. So I go into RADAR and it tells me the "what's." Every Monday we do this. What reports are due, are overdue? Are there any? Then we prioritize those and get an understanding of why they are overdue. Maybe the person just wasn't here and so you tell them that next time make sure you do it before you take your days off, or whatever. Then you are allowed to see what is coming up in a week, two weeks, three weeks, or to plan your work to avoid that. So we do that on a weekly basis. That's from a reintegration work point of view.

Administrator 11: We have a performance measurement tool that we use and we are developing that daily right now. Basically, each month in our performance assurance sector we have an incredible amount of information in terms of our compliance right at our fingertips and what the regional administrators here would be responsible for is monitoring that information and developing strategies to bring us into compliance where we are not already in compliance. We spend an enormous amount of time on that and we will be spending an even greater amount of time on that as we continue to develop our methods for doing that. There is some dissension out there on how we monitor our performance. Some see it as we focus more on compliance; we are not really focusing on the real issue, which is the offender. So there is some learning and education that needs to be done in that area because if we are in compliance we are actually working with the offender. So those two things have to come into balance.

At times, it seems that some CSC managers do not see great value in implementing performance measures because they believe them to be, as one interviewee stated, dehumanizing, and because they may be having some difficulty in adapting to the use of such techniques and tools. However, for the most part, the CSC administrators found the tools available to them, be they already in existence or tools developed for specific needs, to be invaluable. Many of these administrators found that the information generated from performing a variety of such measures or using such tools as RADAR was valuable in monitoring day-to-day events, including timely reporting, compliancy rates related to ETAs, UTAs, or conditional releases, whether or not they are meeting their standards for training, and so on. Can you think of what benefits having access to such a large amount of information would hold for an administrator?

Investigations, accreditation, and audits are also a large part of maintaining accountability, as described by correctional administrators:

Administrator 12: There is a performance assurance sector. I think we have a good system of accountability, not withstanding that there are areas that need improvement and I think there is still some things we could be doing more of. We had a staff-offender involvement. It was a kind of horrific one where I think we should have studied that case to find out what happened. How could this happen? What could we learn? And I think we could have done that kind of thing, but we tend to feel that the sin has been committed so let's close the sin up quick. It's not because we want to sweep it under; it's not that. I just think we don't know how to deal with it. I don't think we are confident enough to tell you the truth. But this has happened, so let's examine it. Let's find out how a person of this training, of this calibre, becomes involved with this offender, of all offenders to the extent that they did, over the period that they did. How could that happen in our organization? What were the signs that we overlooked? So I was anxious to do that, but the sensitivities are very large on those things. But when it comes to an offender going U.A.L., [unlawfully at large] or an offender committing murder or rape we do national investigations that are pretty thorough, although the people need more training in all this kind of stuff they are doing. We've got a good system. Again, our system stands on the base of the people who are doing it. With the time and money to train them and do it to the level that we can fantasize, that we can envision, there's not that there. So, I don't think there is anything wrong with our procedures in my experience.

Now, you can get into the philosophy of do we measure the right things. Are we measuring the right things? There are some debates around that. What they look at depends on why they are coming in. So it depends. We would have to go through the various categories to depict that for you, but there are a couple of things that are used as indicators, things like frequency of contact. That is to say, are we seeing the guys as often as our policy says we should? Collateral contacts … are we just listening to the guy or are we checking with the police, his mother, his employer, his girlfriend, whatever? And where we see the guy i.e., fifty percent in the office, fifty outside the office. Getting our reports in on time. So we measure those sorts of things. Our measurement system is not as perfect as it should be for the conclusions we sometimes draw. So that's one problem. The other kind of thing is that there is debate about whether or not you are literally measuring the thing, or are you measuring what you can measure. See, in Ottawa, they can hit a button and theoretically they can tell you the frequency of contact on every offender across the country, not withstanding a few flaws in the system. It would work to the extent of let's say ninety percent as long as we input it correctly. The problem is people inputting are parole officers, social workers, programmers—they are not the trained, disciplined clerical people. So they make mistakes, they put the wrong date in, their typing skills are less than satisfactory, and so you get a whole lot of what we call data quality errors. So when Ottawa is taking it off, they act as though these things don't exist. There is no margin of error because the system itself was set up as a word processing system, not as a data quality system. I mean, if this was the system in the bank, God help us, we wouldn't have our money in the bank because we could get either very lucky or very unlucky. So, they are trying now to improve the system so that the data quality automatically—the system itself will automatically pick up on the human errors as you punch in, or you don't fill in a blank, or a table or a box.

Now, we have systems of professionalism and we have back up systems to that. Like a supervisor that is supposed to do it all, but who has got the time and the patience to do it all? So, the parole officer is right ninety percent of the time, thank you very much. Now the commissioner wants flawless execution at one hundred percent, and we are saying good luck. Yes, we should, but would all our systems do that, please, like the computer itself, like the funding system, like all of the other kinds of systems? You get them all working at one hundred percent, we can get to one hundred percent too. But if it is only us that are operating at one hundred percent, but all the other things can click along as they have been, we've got serious disengagement. Are you going to spend the time perfecting your reports or are you going to see the guy?

Administrator 12 highlighted some broader issues with maintaining accountability, including a discussion on the opportunities to do case studies of offender-officer involvements. Further discussion is provided around the important topic of accountability including the requirement to also complete performance appraisals on those individuals holding positions of management and leadership in CSC.

Administrator 13: The RAP reports monthly to the Regional Management Committee re a variety of performance measurements, i.e., number of staff on long term acting situations, number of anomalies re bilingual positions showing as filled versus the reality, vacant positions, length of time to deal with grievances, completion rate of performance appraisals (which are done annually on all staff). There are also *ad hoc* reporting requirements from National HQ.

Administrator 14: We have what is known as a *yearly accountability contract*, and the deputy commissioner has an accountability contract directly with the commissioner, and I have an accountability contract that feeds into his contract. Therefore, there will be objectives and issues that are outlined on the contract that we will feed into. My research administrators all feed into my accountability contract and I measure these R.A.'s on their ability to do that, so it's like a feedback mechanism all the way along. For the last five years, the accountability contracts have been refined, because it is a new process, and so finally this year I believe they have the finished product. So quarterly, we will be asked to make sure we are updating the accountability contracts and if things have been added or subtracted, the performance assurance sector is the one that really looks after that.

Administrator 15: Audits are critical but they aren't the only measurement practice—there are all sorts of performance measures. We have a correctional results section on the Infonet which looks at a variety of measures, including timeliness of release, number of grievances, number of institutional assaults, number of escapes, etc. Almost any aspect of our performance can be turned into a measurement criterion and is, and correctional results is a massive package which focuses each month on something different. Excom, (the executive committee made up of regional deputy commissioners, the commissioner and her senior advisors and senior staff at National Headquarters, including the senior deputy commissioner for women, director generals and assistant commissioners) reviews a different element of the correctional results once very month when they meet. So for example, one month they might look at performance measures related to case management, the next month performance measures related to security or health care, and so on. Each of the major areas within the organization is represented by somebody at that meeting. So the group is not large, probably fifteen to eighteen people.

Within programs, we have a whole variety of standards as well. For example, when a program is completed we have ten working days to complete all of the program reports for the offenders who participated in that program. The program therapist, the person who delivered the program, has basically ten working days to write up an evaluation of how each offender did in that program from start to finish, recommendations that they may have, if any, related to the need for additional interventions or treatment, or how they see the risk being mitigated by offender participation in the program. That information goes forward to the parole officer, who of course does the overall assessment and overall case prep for release decisions. That's one example of a performance measure.

Another measurement would be whether or not our program staff are meeting their targets in terms of program delivery. They are supposed to deliver a certain number of programs per year. Are they doing that? Another performance measure in case management, for example, is frequency of contact. If an offender was supposed to be seen four times a month, was he or she seen that often? Basically, our performance measurements are our policies turned around. What does the policy say is our requirement in this and then we measure this against the performance, and if it is up to par, then fine, but if it isn't, then what is the action plan developed?

Another type of performance measure could be a site accreditation as well, because it measures performance against a standard that has been set for program delivery. There are a lot of financial performance indicators as well, and obviously coming in on budget is one, or meeting overtime targets as well, which is always problematic. Performance measurements exist throughout the Service and everything we do is assessed against a number of things in the order of importance: legislation policy and the mission. Therefore, those three elements are the three factors against which we are measured and performance assurance is all about maintaining high levels of compliance.

Many performance measures and indicators have been discussed by several of the administrators thus far, and these discussions have highlighted the importance of such appraisals in the overall operation of CSC—appraisals that include employees, management, standards and legislation, compliance issues, case studies, and reviews of offender characteristics, programming, and eventual release. Accreditation or audits are discussed further in the following interviews. Several organizations, both large and small, have regular audits on specific facets of their operations and some have an accreditation done by professional and often external agencies qualified to perform such tasks. Agencies that are successful are generally awarded a certificate signifying a one or three year accreditation qualification, although this may vary. Accreditation is discussed in more detail in Chapter 5.

Administrator 16: We were fortunate in the last couple of audits on administrative segregation to be one hundred percent compliant. There was national audit and after that a big push came on: how can we help you? So the latest development is at the commissioner's request, is the development of self monitoring tools in each of our most important areas of our mandate. So we have to the end of January to respond to it. It will be time consuming—that is an issue—for staff to comply with. Not to comply with, but to get the survey done. So they have done all these management monitoring tools, using of restraint, fire and safety, etc. They are still only in draft but they've been completed to assist us on site. So you look at what the criterion is, what the requirements are, policy references and how to monitor it.

Administrator 17: Well, again it starts with the—every member of the management committee at the regional level and the senior level. We are all accountable through our own performance agreements, so the areas of performance to be measured are identified early in the year. Those are set at National Headquarters and they are pretty much generalized to every warden across the country because we are all under the same laws and policies. There are also identified specific objectives that will be specific to your unit or what you wish to accomplish. Like for me, the successful opening of the secure unit would be one of them.

Administrator 18: We were involved in ensuring the sites are accountable. For example, recently we did an audit on personal and portable alarms in the institutions. Actually I think we have done a couple, but it is more to know that they are in compliance, to ensure that they are in compliance so they do it on a regular basis, check themselves. We also did it on training of our emergency response teams, and again those are site specific, like each institution has an emergency response team except for the minimum. So we were number one ensuring that the correct training, the basic training and the yearly training and again, it is ensuring that they are in compliance.

A short time ago, probably a year or eighteen months ago, we were asked to develop some audit tools that the institutions could use so that if I was moved to my unit manager position here, I could take this audit tool and know that from a security point of view I had to do A to Z and I could use it as a checklist. So we've done that, as have all the divisions—or they were supposed to, I should say! So the sites are sort of aware of that. Now, to actually figure out where we go—when we did the PPA [Personal Portable Alarm System] one, the IERT [Institutional Emergency Response Team] one, and included in that was urinalysis in the community to ensure they were in compliance—that actually came from National Headquarters and quite often it comes from there are issues in these areas. As a fall out from that, we have done one and then there was a list of about two pages, and as regional administrators we sat down and said we need to pick and choose what we are going to audit. So we prioritized what we should be, and it was really hard to do that because when you look at it, everything was important. But we really needed to pick out what is most important. Like use of force is very high profile. I mean everybody has seen the videos from Kingston Penitentiary, the women's facility—or, sorry Prison for Women—a few years ago, so that is always high. But we have such a process in place for that now, like, that is done on a regular basis. So that is where the most recent ones that we were involved in came from.

We have a Regional Performance Assurance Division here which is very small. They used to have auditors but they are all associated with National Headquarters now, so we don't have any auditors here. However, what we have—National Headquarters would send to the R.A., performance assurance: here is the things we want monitored or audited and he would share it with the relevant R.A. So we would do the security ones, someone else does the reintegration ones.

Administrator 19: We have performance measures that we are required to adhere to. We have, through our program standards, we have had site accreditation. So an independent body will come and look at the different standards. Do we meet them or don't we? That is done every two years. So all our sites except Newfoundland have gone through that process and have been accredited for programs—the core programs that we offer.

Administrator 20: We have touched on this as well. Our new deputy commissioner wants us to be more focused on our commitment to comply fully with our policies, and performance assurance has a huge role to play in all of this. Any audit that I do, from a security perspective, I share the results with the deputy commissioner and others, and I certainly let them know ahead of time that I will be doing such audits and, of course, we are responsible for reporting to Ottawa as well.

Every R.A., is expected to do a five to ten minute presentation on how they are doing on the various security policies. For example, we might present on how we are doing with our arrests or perhaps a short piece on the use of PPAS (Personal Portable Alarms) and whether we use them or just throw them in a desk drawer. So for example, we audit the count procedures for a site and found that they were delinquent on these procedures, and of course they received the "slap on the wrist" administratively, so to speak, for that. So I say to my staff that when they go out visiting institutions or into the field, to just take a look around and do spot or area checks of the various procedures, i.e., are they doing the *counts* correctly, and we have found horrible deficiencies in some departments, which we have let the wardens know about. We are not out there to do finger-pointing at specific institutions—that is not the intent here. Nevertheless, if we visit one site, for example RHC (Regional Health Centre), and find deficiencies there, then every warden should make a note of that and go back to their own site and check that the same deficiencies do not also exist there.

Administrator 21: We do good corrections; where we can improve will only make us better and we need to get people away from the idea that we are just ticking boxes on our audit tools versus why we are ticking boxes. There is a reason why we are doing it, and it is because we are responsible and accountable to the law first and foremost, and by doing it, we will enhance our performance in the long run to work with offenders and safely protect the community. There is a lot of education that needs to happen on that, from historical methodologies and verbal communications to actually showing our performance to the taxpayers who are paying us for the services.

Although we often identify the usefulness of such monitoring or auditing tools or processes as having the capability to present the problem areas or the areas that require improvement, such tools and processes are equally effective in highlighting things that are going well or things that are being performed in a positive, consistent, and efficient manner.

Administrator 22: CSC has a really strong audit function, ranging from regional audits to national audits, to the audits from the auditor general's office. We had a visit from the auditor general and he audited our region in a variety of areas. For example, to look at the federally sentenced women agenda; audited correctional programs and reintegration; audited the community and they looked at a couple of institutions as well. They have a very broad range of interests, but in this particular case they had an interest in reintegration, so they spent some time looking at a whole variety of things such as supervision, frequency of contact, program intervention—not just the types of programs we offer but how we determine where we will offer them, timeliness of programs, effectiveness of programming, and how we respond to needs. The auditor general puts out an annual report and it is an extensive assessment of CSC against some of the basic principles of what we are supposed to be accomplishing. This report is available on our website or by contacting the auditor general. Each annual report, which is quite extensive, is on one aspect of correctional practice, i.e., programming, security, or case management. CSC has not always had a favourable result from the auditor general's department. For example, in the 1996 Report there were a lot of criticisms levelled at the CSC, but when the Report came out a couple of years later, it was quite favourable in terms of the progress we had made. We will continue to see progress because we take these audits quite seriously, not just those from the auditor general, but our own internal regional and national audits.

We don't look at audits as efforts to embarrass or humiliate CSC, or to point out weaknesses or deficits, or to punish or to take away performance pay or anything like that. Rather, we take these as excellent opportunities for an outside look at what we do and a balanced look at what we do in terms of where we need to improve and how we can do so. Auditors recommend actions and our job is to take a look at all of their recommendations and to determine what we agree are legitimate concerns. In some cases recommendations and observations that are made are done so without the full knowledge of what actually transpires in that particular area. Therefore, the recommendations are flawed because they are not fully informed, but in the vast majority of cases their recommendations have substance. Some of them are right on and we shake our heads wondering how in the heck we didn't know that was happening or how we overlooked it, or perhaps we knew for a few years that something was happening and didn't do anything about it. This is the kind of thing that shakes you up and brings to the fore, those very issues that you need to focus on, and sometimes they are very critical issues. Then there are other recommendations where we might agree and think it would be great to achieve them in an ideal world, but the costs of that ... or the implications of that ... are these and if we follow your recommendation we may have a problem over there.

Our preference is to live with current reality, and so we would reject some recommendations outright or accept some fully and sometimes create very complex and comprehensive action plans to address them. Sometimes we might accept parts of them and agree to go part way through accomplishing the goals and hold back on the rest because something else may need to happen first, or we may be waiting for funding, etc. In the end, these audits make recommendations and inform, and CSC has been very responsive to audits, and for me personally, I always enjoy seeing audits because in part I believe we do a pretty good job and you like to be commended for that. At the same time, you sometimes lose sight of things that aren't going well because you are so immersed in the day-to-day operation or you get too busy at certain things and don't pay enough attention to other things.

Administrator 23: Part of the performance measurement process is also to investigate things that go wrong. We need to determine what it was that went wrong, why it went wrong, and if anything critical should have been done differently. This is where you get your formal investigations and those are very informing. There are regional and national investigations, depending on how serious the incident is and what the potential impacts of the event will be. In addition to this, our OMS—Offender Management System—contains an enormous amount of data, and attached to the OMS is a RADAR system which is a quick, inquiry system, which allows you to ask about certain things, where the information is drawn from the OMS and these reports are pre-prepared for us. For example, I could get a report on how many outstanding program reports there are for Mr. X delivering substance abuse at a certain Institution and I can go into that system and it will tell me, for example, that I have three reports that are overdue beyond the 10 working days that I had to complete them. It is that specific and detailed. That is an important thing to know because RADAR is a tremendously informative system which has more than just program elements. It also has case management. So if you wanted to know how many Correctional Plans were overdue for offenders at Matsqui, you can go in and ask that question. Not only will it tell you how many, but it will tell you which offender plans are overdue, and which staff are responsible for those. It is an excellent management tool. It's a performance measurement too, but it is mostly meant for managers to monitor on an ongoing basis because the results of RADAR are not really used as an audit, per se. Rather it is a tool to prevent audits from showing you negative results.

So a good manager will spend some time taking advantage of looking at RADAR on a weekly basis, and might spot some potential problem, like having twelve detention hearings that are late, or identifying an offender whose case prep hadn't been done on time, or having three offenders whose Correctional Plans are overdue by a week and they all belong to Mr. Smith. It's not meant to be critical; it's meant to ask questions and prompt the manager to call, for example Mr. Smith, to see what's going on. Perhaps he's been in the hospital for a week. It's a very useful tool and the correctional results is very much like that and it is updated on a monthly basis as well, drawing its information from OMS in part, but also from separate databases. Performance measurement in my view is one area where CSC is very strong.

The comments from Administrators 12 to 23 discuss numerous tools and approaches to establish accountability. In these comments, can you identify any congruencies between these tools and approaches and the essence of accountability defined by Belanger and colleagues (2001) in identifying key results, measuring performance, and reporting to the public and parliament on performance compared to the original key results identified? What strengths and weaknesses do the administrators identify in relation to the system set up by CSC to strive for accountability?

Although some of the interviewees believed that accountability was affected by errors—particularly human errors in data entry—they also believe that the system is on its way to remedying flaws. That being said, the administrators largely agreed that accountability was necessary. Accountability is set out in performance agreements developed at National Headquarters and often involve the identification of objectives specific to a particular unit or department. Regional administrators are expected to produce regular reports on their various sectors, such as the implementation of various policies. As one administrator said, "we are responsible and accountable to the law first and foremost, and by doing it [various quality and performance audits] we will enhance our performance in the long run to work with offenders and safely protect the community."

Character

We have discussed the makeup of "AIM"; it is comprised of Mission and Values, Leadership, and Accountability. After *aim*, the second pillar of successful organizations is *character* (Ingstrup, 2002). Character is built on three areas—people, communication, and trust.

People

As will be discussed in greater detail in Chapter 7, the people working in CSC are the key to good corrections. Effective organizations are good at identifying the right people with the right skills and attitudes, developing, training, and mentoring them, and, finally, appraising and rewarding them when they have done a good job. One interviewee commented on this area:

Administrator 24: One thing I would like to see—and I am hoping we will move in this direction—is a much enhanced training and development program within CSC. It's one of the weakest areas in corrections and we invest a very small amount of money in training. Many organizations spend a significant amount of their corporate budget on training. CSC spends around four percent and it shows. You get people who don't know much about programming and this leads to bad referrals, or you get people who don't know how to write reports effectively, prepare a case to the board or deal with a detention hearing or a judicial review. The turnover is fairly dramatic and every time you get a new staff there is more training involved. I don't think we invest the kind of energy in training—in this organization—that we need to. I'd like to believe the organization will see this as a weakness. I've spoken to the auditor general when he was here and I hope other people did as well, and that it will be in his report. Then perhaps

CSC will see that and may decide to increase the funding allocations for training. It wouldn't take a lot to see a difference. This could increase staff morale and satisfaction because we do lose people ... they find themselves overwhelmed. They get thrust into positions they are not ready for and feel like they are going to fail or not succeed. No one wants to work in a job where they feel they are behind all of the time, or that they are failing, or that they will make a mistake one day that will come back and embarrass them or get somebody killed. Those are the kinds of pressures people feel and this is an important issue for CSC, and this is an issue that I would like to see them focus on.

Mobilizing the commitment of the staff to the new vision is crucial to managing organizational change successfully (Shepherdson, 1995). The Correctional Service of Canada's success in achieving this commitment was measured in the 1996 All Staff Survey:

> Organizational commitment remained relatively strong with an increase from 61% to 65% of staff who felt loyal and proud to be a CSC employee. There was also strong support for CSC's objectives. About 63% of staff said that CSC's corporate objectives accurately describe what the priorities of the organization should be. Seventy percent of staff expressed agreement with the Mission in both 1994 and 1996. While there was variation by occupational group, support for the Mission exceeded 85% for five of the nine occupational groups. Agreement with the Mission was highest among managers (AS-06 and above; 90%) and lowest among correctional officers (51%) in both 1994 and 1996. The management group (AS-06 and above) was the only job category to show a notable decline in support for the Mission during the two year period (94% to 90%). (CSC, 1997, p. 16)

Similar information is also available from the 2002 and 2005 Public Service Employee Surveys which looks at individual sectors and sites in terms of survey results. [Note: Since the 2007 reorganization in CSC, AS-06s are now project officers, WPSs, CX4s, and AS-07s are managers.]

Communication
The second important factor in building character in an organization is communication. Ingstrup (2002) discussed the importance of communication, ensuring that it is prompt, open, honest, and to the point. Communication needs to be systematic and is a responsibility of the leaders of the organization.

Communication is a two-way flow of information that includes keeping others informed as well as presenting them with opportunities to participate. Two correctional administrators commented on its importance:

Administrator 25: So that brings up another point of importance in terms of correctional administration, is that we need at least one hundred twenty percent in communications skills. What I mean by that is that this is the biggest complaint in any of our organizations as to what would they change if they could, and the response is communications. People do not know how to communicate properly, and part of this is because we rely more and more on email and on electronic systems, so you never speak to anybody anymore. We have correctional officers who never see their supervisors— they may get an email from them every once in awhile. However, really knowing how to communicate appropriately is so very important. Also, around communications too, it is the whole thing of the media. Having media relations training is absolutely crucial for all of our correctional administrators. You may not be called upon to actually have to speak to the media, but you should always know what it is about the particular incident that you are involved in that could (a) be a potentially sensitive issue and could be picked up by the media, because then you should be reporting that to the media relations person, or (b) if you had to write a media clip, what would you put in it? What are you allowed to put in it and what is not allowed to be in Correctional administrators should know all of this. Therefore, that type of training is really important stuff too. Moreover, the media has a tendency to not only track stuff in corrections, but in particular correctional settings as well.

Administrator 26: CSC has not been a good communicator in being able to sell our product. It is a hard product to sell. If I go to you in the community and say that I am going to release ten lifers or ten rapists and they are not going to hurt you, it is a hard product to sell. In the past I think we were secretive; we weren't sharing as much as we wanted to. I think we have to open our book, we need to speak more, get our partners involved a little bit more in helping us communicate and things like that. Because ninety-seven to ninety-eight percent of the offenders are going to return at some point in time. I would rather that they return knowing that they are not going to hurt your grandmother, my grandmother, your kids or my kids and those sorts of things. We have got to empower the public to believe that we are good at what we are doing. We know that we are good at what we are doing and now we've got to get the public.

Both Administrator 25 and 26 speak to the issue of communication with the public, in particular through the media, and how CSC has historically not been a good communicator. Why do you think it is important for CSC to be a good communicator with the public, and why is training for correctional administrators in dealing with the media also important?

Trust

The third factor in building character is trust. Belanger *et al.*, (2001) found that four elements were key to developing trust—empathy, competency, integrity, and openness. Building trust is a complex and fragile task. One negative event can destroy all previous efforts. Therefore, trust needs to be constantly nurtured.

Various levels of trust must exist within an organization, for the highest level of efficiency and effectiveness (Ingstrup, 2002). The first level is personal trust; in other words, people are trustworthy and act in an ethical manner. The second level is professional trust, which occurs when the individuals working within the organization and the organization itself is viewed as being good at what they do. Political trust is the third aspect, and it occurs when politicians are confident in the ability of the organization to do its job and meet its mission. Finally, there is public trust—the degree to which the public trusts the organization's ability to perform competently. This level of trust is largely influenced by the media.

The interviewees expressed a number of opinions about the various levels of trust within the Correctional Service of Canada:

Administrator 27: I do think public opinion is shifting a little bit again in terms of corrections, perhaps more so than in the past. Certain politicians are making huge cases in relation to corrections operations and issues, by and large very uninformed cases, but they are doing damage to perceptions in general. This, in combination with some of the media responses, has not always presented corrections in a favourable light. So I think recent incidents, like the social that happened in the prairies and another one in Ontario where the inmates were reportedly drunk, potentially lead the public to become slowly disenchanted with corrections. Unfortunately, these are incidents that should have never happened. These are not incidents that we support as an organization; they are mistakes made by people who are in positions of responsibility. They come back to reflect very badly on us and it does not matter that we discipline the people and so on. It just leaves a bad taste in people's mouths. If enough pressure mounts up and enough pressure gets directed, there may be pressures to cut back on programming, to reduce expenses, to treat offenders a bit differently. Take away privileges—no more arts and crafts, or temporary absences, or sports activities, or the use of weights in the workout room.

Forget about the fact that these may be fitness activities or a lifestyle enhancement that in many ways helps offenders to develop a more positive self-image, which they may not have had and which might have been part of their overall life problems. Some of these guys have gone on to be umpires in local community softball teams, referees in soccer leagues, and some have gone on to open their own stores for making moccasins or selling their carvings. It's not as though we do not have success stories, but what you hear about are often the failures. I am a little worried that if we are not careful and CSC doesn't do a better job of promoting its own positive image and successes, we may end up being forced into a position where we may have to pull back a little on our reintegration agenda. For example, the decision to put all lifers in maximum security for the first two years in my view is a questionable decision; you should always assess on a case by case basis. But to make a *blanket statement or policy* is inconsistent with our individualized treatment approach. I think the commissioner was forced into it by the Minister and other various political agendas. It will be interesting to see what comes of this in a couple of years. Maybe it won't change at all. We always seem to go through the ups and downs in terms of public perception, and some years seem to be more favourable than others. However, currently I feel we are in a bit of a downward slope and it all depends if we come out of this or it gets worse, in which case we may see some changes.

Society must realize that the correctional system does not create criminals; society/families creates criminals and correction's task is to take the problems that society creates and try to correct them and to turn them back into people that society can utilize in an effective and beneficial way again. And oftentimes I think society gets mixed up and thinks that corrections is at fault for these people coming back into the community and sometimes committing more crimes. It is not our "fault"; sometimes we cannot be successful in the time we have or the person is so damaged they are beyond helping. To summarize, one of the directions that CSC has to go in is towards a much-enhanced image, and that means we have to respond to inaccurate stories by some politicians and media sources. We have to provide enough good news stories to the media and the public to sort of say, yes we have some failures, but there are many positive things happening to. We have to brighten up our image and CSC needs to invest in training and in P.R.

Administrator 28: The best example of that [political involvement into what we know to be correct] for me is when the solicitor general bowed to whatever pressures there were and made a unilateral decision that all lifers would now spend a minimum of X number of years in maximum security institutions. That's not right. That goes against everything we know. But we allowed that thing to happen. I think that is the most ethical problem we have to face ... and I can see more of that coming down the road.

Although some of the administrators have stated the importance of media in creating a more positive public image for CSC, others believe that within the "community of corrections" perceptions of the work being done may be counterproductive to building a healthy, working community. It is most difficult for front line staff in particular to do the work they are required to do when they possess a level of cynicism about the part they play in offender management, rehabilitation, and reintegration.

Administrator 29: One of the challenges of CSC is to try to create an understanding of who we are within our own community and that is something, for whatever reason, we have not managed to achieve at the level that we would like. We know we are respected around the world as having probably one of the best correctional systems anywhere, and we are more successful with respect to our programming than almost any jurisdiction. There is a high level of cynicism in the population at large about corrections, and the fact that people think we are "mollycoddling" or whatever, and this is an issue that is raised regularly, at least by the opposition party, so it creates an atmosphere where there is a lot of prodding by Canadians and often by our own staff. And this is one of the challenges as an administrator—to keep your staff "up" when they go home and talk to their friends and people around them in their community who are saying we are not doing an exemplary job when we think we are.

This is very, very sad, because if you are a professional who believes in what you are doing then you should be out telling everybody about it. But when our own politicians don't seem to support us and don't seem to appreciate the success that we are having, it becomes very demoralizing for staff. We are continually trying to develop more partnerships with communities and involve communities more within our facilities for example, by way of recruiting volunteers, and have developed some partnerships with universities for example, because the reality is offenders are citizens of a community and will be returning to their communities somewhere. Corrections doesn't have the luxury of choosing their own clients; we get who we get.

The more that we can create orderly transitions and clarify the terms of ownership of the problems, the more likely it is we will have successes. All too often, these people have existed in an environment for twenty-five or thirty-five years, where all of the various social systems have failed in terms of assisting these guys to lead socially acceptable lives, and we get them for often a fairly short period of time and we are expected to achieve perfection.

Even though I believe we do a good job, often we do not have enough time and we have to release people whether we want to or not—for example, those who we know are still dangerous have to be released if their sentences are expiring—and many times we can predict who will reoffend and who will not, but there is nothing we can do about it because we don't control who exits the door unless they are out on a conditional release. So it is a very frustrating reality for people because often the faces that are associated with serious crimes in the communities are often the faces we would very much like to keep, but we have no choice but to release them because they are finished, and sometimes we have to release them on statutory release because they don't meet the detention criteria either. But we don't want to detain them either because if they get out of detention at Warrant Expiry, there is no supervision, so often it is much less risky to release them at statutory release because at least they will have the supervision and control as they move out into the community, knowing full well that some of these people will probably get reinvolved. But the reality right now is that if we have a determinate sentencing structure that's just something you have to live with. It's a systemic reality, and to be critical of corrections because of the fact that some of the people, when they get out, may commit a crime, it is not necessarily a reasonable portrayal of what we achieve.

Each of the administrators discusses the issue of political trust, or lack thereof. Can you discern from their comments what impacts a lack of political trust can have on the correctional system?

Execution

Last, creating aim and character is not enough. An organization must be able to execute. To have *execution*, "collectively the members of the service must have the skills to translate ideas, attitudes, creativity, energy, and intellectual insights into well-directed actions that produce results as defined by the mission" (Ingstrup, 2002, p. 7). In order to translate ideas into action, organizations must develop the management and leadership within the organization (Chapter 7 discusses the training of management in greater detail). Leaders need to be able to adapt management or correctional tools to fit a situation or problem.

These leaders use teams to solve problems and come up with creative solutions, and they must be able to manage the organization through periods of change to keep it developing and growing. Ingstrup (2002) believed that

> an organization which is not improving, is decaying. Constant change is part of what makes an organization good and the only way in which constant change becomes constant improvement is when the mission is clear and present in the minds of people, when the operational values are being adhered to and when the organization is comfortable with a relatively high pace of change." (p. 9)

Conclusion

This chapter has discussed the three pillars on which successful organizations are built—aim, character, and execution. To establish aim, an organization must have a clearly defined mission statement and values, and the leadership and accountability to bring the words in the mission and values to life. Character must be established through the development of good employees, clear communication, and trust. Finally, an organization must be able to execute—to translate ideas, programs, creativity, and so on into actions that produce results consistent with the mission statement.

Study Questions

1. By using the comments of the correctional administrators quoted in this chapter, assess how well the Correctional Service of Canada is implementing one of the three pillars of successful organizations.
2. Choose one of the pillars of successful organizations and discuss possible consequences within the Correctional Service of Canada if this pillar was removed.
3. One administrator said that performance measures can be dehumanizing. Can you think of any examples of this and explore reasons for why he/she may feel that way?
4. Discuss how the three pillars of successful organizations support "what works" in corrections.

Bibliography

*Items with asterisks are also suggested readings for this chapter.

Belanger, J., Baillard, V., Steinberg, S., Dinsdale, G., and Giroux, K. (2001). *Building Trust: A Foundation of Risk Management*. Ottawa: Canadian Centre for Management Development.

Bridges, W. (1991). *Managing Transitions*. Mill Valley, CA: William Bridges and Associates.

Correctional Service of Canada (1997). *Results of the 1996 CSC Staff Survey: A Synopsis*. Ottawa: Correctional Service of Canada Research Branch. http://www.csc-scc.gc.ca/text/rsrch/briefs/b17/b17e-eng.shtml

Correctional Service of Canada (1991). *Our Story: Organizational Renewal in FederalCorrections*. Ottawa: Canadian Centre for Management Development.

Duguid, S. (1993). Cognitive dissidents bite the dust—The demise of university education in Canada's prisons. *Convergence* 26(3), 51–65.

Fleisher, M. (1996). Management assessment and policy dissemination in Federal prisons. *Prison Journal* , 76(1), 81–91.

French, B. and Stewart, J. (2001). Organizational development in a law enforcement environment. *FBI Law Enforcement Bulletin,* September 2001, 70(9).

Golembiewski, R. T. (1998). OD in prisons: Expanding the self while the person is confined. *OD Practitioner,* 30(2), 7–11.

Gondles, J.A. (2000). Standards and accreditation: A collaborative effort. *Corrections Today,* 62(5), 6.

Government of Canada. 2002 Public Service Employee Survey. http://www.psagency-agencefp.gc.ca/arc/survey-sondage/2002/results-resultats/04/index-e.htm

*Ingstrup, O. (2002). *Good Corrections: Implications for Leadership and Training*. European Committee ·on Crime Problems—13th Conference of Directors of Prison Administration. Strasbourg, 6–8 November.

Martin, P.L. (1999). Leadership, management and corrections. *Corrections Today,* 61(7), 94–95.

Opengart, R. (2001). OD in corrections. *Public Administration Quarterly,* 25(2), 138–153.

Senge, P. (1990). *The Fifth Discipline: The Art and Practice of the Learning Organization*. New York, NY: Doubleday Currency.

Shepherdson, D. (1995). *Meeting the Challenge: Managing Change in the Nineties*. Ottawa: Canadian Centre Management Development.

*Stoyko, P. (2001). *Learning Organization—A discussion Paper for CCMD's Action-Research Roundtable on the Learning Organization*. Ottawa: Canadian Centre for Management Development.

Tupper, A. (2001). The contested terrain of Canadian public administration in Canada's third century. *Journal of Canadian Studies,* 35(4), Winter 2001, 142–160.

Wiebe, R. (2000). *The Visionary Legacy of Ron Wiebe: An Unfinished Conversation*. Ottawa: Correctional Service of Canada. http://www.csc-scc.gc.ca/text/pblct/ronweibe/index_e.shtml

Suggested Readings

Department of the Solicitor General of Canada (2003). *2003–2004 Estimates: A Report on Plans and Priorities.* http://www.tbs-sct.gc.ca/est-pre/20032004/SGC-SGC/SGC-SGCr34_e.asp

Department of the Solicitor General of Canada (2002). *2002–2003 Estimates: A Report on Plans and Priorities.* http://www.tbs-sct.gc.ca/est-pre/20022003/rSGC___e.pdf

5 Policy-Making in Government

This chapter contains factual information about policy-making and a number of interviews that illustrate the real life views of CSC administrators. The goal of presenting both types of information is to provide you with the means to debate and think through the merits of policy and the methods of policy-making that are introduced in this chapter. Through comparing and contrasting the material, you can begin to form an opinion about the appropriateness, clarity, and practicality of a policy, as well as the competencies and skills of staff that enact policy. You may wish to consider ways and means to overcome them—that is, to engage in the policy making process yourself.

Informed policy-making is what underpins all of correctional practice, beginning with the Mission Statement and the implementation of procedures to meet policy objectives. This chapter also discusses the effects of such elements as political power and pressures, ideology, theory, and research, and their influence on policy-making. It is important for you to consider these factors as you read the interviewees' comments, particularly in terms of corporate and specific policies that have consequences in certain areas of correctional practice.

Process of Policy Development

Canada is a parliamentary democracy based on the collective and individual responsibility of members elected to the federal House of Commons, which, along with the laws and regulations of the *Charter of Rights and Freedoms*, provides a crucial framework for public service roles, responsibilities, and values. Arguably, the principles of responsible government work in a quiet, positive way every day, maintaining ministerial authority over officials. In this sense, these principles are the cornerstone of democracy in a parliamentary system, establishing the authority of elected persons for the conduct of the government.

In supporting the democratic process, public servants have a dual role to play. One role is to carry out the programs and policies of the government of the day. The other is to provide ministers with a full range of analysis and advice that will help them make the best possible decisions—including policy decisions—for the public good. This dual role is played not just at the top of various departments, but at all levels of public service where there are employees and supervisors. It may also involve telling ministers things they do not wish to hear. During the normal course of events, it is the public servants' role to inform ministers as fully and accurately as possible about the consequences of certain policy options, including warning them about possible negative or harmful consequences of proposed actions or initiatives. In other circumstances, which are rarer, public servants have a duty to inform a minister if the proposed action would potentially be unethical, illegal, or unconstitutional.

Once a government is elected, it has a mandate from the people to enact the policies it has proposed. As part of the executive branch of government, civil servants have the task of implementing and administering the government's policies; they are the major point of contact between the individuals and the political regime. In liberal-democratic states such as Canada, there has always been—and no doubt always will be—tension between politicians and bureaucrats over their respective roles in making public policy. The reason for this is fairly simple, even if the practice is anything but; it is virtually impossible to define precisely the division of responsibilities between ministers and their senior bureaucrats. This relationship is constantly in a state of redefinition and renegotiation from government to government and from minister to minister in the same government. However, one thing is clear: bureaucrats play a significant role in the policy process, while the politicians are ultimately responsible to the public. Landes (1995) stressed three points about the importance of the bureaucracy in making public policy:

1. The public service or bureaucracy plays a key role in the initiation, development and implementation of public policy. A bureaucracy is a hierarchically-organized institution based on written rules and staffed by officials paid from public funds. In analyzing bureaucracies from a comparative perspective, three basic problems must be looked at: first, how is the bureaucracy structured; second, how is the public service controlled and by whom; and third, is the public service neutral or non-partisan. [That is to say, according to Landes, the bureaucracy should be free of political interference, impartial, and a defined set of procedures should be applied to specific cases]

2. Policy-making and the role of the bureaucracy in that process can be investigated by using two models: the rational-actor model and the organizational-politics model. The rational-actor model focuses on the maximization of the means-ends relationship, while the organizational-politics model stresses the concept of satisficing (to choose a course of action that is good enough, given such constraints as time, money, information, and effort). The organizational-politics model emphasizes the importance of parochial priorities and standard operating procedures in analyzing the decision-making process.

3. In Canada, the political executive, aided and abetted by the bureaucracy, dominates the policy process. Royal commissions and related bodies may be used to avoid policy rather than to create it. Generally, public policy is little affected by ideology. Instead, policy is incremental in nature and administered by generalists. While recent reforms have sought to move Canada toward a rational-actor model of decision-making, few observers would conclude that the trend has been overwhelmingly successful. (p. 196)

According to Landes (1995), therefore, the roles of the bureaucracy in implementing public policy and of the political executive in its initiation and development have made the executive branch of the government the dominant force in the political process of autocratic, democratic, and totalitarian systems.

One prominent politician in British Columbia commented in an interview that policy development is influenced by the following:

- cost factor—use of public resources
- ability to achieve required outcomes in the least intrusive, deregulated manner
- ability to standardize
- priorities, given limited time, resources, and so forth
- prevailing government philosophical or ideological stance

However, at present, government policy development seems to include moving social policy development into the arena of economic policy development, driven by financial costs and, therefore, cost-benefit analysis.

Landes (1995) defined policy as "an explicit set of preferences and plans drawn up in order to make the outcome of a series of future decisions more nearly predictable and consistent" (p. 131). It is a set of preferences that has consequences for the community. Policies may focus more on "intentions" and reflect the vision or goals of the government or an organization without identifying the procedures (protocols/regulations/steps to be taken) necessary to implement them. Mission statements are often policy statements or policy intentions that guide the organization. They contain core values that reflect collective and individual rights. Guiding principles dictate how policy statements will be put into operation.

The process of policy development generally starts with identifying a problem in need of a solution; however, problems often exist for a time before they reach a threshold, and these problems are often fuelled by extensive media coverage, which ensures policy-makers will intervene. In addition, some legislators and other political actors may engage in the policy process not only to respond to perceived social problems, but also to advance their own political interests and careers. Since the development of new policies often affects the goals of existing policies, it should take into account which policies have priority and should achieve a balance where possible.

According to some of the CSC interviewees,

Administrator 1: Policies are generated by people in committees at a particular time in the organization's life, and also by the particular strength of the commissioner or the minister or how deeply politics are involved and the purity of what we are trying to do. Because the politics can bastardize it—there is no other way of saying it, but they do bastardize it because that's another world—and when that is inserted into this world, it twists it. And that's neither right nor wrong, that's just the dynamic.

Administrator 2: To me, that stuff is all great. Now, as an organization today, we don't pay as much attention to it as we used to. In order to get it up and going (policies), the commissioner and the Ottawa people had to push really, really, really hard. The further you are away from Ottawa, the lower the voice, the lower the intensity. So it takes a lot longer to say no, look, this is of value, this corporation says this is of value. This corporation says this is the way we want to behave. Help us behave that way and if you don't know how to do it, let's get you trained to do that kind of a thing because this is who we are. Now, various line managers along the line, or functional managers along the line, interpret that through their own filters and then manifest it out to various kinds of degrees of purity.

In examining Administrator 1's comments, it is useful to compare this view of policy generation with what Landes defined as the three basic problems that should be discussed when analyzing bureaucracies and their key roles in policy-making. How might Administrator 1 respond to these three basic questions, given his/her views? Likewise, Administrator 2 suggests that policies are made by individuals whose proximity to correctional institutions may be marred by great distances. These distances can be both in terms of actual distance and by position within the hierarchical organizations. How does this translate into the application of such policies by the line level staff? Landes further discussed the role of the political actor in terms of the development of policies; are his views reflected in Administrators 1 and 2's comments?

Political and Ideological Influences on Policy Development

Maintaining the vision or goals in policy development may be complicated by the presence of competing ideologies. According to Miller (1973), an ideology is a set of general and abstract beliefs about the correct or proper state of things, particularly with respect to the moral order and political arrangements that shape individuals' positions on specific issues. Landes (1995) has described ideologies as sets of ideas held by a number of people; they spell out what is valued and what is not, what must be maintained and what must be changed. Accordingly, they shape the attitudes of those who share them. Although Landes would argue that prevailing ideologies do not currently have a prominent role in policy development, it seems that some of the major dividing points within the political sphere may centre on issues such as class, religion, race, and ethnicity, in addition to any particular ideology. These divisions may produce political subcultures whose views may differ from the dominant political culture, and these different values and beliefs may conflict. Currently, such conflicts based on ideologies can be illustrated by debates regarding "legalizing gay marriages" and "providing needle exchanges within corrections settings."

Ideologies often have strong emotional and unexamined presumptions that are generally not consciously recognized. Miller (1972) stated that the formation of ideologies is strongly influenced by environmental experiences and informational inputs, and that once they are formed they are often resistant to change, and hence evolve into "self-contained and self-reinforcing systems" (p. 142). It is important, therefore, to understand—or at least be able to identify—the prevailing and competing ideologies that make certain assumptions about the nature of crime and the methods of dealing with it that are inherent in public policies such as those in the criminal justice system and, in particular, the correctional system in Canada. However, although ideology is an inherent element of the policy-making process and may enhance drive, dedication, and commitment, they may also introduce rigidity, intolerance, and a degree of distortion. To limit the detrimental effects of ideologies while optimizing their strengths, it is essential to develop the skill of separating that which is "value" from that which is "fact" in ideological statement. While it may be impossible to be free of ideological predilections (and possibly it would not be desirable), the purposes of effective policy and practice are not served when we are unable to recognize the degree of legitimacy, validity, and humane intent such ideologies possess. So who is doing the defining, what meaning they are attaching to policy statements, and which ideology is underpinning the entire policy development process are all vital questions to ask. *Ideology can be viewed as the permanent hidden agenda of criminal justice policy development.*

Policy development is also influenced by political positions based on prevailing political ideology and longevity of political parties and their leaders. Thus, differences in government—ideologically and historically—and whether they choose to change or develop a relevant policy have often led to or ended policy initiatives. For example, movements through the various political spheres over time, such as from the Keynesian welfare state, which had as one of its principles *the provision of services primarily by the government to all people at some recognized basic standard for all* to the current neoliberalist political realm, as some might describe it, may bring about many changes, some of which may have powerful influences on current correctional administration practices. According to Glor (2001), as a result of the unsettled nature of politics in the 1970s through the 1990s, "dominant paradigms/ideologies—long term programs [and policies] that had been previously institutionalized, routinized and integrated, were all at risk" (p. 20). Table 5.1 summarizes the political picture from 1968 to the present.

Table 5.1. Government of Canada Political Parties, Leaders, and Length in Power

Government of Canada	Government Leader	Duration of Government	
		Years	Dates
Liberal	Pierre Trudeau	11	1968–1979
Progressive Conservative	Joe Clark	<1	1979–1980
Liberal	Pierre Trudeau	4	1980–1984
Liberal	John Turner	<1	1984
Progressive Conservative	Brian Mulroney	9	1984–1993
Progressive Conservative	Kim Campbell	<1	1993
Liberal	Jean Chretien	10	1993–2004

Government of Canada	Government Leader	Duration of Government	
Liberal	Paul Martin	<2	2004–2006
Conservative	Steven Harper	2	2006–

Source: Mumford, 2006

Neoliberalism identified with the expansion of market economy, globalization, separate groups and separate goals, and the limiting government interventions in the social arena. One of the main focuses of current government in Canada has been to reduce inflation and eliminate government deficits. Public policy development has emphasized *monitoring* (flexible) versus *evaluations* (seen as more static and judgemental by some), moving from highly regulated to less regulated practices, risk versus need, and more rigorous cost-benefit analysis. The government has shown a growing interest in moving away from the obligation to provide services and to finding ways to provide the same services through contracting out and involving nongovernmental organizations (NGOs) and/or the private sector. According to Jessop (2002):

> Neoliberalism promotes market-led economic and social re-structuring. In the public sector, this involves privatization, liberalization and imposition of commercial criteria in the residual state sector; in the private sector, deregulation is backed by a new juridicopolitical framework that offers passive support for market solutions. This is reflected in: government measures to promote "hire-and-fire" flexitime, and flexi wage labour markets; growth of tax expenditures steered by private initiatives based on fiscal subsidies for favoured economic activities; measures to turn welfare states into a means of supporting and subsidizing low wages and/or to enhance the disciplinary force of social security measures and programs; and a more general reorientation of economic and social policy to the private sector's "needs."
>
> In other words, welfare states are seen as costly, overburdened, inefficient, incapable of eliminating poverty, overly oriented to cash entitlements rather than empowerment and so on. Policies should emphasize moving people from welfare into work, that link social and labour market policy, and that provide incentives to learn and/or prepare for a new job. Arrangements should be instituted to encourage families, neighbourhoods, informal or market-based and market-sustaining solutions to the problems of social reproduction.
>
> In addition, social partnership is disavowed in favour of managerial prerogatives, market forces and a strong state. Neoliberals also

support free trade and capital mobility. They expect innovation to
follow spontaneously from freeing entrepreneurs and workers to
seize market opportunities in a state-sponsored enterprise culture.
(2002, pp. 461–65)

Generally, this description of neoliberalism can help us develop a more
specific comparison of the criminal justice policies that result from left and
right ideologies.

As we can infer from the above, to *left* ideology, in contrast to a neoliberal or
conservative perspective, private lives and their expression in entrepreneurship
and the growth of capital are not as important as the welfare of the whole. A
left ideology places criminality as one of a number of negative results of capitalist economies which create unjust social structures. The key to correction of
these imbalances is to vest government with power over corporate behaviour
and thus control the economy through planning or strong legislative guidance, and through these controls to create a more even distribution of wealth
and thus reduce crime. A right or conservative ideology, on the other hand,
would see the individual as the key piece of the puzzle, not the collective. The
individual makes choices and is a responsible agent; individual decisions lead
to right or wrong action—specifically in the commission of crimes. Members
of disadvantaged groups do not necessarily commit crime; individuals commit
crime. In addition, power is vested in an order which is legitimated through
overarching moral values, values which produce a strong sense of right and
wrong. The criminal breaks these values.

Conservative ideology maps crime as the result of the erosion of discipline
and excessive social permissiveness. Crime arises from this excessive leniency;
this is shown in the law's favouring of the offender over the victim which results
in penalizing the victim. The sanction of 'criminality' is a valuable deterrent
as it distinguishes victim and offender. Left ideology on the other hand views
criminality as a more complex interaction where the state is given the power
to define, or label who and what is criminal; this in turn promotes the growth
of the justice system and creates a hierarchical and centralized structure in
which too many who are not responsible are incorrectly labeled as criminals;
there is a discriminatory class bias in this labeling.

Left ideology also views injustices of society like poverty, racism, and ghetto-
ization (the process where minority groups are forced out of the mainstream
and usually into specific areas within a city) as fundamental causes of crime.
Inadequate or unjust social structures do not meet basic social needs and frus-
trate merit. Crime grows in this fertile soil of social injustice. A conservative
ideology favours a return to structures considered valuable; self control, disci-

pline and social sanctions are used to maintain venerated social practices and institutions. The criminal justice system cannot create a new society. Crime is a result of the breakdown of valuable institutions like the family, the result of weaker controls and permissive values. A too permissive criminal justice system allows crime to be profitable at the expense of social order.

In terms of crime prevention or the reduction of crime, left ideology would remake social structure through investing time, effort and money in meeting the needs of the disadvantaged, often through large scale work projects or social welfare spending. For the left, the criminal justice system needs to be made humane and rehabilitative not punitive. For a conservative or right ideology, the social order and its structures need to be lived up to and maintained through the courts and through law—thus the emphasis on law and order. Traditions are important in providing security and should be asserted through making the cost of crime greater and thus a meaningful deterrent—stronger sanctions will produce less crime.

The focus of right ideology tends to be on the victims of the crime. The criminal should be punished in order to protect the innocent and provide redress to the victim. The left focus tends to be on the criminal, making sure that the offender, who is disadvantaged either in terms of class, race or income, is reformed in order to prevent further crime and through this route to prevent further victimization.

The left ideology also forwards the protection of individual rights, human rights, and notions of humane treatment of the less advantaged through activist views of justice and through being proactive in terms of social change—the justice system exists for the betterment of humanity. The conservative ideology stresses the current order and its past, the strong application of values of a system which has been achieved through a rich and worthwhile history in which freedoms have been won at great cost. A justice system exists to fairly judge and punish crimes against this order—but on conviction, crime should be punished.

For the right ideology, if the criminal justice system needs to be reformed it is in order to release its full potential to prohibit crime. The criminal justice system is hampered by liberal thinking; criminals can be let off on technicalities. Judicial discretion should be reformed to ensure that correct levels of punishment occur and that justice is done. For the left ideology, in contrast, reform means reshaping and controlling the criminal justice system itself so that it is a force in social reform. These are significant differences in outlook and they result in very different views of the criminal justice system.

When a new political party is elected and forms the government, there is potential to introduce new actors and new ideas. Thus, there is the possibility that big changes may be made and the emergence of new actors, either from within or outside the organization, is necessary for major policy or goal changes. If there are no new actors but new ideas are initiated, a process of *disjointed incrementalism* occurs; that is, relatively small changes happen. Conversely, if there are new actors but no new ideas, there may be a change in structure, but it will not likely result in new policies or goals.

Impact of Correctional Theory and Research on Policy Development

Theory

According to Ekstedt and Jackson (1996), theories of crime causation are closely linked to those regarding sentencing of offenders and administration of sentences. They argue that, "depending on which theory is predominant at any given point in time—whether the *individual deficiencies model, the medical model* or *the social causation model*—there will be fairly divergent outcomes in program development" (p. 41) and the policies and procedures that guide them. In the Daubney Report of 1988, which sought to identify the goals and objectives of corrections through the inclusion of discussions with relevant stakeholders, the principles that emerged with respect to sentencing and punishment may be briefly summarized as follows:

> *Just Deserts*: the principle of proportionality should be upheld when sentencing offenders and the purpose of sentencing is punishment.
> *Offender Responsibility and Deterrence*: punishment as it currently stands does not allow the offender to take any responsibility for their actions, nor is it conducive to the offender making amends to the victim/community. However, severe punishment does serve the purpose of both general and specific deterrence.

> *Victim/Offender Reconciliation*: making amends for offending against the victim/community should be done through reparation, which allows the offender to become part of the healing process and further allows the community to assume some responsibility for offender reintegration. Reparation can be made in many ways—for example, financially—through completing community service hours or community projects, offering apologies, or, in the case of some property offences, returning stolen goods.

Denunciation: the emphasis here is on offender accountability and on acknowledging the extent to which the community abhors the offenders' behaviours or actions. Such community views of offender behaviour are often expressed verbally, as is the case in "shaming" practices, for example.

Incapacitation: this principle primarily involves increasing the frequency and/or severity of the punishment through lengthier or harsher sentences for offences and using imprisonment more frequently as the mode of punishment.

The Daubney Report commented on the efficacy of each of these principles in connection with correctional practice. In reviewing the statements of those individuals who provided information for the Report, the authors (the Standing Committee of Justice and Solicitor General) acknowledged the importance of using alternatives to incarceration, especially for individuals convicted of non-violent offences. They also saw alternatives to incarceration as the best way to encourage the process of rehabilitation and "voluntary" participation. Included in its recommendations were several values and opportunities that the Committee felt were essential to developing principles of sentencing and correctional management:

1. Acceptance of responsibility by offenders for their criminal behaviours and its consequences;
2. Victim reparation and victim/offender reconciliation;
3. The habilitation or rehabilitation of offenders (offenders who have never been habilitated cannot be rehabilitated); and
4. A consideration of denunciation and incapacitation where appropriate and necessary. (Ekstedt and Jackson, 1996, p. 45)

Although theories may have some influence in the development of policies guiding correctional administration practices, according to Ekstedt and Jackson, it is difficult to relate "philosophical explanations to working systems" p. 48. Therefore, theoretical assumptions are often in conflict with the beliefs and working assumptions of people employed within the correctional system. However, that being said, theory has had some impact on the current shift, from carceral to noncarceral programs as a way to meet both sentencing intent and public expectations. This move is partly based on a sentencing theory that places more emphasis on community responsibility for reintegration of the offender and less on the responsibility to provide rehabilitation within an institutional setting.

Research

Academic research is sometimes done at the policy evaluation stage where the research objectives are well specified and, therefore, it is where the greatest impact of research is. However, it is possible that although research is essential, it should be done when a problem is identified because it could influence the nature and direction of a policy initiative. Such research may support the government's position, or it may oppose it or suggest a significant modification at the early stage in the policy-making process. For research to have a meaningful impact at this early stage, researchers need to develop an understanding of the key policy issues involved in order to have sufficient time to conduct studies that may affect the thinking of regulators.

Including academia in the process of policy-making initiates a process known as evidence-based policy-making. But the question arises: What is meant by "evidence"? Hudson (2003) described research as a systematic investigation that increases knowledge and states that, although it is often synonymous with evidence, there is simply no consensus over what actually constitutes evidence. For example, Hudson stated that in policy-making, "expert opinion, common-sense knowledge and theorizing with dubious empirical basis" (p. 65) may all constitute evidence.

Hudson (2003) went on to explain that there is currently an insufficient connection between research and key policy issues, and therefore, that research has little effect on daily practice in areas such as criminal justice, health, and education. However, within the field of criminal justice, the "what works" movement has generated more interest in the role of evidence or research in shaping policy decisions. More frequently, research includes both qualitative and quantitative research, including ethnographies, participant observation, survey research, longitudinal criminal career research or post-release research, experimental research, meta analysis, and, of course, rigorous systematic review of existing research. However, all research methodologies can be time consuming and costly, and policies are frequently developed and implemented before research is completed. Nonetheless, research is necessary for high-quality public policy development.

Differences between policy-makers and researchers are thus marked, despite their convergence on the significance of evidence as a basis for change. The crux lies in two questions: "whose evidence?" and "what is to be counted as evidence?" At best, policy-makers may wish to limit the influence on the research to those whom they choose to support; at worst, they may see no place at all for scholarly research in the advancement of correctional practice. Perhaps the research community needs to become more politically sophisticated and advance a clearer vision of its social function to realize its potential contribution to correctional policy-making.

Process of Policy Making

According to Haztak et al., there are six key elements in the policy-making process: (1) Identifying the problem, (2) building a policy mandate, (3) exploring policy options, (4) Executing the policy, (5) evaluating the policy and (6) enforcing the policy (p. 171).

As mentioned elsewhere in this chapter, public policy-making begins when a problem is recognized or when an issue gets extensive media coverage and results in interventions by policy-makers. According to Hastak, Mazis, and Morris (2001),

> ... problem identification involves an assessment of the importance of the problem to society (costs to society) which is influenced by a variety of forces such as the political climate, media appeal, public opinion, group focus and ideological orientation of agency personnel. (p. 171)

The identification of the problem is often followed by a conference or a forum of some type in which stakeholders contribute their various perspectives, or the policy-makers may use a panel of experts. The result may be a report that offers recommendations or potential solutions to the problem. From this point, several options about ways to implement a solution or solutions may be explored, and policy-makers may engage in the process of cost-benefit analysis to determine the most suitable option(s). The next step is the selection of a broad policy option and a further examination of the implications of activating it. The draft policy may be circulated to key stakeholders for feedback, and once revisions, if any, are made, the policy is adopted and executed. After the policy has been in place for a period of time, the impact is often assessed. Hastak *et al.*, (2001) stated that there are three primary reasons policies are evaluated:

- to assess the outcomes of a policy to determine whether the policy meets its objectives,
- to provide feedback so that the policy may be modified to improve its effectiveness, and
- to identify the unintended consequences and permit changes to avoid these undesirable outcomes.

According to Hudson (2003), modern policy-making should be:

1. Forward looking (looks at least five years ahead at the likely impact of the policy);
2. Outward looking (e.g., draws on the experience of other countries);
3. Innovative, creative and flexible;
4. Evidence-based (reviews existing research, commissions new research, consults relevant experts and considers a range of properly costed and appraised options);
5. Inclusive (takes account of all who are directly or indirectly affected by policy);
6. Joined up (goes beyond institutional boundaries to the government's strategic objectives);
7. Required review and evaluation; and
8. Adjustable (learning from the experience of what works and what does not work). (p. 67)

CSC Corporate Policies

As a result of the CSC 2007 reorganization goals and focus on correctional transformation, a 2008 Policy Review Task Force was created (*Let's Talk*, May 2008). The goal of this task force is to "ensure that the Service's policy framework supports the transformation of corrections to, in the end, achieve better public safety results" (p. 18). Much of the work will be focused on the Commissioner's Directives, using a comprehensive and analytical process to determine the appropriateness of the CDs and to ensure best practices are reflected in the wording whenever possible. The mandate of the 2008 Policy Review Task Force is to:

> conduct a comprehensive review of CSC's policy framework in order to ensure that CSC's policy direction is clear and empowers staff to accomplish their work with confidence, and that the policy development function is efficient and responsive to change. The review will be conducted within the context of the recommendations put forward by the Corrections Review Panel and the Institutional reorganization exercise. (p. 18)

Corporate policy is a general term referring to policies specific to a corporation, association, or organization—in this case, CSC. Corporations form unified or collective bodies of individuals, and corporative government or political systems often are the same. In response to a question regarding corporate policy developments and the implication they have for correctional practice, interviewees made the following comments:

Administrator 3: My answer is going to be that virtually all policy has an impact—if it doesn't have an impact then it shouldn't be there. A kind of turning point for me—this is an area that gets a lot of significant attention when it happens. I have the only authority to segregate an inmate, and when that happens things have to happen right away. Segregation for the CSC is kind of like a pivotal point. It came from the Arbour Commission, and what she found was that CSC had these wonderful policies that talk about inmates' rights, phone calls, and visits by the institutional head, sharing of information—none of them were followed. I remember there was a task force that came out of that and they came around to this institution. Part of it was to interview seasoned correctional officers and one of these correctional officers began to talk about policy. He said, "well, you know policy—they really are only guidelines. You kind of pick and choose what you are going to use out of them." That was way back in the early '90s. So we have moved from that. We had a lot of work to do right from the top down in terms of the rule block, and that's what that is—that's the law. The only person that can segregate an inmate is the warden. We've become very cognizant of compliance to policy. See, the problem is that if I pick and choose, if I say, "well I'm going to follow segregation policy" to the team, but other policy I'm just going to pick and choose what I'm going to be in compliance with, staff will take that and it will go back to what that correctional officer was saying because that's where they learned it.

Although it is true that a warden can segregate an inmate, after normal business hours a correctional manager can also initiate this procedure. Most institutions have standing orders delegating this authority to other positions as well.

Administrator 4: There are lots of those (corporate policies). They are as complex as accreditation and programming because there are a whole lot of rules that you have to maintain. When the budget crunches, we become discriminatory as to what rules we are going to maintain. I think it's okay to do that. It's like saying what policies are you going to follow or what laws are you going to follow. Just various degrees of that theme. So, of course they are affected, but you can have simple things like procedures that sound like a good idea five years ago or ten years ago that are costing us so darn much money. For example, one of the things that we do in order to be transparent, is that we bring in to our national and regional investigations a citizen from outside. They don't know corrections, they don't know our procedures, and all they've got to go on is the TV programs they watch or their own value system that has been created. So we bring these people in and give them an allowance and travel and the added value? Somebody thought this was an example of transparency. I tell you, I shake my head at that.

Another thing that we do is for every offender that comes into our Community Correctional Centres who, outside a twenty-four hour period leaves, and doesn't come back (what we call UAL—unlawfully at large—he came into the halfway house and the second day he took off), we have to do a file review to see if there is anything we haven't been doing, something that we don't know or something that we should be secure—like maybe the guy was a predatory rapist. Well, finding out that takes that [snap of finger] much of the time but doing these file reviews that go on for three to four pages usually takes a competent senior parole officer a day, depending, because some of these guys come with five files. The senior parole officers are terrified that if they miss anything here and then this guy goes out and does something horrific and it results in a national investigation, they will be cited here as not being as thorough as they should have been. So it takes them a day or two days, depending on the file, and then they have to write it up. Plus, we've got clerical time in association with that kind of thing. We have found, in three years of doing this that there is often nothing that we could point at that we could change to ensure that these guys don't escape or UAL. We operate by what is called Commissioner's Directives. So this was in a Commissioner's Directive.

In a time when the concept of "transparency" is a well-used term in most areas of government business, it may be that not all of the administrators feel the same way about the value versus the cost. For example, if transparency translates into the cost of having uninformed citizen involvement in providing input into policies and procedures or overall CSC operations, perhaps there is a need to re-examine the value for dollar invested just for the sake of having public involvement. However, there are other perspectives discussed further on in the book that suggest citizens have been deprived of the opportunity to provide meaningful input into the decisions and processes exercised by CSC.

Administrator 5: Well, the security sector wants to update—they not only give money, but they also set the rules for their sector. They decide that we should be doing that for CBRFs (community-based residential facilities) –those are the agencies that we contract with. We said, "for God's sake don't do that." It's bad enough that we do it over here. You are going to double the workload. We aren't finding anything. However, it is easy for them to write the policy. It's easy for the commissioner and people up there to say "good policy." We are the ones who have to work with no extra funding to do the policy and are saying, "my God, please examine this." But it is like you are writing into the void when you say "would you please take a look at this?" And then when they write a draft one and consult with I don't know how many people, I can't imagine many people saying, "oh yeah, let's extend it to CBRF's." I would like to see who did that and hear their rationalizations. So I have to assume that in the face of these oppositions, they still went ahead and did it anyways. What happens when enough of that occurs, policies come down and you say I've got other things I can keep myself busy with besides this, so you get this disengagement that occurs, and the problem is the longer you are in the organization, the more opportunities there are for those types of situations. Younger people who are getting in are thinking okay, next time they will listen or the next time I will say it differently or say it better or maybe present my argument in a more logical way. So, there are a few of those kinds of things, of course, that are causing us additional pressure.

Administrator 5 speaks about the concept of "transparency" in terms of bringing citizens into national and regional investigations. But where did the idea of transparency originate? One of the important points that Hudson (2003) made, previously, mentioned in this chapter, was around modern policy-making needing to be evidence based. Based on the information presented by the three administrators, what might their view be regarding the use of research, experts, consultations, and so on in the development and implementation of corporate policies? Can you find examples of ideological assumptions in these responses? Are they congruent with what is reflected in CSC's Mission Statement? In other words, do they speak to the legitimacy and validity of the ideologies underlying the Mission Statement? Given what has been said by these administrators, can you separate what is "value" from that which is "fact"? There are several instances in the interviews where administrators speak about the use of discrimination in terms of choosing which policies to apply, in part or fully. Can you identify some of these instances?

Some corporate policies identified by administrators as not very helpful or cost effective were those that required the involvement of citizens largely unacquainted with correctional practice in situations where national and regional investigations were initiated. Another example administrators gave was having to complete extensive file reviews on offenders who were unlawfully at large to see if CSC staff missed something before giving the offender a conditional release. In general, the consensus from the interviewees who responded to this question regarding corporate policies was that the policies are often initiated by people with no real life corrections experience, and that there is often a failure in communication when staff who are responsible for implementing such policies attempt to inform the policy-makers. In addition, implementing some policies requires additional funding, which is often problematic, as is discussed briefly in the next section.

Treasury Board and other Resource Allocations

The Treasury Board Secretariat (TBS) is a central government agency. Its mission is to help the Government of Canada manage its human, financial, information, and technology resources. Comments from interviewees note the importance of having Treasury Board approval before they are able to implement policies and procedures:

> **Administrator 6:** Sometimes we get new money to meet the needs. In the last five years, we've gone to Treasury Board on numerous occasions. We just went to Treasury Board for learning disabilities. We weren't assessing for learning disabilities and we went to Treasury Board and we got money for two years to do a pilot to flush out what kind of numbers we could identify, and based on that, we've got one more year under that pilot and then we will go to Treasury Board to see if we can secure permanent funding to be able to address the need of learning disabilities in our offender population. So it is a combination. Sometimes we will readjust—for example, the Violence Prevention Program. In the last five years when we went to Treasury Board, we said this is a section of our population we are not addressing. Here are the numbers. Here is how many we want to treat and then we made a proposal for a few million dollars and Treasury Board said yes, that makes some sense, so they freed up some money for us and we needed more so we moved some money around.
>
> I don't think our budget allocations prevent us from reaching our goals. It's speed—it's the people in the process that prevent us from reaching our goals. The people twist the budgets, the people twist the values, and the people twist the procedures and processes. It's the people that are doing that kind of thing. The budgets are sufficient. It's how we manage them, it's how we spend it, and it's where we spend it. It's all those kinds of things. Treasury Board has said we aren't throwing any more money. You get your act together. You are mismanaging here, here, and here so you get that together and then come see us after that and we will give you some more

money. They are holding us accountable like we have never been held accountable before, so [that is what is] causing these things.

Although Administrator 6 suggests that funding opportunities are based on evidence to support such requests, Administrator 7 believes that if the request is not based on CCRA policies, it is less likely to be supported or receive sustained funding.

Administrator 7: We try to identify the funds based on CCRA policies—our Act, our policies, those things. It's not my money, it is tax dollars that I manage, so it's your money. To be fiscally responsible, I want to make sure that what I do is required by law, by policy—if not, I've got to question it. What I do is based on the CCRA, which indicates that I have to identify the needs of the offender. Once that need is identified, address them, so find money to do that. If it is not in the CCRA policy, then I have to revisit and it would be the first one that I would want to look at, to cut or eliminate or reduce if we run out of money. So we manage based on those.

This one area has been contentious for me because when you look at all of the policies in CSC, approximately sixty percent of the policies apply to my department. And yet, when you look at the small amount of staff I have, who are expected to go out and observe and see whether other departments are in compliance, it doesn't seem to make any sense. And for example, the regional administrator of reintegration, for the purpose of the operation, has a lot of online tools that they can access, such as RADAR—where information is monitored in RADAR. It would be helpful if we had the use of online tools to monitor compliance rates…. For example, in terms of the *use of force*, we have to literally sit there and watch video tapes, which can tie up one person for a whole week, just going over those tapes. So monitoring those policies slows down my department. However, we started with one person in this department and now we have grown to four, so we are making headway and I do have some support in getting more staff into this department.

Therefore, this will be a little bit of a challenge for us, and of course we do not have those online tools. However, that may actually come, because CSC is constantly advancing, and even in the four years I have been in this position, even this department has grown. Moreover, even the National Security Department in Ottawa has seen growth in their security department over the past few years. So for example, when I started in this Department four years ago and looked at the list of people at HQ in the Security Department, there were six people on that list … today there are now thirty ... so that really demonstrates how security has grown, both nationally and regionally. And so those requests for information that come to us from Ottawa also come with new and often changes to existing policies and practices, especially in the last two or three years. Therefore, it has been an ever-changing department, for sure.

Administrator 8: Corporate policies dictate how we do things. I don't really know what more to say besides that. Everything we do is regulated by the mission—I mean the CCRA, the regulations, the Commissioner's Directives. I mean, they are our Bible. So there is a big impact there. We follow that. All of our policy is a trickle down from that. Again, the CCRA really dictates how we do things, how we do a search, when we can do a search, when we can do urinalysis. We don't do it when we feel like it. And then when we do it, we have to do it according to what's in the CD in terms of the "hows." That kind of stuff. So there is a major impact there.

Administrators 6, 7, and 8 have different opinions of what role the Treasury Board plays in terms of CSC implementation of policies and procedures. Can you identify instances of how, specifically, policy is implemented by the three administrators and how each interprets the role of the Treasury Board in that process? The CCRA is a strategic document in terms of CSC carrying out its responsibilities. How do the three administrators acknowledge this importance in relation to the process of policy implementation?

The ability to implement policies sometimes creates pressures for various sectors or departments within CSC, such as the lack of resources, be they people, tools, or funding necessary to follow through. However, other interviewees discriminate between policies they are able to implement and those that create some problems by basing decisions on the requirements of the law or the CCRA. If a policy requirement is not consistent with the CCRA, it may be the first to be cut or eliminated if funding is a factor. Still others see the budget as being sufficient to allow the attainment of goals detailed in policies and believe that they are successful in implementing these because of their ability to adjust or to move the money around in their budget.

Mission Statement
As mentioned in the chapter on *Principles of Management*, the Mission Statement is about people—their potential and tapping that potential. It moves from the individual to the organization to the wider collectives of Canadian society, the justice system, and national and international corrections. It recognizes the

past but moves towards the future. It grounds the Service in its wider world. The statement reads as follows:

> The Correctional Service of Canada (CSC), as part of the criminal justice system and respecting the rule of law, contributes to public safety by actively encouraging and assisting offenders to become law-abiding citizens, while exercising reasonable, safe, secure and humane control. (Correctional Service of Canada, 1991, p. 2)

According to some of the interviewees:

Administrator 9: One of the primary elements of the Mission Statement is the whole notion of helping offenders to reintegrate back into the community, so obviously, being involved in programming, we feel that we are at the heart or core of what corrections is all about or certainly what the mission is all about. Nobody works in programs without believing in the capacity of pretty much all offenders to change and become law abiding citizens, which is very much consistent with our mission. In the program area, the fifty-eight people that I have are totally committed to the mission and demonstrate that every day in terms of the work they do in the class. You simply couldn't do this work and not believe in what you are doing. So for us, I think the Mission Statement is integrated automatically; it is tougher in some other areas where people are doing, for example, security work, as it is more difficult for security officers to integrate the mission into their day-to-day regimes. They have more of a custody and control responsibility, or it would be easy for them to focus on that aspect of their job instead of perhaps the reintegration aspect. For us, however, that certainly is not an issue.

Administrator 10: We talk about them (corporate policies) all the time as a senior management team when we are forced to make decisions, and I use it, the mission in particular guiding me in terms of making decisions about sending inmates to segregation, or sending them to an institution or things like that. Transfers and temporary absences. Policies intertwine all the different activities that we are involved with.

Administrator 11: The Mission Statement—we had a change in the Mission Statement and it was in direct relation to the Arbour Inquiry. So did it change the way we do our business? I hope it did—improved what we did, and made us more accountable for ensuring we are applying the rule of law in all of our policies. Our duty to act fairly is another one. We have that duty to act fairly. We are responsible to the public and we are responsible to adhere to Canadian law and policies.

Reference is made to the Mission Statement as the "Bible" of CSC by some of the administrators, which really illustrates the importance of this document in overall correctional practice. How is this reflected in How is this reflected in Administrator 9's, 10's, and 11's interviews? In other words, can you identify consistencies or inconsistencies between each of the interviews and the Mission Statement? What part of the language of the Mission Statement reinforces the need for CSC to be accountable? Is that need for accountability demonstrated in the administrator interviews?

Commissioner's Directives

Subject to the provisions of the CCRA, the commissioner may make rules for the management of the Service and generally for carrying out the purposes and provisions of Section 97 (CCRA) and the regulations. The commissioner may designate as Commissioner's Directives any or all rules made under Section 97 and the Commissioner's Directives are accessible to offenders, staff members and the public.

Interviewee comments:

Administrator 12: Commissioner's Directives are a little tougher, obviously, because they focus on so many individualized, specialized areas and, to the largest degree, the directives that affect the programming division are those which are consistent with the mission and with the goals of the program. However, there are some policies that are very difficult for us to implement, for example, the policy on ethno-cultural offenders, which speaks to developing culturally sensitive programs, activities, and services to support this population. Unfortunately, no money is attached to that policy and it becomes a tremendous challenge year after year to find ways to achieve what the spirit of the policy is without actually having money to invest in the policy direction. This creates frustration for staff, not just in the programming area, but in other areas. Where a policy says that we should be maintaining a particular standard, we strive towards it; we do not do the opposite. We often feel that we are unable to achieve the policy to the fullest degree because of funding pressures. This is one of the unfortunate realities—we set policy because we know it is the right thing to do and also because it is something we know we have to aspire to, but we aren't always able to achieve what we set out to do in the fullest possible way. That is why we have audits, why we identify deficiencies, and we identify how to overcome those deficiencies and so on. Performance measurement has a role in this, certainly—to track and identify areas where we have strayed too far and to suggest that we need to work to get back on track.

Administrator 13: Commissioner's Directives—those too can change; they can incorporate the evolution perhaps of corrections too, so we have an opportunity at the Regional Management Committee where everyone is coming in to express to our deputy commissioner who will represent our region at the table of the Executive Committee if we have concerns with implementation. Sometimes a CD can come down which will have a large cost implication and we may not have had confirmation that that cost will be either looked at, or do we have to absorb that cost, how are we going to do that. So there are implications in different ways.

Ideally, Commissioner's Directives provide a roadmap by which the policies articulated in Section 97 (CCRA) need to be implemented. Both Administrators 12 and 13 express frustration with this process because on the one hand there is a desire to "do the right thing," but on the other hand, there are resource limitations. Given that Commissioner's Directives are accessible not only to staff, but offenders and the general public as well, can you think of some potential conflicts that may arise between expectations around implementation of these directives and the realities of resource allocation?

Standing Orders and Post Orders

A Standing Order is generally a standard procedural instruction outlining general routines and is constantly in force. Post Orders, as noted in the interviewee comments, are instructions that describe in greater detail how to apply the Commissioner's Directives. Here is what the interviewees had to say:

Administrator 14: We have what are known as Standing Orders, which are general instructions outlining our general operating routines. They describe site specific, for example, how often our rounds are done for example by staff, how often our counts are done, our movement—it's site specific.

Post Orders are the same but they are more specific instructions for staff. The CD will spell out the policy, the objectives, and the intent of it all. Post Orders will describe in more detail how to apply the CD.

Minimally, every two years there is a revision that happens, but as well if there is a change, like we have just, for an example, had to create our own Post Orders and Standing Orders for the secure unit that could impact on our other Post Orders, so then we have to amend our Post Orders and Standing Orders to comply and to modify, I guess, the routines from there. Another example is movement within the institution. We have women that will have access to our gymnasium and our leisure room. We have a library, fitness room, gym, classroom, that sort of thing, and they will have access to these three times a week. Prior to us opening the secure unit, the women had access seven times a week. So when we have movement of the maximum security population, they are not to interface with medium and minimum populations, so the rest of the women have to be up in their houses. So we also have to regulate movement when they are coming through so that also means that they will be coming through, the front entry here, so our front desk has to include, okay, when there is movement, don't unlock the front door, and there are no deliveries that come in until movement has stopped. So that is all cross-referenced with other Standing Orders to make sure that if there is any effect on the other ones, that you go in and modify them so you can do that any time. If the profile changes, you may modify again.

They are all available to staff, and as changes go out staff are all notified, and part of the Standing Order or Post Order that has been modified is identified to show which change has occurred.

Administrator 15: Well of course, we are governed by the corporate policies. The Commissioner's Directives actually give us the direction as to what we can do and how we can do it. The CCRA gives us the ability to or gives us the authority in law as to what we are able to and not able to do with offenders, so we are very much governed by policy. We have policy documents for everything and we are always trying to get them into a manageable semblance in order to work with them. The Commissioner's Directives are what guides us, and every institution has their own Standing Orders, which shows how you will operationalize the Commissioner's Directives in the institution. We used to have a number of Regional Orders as well, but we have done away more with them because the Commissioner's Directives guide us—there is really no need for another layer of policies unless it is something totally specific or unique. Therefore, it is the institution's Standing Orders and the Commissioner's Directives that really govern us.

Administrator 16: In the institutions they have different policies—for example, a policy on segregation, which is a specialized function—they would have something there known as post orders. These orders really identify how the unit is operated, what is being allowed, and what is disallowed in this unit, within the context of the directives. Therefore, it really is about how to operationalize the directives. Therefore, we really do not breathe without checking the policy first! That is really what we do here at Regional Headquarters. That is, we do a lot of policy interpretation for the institutions, or for the wardens. So for example we might get a phone call from someone like a warden who may say, "this is what we are doing and this is what we think might be great," and what we do is to see what the CD says on that and also obtain a legal opinion on that, etc., prior to that warden or institution making another move. New wardens are especially a lot of fun because they come in so energized, ready to change the world, and have this or that idea, and I think, 'oh boy, now how do we operationalize some of those good ideas?' Moreover, some of them manage to do that; it works well. And others, they may think to themselves, 'maybe not'—put it on the shelf for now.

Administrator 17: Post Orders and contingency plans have to be altered with the redevelopment to take that into account. We have local policy— Post Orders and Standing Orders virtually at every management meeting which is held every two weeks. So staff and managers, they are looking at our policy and some of them are very minor changes but others are fairly significant.

However, when Standing Orders or Post Orders need further clarification, administrators will often refer to the Mission Statement, *Charter of Rights*, other legislation for some direction or sometimes clarification comes from precedence.

Administrator 18: If there is a conflict in policy you go to the higher level documents, ultimately the Constitution, the mission, and Acts of Parliament. As an organization we have done a pretty good job of lining that stuff up. I know at the institutional level we have gotten rid of a lot of Standing Orders, a lot of local policy that basically restated what the Commissioner's Directives said or what higher level policy documents say. Our staff are quite comfortable with—I just came back from the IPSO who had three or four different policies from major acts. He was looking at security classifications, security clearances, and our staff are very adept at going to acts and regulations to guide them. There is also a lot of stuff on the info net now.

Administrator 19: We have developed a role statement based on the Mission Statement, which is specific to the department. Some pieces pertain to this specific unit. In terms of the Commissioner's Directives, not many of these deal with Human Resources issues. We are mostly guided by legislation and precedence based on logic. Some of these pieces are the *Public Service Employee Act and Regulations, Public Service Staff Relations Act and Regulations*, and other pieces which refer to language issues, employment equity, etc.

The work/role/processes are not driven by operational expectations of the organization but mirror the same process. If the Mission Statement changed drastically, this could affect the Human Resources operation, and this is also true if the Commissioner's Directives changed, however it is less likely to have an effect. Corporate policies can change our priorities and change how we do things this year versus last year. Corporate policies are developed with tremendous consultation within departments and unions prior to implementation. Human Resources recommend implementation dates, for example.

Administrator 20: We cover the majority of the policy framework in this division—CCRA, the National Parole Board Policy Manual, and our Standard Operating Practices. The *Charter of Rights* certainly plays a huge role in our division. The Duty to Act Fairly document really is huge in terms of the information sharing requirements for offenders going to the Parole Board for decisions—that is becoming an increasingly significant portfolio for us. I would say that there are not too many things that are not driven by policy in our area.

A decision was made by CSC to implement changes to case management policy documents, including Standard Operating Practices (SOP), beginning in 2005. As a result, SOPs were reformatted into Commissioner's Directives, producing more effective, streamlined policy documents.

The Impact of Corporate Policies on Correctional Operations

Corporate policies are important in safeguarding the interests of the stakeholders, who are in this case the public, and allow for the transparent disclosure of the CSC organizational and management structure. Current thinking recognizes the obligations to society and this has driven the study and practice of good corporate governance to the levels it has reached today in CSC. Perhaps it is also such thinking that accounts for the hectic pace at which developments have taken place and are currently taking place in the practice.

According to the interviewees:

> **Administrator 21:** How corporate policies affect my area of responsibility depends on how seriously I take all that and how much I can remember all of that when I'm doing any one thing. I think we have—I hope this doesn't sound too Pollyanna—I think we have a wonderful, wonderful, wonderful "Mission Statement" that contains what we are trying to do and how we should be trying to do that. I think there is some wonderful, wonderful wisdom in that book. Now, me as a human being, sometimes I don't have the ability to do it to the level that, in my view, is inherent, or implicit in the document. Like one of the kinds of things I remember when I read it thinking, 'my God, this is the mother of them all,' is lead by example. Well, some days are better than other days. Maybe it's the apple I ate, maybe it's the chocolate bar I ate, maybe I'm really upset because my car isn't working ... for whatever human reason. Maybe I've seen things in one way for so long that I don't know how to see them another way.... Whatever the human reason is, I'm not just as good that day as I would like. So, I don't see that there is anything wrong with the document; it's something wrong with me, but not the document as I see it.

Issues of Accountability

> **Administrator 22:** So, I think all the values and all the corporate policies are there for us to be the best correctional service that we want to be. Our failure is, I think, in the fact that the degree that we hold people accountable for all the things that we have to hold people accountable for ... it's horrific. It's simply unadulterated horrific in a bureaucracy. And there are new things coming in all the time that if you just take the concept of the learning into account, it becomes overwhelming. For example, when they brought in section 127 or 128 of the Labour Code that made managers financially and morally accountable for safety within their units. All these laws—privacy, human rights—are all good things. I work in a perverted system. I work looking after offenders who break the most fundamental of laws, either because of cognitive distortion, biological reasons, opportunity, and all kinds of reasons. We who are working with them—the police, the court system, the corrections system—are close to these levels of distortions and you get tainted. However, it has been my experience that most organizations that I know have ten percent of the people who are criminal when it comes to following the organizational laws and policies. When you are in a bureaucracy ... I could stack that desk up four feet with all the

laws, policies, and the regulations. Not just of my organization, but of all the other ones that I have to be responsible for. Just the pure process of remembering them all is horrific.

I have to ensure and be accountable re: following corporate policies so ... I'm not Harry Truman, but the buck stops here and I have to ensure that we are compliant, in that so when there are changes to any policies obviously we have to ensure that this information gets down to staff and that they are not only informed but aware and integrate what it is that is coming down. There are certainly some changes that affect us to a greater extent than others.

Administrator 22 points out the contrast between the stringent level of accountability required of CSC staff as established by corporate policy and law and the lack of accountability exemplified by the offenders they work most closely with. What might some of the consequences of this be if you examine, for example, the policies governing conditional releases?

The Mission Statement and corporate policies discussed in this chapter are the gold standard of correctional practices, meaningful and wise in their intentions. However, it is up to the individual to enact these policies in a realistic manner in a variety of correctional settings. Despite all of the best intentions of the policies and the policy initiators, according to Administrators 12, 21, and 22, what might interfere with the process of initiation at the field level? Are there specific examples to support your claims?

Consequences of Specific Operations Policies

The next section presents the views of several of the interviewees with respect to specific policies that impact their respective areas of responsibilities.

Administrator 23: So policy that directs—that says "thou shalt"—it doesn't matter what it is, you have to be in compliance. Unless it says that you have discretion to do this, this, and this or if the policy is silent, then you go back to the spirit of the mission and things like that. That's where we are now from my perspective with policy. It's been a grind.

CCRA and the Mission Statement

The real value in having a Mission Statement is to provide clear direction for board members and staff of the National Parole Board—in how to achieve excellence in the field of corrections in general. This is supported by the CCRA, implemented in 1992, which provides a number of principles that serve as guides to delivery of service by correctional staff.

Administrator 24: CCRA that I just mentioned would be one. The whole operational portfolio and how it is represented in the Act and our policy document, indicate that we have to free up some money to meet the needs of the Aboriginal offenders, both spiritually and programming needs. So, I'll take the programming needs: since the CCRA included that the Service is responsible for identifying the need that leads the offender to creating criminal activity; once those things are identified, I have to treat them and I have to free up or the CSC has to free up money to make sure that we are able to attain that. Otherwise, we would be liable because we are not meeting the needs under the Act. That occurred two years back. The CCRA I think is four, five, or six years old.

The mission document is another one that dictates that we have to treat people with dignity and those types of things, so whatever we do, we try estimating by what is included in the mission.

Accreditation

Accreditation is a process whereby correctional facilities can measure themselves against nationally or internationally adopted standards. Some of the benefits include identifying and assessing a facility's strengths and weaknesses, identification of obtainable goals, an increase in community support, and a higher level of staff professionalism and morale. In terms of identifying specific policies that had consequences in various correctional operations, the policy governing program accreditation seems to garner much interest and many comments. As many of CSC administrators stated:

Administrator 25: When a site is accredited it can be for one, two or three years, depending on the score that is achieved in the accreditation process. Also, a site can be awarded a "conditional" accreditation, which generally allows a specific timeline for a site to get up to par on a very few specific standards while the other standards have been fully met. Each one of those standards is assigned a range of values. So if you get a perfect score of two on all of the mandatory standards, and a certain percentage on the non-mandatory standards, you would probably be awarded a three year accreditation which would mean you would not have to go through this process for another three years, which is certainly better than having to do it each year. However, the fact is that three years can be a long time and things can deteriorate, and that is why they don't want to go any longer. Once you leave something for three years, whether people intend to or not, people slip away from the program design or the way it was intended to be delivered, and slowly but surely you erode the integrity of the process.

Administrator 26: The issue of accreditation is, of course, very important because we are in a hospital setting. Very important because professional standards of practice are something we have to expect and all professions work through their own particular standards of practice. The demands of professionalism, whether they are correctional staff, nurses, or psychologists, requires them to behave in a manner where they are role models, where they are fulfilling the very standards of practice and without this we will not have success. I see accreditation as a "report card," where if we are following good standards of practice on an ongoing basis, then accreditation is nothing other than a statement that we are doing what we are supposed to be doing. So I see accreditation as a valuable tool and similarly, I am very pleased when the staff want to work within their professional association because again, that speaks to professional ethics and to respecting the fact that they have a profession that demands a certain level of accountability in terms of the way they apply their practice.

Administrator 27: The best policy I can use to answer this question is the policy around program accreditation, which is an outstanding policy if you are a programmer and you believe in the integrity and quality of programs. What the policy says is that all of CSC programs will be accredited against a series of standards imposed by an international panel, and that panel is made up of experts in the field related to that program. So there is a special panel for sex offender programs, another special panel for substance abuse programs, and a different panel for living skills programs, one for family violence, and so on. These panels are composed of a blend of people who are experts in those respective fields, i.e., substance abuse for example, and management executives or top managers in various correctional jurisdictions from around the world where a substance abuse program operates. So you have a combination of content expertise and the reality of life within a prison, correctional operations expertise, etc. Therefore having to comply with the standards set out by such panels of people, for example, is what makes our various programs so successful. People come from all over, such as Europe, Germany, England, Scotland, New Zealand, Australia, the Netherlands, U.S., and none of them are associated with CSC directly. They are all independent experts in their respective fields and they put together a set of expectations or standards around a particular program. Our programs would have to come into compliance with those standards. In addition to this, an evaluation design for the program must be present so that the program's effects on recidivism can be measured.

Accreditation is generally seen as a positive process—one that can highlight areas of efficiency and effectiveness as well as areas in need of improvement. However, accreditation may also produce some unanticipated consequences in the form of delays in the initiation of some programming, especially those based on pilot projects awaiting accreditation status.

Administrator 28: The process is basically called program accreditation and there are two aspects to this process. There is the accreditation of the program itself, in terms of its content, the design, the model, the length and intensity of the program, the modalities that are utilized—those are a whole variety of the elements of program accreditation. Then there is the site accreditation, which is an accreditation of the environment where the program is delivered, in terms of the physical plant, the facilities, the qualifications of the program deliverers, the method of delivery, whether the program is delivered, against a consistent or standard manual, the degree to which the staff are trained, etc. First of all, a program must be very solid in terms of its design, and then you have a method of delivering that program, which ensures that the design is honoured and the integrity of the program is maintained wherever it is delivered and under whatever circumstances it is delivered. In addition to this, an evaluation design for the program must be present so that the program's effects on recidivism can be measured at points later on. So accreditation is an area of significant interest to corrections right now and one that should probably be looked at in a university setting.

Those of us involved in programming, or in fact those of us involved in corrections, would argue that the policy is in fact a wonderful initiative because it ensures the quality and integrity of programming within the CSC to the point that we are recognized internationally as one of the leading correctional jurisdictions with respect to program interventions and the quality and impact of those programs. The evaluations of these programs or interventions also bear out that they are working in terms of reducing recidivism. Therefore, the impact of that policy has been positive in that regard.

There are also what might be considered to be negative impacts, which come about as a result of imposing strict standards and guidelines on a program, its design, and delivery. You run into a number of problems. These include the length of time it takes to obtain the accreditation by the international panel, and in some cases, it has taken a year or two to get that approval. Secondly, there are credibility issues. Every time a program is not accredited or as long as it is not accredited the National Parole Board wonders about the impacts of this program—if it is not up to par—and if that is the case, then it is not doing what it says it is supposed to do. Maybe they shouldn't take for granted that anyone who finished the program would have necessarily learned adequately from it, and so there are those concerns. It also delays the ability to introduce the program on a full-scale basis. Normally we pilot programs until they achieve full accreditation status and this usually means we only run them in one or two sites in each region and we don't introduce them across the board. It certainly reduces our capacity to meet the needs of offenders in that particular area because of delays associated with having to be accredited.

And then you have the site accreditation issues, where there are all sorts of expectations around class size for example, you are limited to ten to twelve people per class. You have to have a certain size facility and there has to be pre- and post-tests done to establish measurements in skill development resulting from the program. The pre-program interview process for the Cog Skills Program has gone up from what it used to be, so what used to be one half to one hour is now two and a half to three hours, and therefore you can only really interview two individuals per day. In the past, you could interview almost ten in a day. Now it takes much longer to screen people for a program, and quite frankly you probably screen more offenders out because the screening is more thorough. The more intricate the accreditation process becomes the more demanding it becomes and the greater impact on programming generally, and the slowing down of the process. Certainly, the complaint that we get now from a lot of the managers is that it is taking too long to get people through the programs and the reason for that is there are too many standards to meet and too many hoops to jump through. On the one hand it is a great asset, and on the other hand it is interesting how it has hurt the system. Of course, any management policy needs to be assessed on both fronts; what has it brought in a positive way, to the organization, but what has it created in terms of negative implications too? This could apply to policies around methadone, around use of force, around regional investigations and so on.... All of those have positive aspects which are very important. However, they often bring negatives, unfortunately, and that is the basis upon which most policies should be assessed.

Generally speaking, CSC administrators believe the process of accreditation to be valuable for various departments and for the organization as a whole. Successful accreditation by a panel of international experts in penology is based on the integrity of the various departments and their ability to comply with a set of professional standards. Nowhere is this more evident than in the area of programming, where CSC is "recognized internationally as one of the leading correctional jurisdictions with respect to program interventions, and the quality and impact of those programs" (Administrator 28, p. 137). What might some of the implications be of having a panel of international accreditors evaluate CSC and its programs?

The administrators also pointed out that the downside of accreditation is that it may take a very long time to receive, sometimes up to a year or two, or a program may not be accredited or fully accredited. Both of these factors influence the ability of offenders to receive the programming they require and be prepared for eventual release. In addition, the imposition of additional standards and strict guidelines may make it more difficult to process offenders so that they can take the programs in the first place.

In terms of accreditation policy, concepts such as accountability, professionalism, standards of practice, quality, etc., are frequently mentioned by the administrators. Therefore, it is on the basis of the positive consequences resulting from the program application as well as the programs themselves that the process of accreditation occurs. However, as Administrator 28 states, it is the negative consequences that result from these policies or programs that should form the basis for their assessment. What are your views on this and can you provide some specific examples?

Use of Force

The policy governing the use of force and, in particular, use of force by the Institutional Emergency Response Teams, has also generated some comments. Here is what some CSC administrators had to say:

> **Administrator 29:** Use of force. For example, the current policy that we have came in, about—I think it's coming up about two years. It had a significant training and workload impact on the sites here because we were required to review every use of force that came in. At the sites it meant managers—from wardens to deputy wardens—all had increased workloads. It had a significant workload impact for them and for us.
>
> Before, there was no requirement to videotape pre-planned use of force. There was no requirement for the institutional, regional, and national reviews, and there was no requirement to send it to the correctional investigator. It would stay at the institutional site unless an offender submitted a complaint or a grievance.

Now, every use of force incident, whether it is pre-planned, which has to be videotaped, or the spontaneous, for which all of the paperwork still has to be completed with an explanation as to why it wasn't videotaped, must be sent here, to Regional, as well. So that whole process was new. The other part of this is follow up on them because we have identified issues, right, and we've developed this new procedure. There is a whole bunch of new players in it and it affects everybody right down to the correctional officer level because those are the people who are using the force. Once issues are identified, then there is a whole procedure to follow up on those issues and that is all recorded as well and it is shared with everybody. That was like major, major.

We actually tracked the workload impact for a while and it does vary. We spent here at Regional Headquarters, about one week, about forty hours a month reviewing use of force, dealing with issues, follow up issues, etc. So that would be dealing with National Headquarters, dealing with the correctional investigator, dealing with sites in terms of addressing the issues.

Administrator 30: I have talked about it in great detail already, and that is the use of force policy. This policy is something that is fairly new it's only three years old, and in the old days, when force was used on the inmates and a correctional officer would submit a report and that was it, they had to be accountable for such use of force, but there was never any process to follow. Nowadays, of course, the process involves physically interviewing the inmate face-to-face, for example. The policy has an impact on health care, for example, because they may have a requirement to record with respect to use of force incidents, and the coordinator of correctional operations has to submit a detailed use of force package to Ottawa for review there and it goes to the correctional investigator. So the introduction of this one policy just three years ago has impacted the lives of others. Where once you might have had a couple of reports you looked at and said, "yeah, okay I support the use of force" to a process now, where many different levels are required to review that file. So the accountability has really changed and it is for the positive in my view. You used to hear of rather unpleasant stories in the past, about incidents regarding the use of force, and this just does not happen any more; people are very accountable. Therefore, this is the example of one policy that has had a huge consequence.

Consistent with the intent of the 2007 reorganization, the coordinator of correctional operations has been replaced by the position of correctional supervisor.

Cell extraction by appropriate personnel was one of the main issues that arose during the P4W (Prison for Women) incident. Likewise, the use of force issue is also being hotly debated among politicians and citizens alike when it comes to local police forces.

Administrator 31: Another example of a policy would be having the IERTs —the Institutional Emergency Response Teams—do all the cell extractions. It costs a bit more because we have to use specific individuals. There are twenty-two people trained in Atlantic. You need a minimum of five to do that. So if you've only got three on staff, you've got to bring two in. You are looking at overtime, meals, and mileage. But in the long run, those people are better trained, they do it more often, and it reduces the number of injuries to both staff and inmates. Normally it has a calming effect at this point because when the inmate sees the IERT they know it means business kind of thing, and they are less likely to fight them than they are line staff.

Based on the comments made by the interviewees, it would seem that the initiation of this policy has created workload pressures primarily because of the process involved in examining any use of force event. The process now involves physically interviewing the offender, examining videotapes, and complying with many other requirements of the "use of force package," which must be completed and sent to the correctional investigator. On the other hand, the positive consequences of such a policy has been to clarify the process involved in using force within institutions and the decreased numbers of incidents requiring such force. As a result, CSC has seen a reduction in the number of injuries to both staff and inmates.

Human Resources

Administrator 32: In speaking about changes in corporate policies changing how we do things, an example would be in the change in how we assess people who want to be correctional officers. The changes meant that all of those who had been previously assessed and were on file had to come to be reassessed with the new criteria. Also, there is a change in policy re the educational level standards, i.e., requirement for a degree and sometimes a specialized degree, i.e., criminology, without which potential advancement might be impossible. And HR needs to deal with the fallout of these policies.

According to the CSC website, correctional officers must have at least Grade 12. However, a degree in sociology, psychology, or criminology is preferred; some research has suggested that officers with university degrees "performed significantly better on knowledge, abilities and skills testing" than those without post secondary education (CSC Research Reports, 2002).

Victims' Rights as an Integral Part of Offender Transfer or Release

An emerging area of interest is the rights of the victim versus the rights of the offender, particularly during the pre-release phase. Often, parole decisions were made behind closed doors, and while some might argue that this practice still continues and is justifiable, others may argue for an opportunity for observation or input from the victims of such crimes.

> **Administrator 33:** Some of the areas would probably be the balance of considering victims' rights within the management of an offender and preparing him for release. While we have to obviously hear from the victim and their concerns, we have to balance that with, first off, the offender's right to be released and safe reintegration as well. That's always a difficult struggle. So what we are really trying to do is to focus more on the whole circle of supports—restorative types of justice models—to try to incorporate those, and that's really where we are trying to head. We actually have a Victims' Advisory Committee in this region that has been instrumental. So although the offender's release date is legislated, we do take the victim's rights and concerns and they get incorporated into the risk assessment on him/her. So if, for example, we are looking at transferring an offender to minimum security and the victim resides in that community, we would take this information into consideration as part of the transfer. That's not saying he wouldn't be transferred, but the information would have to be considered. What we are trying to do is to make sure we balance all of the information to ensure that every player that is part of this offender's community is involved in that healing, from both avenues. It's a really interesting topic of discussion in corrections that is coming to the forefront.

Lifers

According to the Annual Report of the Correctional Investigator, 2003–2004, the "two year rule" applies to amendments to the Custody Rating Scale so that newly admitted offenders serving life sentences will automatically serve at least their first two years in a maximum security facility. Some of the arguments against this rule is that it violates the CCRA and further adds to the already existing problem of overcrowding in institutions. Despite recommendations from the Office of the Correctional Investigator and others to rescind this policy, it is still in effect.

> **Administrator 34:** Another corporate policy change which will affect me as well, which is fairly new—it is only a year or two old now—is that anyone sentenced for first or second degree murder will serve two years in maximum security, so that will affect us here as well.

> **Administrator 35:** One of the policy changes that we've seen in the last couple of years has been to classify our Lifers—convicted of first or second degree murder—to maximum security automatically, which is something new. Before, we would do our risk assessment and make the appropriate placement based on risk, which is much different from looking at the actual crime committed and placing them based on the actual crime. So that has been a real struggle for people to try and understand where we are going with this. It is a real shift in our thinking from individual assessment to "let's look at the crime." The rationale involves the fact that we are looking at sentence length more than anything in terms of if he has twenty-five years or fifteen if he gets through his judicial review, so how do we take these offenders who have committed a very, very serious crime and manage their sentence that is fair to the community and fair to the offender? Two years into maximum security is deemed a starting point to start to do this. In other words, all Lifers are reviewed two years after they are placed into maximum security.

Segregation

Although there is a policy in place that specifies the required procedures and reviews for offenders being placed into segregation, there are still some issues which pose significant challenges for those abiding by this policy. Some of these issues include the ability to re-house segregated offenders back into the general population, how to apply segregation processes to both voluntary and involuntary offenders given space constraints and the whole issue of single versus double bunking, and the implication for those requesting voluntary segregation.

> **Administrator 36:** Segregation policy. This policy is very specific. For example, there are laws that govern the reason an offender can be placed into segregation, there are policies guiding how long they can be in segregation and for what reason, how they come out of segregation. There are policies around the type of accommodations that must be in place in segregation— what they are allowed and what they are not allowed. In addition, because

these inmates are still part of our population management, what do you do when all of your segregation beds are filled in every institution and you need to get these guys back into general population? How do you do this when your medium security beds are all filled? Therefore, this policy really influences or drives the population management as well.

We also have two types of segregation placements, which are voluntary. These are the guys who are running for some reason—find they are unsafe in the environment they are living in—and then there is the admin[istrative] segregated offenders. So what should we be doing with these two groups? Administratively segregated inmates are those who have done something in the institution to cause danger to himself or to others. Therefore, he is involuntarily segregated and there are all sorts of paperwork and rules that must accompany him. He has an opportunity to present a rebuttal to this according to the law, the warden has to review this process or decision, and there are all sorts of rules around this procedure. Voluntarily segregated guys are a bit different—sometimes they are the guys who are in debt, or sometimes they are the marginal types of guys who really cannot function and they are being picked on and stuff like that.

In fact, the two types of segregation are administrative, including voluntary and involuntary, and disciplinary segregation. The use of administrative segregation must be justified according to Subsection 31(3) of the CCRA. Section 44 (1-F) specifies the conditions necessary to impose disciplinary segregation, which may be imposed as the result of the offender being convicted of a serious disciplinary offence (Correctional Service of Canada, Research Report 2004 N.R-158).

> **Administrator 36** (cont.): We need to look at alternatives for this group and right now we are looking at programs for those who are voluntarily segregated, who maybe cannot live in a general population, that don't need to live in a restrictive environment such as a segregation unit because it is very restrictive. How do we get them into a different living environment where they can live in an environment that is least restrictive as possible but not have to live in a segregation type of environment as they currently exist? The rules of segregation, for example, might include one hour of exercise per day and that sort of thing, so it is really restrictive. The thing that really drives us in terms of segregation is that we are not allowed to double bunk in there because it is such a restrictive environment. The commissioner has decided that this is one thing that they do not want to see. However,

that also drives the population agenda again. For example, we do have some guys who want to go to voluntary segregation because they are single bunks and so what do you do with them? Therefore, the segregation policies for our area are huge.

Transfer Policies

Administrator 37: The transfer policies are also huge; for example, the rules around transfer, how you get an offender to transfer, how we transfer for the Parole Board, is it an involuntary transfer—somebody who doesn't want to go somewhere, but we are placing them elsewhere for a reason—out of region transfers, inter-regional transfers. This is another huge area that we take a lot of time with and it causes us to exercise a lot of cooperation between regions, between institutions, etc.

There seems to be some consensus among the administrators that specific policies are not without their challenges. Adequate resourcing is one topic that frequently emerges in terms of being able to fully implement specific policy intentions. On the other hand, most administrators agree that these policies are essential in establishing the day-to-day business of correctional operations. In terms of the specific policies being discussed in this chapter, are you able to identify and discuss some of the commonalities in terms of facilitators and barriers to successful implementation of these policies?

Conclusion

Dr. Margaret Jackson of Simon Fraser University's School of Criminology, points out that there are examples of failed policy resulting from an inability on the part of the implementers to understand the "real" reasons for its existence or its meaning in any context familiar to them. This is a problem for corrections in making meaning of policy for its staff. Another possibility for failed policies is that research has not been informing policy development. Although academic research could be a vital component of policy-making, particularly when implemented prior to actual policy development, there is often a lack of consensus and a range of interpretations around what constitutes research that is relevant for policy development. Qualitative research, for example, has frequently not been perceived of as being as legitimate or relevant as quantitative research. In addition, policy may fail not only from a lack of incorporation of research, but because research findings themselves may not be disseminated effectively to policy makers in the first place.

Policy-making is a cyclical process. In other words, once implemented, policies may solve some problems but they are just as likely to give rise to new ones. Evaluation of policies can also be a precursor to the identification of new problems. As it is within most areas of public service, a multitude of factors interact to shape and direct policy, including correctional policy. Some factors, including the impact of theory and the influence of political parties, political agendas, and prevailing ideologies, may intervene in the policy-making process. Therefore, it is essential to establish an understanding of the policy-making process to guide the effective planning and management of correctional programs. Perhaps Ball (1994) said it best:

> Policies shift and change their meanings in the arenas of politics; representations change, key interpreters (secretaries of state, ministers, chairs of councils) change (sometimes the change in key actors is a deliberate tactic in changing the meaning of a policy) ... [Policies thus have] an interpretational and representational history. (p. 17 as cited in Hume, 2001)

Study Questions

1. Using material from the text, discuss the role of government and the civil servants in terms of policy-making.
2. What are some differences between the rational-actor model and the organizational-politics model as it applies to policy-making?
3. What is a policy? Describe its function(s) and give an example to support your answer.
4. Discuss and give examples of how the Conservative, Liberal, or other major political party's ideology might influence correctional services policy-making.
5. Should theory and/or research play a role in the policy-making process? Why or why not?
6. Choose one CSC policy as discussed by the administrators in this chapter and discuss the policy intent.
7. How might Commissioner's Directives and Post Orders collide? Can you think of some specific examples?
8. In light of discussions in this chapter about the role of political actors and ideology in criminal justice policy development, what might be the impact of a change in federal government on the CCRA, Commissioner's Directives, and ultimately, Post Orders?

Bibliography

*Items with asterisks are also suggested readings for this chapter.

Correctional Service of Canada (2002). Research Reports. Profile of Correctional Officer Recruits. http://www/csc-scc.gc.ca/test/rsrch/reports/r102/r102-eng.shtml

Correctional Service of Canada. Our Story: Organizational Renewal in Federal Corrections. Ottawa: Canadian Centre for Management Development.

Correctional Service of Canada (2007-10-11). Policy Bulletin 238. http://www.csc-scc.gc.ca/text/plcy/cdshtm/b238-715-718-719-eng.shtml

Correctional Service of Canada. (May 2008). Let's Talk, 33(1). http://www.csc-scc.gc.ca/text/pblct/lt-en/index-eng.shtml

Ekstedt, J. and Jackson, M. (1996). *The Keepers and the Kept: Introduction to Corrections in Canada.* Toronto, Ont.: ITP.

*Gilsinan, J. (1991). Public policy and criminology: An historical and philosophical reassessment. *Justice Quarterly*, 8(2), 201–216.

Glor, E. (July 2001). *Innovation Patterns.* Paper presented to the 1997 roundtable International Institute of Administrative Sciences, Québec City.

*Hastak, M., Mazis, M.B. and Morris, L.A. (2001). The role of consumer surveys in public policy decision making. *Journal of Public Policy and Marketing*, 20(2), 170–185.

Hudson, C. (2003). Basic skills provision for offenders on probation supervision: Beyond a rhetoric of evidence-based policy? *British Journal of Educational Studies*, 51(1), 64–81.

Hume, W., and Bryce, T. (2001). Scholarship, research and the evidential basis of policy development in education. *British Journal of Educational Studies*, 49(3), 329–352.

Jessop, B. (2002). Liberalism, neoliberalism and urban governance: A state-theoretical perspective. (p. 453–469). *Antipode.* Oxford, ENG: Blackwell.

Landes, R. G. (1995). *The Canadian Polity: A Comparative Introduction* (4th edition). Scarborough, Ont.: Prentice Hall.

Miller, W. B. (1973). Ideology and criminal justice policy: Some current issues. The *Journal of Criminal Law and Criminology*, 64(2), 141–162.

Ryder, D. (1996). The analysis of policy: Understanding the process of policy development. *Addiction*, 91(9), 1265–1270.

Tait, J. (1996). *A Strong Foundation: Report of the Task Force on Public Service Values and Ethics.* Canadian Centre for Management Development.

Whittington, M. and Williams, G. (Eds.) (1995). *Canadian Politics in the 1990s.* Toronto, Ont.: ITP.

Wincott, D. (2003). Slippery concepts, shifting context: (National) States and welfare in the Veit-Wilson/Atherton debate. *Social Policy and Administration*, 37(3), 305–315.

Suggested Readings

Davies, H., Nutley, S., and Smith, P. (2000). *What Works? Evidence-based Policy and Practice in Public Services.* Bristol: Policy Press.

Tilley, N. (2000). Experimentation and criminal justice policies in the United Kingdom. *Crime and Delinquency,* 46(2), 194–213.

Whiteford, H. (2001). Can research influence mental health policy? *Australia and New Zealand Journal of Psychiatry,* 35(4), 428–434.

6 Comparative Correctional Practice: Canada and The United States

To set the context for this chapter, a brief overview of some of the international incarceration rates is first presented. A more in-depth comparison is then made between correctional practices in Canada and the United States. Four major themes identified by CSC administrators are included in the discussion of correctional practices: *incarceration versus decarceration; dynamic versus static security; rehabilitation and reintegration versus punishment; and education as a priority in prisons.*

International Incarceration Rates

According to Walmsley (2003), approximately 8.75 million people are held in penal institutions around the world. When considering the world population, this equates to 140 per 100,000 or one out of every 700 people in the world. More than 63% of the world's countries have rates below 150 per 100,000 according to Walmsley (see Figures 6.1 and 6.2). Countries and territories with the highest rates do not necessarily have the most punitive criminal justice system—they may have more serious crimes or be more effective in processing offenders who have committed serious crimes.

From 1992 to 1993, Russia replaced the United States as the world leader in rates of incarceration. Mauer (1994) believed that

> a variety of factors have led to the increased use of incarceration in Russia. News accounts have discussed the rise of organized crime, coming at a time of much economic and political instability. As the country moved toward a market economy, the social disruption and loss of a limited social 'safety net' for some may have contributed to higher crime rates. In addition to using incarceration for all types of

"recognized" criminal offences, Russia also incarcerates political prisoners. Although figures for this group are not available, this practice
has probably contributed to the overall increased incarceration rate.

In addition, Mauer suggests that the high rates in Russia may reflect harsher
sentencing practices rather than an increase in overall crime; in other words,
offenders are being imprisoned for "trivial offences" and serving lengthier sentences.

Figure 6.1. Rates of Incarceration across Selected Nations in 2004 (number of
people in prison per 100,000 population).

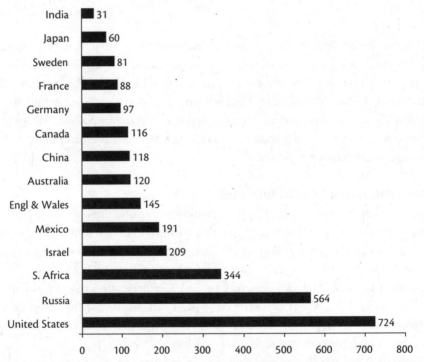

Source: International Centre for Prison Studies, http://www.kcl.ac.uk/schools/law/research/icps. Current
data available as of 2005.

In the 1990s and 2000s, the United States continued to occupy one of the
top two spots in incarceration rates worldwide. In 1992, the U.S. had a total of
1.3 million inmates; at an estimated annual cost of $20,000 per year per inmate
at that time, the national cost of imprisonment in the U.S. was approximately
$26.8 billion (Mauer, 1994). By the mid 2002s, the total number of incarcer-

ated inmates was approximately 2,000,000, and reached a "record high and unprecedented 30 year rise in use of incarceration" (Mauer, 2003, p. 1).

Figure 6.2. Ten Leading Nations in Incarceration Rates in 2004

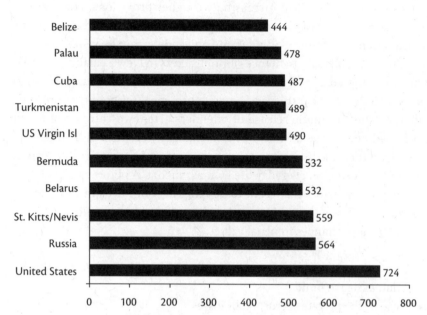

Source: Rate for the US from Prisoners in 2004 available at www.prisonstudies.org. Current data available as of 2005.

Appendix C also presents an historical view of incarceration rates for several countries, over the ten-year period from 1985 to 1995. Of the western nations listed, the United States had a 92% increase in incarceration rates over this ten year period while the Netherlands had an 86% increase. Although the rates of incarceration have grown tremendously in the United States compared to other countries, according to Pratt (2002), they have also increased in other English-speaking countries. Moreover, the prison population has increased in 118 out of 173 countries worldwide. In some of these countries, such as South Africa, Cambodia, Mexico, Brazil, Poland, and Greece, this increase has been quite substantial.

Before the 1970s, many English-speaking governments were intent on reducing incarceration, which was seen as expensive and inhumane, and developing alternatives such as community-based sanctions. However, by the early 1980s, incarceration once again gained favour among the public and politicians. Prisons were seen as valuable institutions, not for the rehabilitation of offenders but rather as a way to keep them off the streets for longer periods. According to Pratt (2002), "... punishment, like other aspects of modern life, had to be 'globalized', i.e., trends that can be found in the United States, were likely to be replicated in other countries" (p. 65). Concepts and terms such as *zero tolerance* and *three strikes* began to emerge as the new language of punishment, perhaps as an indication, as Pratt suggested, of growing intolerance toward offenders, which was transformed into increasingly tougher provisions. For example, England adopted a two-strikes policy for property offenders and longer terms for repeat offenders; the use of indefinite and indeterminate sentences grew. New Zealand extended life sentences for murderers in New Zealand from 10 to 17 years and adopted one strike mandatory incarceration for young, first-time property offenders and car thieves. Some English-speaking countries proposed abandoning the automatic release of offenders after two-thirds of a prison sentence had been served. Many of these changes were fuelled by a sense of inequality, an increase in anxiety about perceived and perhaps real threats by others, and intrusion on everyday life by mass media. As Pratt summed it up, "... we conjure monsters that seem to be lying in wait for us in the shadows of everyday existence" (p. 65). However, as he indicates, economic factors also precipitated these changes in penal values:

- new generation prison architecture, which makes prisons less costly and easier to build
- use of the private sector to cut losses
- emasculation of prison unions and the curtailment of the perks and privileges that they had previously won for their members
- a readiness of governments to spend revenue on prison development while cutting back expenditures in other areas of social responsibility (2002)

While this trend toward increased incarceration extends across most English-speaking countries and some non-English-speaking countries as well, Pratt suggested that this "new axis of penal power" (p. 66)—the alliance between government and the general public—has been cemented more firmly in the United States than in any other country.

Correctional Practice: Canada Versus the United States

Although many of the discussion points in this chapter overlap, they are discussed separately as much as possible in order to give you a better understanding of each issue presented. Likewise, for each specific category, there is a blend of interviewee comments and existing research.

Administrator 1: I have often heard that we [Canada] have the corrections model for the world and I believe there is some truth to that.

According to a July 2003 press release from the Bureau of Justice Statistics (Harrison and Beck, 2003), the U.S. prison population rose 2.6% during 2002. At the end of 2002, there were 2,166,260 persons in juvenile facilities and jails. According to Mauer (2003), the U.S. locks up its citizens at a rate of five to eight times that of Canada and Western Europe. The breakdown of various U.S. institutional populations is shown in Table 6.1.

Table 6.1. Incarcerated Population in U.S. Federal, State, and Local Facilities in 2002

Facility type	Number of incarcerated individuals
State prisons	1,209,640
Federal prisons	151,618
Local jails (as of June 30, 2002)	665,475
Juvenile facilities, public and private (as of October 2000)	110,284
US territorial prisons	16,206
Bureau of Immigration and Custom Enforcement (BICE)	8,748
Military facilities	2,377
Indian country jails (as of June 30, 2001)	1,912

Source: Harrison and Beck, 2003.

Harrison and Beck (2003) further reported that although these figures represent a 2.6% growth from the previous year, the rate is still lower than the average annual growth of 3.6% since 1995. At the end of 2002, it is estimated that there were 476 inmates per 100,000 U.S. residents serving sentences of at least one year in federal or state prisons compared to 411 inmates per 100,000 general population in 1995. In addition, the number of females incarcerated in the U.S. in federal or state prisons as of the end of 2002 was 97,491, which made females approximately 6.8% of all prison inmates (compared to approximately 4% of the population of federal offenders in Canada). From 1995 to 2002, the female inmate population in the U.S. increased 42% while the male inmate population grew by only 27%. The overall increase in the federal system, which was estimated to be 61% from 1995 to 2001, is largely attributed to an increase in the number of drug offenders (48%) and immigration offenders (21%). The inmate population in the U.S. is now six times that of the 1972 total of 330,000, which preceded the "get tough movement."

Mauer (2003) emphasized that the focus in the U.S. has been on punishment rather than on rehabilitation. Furthermore, he stated that, "in Canada, for example, the federal prison system has instituted a comprehensive policy of prison assessment and programming, with the goal of achieving early parole release" (p. 11). Still others have described the system in the United States as "an inexplicable deformity" (Mauer, 2003, p. 13) compared to other Western countries, many of whom have concentrated their efforts once again on the goal of rehabilitation of offenders (Mauer, 2003).

According to the CSC Performance Report for the period ending March 31, 2004, 4,281 offenders were admitted to CSC facilities during 2003–04. The total federal offender population as of March 31, 2004 was about 12,413, which was the lowest figure in more than seven years. Figure 6.3 illustrates the federal offender population for the last seven years (1997–2004). The rate of incarceration has dropped by 12.5% between 1996–07 and 2003–04.

Figure 6.3. Federal offender population 1997–2004 (continued to drop).

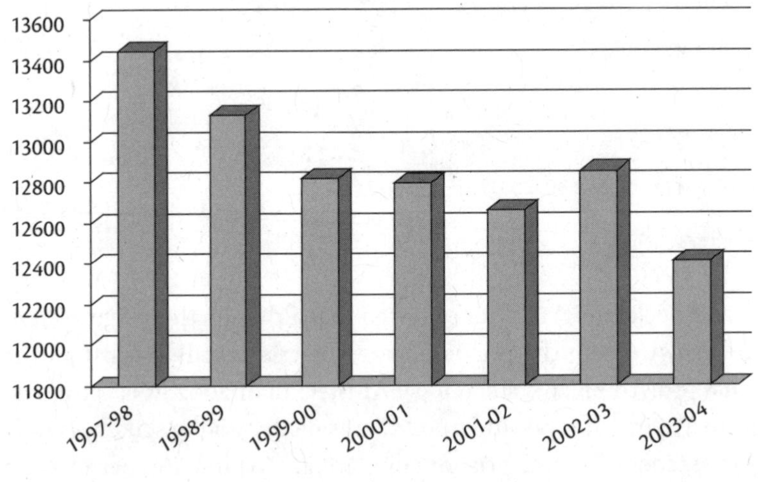

Source: Correctional Services of Canada, Speakers Binder, Section 7 Statistics

According to Landreville (1995), the rate of incarceration in Canada in 1972 was 90 per 100,000 general population. By 2000, it had risen to 118 per 100,000 (compared to 411 per 100,000 in 1995 and 476 per 100,000 in 2002, for the United States). One CSC administrator said:

Administrator 2: The thing that impacts me the most is the incarceration rate. I was looking at it the other day; I forget the numbers, but the discrepancy between the Canadian rate of incarceration per one hundred thousand and the U.S. And when you look at the statistics on crime, that has not had much of a positive impact on American way of life, whereas our crime rate is better compared to theirs. I am certainly convinced that simply locking a person up in jail and not doing anything other than that does not protect the public in the long run. Canada's approach where we incarcerate, do an assessment, and try to target criminogenic factors has, in my view, had a positive impact.

Administrator 2 expresses a viewpoint that is consistent with Section 3 of the CCRA. Based on what you have read in the chapter thus far, how might the Canadian view on the purpose of the correctional system differ from that of the United States?

Although Canada's incarceration rate was higher than the rates in many western European countries, it was still much lower than the United States. The average annual cost of incarcerating an inmate in a Canadian federal institution during 2003–2004 was $80,965 for men and $150,867 for women (*Speakers Binder*). Costs are greater for women because their numbers are fewer (based on economy of scale) and there exists a legal requirement to provide programming and services equity.

Some of the following comments made by CSC administrators during the time of the interviews suggest a fear that Canadian politicians may be moving toward support for an American model—that is, towards a "boot camp" mentality. Furthermore, some of them may be promoting fear among the public that crime—especially violent crime—is increasing, and that the solution is the proverbial "lock them up and throw away the key"—in other words, longer and more punitive sentences. However, CSC administrators also acknowledge that there are exceptional programs in some U.S. state-run institutions, such as those for treating substance abuse in Minnesota, that demonstrate progress or movement away from the general incarceration movement in the U.S. Nonetheless, CSC administrators agreed that Canada has exceptional programs as well and, in fact, focuses primarily on the needs of the offender in terms of programming to enhance post-release success. Here is what some of them had to say:

Administrator 3: Let me quote Leonard Cohen: "it's the best and the worst." That is what the U.S. system is. They have a lot of research going on in areas that I think are great. I remember coming across one research study on sex offenders—ten thousand offenders in one state who were under a particular program, which just underwent a sophisticated evaluation. I think that's wonderful corrections in a much needed area. They build institutions.... A fellow was just telling me he went to see—he's interested in the architecture of institutions and its effect on people; he went to see one institution in the states, seven thousand offenders in one institution. No wonder. They have the three strikes and you are out. I mean, what kind of a mentality devises that? That is so far from anything that I hold as real or true or of value. But it's a good sound bite and it gets people elected. Canada is now using that kind of bullshit tactic.

Note: According to several criminal justice reports, Angola Prison in the state of Louisiana houses the largest prison population, some 5,000 individuals.

Administrator 4: They are using corrections as a whipping dog—in some cases it should be because we've made terrible mistakes and maybe we haven't moved as quickly as we should have in correcting some of those terrible mistakes. But when I see our politicians taking a page out of the American political system in terms of how to gather attention under—what do we call it, "Peace and Security," something like that—I shudder. I have heard the solicitor general of one of the provinces. The guy is to the right of Attila the Hun. When I think that we are going that way.... It's not that we can't learn things from the Americans in terms of boot camps, but all our research says that doesn't work. It doesn't mean that it doesn't work for all people. There are some people that can benefit from that like some people can benefit from AA and some people need a cognitive-based program. So let's differentiate. Let's not bring politics into corrections. Let's have an accountability system of course, but when you start lying—not that politicians and bureaucrats lie—but when you go against the facts about "the streets are unsafe...." The streets are safer today then they were ten, twenty, thirty, a hundred years ago. We are safer for everybody.

Administrator 5: Everybody has been corrected—by parents, by church, by school, and then of course by the state, and we grow up with it ever surrounding us and then we sensationalize it in the newspaper, God Almighty, or on television, or in the radio, because you want to get people's attention to sell soup. So boom, sound bites and sensationalization and who gives a hell where the truth lies—that's somebody else's problem. I've even been disappointed in programs like *The Fifth Estate*. But it's like everybody; you haven't got time to do the job properly so you do what you can in the time that you've got. It's no more difficult for them than me, but politicians getting involved, using it that way, at one level I think is wrong and at another level it is inherent in our society that they can stand up and say those things and people can decide. It's just that I think that they should decide on the basis of fact and reality as opposed to fear and sensationalization. However, it's a dreamer's world.

Now, I also realize there are some pretty progressive and good correctional facilities in the U.S. Unlike the U.S., our federal correctional system is fairly homogeneous. In other words, our institution and how we operate, what we do here, looks very similar to Warkworth Institution in Ontario and Cowansville in Québec and so on and so on. Whereas in the U.S., there is hot bedding in Texas, and capital punishment and really progressive substance abuse treatment, or prisons devoted to substance abuse treatment, that have very good success rates in, say, Minnesota. So there is a huge continuum and we don't have that in Canada. I think it's good. And of course probably the underlying reasons are critical why the system that I described exists in the U.S. It is a state's decision how they run their prisons.

While Administrators 3, 4, and 5 seem to generally agree that a focus on punishment, as illustrated in some U.S. models, is more costly and simply does not work, they also suggest that our streets are generally safer for everybody compared to those of the U.S. It is political self-serving and media hype that cause the public to support a stronger, punitive stance for offenders in Canada. Given the current political situation and crime rate in Canada, do these administrators' views reflect the Canadian reality?

Others have pointed out the differences between staff quality and working conditions in Canada and the U.S. by remarking on the level of education required and the job satisfaction that results from better pay and a less stressful environment, as is found in Canada.

Administrator 6: One of the responsibilities that we have as correctional administrators is to decide what it is we are trying to foster in offenders and to support, guide the development of processes that will encourage and enable offenders to be more successful upon their release. Otherwise, it becomes very easy to emphasize other stuff, for example to emphasize the budget restrictions, and very easy to emphasize the human relations problems because it is the staffing issues that wear you down. For example, we are even more unionized in some ways than they are in the U.S. Our correctional staff here makes a good wage compared to what the U.S. prison employees make, although our correctional staff may not necessarily agree with that.

Of course, our skill sets and what we require in terms of educational background is also much higher here in Canada as well. So when you are talking about job satisfaction, you have the ability in Canada to say that you are *in a profession....* In the U.S., in a number of cases, I think the employees see themselves as being *in a job,* and whatever level of job satisfaction that may come with that. Correctional administration has a lot of responsibility on the human resources side of the house to make sure we have the proper work force and to make sure we continue to have it. We need to realize that the baby boomers are just about done now and we are into the Generation Xers, and it is a completely different category for them. They will come to work for us for five or six years until they get out of the profession what they wanted to learn and what they wanted to offer and then they will move on. It is a changing workforce and we have always been used to people who come and stay with us for fifteen to twenty years.

One of the ways to interpret what has been stated by administrators in this chapter is that Canada's federal corrections system is made up of an organization of institutions operating on the same mandate, same policies, etc. as compared to the U.S. system. The U.S. system is described as being operated by different states in different ways—that is, it lacks consistency and continuity as a "system." In addition to this, some administrator comments suggest that education, training, and qualifications of staff at CSC institutions are generally higher than for their counterparts in the U.S. This leads to a more professionalized staffing complement in CSC. However, others might argue that there are inherent biases within the statements made by the administrators, who may have a vested interested in presenting the Canadian system as more functional than that of the U.S. In terms of what you have read in this chapter and what you have experienced where do you think the truth lies?

Administrator 6 discusses the differences between staff in corrections in the U.S. compared to Canada and uses concepts like "having a profession" vs. "having a job" to illustrate some of these differences. The inference here seems to be that in Canada, CSC staff have pride in the work that they do and remain committed to their profession. Chapter 4 also presents information that suggests that the organizational commitment demonstrated by CSC staff remains relatively strong. In view of this, how would you explain Administrator 6's further comment that the Generation Xers work a shorter period of time for the organization, get what they want out of the profession, and then move on, unlike earlier generations who sometimes stayed 15–20 years?

Incarceration Versus Decarceration

Rapid expansion of the prison population during the 1980s caused increased pressure on U.S. prison populations, a trend that has carried on into the current century. In their July 2003 report, Harrison and Beck stated that in the United States "… 17 states reported increases of at least 5% in their prison populations during 2002 … these were led by Maine (11.5%), and Rhode Island (8.6%). Overall, state prisons were operating between 1% and 16% over capacity at year end 2002, while the federal system was 33% over capacity." The fact that the wealthiest society in human history maintains the highest use of imprisonment presents a clear indication of troubling circumstances. Crime rates alone do not explain the increase in prison populations.

According to Mauer (2003), new policies such as mandatory sentencing, truth in sentencing (meaning that a person must serve 85% of their sentence prior to release), and three strikes and you are out (which requires a life sentence upon conviction of a specified third felony offence) have all played a large role in making the U.S. justice system more punitive. In addition to this, there have been restrictions on parole releases, earned good time, and other policies which have increased time served in prison. Moreover, nowhere are the harsher sentencing practices demonstrated more vividly than in the case of drug offences. For example, "… in 1980 [U.S.] prisons and jails held about 40,000 inmates for drug offences…. By 2003, that figure increased tenfold to about 450,000 inmates, nearly a quarter of all inmates" (Mauer, 2003, p. 7). Criminal justice policy, and particularly sentencing policies, increasingly appear to explain many of the changes in prison populations in the U.S. that have been observed over time. Here are some further comments made by CSC administrators:

> **Administrator 7:** So, my issue between them and us would be the involvement of politics, predicated on research. It's a big country, a lot of people and if you figure that ten percent of the people are going through the system, are churning through the system at any given time—three hundred million Americans, that leaves thirty million in their correctional system. That's a lot of people, a lot of people. A horrific amount of people. And the truth about prison and what's going on, what's happening is that it makes people worse, it does not make them better. Yes, put the Bernardos, those people away for God's sake, because that's the best you can do to protect society. But there is a whole lot of people in between that don't need that level. One of the things that is encouraging to me is what is happening in provincial corrections throughout Canada with the exception of Ontario— what I see in terms of post arrest, bracelets and all of these other kinds

of things, a lot more tools are being used to keep people out of prison. I think that's good.

Administrator 8: Other states I think from time to time we learn a few things from. Minnesota comes to mind as being fairly progressive and other states still use a very conservative and political influence to determine their policies. You look at statistics in the U.S. and there are over three million people incarcerated. If we worked to incarcerate at the same level of incarceration—we are thirty million so we should have what, three hundred thousand incarcerated? We roughly have, at least federally, not even one-tenth of that. And has crime increased? No. The statistics tell us that crime is on the decrease, violent crime is on the decrease. So I think what we are doing is working and the long term goal is to ensure public safety, so I think that the approach that Canada has put in place—tried lower incarceration rates with alternatives, whether conditional sentencing or amendments to criminal codes—is working, has had a desired effect as opposed to following our closest neighbour.

Administrator 9: In terms of their treatment approach, they [the U.S.] over incarcerate. I think they are building more prisons where they are using the least restrictive method of incarceration. So those would be some of the major differences that I would see with the States from the prisons that I visited.

From what we know about Canada's current crime rate and sentencing practices, how might we predict the effect on future rates of imprisonment? Would these predictions be consistent with the views expressed by Administrators 7, 8, and 9?

According to Mauer (2003), the high rate of imprisonment in the United States can be explained by several factors:

- a higher rate of violent crime than other industrialized nations
- harsher sentencing practices than in other nations, particularly for property and drug offenses
- sentencing policy changes over a period of three decades, particularly the shift toward mandatory and determinate sentencing, restrictions on judicial discretion and a greater emphasis on imprisonment as a preferred sanction

- policy changes adopted as part of the "war on drugs" leading to a vastly increased use of the criminal justice system as a means of responding to drug problems. (p. 16)

As mentioned earlier in this chapter, the U.S. has experienced an increase in the rate of incarceration higher than that of most comparable nations, and this increase is more likely due to the changes in policy discussed previously, although, as Mauer has pointed out, there is a higher rate of violence in the U.S., which has also influenced rates of incarceration. As a result, more people are being sent to prison with lengthier sentences. From 1980 to 1996, the inmate population increased dramatically; 88% of this rise was a result of sentencing policy (increase in determinate sentencing and decrease in judicial discretion), and 12% due to changes in crime rates. Other possible reasons for an increase in incarceration include:

- an increasing fear of crime
- loss of confidence in the criminal justice system
- disillusionment with positive treatment measures
- strength of retributionist philosophies of punishment

Attitudes can also be influenced by short term dramatic events, often highlighted by the media. This results in public pressure to move to more punitive measures.

Some of the lessons learned due to the "get tough" stance illustrated in U.S. sentencing practices are as follows:

- mass incarceration has had only a modest and diminishing impact on crime
- incarceration has a broad range of collateral effects on society, for example, impact on families of prisoners, huge impact on communities due to missing or absence of population of young men
- costs of incarceration affect other social priorities, for example education, social services, health, etc.
- privatization has not proven to be a panacea for rising prison costs
- mass incarceration affects democratic society—in the U.S. persons convicted of a felony generally lose their right to vote for a period of time. In some states, they lose their right to vote permanently (Mauer, Oct. 2004)

In Canada, the causes for the rapid growth in inmate populations have been attributed to some of the following factors:

- at the provincial/territorial level of the system, more custodial sentences were being given and for longer periods of time; there has been significant growth in charges for sexual and other assaults
- federally, there have been fewer conditional releases granted and more revocations of conditional release, resulting in more time being served by more offenders; in addition, there has been significant growth in the proportion of offenders serving sentences for violent offences, including homicide
- the crime rate in Canada began to decline in 1991, so the sudden growth in inmate populations was most likely attributable to a combination of other factors, such as:
  - a rapid increase in prison and penitentiary admissions
  - changes in the length of the average sentence handed down by the courts
  - changes in the average length of time served in custody by offenders (Boe, Motiuk, and Muirhead, 1998)

Another factor that needs to be considered when looking at the growth in inmate populations is the cumulative effect of life sentences.

Figure 6.4. Annual admissions to federal custody on warrant of committal

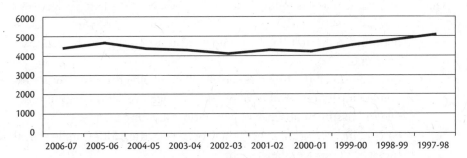

Source: Corrections and Conditional Release Statistical Overview, 2007, p. 41

The increase in admissions to federal custody is coincidental with the younger demographics among males in society.

A more punitive policy has led the U.S. to a position where more prisons are being built to house the increasing population of offenders. In the U.S., one out of every 138 residents was incarcerated and the average time served rose by

30%. In addition to this, in 2004 the increase in the prison population led to overcrowding by as much as 40%. Fifty-five percent of those serving sentences in federal institutions were there for drug offences. Moreover, women who are sentenced to incarceration are generally convicted for drug offences, and the increase of rates of incarceration for women have nearly doubled the increase of incarcerate rates for men, over the past two decades (Mauer, 2003).

However, Landreville (1995) believed that alternatives to incarceration are not necessarily the solution to decreasing prison counts, although it might affect prison flow. He argued that these alternatives are often applied to offenders whose sentences would be shorter in nature—for example six months or less— and that in order to affect the prison count or population, alternatives would need to target longer-term offenders. For example, Canada's decision after 1976—when the death penalty was abolished—to give those offenders convicted of homicide longer sentences has served to inflate prison population counts. In addition, making it more difficult for long-term offenders to obtain parole keeps them in the prison environment longer and does not allow for much of a reduction in the overall population.

Landreville's (1995) point is that if Canada continues to bestow longer sentences on offenders, especially those convicted of violent crimes, we too may be faced with prison overcrowding in the future. Already some institutions such as RRAC (Regional Reception and Assessment Centre) are double bunking to accommodate this increase in offender populations. Alternatives therefore need to target longer-term offenders as well as shorter-term offenders. But Landreville also believes that these alternatives should be put into place because they make sense to the overall goal of offender responsibility and restitution, and not just as a substitute to alleviate any potential overcrowding in prisons. Nonetheless, as CSC administrators have repeatedly said, the focus on offender rehabilitation, pro-social intervention, and reintegration into the community is likely to keep Canada from experiencing the problems of prison overpopulation currently facing the U.S.:

Administrator 10: The numbers of offenders who are incarcerated in the U.S. are dramatically greater per thousand than is the case in Canada. I read somewhere recently that one in every thirty-two Americans in the next ten years, will be incarcerated which works out to about three and one-third percent of the entire American population or six to seven million people that will spend some time in a correctional facility, and that really is amazing. What this says to me, is that whatever we are doing in Canada is keeping those numbers down. Our federal corrections population has not grown dramatically over the last several years and we don't anticipate huge growth over the next several years. In the American system, they have been building jails at a rapid rate and they cannot even keep up with the demands. U.S jails are overflowing and every year there are more people incarcerated, so something is not working down there and is working up here. I believe it is the focus on reintegration and pro-social intervention.

Although we do not want to put all American prisons under one group, I think as a rule, American prisons are far less oriented towards reintegration and correcting deviant behaviour in comparison to the Canadian system. Our whole focus here is around correcting antisocial behaviour in terms of overcoming criminal values and developing new pro-social values. In the States, in many of their jurisdictions—and I won't say all of them because there are a few states that have come a distance in this regards—but generally the focus is very much on punishment, simple incarceration, detention, and protecting society by keeping people behind bars. But of course at some point offenders are eventually released back into society. I have even heard stories, which I believe are true, of American prisons becoming so full that management, knowing more offenders were coming and they had no way of housing them, simply took the least dangerous offenders in their inventory and released them back into the community to make room for the worst guys that were coming in. That to me is obviously not serving the public well through protection or reducing the likelihood or frequency of crime.

According to Administrator 10, between the late 1990s and into the early 2000s, the number of federal offenders admitted to correctional institutions was decreasing and the prediction was that, unlike the U.S., these numbers would continue to decrease. In contrast to what was surmised by this Administrator, those numbers have shown increases over the past three to four years. Likewise, as was mentioned earlier in this chapter, overcrowding is also a reality in some of the institutions, which have resorted to double bunking as a population management strategy.

Table 5.2 in Chapter 5 summarizes the Liberal versus the Conservative view on crime and punishment. In looking at the "focus of attention" segment in Table 5.2 and in the context of the current political climate, would we expect to see any changes in the rates incarceration rates/numbers, and if so, why?

In addition to the concerns regarding increasing incarceration and the possibility of overcrowding within prisons and penitentiaries, there is a concern about the use of dynamic versus static security in mediating the development of violence within a prison or penitentiary setting, which is discussed briefly in the next section.

Dynamic Versus Static Security

In the U.S., the *inmate capacity* of a prison is defined as the number of inmates in jail divided by the rated capacity (Tartaro, 2002). The *design capacity,* or the number of inmates a prison or jail can hold, is determined by the institution's architect, whereas a *jail's rated capacity* is determined by corrections officials or national corrections organizations. Lastly, the *operational capacity* is the number of inmates a facility can hold while being managed properly, a number that is often determined by corrections officials (Tartaro, 2002).

Several studies in the U.S. have tried to determine the relationship between density and violence as well as density and physical and psychological health status of both the offenders and staff in prisons, often with mixed results. Although Tartaro explains the differences between crowding and density in greater detail, these details are not included here. However, some U.S. corrections officials felt that as soon as prisons reached 80% of their capacity, resulting in the loss of extra cells to put troublesome offenders in (i.e., separate them from the general population), the effects of crowding were felt. Crowding has often been associated with increased violence among offender populations, as has the placement of more than two offenders in a cell. However, one variable that seemed to produce a decrease in the level of violence was more direct supervision of the offender by the correctional officer, which was made possible by a lower inmate to correctional officer ratio. It increased the likelihood that the correctional officer could build a rapport with the offender and learn more about his/her personality. In support of the process of dynamic security, CSC has ensured that such a process of relationship building has every opportunity to develop between the offender and correctional officer through one of its commissioner's directives:

Commissioner's Directive 560—Dynamic Security

Policy Objective:
1.   To optimize institutional security and the safety of staff, offenders, and the public through interaction between staff and offenders and through the sharing of information among staff members.

Responsibilities of Staff Member:
1.   It is the responsibility of staff members who work directly with inmates to develop an ever-increasing knowledge of the offender through mean-

ingful interaction, and thereby diminish the likelihood of unexpected behaviour on the part of those offenders.

2. Information and observations of behaviour of significance for the on-going understanding of individual offenders shall be shared with other staff members for whom such information may be of importance.

Operating Procedures:

1. Operating procedures shall be established in such a way as to facilitate the greatest possible degree of interaction between staff members and offenders. (*CSC Commissioner's Directive 560* http://www.csc-scc.gc.ca/text/plcy/cdshtm/560-cde-eng.shtml)

The following are comments made by two CSC administrators:

Administrator 11: I will speak to the danger factor in prisons as a comparison. I do not have a lot of experience in U.S. corrections but have certainly seen reports.... So we read a lot about how dangerous it is in those prisons. And when you throw thousands of men into a prison and you put them five, six deep into a cell, and there is no programming, no dynamic security. Most American prisons are like warehouses and the inmates are stuck in there like animals ... the entire environment is negative and it is violent. I am sure we all have visions of what the American prisons look like and there have been many documentaries done on television, for example, depicting the nature of such prisons. In comparison, looking at Canadian corrections is like night and day, or black and white with respect to the U.S. prisons.

Administrator 12: There is also no question in my mind that American prisons are more dangerous environments and that gang activities and general violence are more apparent within their institutions. Of course we have some violence as well, but our prisons operate on a dynamic security model. There is a lot of interaction between staff and inmates—more so than in the American prison system. The fact that we have treatment programs and quality health care, etc., solid staff/offender interaction, suggests that there is significant emphasis placed on the dignity of life, and so you would expect that the offenders in our system would respond more favourably to that than an environment in which there is less of that.

In previous chapters we have discussed the importance of ethics, codes of conduct, choosing the right recruits for the profession, and the importance of a balanced offender/officer ratio. However, other elements may have played a part in limiting episodes of violence in Canadian institutions. Can you think of what some of these might be? Do you agree with Administrator 11 that the differences between U.S. and Canadian prisons is like night and day, and does that comment still hold true today? Administrators 11 and 12 voiced some strong opinions about the US prison system in comparison to the Canadian system. How valid do you think these comments are and why?

In terms of institutional construction, CSC has moved from institutional design concepts that first promoted the use of dynamic security, to static security, and back again to dynamic security. Prior to the 1940s, penitentiaries were modelled after the Auburn model, which allowed offenders to eat and work together during the day, but housed them in single cells at night. Offenders were forbidden to engage in verbal or non-verbal communication. However, during the 1950s, institutions had smaller ranges composed of larger cells and dining rooms that could also serve the purpose of offender lounges. Movement throughout the institution was controlled with dynamic security and manual locking of barriers. In the 1960s, prison construction returned to a design typified by those in California, including the use of "bubbles" and remotely controlled means of limiting offender movement throughout the institution. Staff contact with offenders was severely limited and separate corridors for staff became standard features. These institutions often provided goods and services to neighbouring institutions using offender labour in a variety of activities that were not necessarily conducive to their eventual reintegration into a labour market (Posner, 1991).

By the 1970s, new approaches to reduce confrontation, enhance rehabilitation, and create a more humane environment evolved with a movement once again toward a more dynamic security approach. Although there were still a few institutions where correctional officers were in bubbles, other staff members interacted with inmates on the floor. The current trend seems to include the retention of a few high-security, highly controlled institutions for those offenders who require such environments, and they are characterized by greater supervision and diminished staff/offender interactions. However, the great majority of institutions are designed to be medium or minimum security in nature, preparing offenders for eventual reintegration into the community and ultimately to reduce the relative use of incarceration as a major intervention in corrections. This type of model will ultimately encourage and support a model of dynamic security (Posner, 1991). Some of this sentiment is captured in the following comment made by a CSC administrator:

Administrator 13: We have visiting officials coming from international destinations to look at our model, and that model has in some ways been damaging to us in the way that the media perceives it. However, like it or not, these inmates will be released back into the community at some point in time. We are known for our ability to reintegrate successfully the majority of our offenders back into society because of the type of model we use when working with them.... I suppose one could argue that the opposite of that model would be the "punitive/warehousing" model used by the U.S., and I think the results really stand out in our stats. When you look at violent incidents—riots, hostage taking, murders, assaults—they all still exist. However, they have decreased significantly over the years.

So when you talk to correctional officers that have been around thirty to thirty-five years, when they compare operations to today, including the relationship between management, staff, and inmates, most people will tell you there was a fine line between correctional practice and militaristic practice with respect to the types of things that happened, including the overall atmosphere or working environment. In today's correctional practice, all levels of staff interact very closely and I don't think there is a warden in this region that you couldn't go up to his/her office and just say "hi" or talk to them, whereas when I started sixteen years ago, you just didn't do that. Therefore, the barriers have been broken down, not just between inmates and staff, but also amongst various staffing levels themselves and between management and staff as well. In addition, I think this a very positive thing.

Administrator 13 makes reference to the fact that we are recognized internationally for the corrections model we have here in Canada and then goes on to say that this model "has in some ways been damaging to us in the way that the media perceives it." Can you explain what this statement might mean?

Another difference between the U.S. and Canadian institutions that leads to a more positive outcome for offenders, as well as corrections staff and the public in general is the belief in rehabilitation rather than punishment as a goal for Canadian corrections. This is discussed in greater detail in the next section.

Rehabilitation and Reintegration Versus Punishment

A study published by Kelley, Mueller, and Hemmens (2004) examined the U.S. statutes governing correctional practice in several states with respect to rehabilitation versus punishment. What they concluded was that during a ten-year period (1992–2002), although rehabilitation was the predominant correctional requirement, punishment and control was a re-emerging theme in

2002. Some of this can be explained by the increasing correctional population versus the shrinking budgets which make it difficult to sustain or even justify longer-term rehabilitation programs. It is also quite likely that with the current movement toward a punitive ideology, especially in view of the U.S. political party in power and the war on drugs, which has put increased pressure on the use of incarceration as a solution, the punishment or control/custody mandate of correctional practice will continue to increase.

This issue of rehabilitation versus punishment is still one that is debated among the public and politicians, as discussed to some degree in Chapter 1. However, it is worth mentioning that several of the CSC administrators commented on the positive outcomes achieved by a focus on rehabilitation—outcomes such as a reduction in recidivism rates. Many administrators also believe that investing in programming and post-release planning has resulted in a reduced offender population and a decreased need to build more prisons, unlike the U.S., with its focus on punishment and lengthier, harsher sentencing practices that sometimes results in the "warehousing" of offenders. For example, one interviewee said:

Administrator 14: When you have professionals, like Dr. Michael Jackson, for example, supporting our position, advocating for the primary focus in prisons to be on reintegration and rehabilitation, and taking on the outspoken politicians of the world, it is incredible to see. In addition, of course having people like that fully supporting us lets us know we are moving in the right direction with the way our Canadian correctional work is done.

In addition to the use of dynamic security, which relies on the development and nurturing of interpersonal relationships between offender and correctional staff, rehabilitation focuses largely on the provision of appropriate programming to fit the unique needs of each offender. Some CSC administrators noted:

Administrator 15: In Canada there is specialized programming that requires us to move inmates, and that happens there is a process to do that—probably too long and complicated, but there is a process that works.

Administrator 16: We have invested a lot of research into the programs that we currently deliver. I would like to think that that has a strong bearing on recidivism rates. Are we seeing the return of as many offenders? I don't think so. It is easy to stay positive in this business when you remember all that. To me, I'm still seeing way more many individuals never come back than come back so I like my job!

Administrator 17: Canadian corrections is very much focused on re-integration and programming, etc. The shift from when I started fifteen or sixteen years ago—at that time correctional officers and inmates very rarely talked to one another, whereas today inmates and guards are on a first name basis. It is not uncommon now to see inmates and correctional officers walking down the middle of the jail, talking and laughing with each other—so it is a very dynamic type of interaction. In addition, we have a variety of committees who are committed to identifying the problems and bringing them forward so we can resolve them right away. We do not let the problem fester, or persist and grow so that it becomes so problematic that you end up with a riot or something. So staff in Canadian corrections work closely with the inmates to bring the problems to the forefront and to re-solve them. Moreover, a lot of this has come about because of the programs that have been brought in and the interaction that occurs between inmates and staff. Therefore, we have more of a rehabilitation focus, whereas the Americans have more of a punitive focus within their institutions.

Of significance, then, is the shift from a model that supported a rather distant and impersonal style of communication between inmate and guard to one that recognizes the importance of improved communication. Such communication is essential in order to enhance not only reintegration potential for the inmate, but also to assist and improve in any potential conflict resolution between the inmate and others, including guards.

Administrator 18: The variable I am most proud about, in terms of Canadian corrections is that we are probably the only country that I'm aware of that has a requirement for program participation and involve-ment—as a requirement—in the Act. Offenders have to be treated and be given the opportunity to participate in programs. It is incumbent upon us as a country and as corrections services professionals to provide that opportunity to offenders, and not only provide it, but have the expecta-tion that they will be involved, which is quite unique. When we wrote the CCRA, this was one of the things that was a big thing for us, was to write this right into the Act. I was lucky to have a fair bit of involvement in the development of the CCRA and this was an area that I thought was really crucial, whereas in most jurisdictions the emphasis is much more on punishment or on separating people from the community for a per-iod of time and essentially being a denunciation in terms of case specific circumstances. We make the effort to look at what the opportunities are to take this individual and see what we can do in terms of addressing the variables that caused the criminal behaviour in the first place. We look at whether we can address the deficiencies in terms of his/her skills and also provide very strong supervision.

Participation in programming is voluntary; however, failure to complete programming has sometimes meant that offenders are denied access to early release opportunities.

Administrator 19: I must admit that my knowledge is very superficial and it comes mostly from talking to people who have visited the U.S. But I mean, if you look at our prisons compared to them, our, the Canadian approach is much more directed at reintegration and programs, correcting the issues that brought the offender in. Their prisons have hundreds and thousands of people, where ours are much smaller. It is a completely different approach. I guess that would be sort of the two things that jump out at me.

Some real concerns are expressed regarding the practice of giving pardons or even providing less than adequate sentencing for some offenders, (e.g. violent offenders) that occurs in some parts of the U.S. This is because such practices are based on what is described as potential over-incarceration of offenders, which further leads to over-population in U.S. prisons and penitentiaries rather than on good correctional decision-making processes. Some discussions in this book have indicated that, particularly in the U.S., offenders being incarcerated, might otherwise benefit from non-carceral sentences.

Administrator 20: Well, we certainly differ on our opinions of how we can safely protect the public, and certainly reintegration and the way we come at it in this country by comparison is vastly different. We protect the public by reintegrating offenders through supervision in the community so that we can manage them and monitor them properly prior to them hitting their Warrant Expiry Date and being completely on their own with no support network. We have managed to stabilize our crime rates and recidivism rates. We have seen a slight increase I think, but certainly not in the violent crimes. And if you look to the U.S., where it is "incarcerate, incarcerate, incarcerate," and the crime rate there, just continues to climb.

According to a report put out by the Federal Bureau of Investigation, a ten year (1997–2006) comparison of crimes in the U.S. presents a picture of decreased crime rates over time in both violent and property crimes (U.S. Department of Justice).

> **Administrator 20** (cont.): We were just reviewing this morning their abolishment of the sentences by one state—giving pardons. We are seeing these as trends and basically the fact that they have incarcerated so many offenders they are having to open up the doors. So the "can't keep you anymore" position and the safety of that for the public versus the approach that we take are certainly opposite. Yet our public pressure in this country is more toward locking them up. We clearly see that it's not working and so the real struggle for Canada is to get out there and to say to the people that what we do is really about protecting you. You may not see that due to the fact that we are releasing them in what you may consider "early in their sentences," but in the long run they are going to be much more conducive to being in a community environment, not committing a crime four years from now than they would be by releasing them out the front door and saying, "you have completed your sentence and now you are a free citizen." So we really have to get out there and work with educating the communities to be involved in those types of support networks. So in looking at the bigger picture, this is not to minimize the significance of crimes that happen out there, but we have to look at it in the context of comparing the safety of what we do in comparison to what the States do. It certainly is a contentious issue.

Although the administrators are very strong in their opinions around the differences between the U.S. and Canadian prisons in terms of the punishment versus reintegration, you might recall that in Chapter 2 one of the ethical issues that arose for many of the administrators was the issue of "meeting the measurement criteria." In other words, when looking at the success of reintegration, is this measured on the ability to release the offender by the day and full parole eligibility date, or is it making sure the offender completes all of the required programming even if it means a delay in his or her release? Given that offenders may be released when they meet their release eligibility date, whether or not they have fully completed their programming, do you believe this practice is better or worse compared to the U.S. practice of "warehousing"?

Other CSC administrators expressed optimism about the direction some of the U.S. states are taking in terms of looking at the issues around reintegration and the provision of programming:

Administrator 21: I think that Canada and the U.S. are finally coming together on some of the policies we are following. In other words, they are coming to us for things such as doing programming. Some of the states have begun to realize now that the punitive model just does not work. Death penalty does not work, except for those very few people. The statistics really show this; for example, they have the most restrictive methods in place for decades, such as the death penalty for example, and their crime rate is the highest in the civilized world, and so these are not [deterrents]. They really have produced huge institutions, with little or no programming geared to helping offenders get released and successfully reintegrated into communities, and so they are basically warehousing offenders. They are realizing now that the long sentences and death sentences they are imposing are not working.

These people are all coming back out. In other words, these are their neighbours and our neighbours, and I would rather that these individuals have some skills that are useful in successfully negotiating life, obtaining and maintaining employment—work skills and in controlling themselves. Therefore, the U.S. is starting to come and take a look at some of our cognitive skills types of programming, our sex offender programs, etc. Therefore, these are some of the areas that I think we are starting to collaborate a bit more on.

Therefore, I think these are two areas where our correctional system and beliefs differ from the U.S., and these are in the areas of programming and rehabilitation—the importance of employability. So when you are talking about correctional administration and programming, I think we really have to give some thought as to what it is that we are really trying to foster with the individual, because they are coming out.

Reintegration, of course, would not be successful if it were not for the support of and partnerships with various communities, both in their acceptance of the return of offenders and the provision of ongoing post-release programs to facilitate a successful reintegration process. Some comments by administrators help us to conceptualize the more "militaristic" model of supervision exercised by the U.S. versus the community reintegration model used by Canada.

Administrator 22: The other thing that is beautiful in Canada in terms of our system is the integration of the community side of the operation with the institutional side of the operation. That allows for orderly transition and allows for gains that we worked on very hard in terms of teaching skills to be integrated and practiced in the community with supervision. And because we have relapse programs in every area, whether it be substance abuse, violence, sex offenders, the programs that have been initiated inside carry into the community, and they have the same trained professionals to provide the relapse training to ensure they are always watching for things that are starting to lapse and to continually reinforce the gains that were made inside. To use the experiences in the community as ongoing learning experiences in terms of testing out the skills that had been developed.... And so it provides for a much stronger approach with both supervision and ongoing learning than in most any other jurisdiction. Again, that's one of the strengths of the Canadian federal system. I've had occasion over the past several years to visit dozens of jurisdictions—Japan, Australia and New Zealand, all over the States, Hong Kong—and from the perspective of an integrated approach and with a mission that is overriding across all parts of our services, we are in the strongest position of any of those countries thus far. So in comparison to other jurisdictions as well as provincial corrections, we certainly have the most integrated system in terms of the delivery of correctional services.

Administrator 23: Integration of offenders back into the community—what it comes down to is that we have an incredible amount of community support networks in Canada and commitment from the people who work for us to work with the offender versus the more militaristic type of model, which is typified by parole officers carrying guns in some states, etc. Whereas here, we wouldn't even fathom that in our approach in working with the offender, and I guess that is the key—working with the offender as opposed to monitoring the offender out there. And that is certainly a trend we are starting to see the States pick up on the support is what is really needed rather than the reporting mechanism, which can be very costly.

Although there is an emphasis on the importance of working with the offender and moving away from strict, regimented types of monitoring models such as those used extensively in the U.S., there may be segments of the Canadian public who might believe that in some cases the latter model is more favourable. Would you support the stricter monitoring model, and if so, can you provide examples of where this could be used?

Finally, as one correctional administrator stated:

Administrator 24: Some of the statistics on American crime are quite revealing in that regard. So this is not much of a deterrent, and there is a great comment from Dr. Ed Zamble in one of his publications: "... in the

absence of correctional intervention or programming, prisons are basically a behavioural deep freeze" in which the offender comes out in many
ways, unchanged, and if anything changed for the worse because of the
environment he has lived in, and the bitterness and resentment that he has
experienced and the fact that he has had nothing but negative or antisocial
and pro-criminal peers to associate with all of this time. So what do you
expect when a guy comes out of a cage? He's going to be angry, violent, and
want revenge on the world, and so he commits the same kind of crimes if
not worse crimes.

We are very proud, therefore, to be Canadian and part of the Canadian
correctional system, because our focus is based on a much more humanitarian model and our mission statement, of course, speaks to that. In my
view, that is the most significant difference between the U.S. and Canada in
terms of correctional practice, and that is the focus on behavioural change
which is predicated or based on a theory of criminal behaviour that we
apply, which is based on the social learning theory, i.e., if criminal behaviour can be learned then it can also be unlearned. It is up to us to introduce
interventions that help offenders unlearn their negative behaviours and to
relearn more pro-social behaviours. So although one might say that the
Americans are familiar with the social learning model, and may even agree
with it, they are not all devoted to applying it within their correctional
practices. Not just the U.S., as there are many countries which have made
no attempt to rehabilitate offenders, strictly keeping the offenders locked
up to protect the people for the duration of the sentences.

There has been some somewhat threatening discussion about the fact—if
we keep needing more money, keep going back to Treasury Board for more
money, or keep having these failures where offenders escape, with murders
or suicides in jail, having riots, or hostage takings and so forth, eventually
the politicians and public are going to get so frustrated and disillusioned
they will suggest our programs aren't working. This may lead to pressure
from the government, for us to turn towards a more punitive model—three
strikes and you're out or lock them up and throw away the key, much like
the American scenario in many places. People are sort of putting pressure
on us to be better, to do better, to convince the world that these programs
do work and that we are making progress. It is a frightening proposition
to think that government would ever make that decision, frankly. They
think they are saving costs in the U.S. by not programming, but think
of the tremendous cost in building one prison, or the "cost" of one rape,
or one armed robbery, or one death. How do you measure the financial
costs or dollars attached to any one of those crimes? It strikes me that in

Canada, the fact that the numbers in jails have been steady for so long and our recidivism rates are so low, we really are, in the true sense of the word, protecting society. It is not just protecting them from crime and from violence. Its protecting them from the costs which are associated with that, and which are often very subtle. Therefore, I personally doubt that we will ever follow a non-reintegration model, at least not in our lifetime.

In terms of recidivism rates, over the long run it is almost universally 50%, including Canada. However, Canada seems to have lower recidivism rates in the short term while the offender is still under sentence. Canada's focus is on reintegration of the offender into the community, and this is primarily achieved through the provision of some excellent programs targeting the needs of the offenders. However, the lack of a formal education is also of concern to CSC, and this has led to the development of opportunities for some offenders to further their education while serving time within the various institutions.

Education as a Priority

In his article, Stevens (2000) points out that offenders constitute the largest percentage of uneducated individuals in Canada, citing that nearly "two out of every three offenders have not completed high school and ... 30% of these do not even have grade 8" (p. 29). CSC recognizes the need to provide offenders with basic educational requirements up to a GED level, generally through the provision of adult basic education, and in some cases there is the opportunity to acquire post-secondary education. Some individuals have argued, especially by the proponents of the "just deserts" perspective, that formal education does nothing to alleviate the rate of recidivism; those who favour the treatment/ rehabilitation perspective would argue otherwise. In fact, according to Stevens (2000), "offering individuals under correctional supervision a student-centred educational program provides an avenue for those offenders who want change, an opportunity to advance themselves" (p. 30).

According to Ubah and Robinson (2003), in the U.S. the field also appears to be divided between those who hold an "idealistic/optimistic" view (in other words, those in support of treatment/rehabilitation) stressing its promise and value, versus those who hold a "pessimistic reaction" (those who relate more to the punitive side of incarceration), perceiving it as ineffective. In the U.S., the strong proponents of the punitive side of incarceration were able to achieve some success in pushing forth their view that inmate or offender education fits into the category of "nothing works" analysis. As a result, much of the financial support from the federal level for inmate education, particularly post-secondary education, was eliminated, although a few states have been successful in generating some funds at the state level. However, as Ubah and Robinson point out, further research on the effects of such dramatic cuts seem to suggest that they have produced an adverse impact on offender rehabilitation and on the rates of recidivism. One correctional administrator noted:

> **Administrator 25:** I think that they are doing some better things in the educational area. There are some areas that I'd like to duplicate. It is an area that we are spending a lot of money in, but I think we should be looking at spending a little bit more and educating offenders. In some states, they take the mandatory grade twelve level a little more seriously than us. They might force the inmate to be in education for six months, so they don't get access to anything else. We have a grade twelve policy but it is not applied as forcefully as it would be in some of the states, where "you are going to school for six months and then we will look at other programming." We have it in our policy that grade twelve is the minimum, but if you look at specific cases that assess functioning under grade twelve, they might be or they might not be, in education. But that is more of a management issue than a policy issue because the policy is there. However, I do believe that education is the cornerstone of a progressive society and an efficient agent for social change.

What are your beliefs around the need to provide all offenders with the equivalent of a grade 12 education prior to implementing any other types of programming for them? Can you come up with some arguments opposing such a concept?

Conclusion

This chapter presented an overview of some international incarceration rates and evidence shows that among some nations, in particular Western nations, the U.S. continues to have one of the highest rates of incarceration in the world. Several English-speaking governments followed the lead of the U.S. in the 1980s by also focusing on increased use of incarceration rather than rehabilitation. However, nowhere has this "axis of penal power" been more firmly cemented than in the U.S.

This chapter also presented some comparisons between Canadian and U.S. correctional practices and included discussion on concepts such as decarceration versus incarceration, dynamic versus static security, rehabilitation and reintegration versus punishment, and lastly, education as a priority for offenders. The focus on punitive practices found in some states may be predicated on a theory of criminal behaviour that does not support the position that criminal behaviour can be "unlearned" through programming and other rehabilitative efforts. Nonetheless, it is clear that CSC administrators believe that Canada has one of the most humanitarian models of correctional practice in the world and that it is internationally recognized. CSC practice is based on a mission statement that respects the dignity of all individuals and which emphasizes the value of all human life.

Study Questions

1. Discuss possible factors that can influence the incarceration rate of a country.
2. You are a correctional administrator appearing before a committee on correctional reform. Prepare an argument for why corrections should or shouldn't focus on rehabilitation and reintegration as opposed to punishment.
3. Should education programs be a priority in prisons? Why or why not?

Bibliography

*Items with asterisks are also suggested readings for this chapter

Basic Facts. Correctional Service Canada. http://www.csc-scc.gc.ca/text/pblct/basicfacts/BasicFacts_e.shtml

(*CSC Commissioner's Directive 560* http://www.csc-scc.gc.ca/text/plcy/cdshtm/560-cde-eng.shtml)

Correctional Services of Canada. *Speakers Binder, Section 7 Statistics* http://www.csc-scc.gc.ca/text/pblct/guideorateur/sec7_e.shtml

Coyle, A. (Feb. 2002). An international perspective of imprisonment in the early 21st century. *Corrections Today, 64*(1), 8–10.

Harrison, P. and Beck, A. (2003). *Prisoners in 2002*. Bureau of Justice Statistics. http://www.ojp.usdoj.gov/bjs/abstract/p02.htm

International Centre for Prison Studies. Kings College London Law School (UK). http://www.kcl.ac.uk/schools/law/research/icps

Kelley, L., Mueller, D. and Hemmens, C. (2004). To punish or rehabilitate revisited: An analysis of the purpose/goals of state correctional statutes, 1991–2002. *Criminal Justice Studies, 17*(4), 333–351.

Landreville, P. (Jan. 1995). Prison overpopulation and strategies for decarceration. *Canadian Journal of Criminology, 37*(1), 39–61.

Mauer, M. (Oct 2004). *Lessons of the "Get Tough" Movement in the United States*. Presented at the International Corrections and Prison Association 6th Annual Conference, Beijing, China.

Mauer, M. (2003). *Comparative International Rates of Incarceration: An Examination of Causes and Trends.* Presented to the U.S. Commission on Civil Rights. http://www.sentencingproject.org/pdfs/pub9036.pdf

Mauer, M. (1994). *America Behind Bars: The International Use of Incarceration 1992-1993.* http://www.druglibrary.org/schaffer/other/sp/abb.htm

Posner, C. (1991). A historical overview of the construction of Canadian federal prisons. *Forum on Corrections Research,* 3(2).

Pratt, J. (Feb. 2002). The globalization of punishment. *Corrections Today,* 64(1), 64–67.

Public Works and Government Services. Corrections and Conditional Release Statistical Overview 2007. http://www.ps-sp.gc.ca/res/cor/rep/_fl/CCRSO_2007-eng.pdf

Stevens, D. (May 2000). Education programming for offenders. *Forum on Corrections Research,* 12(2), 29–31.

Tartaro, C. (2002). The impact of density on jail violence. *Journal of Criminal Justice,* 30, 499–510.

*Ubah, C. B. and Robinson, R. L. (June 2003). A grounded look at the debate over prison-based education: Optimistic theory versus pessimistic worldview. *The Prison Journal,* 83(2), 115–129.

United States Department of Justice. Federal Bureau of Investigation. 2006 Crime in the United States. http://www.fbi.gov/ucr/cius2006/data/table_01.html

Walmsley, R. (2003). *World Prison Population List* (4th edition). http://www.homeoffice.gov.uk/rds/pdfs2/r188.pdf

Walmsley, R. (Dec. 2003) Global incarceration and prison trends. *Forum on Crime and Society* 3 (1 & 2), 65–78.

Suggested Readings

Carlie, M. K. and Minor, K. I. (Eds.) (1992). *Prisons around the World: Studies in International Penology.* Dubuque, IA: Wm. C. Brown Pub.

Moyle, P.(2000). *Profiting from Punishment: Private Prisons in Australia—Reform or Regression.* Annandale, AUS: Pluto Press.

Zimring, F., and Hawkins, G. (1991). *The Scale of Imprisonment.* Chicago: The University of Chicago Press.

7 Human Resource Management in Corrections

In this chapter, we focus on the management and staff of the Correctional Service of Canada who have the task of carrying out its mission and bringing to life the words that exist on paper. Philosophically, the Correctional Service of Canada has recognized the paramount importance of its staff in striving towards the mission statement. The third of the five core values that guide the work of the management and line staff of the CSC states *"we believe that our strength and our major resource in achieving our objectives is our staff and that human relationships are the cornerstone of our endeavour."*

As Ole Ingstrup (2000) wrote:

> In our study of the best of the public service, we found the second most important factor, after mission, was recruiting and developing men and women of character. The people in these organizations exude a sense of integrity, trust, caring, openness, and a desire to learn and get better at their jobs.

Thus, on paper the Correctional Service of Canada is strongly committed to its staff not only philosophically, but financially as well. In 2005–2006, the total expenditure of CSC was $1.6 billion—$808 million of that was spent on salaries and a further $162.6 million on Employee Benefit Plans—combined at is almost 61% of the total budget. CSC employs approximately 14,500 staff (as of March 31, 2006). If part-time and casual employees, as well as those who may be absent at any given time, are included, the number of full-time equivalents increases to 15,491 (Correctional Service Canada, 2007). In addition, Correctional Service of Canada has recognized the human resource management challenges it faces in the coming years due to changing offender demographics, projected labour shortages, effective labour relations, and evolving learning needs, and has developed a Strategic Plan for Human Resource Management 2007–08 to 2009–10 (CSC, 2007).

But how does this commitment play out in practice? Key to answering this question is the examination of CSC employees, who have to make discretionary decisions in their daily work that can either support or hinder the implementation of the CSC's mission, philosophy, and policies. For the organization to continue to work in a manner that is faithful to the intentions of the mission statement and policies, recruiting, selecting, and retaining effective and efficient employees is of paramount concern. This area is increasing in importance for the CSC because more than 40% of its staff could leave within the next three years, the majority coming from the senior management levels (CSC Review Panel, 2007).

Recruitment

Today, the recruitment of CSC employees is much more formal than it has been historically. A few of the interviewees described how those coming to work in corrections did not always have the specific skill sets required for the job:

> **Administrator 1:** I was surprised at the background of some of the parole officers in terms of the extent or lack of extent, that they had interviewing or counselling backgrounds in their undergraduate degrees…, I mean, I was shocked to find that one of my staff members had their degree in French. That's nice, I don't know, maybe if you are going to teach French or something, but to what degree do they have the interviewing and the counselling skills inside that program wasn't apparent.

In the Report of the Task Force on Security (2002), the authors stated that the CSC had to adopt an integrated and comprehensive human resource strategy that included developing competency profiles for all positions and an expanded and revitalized recruitment program. The Task Force recommended that "CSC develop a selection process that ensures the hiring of staff who possess all of the core competencies necessary to work in a correctional environment" (Report of the Task Force on Security, 2002). Research shows, however, that core competencies are not the only factors to consider when recruiting new staff. Lariviere (2002) believed that the person-organization fit theory "predicts better overall adjustment for workers whose attitudes and values are congruent with those of their employer" (p. 19)—in this case, the mission statement and core values of the CSC.

According to Riley and Wilder (2002), in addition to developing competency-based criteria for hiring staff, correctional employers need to be able to identify the personal characteristics of potential employees that will lead to success in the corrections field. They state that "people who understand the strengths as well as limitations of the offender population with whom they work, and who possess intelligence, flexibility and interpersonal skills to deal with individual offenders differently but consistently will be successful" (p. 89). The former commissioner of the CSC also noted that "not everyone is ethically qualified for public service, especially in corrections. When recruiting and promoting, examine their ethical track record, their values" (Ingstrup, 2000,). In the 1992 Staff Commitment Survey, the CSC researchers found that "attitudes towards corrections" was the factor most strongly related to staff commitment. In other words, staff who were committed to the Correctional Service of Canada held fundamentally positive views about the field of corrections.

In addition to core competencies and values, a diverse workforce is beneficial in corrections. Johnson (1995) found that "a diverse correctional staff can enhance communication between staff and inmates, add to the cultural awareness of staff, decrease racial tension, provide positive role models and enhance a department's public image" (p. 97). When the *Employment Equity Act* was introduced in 1995, CSC formalized its hiring process by setting employment equity targets for four designated groups: women, Aboriginal people, persons with disabilities, and visible minorities. Since it is a public service employer, the Correctional Service of Canada is expected to meet the employment equity targets of the Employment Equity Division in the Human Resources Branch of the Treasury Board of Canada Secretariat. This division "provides strategic orientation and coordination in support of employment equity in the federal Public Service" (Treasury Board of Canada Employment Equity Division, 2000). Each year, the president of the Treasury Board tables in Parliament an annual report on the state of employment equity in the public service for the preceding year as required under the *Public Service Reform Act*. The CSC also reports on its ability to meet its employment equity targets in its annual performance report.

To try and achieve employment equity targets, competitions for positions can be limited to a specific group, as correctional administrators outlined:

Administrator 2: CSC is a leader in the employment equity field. We have some very clear national and regional targets for hiring of women, minorities, disabled persons and Aboriginals. We have very good policies in this regard and a number of legislated opportunities that allow us to focus entirely on a particular employment equity group if we choose to, for hiring into certain positions. For example, we have the capacity to ask the Public Service to allow us to hire only Aboriginal applicants for an entire Correctional Officer Training Program (COTP) or we could do the same for women or visible minorities. And in fact we have already offered the COTP for solely Aboriginal applicants and for solely women as well. We certainly do take advantage of those opportunities available to us.

Administrator 3: Our work force is supposed to mirror the Canadian public and our clients who are the inmates. We have a disproportionate number of Aboriginal inmates so our staff should have a disproportionate number of Aboriginal staff. We have employment equity targets. Through our personnel committee and the RMC (Regional Management Committee) we look at them and we decide how we are going to address those targets. We've had successes in certain areas and we are struggling in other areas, but it is an ongoing program that is managed at the regional level but we are expected to produce the results.

The following excerpt from the 2002 CSC Performance Report shows some successes and problems:

> CSC surpassed its overall staff representation objectives for women and persons with disabilities last year. Nationally, CSC planned to achieve representation rates of 39.1% for women and 3.4% for persons with disabilities by 2004. Results at the end of fiscal year 2001/2002 indicated those goals were achieved early, with representation figures for those groups calculated at 41.4% and 4.3% respectively.
>
> At the same time, visible minorities represented 3.9% of term and indeterminate employees, 1.8% shy of the national goal set for 2004. Aboriginal employees were also under-represented at 5.6%, 3.4% short of the 9% objective set for 2006. In some cases, employee retention in these groups continues to be more of a problem than recruitment and promotion. (CSC Performance Report, 2002)

A number of factors were cited as having an impact on the CSC's ability to meet the employment equity targets. Sites where there has been a lot of growth tend to be much more representative because they have had the opportunity to target specific groups as opposed to sites where there has been little or no growth or turnover, and therefore fewer hiring opportunities. Difficulties can also arise when applicants do not meet the minimal criteria set for a position or when the individuals who meet the criteria are also well qualified for other departments. Two of the correctional administrators interviewed commented on such situations:

Administrator 4: Recently, the regional administrator of Aboriginal programs was attempting to run some competitions throughout the region for positions they would be interested in hiring for, and we have government support for this; however, it was difficult to find qualified Aboriginal people. Perhaps this is made more difficult by the fact that the model used in corrections work may not be very consistent with the justice model used by Aboriginal peoples. In other words, how we mete out punishment versus how the Aboriginal communities would deal with such issues through, say, restorative justice may differ.

Administrator 5: Similarly, when you look at ethnic diversity within our facilities, for example with Aboriginal people, we are way beyond our national target in terms of promoting diversity. The one area where we have not managed to be successful is in the Prairies, where we have more Aboriginal offenders, and a lot of Aboriginal staff find it difficult to work in the CSC environment because of the "structures, controls," and that sort of thing, because they don't feel very comfortable working in that manner. And the other reality is that for those who meet the education criteria that we demand at the professional or supervisory level, there are so many opportunities for Aboriginals graduating from university that we would not necessarily be their first choice. Even though they may join us, they often get promoted to other opportunities in other governmental departments because there is just such a huge demand right now in government for a fairly limited number of people. So in terms of Aboriginal people, there are a fixed amount of available resources which are highly sought after and we may not be their first choice.

The Correctional Service of Canada keeps track of its ability to meet employment equity targets through *PeopleSoft*, a program that allows it to do a quarterly run to see how many of each target group are employed within what positions and regions.

The 2007–2008 Estimates Report on Plans and Priorities shows an improvement in CSC's attempts to maintain a workforce that reflects Canadian society. As of March 31, 2006, slightly more than 5% of the CSC workforce are from visible minority groups, approximately 4% are persons with disabilities, approximately 7% are Aboriginal, and just under 45% of CSC staff are women (Correctional Service of Canada, 2007).

Though employment equity has been a formal government policy since 1995, there still seems to be some confusion about what employment equity means in practice. One interviewee described how he viewed it:

Administrator 6: There are certainly some examples of staff, who lack the requisite skills, some of which may involve being able to write a basic report on an inmate. So for example, in the case of hiring practices targeting some of the unique populations, by lowering the guidelines or criteria to apply for or even be awarded a position, probably does a disservice to the inmates, the staff-person, and ultimately other staff, as well. So I guess the solution is to find ways around this and to find better solutions and better models, and I think the notion of hiring minorities, etc. is a good principle.

Other interviewees described the confusion that results from the term "employment equity" and the misconception that an individual may get promoted because they belong to a visible minority as opposed to their qualifications. Administrator 7 emphasizes that everyone still needs to meet all of the qualifications for the positions and that there is a need for training in this area to minimize these types of misconceptions:

Administrator 7: We have employment equity programs in place here—we do not discriminate and it is right in our mission document. In fact, we do not even have mandatory retirement ages in federal corrections. People can work here as long as they like and do not have to automatically retire at age sixty-five years or after thirty years of employment or anything like that.... As administrators, I think this is something we would like to see stressed in programs—that we are teaching and training competencies for young managers, and that is, what do we mean when we need "equity?" What do we mean, and what is so different about having employment equity groupings within our ranks. What kind of environment do we have to prepare and have in place in order for employment equity people to come, to stay, and to feel welcome? Because there are many misconceptions, even now, even though we have had the policies in place for years and years. [Years ago, promotions] were not based on merit; it was based on the concept of targets, and they need to meet those targets.

It's those kinds of issues that I think are still here. We have visible minorities within our workforce here. For example we have a high Indo-Canadian population, we have Indo-Canadian staff, and when these staff move ahead, is it because they are qualified or is it because they are Indo-Canadian or because they are Aboriginal? We still get those questions. It does not mean that they are coming in because they are in an employment equity group—they still need to meet all of the qualifications for those positions. But it also means we have some additional opportunities to a point, because they do meet all of the qualifications. We do not lower the bar for those people in the employment equity groups—they must meet the competency requirements of that particular position. Not all of our positions have university requirements but some of them do. For example, we have an Aboriginal-focused facility here that we would eventually like to have an Aboriginal person run, but that person would still have to meet all of the requirements, that we would expect of a director, no matter what. So in the next round of wardens competitions coming up shortly, which are national competitions, we will have a number of applicants, and if one of those applicants happens to be Aboriginal and happens to be success-ful, the deputy commissioner may very well say that because they are on the list, and they have fully qualified, that the D.C. may want them to run the Aboriginal-focused facility. There is nothing different about them inasmuch as they have to meet the standards like anyone else, however again, many people do not understand that.

In addition to that, many of the visible minorities who apply for work do not even want to identify themselves as such on their resumes or applica-tion forms because they do not want to be seen as being hired based on that factor alone. However, as people get to know and understanding how employment equity works that myth is disappearing a bit. But at the line level, i.e. correctional officers on the floor and the clerical people on the floor—not all of them fully understand it and it is not being communicated very well.

While Administrator 7 emphasizes that everyone must meet all of the quali-fications for a position, Administrator 8 explains that there are some exceptions to that rule:

Administrator 8: As a rule, we do not lower our standards in order for these employment equity groups to be able to work in CSC; however, there are exceptions. For example, within the Aboriginal area we did make an allowance for Aboriginal program officers to take on the role of program delivery in the Aboriginal area, without possessing a full degree from a recognized university. But we did require these individuals to possess some kind of qualification, certificate, or diploma from a recognized Aboriginal educational institution, such as the Nechi Institute or an institution of that nature, which demonstrated that they had passed a certain course of study and were now competent in the delivery of a particular program. The reason for that, and even though some people might argue against that by stating that it is reverse discrimination, I personally think it is the right thing to do because when you talk about the delivery of Aboriginal programs to Aboriginal offenders, we are talking about a much different approach, strategy and concept than with the general population. The Aboriginal people who may be affected by this, are so immersed in their culture and spirituality that what you really need is not someone with a university degree in Criminology, but someone with qualifications in spirituality, traditional and cultural practices.

These qualifications are often achieved through extensive experience, living on reserves, seeing what has happened with their people, learning from Elders and Aboriginal institutions, having an extremely strong commitment to the "Red Road" Aboriginal spirituality and culture, and who can impart that respect and sense of dignity to the Aboriginal offenders. Along with that, we need to have a solid program that helps offenders develop skills and to go in a new direction. So in some cases there are concessions made and this is the only example I can think of. In most situations, the standard remains the same but the restriction is simply that no one other than this particular group can apply or will be considered for the position. It is simply a way for us to bring this into balance with the community and with our institutional needs. So the policy, which may have it detractors, is one that I think is necessary in our environment. Corrections is part of the federal government and I think they have the responsibility to take the lead in these areas.

Most interviewees felt that in terms of employment equity, the issue of females in a male-dominated field is passé. As one interviewee says:

Administrator 9: The ratio seems to be about fifty/fifty females to males and when you look at correctional administrators in CSC at this particular time, most middle managers and, progressively, most senior managers, a good percentage of them are female, and most likely the majority will be female in a not too distant time. In particular, among those people who are interested in the field of criminal justice, most males who finish their college or schooling, or criminal justice programs, they tend to select careers in policing, whereas females tend to be moving more toward corrections. And so we have had a fairly large migration of young male corrections officers into policing, whereas we are not seeing the same thing happen in females. As a result, a lot of the bright students who have come into the Service in the last few years, young professionals, have moved very quickly through the ranks and are moving into supervisory and executive positions. And so I think that the issue of employment equity when it comes to females, is a nonentity at this point, certainly within CSC in this region.

Administrators 2 through 9 comment on the application of employment equity practices and targets within the CSC. A number of benefits and difficulties are reflected in their responses. Can you identify some of these benefits and difficulties with regard to employment equity?

According to the interviewees, the CSC does not have any hiring practices that are based directly on religion. However, the CSC does recognize that the needs of offenders are diverse, and as a result, corrections has developed many different ethnic, cultural, and spiritual contracts with Sikhs, rabbis, Catholic and Anglican priests, and other religious groups, as well as multi-denominational groups like the Salvation Army. Therefore, it is often a contract issue, not a staff issue, as CSC does not hire those staff for chaplaincy. We can conclude that religion is a factor in some contract positions in order to meet the religious needs of the inmates, but that it is not an employment equity target.

Though bilingual employees are not an identified employment equity target group, in areas of the country where one official language predominates, it can be difficult to recruit bilingual employees. Although federal institutions are regional facilities, they are under the *Official Languages Act*, and services must be available in both official languages, which means that competitions for job postings are sometimes limited by language requirements.

Recruitment is and will continue to be a major challenge to CSC. In 2006 CSC recruited between 500–600 individuals into indeterminate positions, and it is expected that this number will quadruple over the 2007–2010 period (CSC, 2007). As a result, CSC is focusing its efforts on directed recruitment activities at universities and colleges in order to attract and retain a representative workforce with the appropriate skills to meet the needs of CSC.

Training

Moral thinking is a skill that can be developed. As can insight into the impact of actions on others. Similarly, staff's skills can be increased if we give them training, have them study cases, and think through problems, not just memorize the policy. (Ingstrup, 2000)

The Correctional Service of Canada has a vast array of training available for staff at all levels. In particular, one of the most crucial components of the training is focused around attitudes and values, because in order to create an environment for offenders to have the opportunity to change, they must be treated with dignity and respect. The importance of having quality training programs in this area was described by one interviewee:

> **Administrator 10:** As for training, I think it is one of the most crucial components of any profession in corrections, in particular the training around attitudes and values. It's easy to teach people knowledge, and you can also improve skills to some considerable degree, but it's very difficult to sometimes transform attitudes. First and foremost, you have to hire the right people in the first place and they have to have the proper value system, and then you have to ensure ongoing training so they understand how and what they do impacts on others, and the way they walk the walk will affect the way we have success. To me, it seems perhaps the most important single variable in success in corrections is to—to borrow a theological term—incarnate values in your life, and that's what I see as my responsibility as a leader—to live in such a way in terms of the way I work within the facility that people unequivocally know my commitment to the mission that we are about and the success of our enterprise, and that while we don't have to be happy with what our offenders did, we have to recognize them to be in every sense human, requiring dignity, respect, and acknowledgement if we expect them to change, and we do also expect them to change. And you have to expect accountability and responsibility, but it has to happen in an environment where change is supported, where vulnerability is accepted, where testing is required, and where when people do act out they may try out new things and may be unsuccessful at some things, but they will do so in an environment where values among our staff and professionals are paramount and we can assure the Canadian public that when our guys do leave, they do so with a set of skills that will help them to succeed out in the communities.

As one interviewee mentions, the current approach to training is much more focused than it was in the past:

> **Administrator 11:** We are currently in a transition. Before, there would be some money in the district or the district would garnish money together and provide various levels of training according to various processes, appraisals, which identify some things, or a section supervisor or a manager

wanted to take a group in a particular direction. For example, when I arrived here I wanted the parole officers to increase their knowledge of the core programs that our business provides, so we provided a lot of training in that area. As well, we wanted to get involved in the other kinds of things. I was surprised at the background of some of the parole officers in terms of the extent, or lack of extent, that they had interviewing or counselling backgrounds in their undergraduate degrees. So we started to increase— we had—once a month we would have in-service days specifically for the parole officers.

We also tried to increase the scope and breadth of knowledge of the admin support staff who wanted more involvement than just clerical work so we tried to increase their frame of reference as well. That was six or seven years ago. Since that time, we have lost the money that we had in training, primarily because the organization has said, "look, we are going to direct this a little bit more rather than leave it up to the whims of the local manager. We want national training." So they created colleges, or national colleges, and regional colleges, and they started to organize in our normal bureaucratic fashion. We organized to provide corporate type of training, so most moneys were directed to that sort of thing.

Soon after being hired into the CSC, all employees are required to complete a two-week orientation program. Most individuals interviewed felt that this initial training was useful for new employees, although they felt a few components were lacking. At times, casual staff also attend this training:

Administrator 12: We have an orientation to Correctional Service of Canada. It is primarily driven towards the institutional stuff, so any of our staff members going to that—and they have to go to that—spend a lot of time learning about institutions, which is a good thing. However, they don't spend enough time learning about the dynamics of community corrections. At times we train our casuals up and we train our determinates and indeterminates, even our contract people up, because I think there are a number of good things about the training and if they learn every move from contract to casual to determinate to indeterminate, the training is already done. We look upon it as a positive thing.

Numerous interviewees described how training standards have been developed for compulsory training and mentioned that departments are expected to be 100% compliant to these training standards. In order to keep track of training requirements, managers identify needs and develop action plans for staff on a yearly basis, and these plans are generally reviewed and modified monthly as new staff is hired or other staff is absent on holidays, maternity leave, sick leave, etc. Each standard comes with a time frame, so the window of opportunity for compliance is quite specific.

Training of Staff

The interviewees were asked to describe the various training programs available in the Correctional Service of Canada. The following is a summary of their comments.

Correctional Officers

For correctional officers, parole officers, and supervisors of case management, training begins before they are even hired as indeterminate employees of the Correctional Service of Canada. Prospective correctional officers attend the Correctional Officer Training Program (COTP) at a regional training facility after being screened, evaluated, and selected by CSC. On successful completion of their correctional training program, they become indeterminate government employees working for CSC.

This eleven-week program is mandatory, whether or not the individual has taken any correctional officer course, either at a private college or a community college. Such courses are viewed as an asset, but individuals who want to work for CSC also have to complete CSC's training. The COTP was generally viewed as an effective entry-level training program, though some noted that there is always room for improvement, and more training in other areas—for example, programming, community, and health—would be additional beneficial components.

Correctional officers must also maintain other compulsory training after the initial orientation training in areas such as firearms recertification, self-contained breathing apparatus training and certification, chemical agent training, use of force, escort, suicide training, anit-harassment training, and Emergency Response Team training. In some areas, such as firearms, staff are recertified yearly. In other areas, such as chemical agents, the institution has a yearly checklist and every third year go through a more intense module.

Correctional officers holding certain positions must complete additional training. For example, not all of the correctional staff goes through the Institutional Emergency Response Training (IERT); it is voluntary. However, for a correctional officer who is part of the IERT, in addition to taking all of the regular training of a correctional officer, they participate in an additional ten days of mandatory training every year in just IERT components. Generally, in the security area, they have to requalify on their core SCBA (Self-Contained

Breathing Apparatus) training, in weapons and first aid, and other areas from time to time. This is because if there is some type of disruption or event among offenders or within institutions, with inmates perhaps trashing the range, taking a hostage, or setting fires, officers have to go in and stabilize the situation by making it impossible for the offenders to continue what they are doing. In some of these situations officers have to be able to protect themselves with oxygen masks. So SCBA relates to the use of gas gear, tanks, masks, and so on. Correctional officers working in women's institutions must participate in women's training.

Parole Officers

Every parole officer that is now hired by the CSC must have a formal degree, so they bring a certain set of skills with them. They are then put through a ten-day training program that focuses on case management practices in general, risk assessment, writing and preparing reports for the parole board, interventions and strategies, and program referrals for the offenders. They must have this training before they assume the positions.

Interviewees described how ongoing training for parole officers has been under scrutiny nationally for some time. Current training focuses on case management processes and the manual, as well as the rules and regulations around case management. However, it has now been recognized that these staff have critical roles in other areas, such as making effective program referrals or interacting with Aboriginal or special needs offenders, and that they need to extend their understanding and knowledge of these areas. Consequently, a mandatory five-day annual professional development session for parole officers has been developed to enhance the ten-day training program. This training allows for a greater focus on particular issues. For example, parole officers might have sex offenders on their caseload, so the training might include discussions of new training/initiatives being done within the Service, what kinds of things they can expect to see behaviourally in the offenders after they have participated in sex offender programming, how they would support the programming that the offender has had, and so on. Other topics could include different ways of checking on offenders, motivational interviewing, and getting offenders into work or into a program.

The parole officer training has been redeveloped, and there is a proposal to increase it to a twenty-day training package, which would be a considerable improvement because that will allow them to become aware of many more things, such as program screening criteria, Aboriginal and ethno-cultural sensitivity issues, and many other topics that are not given adequate attention in the current training.

Supervisors of Case Management

According to the correctional administrators interviewed, training for supervisors of case management has been identified as an area in need of improvement. Unit managers have a huge mandate; they supervise correctional officers and correctional managers as well as the case management portfolio. The job is very demanding, but the extent to which managers are able to focus on reintegration is quite limited. Consequently, managers need specific training on risk management and risk assessment so that they can provide leadership to the parole officers in the field. Currently, the unit managers only get that training through job experience. They are offered management training programs, which may involve, for example, staff relations or how to work within the law, but job specific training currently does not exist.

Program Delivery Staff

Correctional administrators said that within program areas, the training packages are highly structured, are all based on research, and all have integrity and validity since they are identical from one region to the next and from one session to the next. For instance, the training a program officer in the Pacific region receives is basically identical to that of a program officer in the Atlantic region. Program officers receive an initial two weeks of training, and when they go into the field and deliver a program, it is videotaped. The tapes are reviewed by the quality assurance staff, who provide feedback. When the program officers do another program, it is also taped and feedback is provided again. They then attend a follow-up session, deliver another program, and at that point they are generally certified. There is also refresher training on an ongoing basis. So training in the program areas is highly organized, and by the time someone becomes certified in a specific area—for example, living skills or substance abuse—he or she has had high levels of training.

There is no recertification requirement for program officers, and they maintain certification for as long as they continue to deliver the program. If they leave for a year or two and want to come back, they have to go back and requalify or at least take refresher courses. Interviewees said that parole officers, program officers, and other staff are expected to take refresher training from time to time because new programs, policies, and strategies are constantly being introduced.

In addition, when the Service introduces a new initiative, such as a new case management process or a new format for correctional planning, there is a nationwide training program and all staff affected must take the training, although this generally happens only for large scale operators. There is an opportunity for staff who want to move through the system to take training that focuses on self-development and skills building, and the emphasis depends on whether the training is specific to development or is job-centred.

Management

Formalized training for management within CSC is a relatively new phenomenon, as correctional administrators pointed out:

> **Administrator 13:** The other thing that we have in place and have had for the last couple of years is the Cornwall Management Learning Centre for middle managers, so that's correctional supervisors or unit managers, deputy wardens, assistant wardens, regional administrators. This training includes anything from specialized crisis management to ethics in corrections to a number of different supervisory orientation including staff relations, budget management, how to deal effectively with the media, conflict resolution, supervisory and middle management training, and project management, and a whole variety of things—a lot of training available there to either assist young managers coming in because we do have that pocket of people nearing retirement age, to strengthen their skills, and reinforce some new learning in senior managers as well.

> **Administrator 14:** Now they have developed some really good courses on things like staffing for managers, how to be a new supervisor, or a correctional supervisor training course, so you know what is expected. It is a huge jump for our CX's for example, to go from a correctional officer two to a correctional officer three, which is a supervisor. As a supervisor, they are now out of the Union, they are now seen as part of the management team, and they have to do the supervision of the institutions and the CX's rank. So it's a huge jump. So many times we have found we have been very lax … you have a very good person who might be a line level staff, either a nurse or a correctional officer—obviously they would make a great supervisor, right? Well, not always true, because they have not been given the training. What has been happening, I think, is that we provide them with the training years after they have assumed the job, and it is not beneficial when that kind of thing happens.

> **Administrator 15:** For management in the programming area there are fewer training opportunities for program managers per se, nothing quite as structured as I've described for the line staff or program delivery people. But there are a range of training opportunities available for managers. In fact, our regional staff college has an extensive calendar of training op-

portunities. Of course, we can also receive training through the public service and other external organizations like CCMD—Canadian Centre for Management Development, and so on, and we take advantage of external training as well. CMLC—Correctional Management Learning Centre—in Cornwall is a major source of training for management.

Administrator 16: I think that some professional training programs we give to our staff have been inadequate. I think that we are now corporately recognizing the importance of providing ongoing professional development and training, and as a result of this the National College in Cornwall has started to provide courses that directly relate to the operational side of the house.

Administrator 16 suggests that some professional training programs have been inadequate. This point is expanded upon by Administrator 17, who gives specific examples of areas requiring training:

Administrator 17: If we are looking at training or courses for correctional administration staff, one of the things we lack is the ability for people to learn how to really handle their budgets, because even in every institution, every unit manager has a small budget and some of the correctional supervisors even have small budgets. How do you work with that budget in this government structure, with an envelope structure they have gone to now, so you have to learn what you can move and what you cannot. Things like how you can put some of your training money together, with someone else's training, money, etc.... What kind of training dollars can we put together by combining it and get some training that is effective and be more efficient with the use of those dollars?

One of the things I always say to our group in Ottawa is that we were starting to do training packages for unit managers, which are the feeder group for deputy wardens and wardens, you really have to have the stuff in there on the management skills and competencies. How do you deal with harassment issues? How do you deal with difficult employees? What is attendance management and how do you make that work for you? We never heard those words. How do you manage a roster? If you are a unit manager in an institution and perhaps came up through the parole officer side of the house, not had a lot of experience on the correctional officer side of the house, you have never even looked at a duty roster, have no idea of how it is built, or how to make one. It is those competencies and I really like competency based learning because it gives people an opportunity to get some of this information before they even apply for some of this stuff. If you want to be a correctional supervisor or if you want to be a unit manager, then here are the competencies you should have because otherwise, if you try to get them after the fact, it will be very frustrating for you and really frustrating for staff. Correctional administration courses are very much needed.

The comments above from administrators identify a number of key training areas for those in management positions. Can you identify those as well as think of any other training areas that would be important for a CSC manager?

Correctional administrators also commented on non-compulsory training—personal or professional development, management courses, language courses, workshops in particular areas of interest for the employee. A yearly performance evaluation is completed for each employee, and part of that process is also to complete personal development plans (PDPs) in which employees have the opportunity to identify training that they would like to take in the upcoming year and discuss this with their supervisor. The supervisor may see other things that the person needs, so they will work toward a consensus to identify the individual's plan. When opportunities come up for workshops or other training, managers refer back to the PDPs. Any elective training always has to take into account two things: the ability to free that person up and the fiscal possibility to send that person to training.

Interviewees described how CSC began a two-year pilot project in response to the Arbour Commission report in 2001 by creating individual learning accounts in which employees could each have an expenditure of $200 each per year or carry it over for up to $400 a year to spend in any professional manner that they choose. For example, if a staff member felt that they needed more computer training, they could use their money to take a computer course. A number of interviewees noted that few guidelines existed for the learning accounts, and as a result some of the money has gone to funding activities such as golf lessons or yoga lessons under the heading of general wellness. They expressed concern that this practice was a misuse of tax dollars. However, other employees have used the learning accounts to buy books, take courses, or participate in conferences. In summary, the learning accounts were quite popular in concept, but the implementation required more guidance from National Headquarters. Interviewees expected that if the pilot program was permanently instituted, stricter guidelines would accompany its implementation. The pilot program has now been suspended.

Courses are also offered through the regional and national training facilities, which are more developmental in nature and not directly applicable to an individual's day-to-day job. The development and implementation of such training courses demonstrates CSC's commitment to self-development for its employees. Computer training, self-development training, and leadership training are not compulsory, and the challenge for managers is that the compulsory training is seen as the nuts and bolts training for people to do their job. The non-compulsory training is seen as career development, and when it comes to setting priorities there is no doubt about what comes first.

Challenges to Training

For managers, meeting the training standards set out by the Correctional Service of Canada can at times be a daunting task, requiring a new approach to be successful. Many interviewees mentioned these challenges:

> **Administrator 18:** Institutional Emergency Response Team training is ten days of mandatory training that must be done every year to keep the guys up and running and familiar with all of the things that are going on. That is a huge budgetary cost, because when we when we pull correctional officers, like, say, sixty correctional officers out of the various institutions for training, and they have to do them as a cadre, a lot of the training is modular, it is costly because of the overtime, backfill, and that sort of stuff. Now we are looking at breaking them up into smaller groups even though we know they have to have a core group of people, and staggering them a bit more differently throughout the year so that we can still get what we need and take advantage of a better cost distribution. It is a departure from our old culture—it used to be that the boys went off and did their training in a collegial, team building type of thing, and now they have to learn to work differently as well.

> **Administrator 19:** A lot of the decision-making that goes into training involves [questions like] is it compulsory, does it impact on compliance standards, and can we afford it? At this point in time, a lot of decisions that are in the mix today are impacted by finances.
>
> The resources to train our substitute staff. Our correctional officers are the most challenging to schedule for training. Because we operate twenty-four hours a day, three hundred sixty-five days of the year, we have two choices to make. To either substitute staff—there is a formula that gives you a certain number of persons to fill a roster, and substitute positions to cover people when they are off sick, on vacation, and on training, and then there is some other things. The real art of it is to—our budget is locked into those resources of substitute positions—and the key is to use them

wisely. Normally what happens is overtime budgets get out of whack due to operational things like disturbances, suicides, and things like that, and if you don't have an attendance management system in place, vacations hit and then you hit September, and you've overspent your budget, you still have your training to do, and you have to come clean. So it's a very management-intensive activity at the highest level.

Administrator 20: So I don't think there is a lack of training opportunities. Probably the greatest drawback to our training initiative is the resources attached to sending people to training. It costs money to send people to Cornwall, Ontario, i.e., CMLC, or to Vancouver for a week or two weeks of training. It means time away from the job, it means accommodation usually, travel costs, the costs associated with tuition, and so on, and quite frankly, I would say that CSC is not a rich organization in terms of being able to afford that kind of training. The opportunities are there, but whether or not we can take advantage of them for financial reasons is debatable.

One of the reasons that training is not a huge area of expense for CSC is exactly what I have just said. If the dollars for program delivery are tight, then we are going to invest the majority of those dollars in the delivery function because public safety depends more on that than on staff training. Staff training then becomes a "nice thing" to have rather than an "essential thing" to have. Having said that though, there are some training requirements in the organization that are essential—such as firearms and first aid training for example—so some things remain mandatory and you do those regardless of what they cost. However, once you get past the mandatory training, training drops off dramatically because of the financial implications.

Although there is a recognition among administrators that training is essential, what they describe as impediments to this are budget freezes or no budget increases and the cost of sending a worker to such training—costs associated with travel, accommodation, and providing backfill for that worker during the training period. Certainly, these are competing interests—the need for training versus the cost of training—which administrators must debate, continuously. In some cases, it is just this type of deliberation or debate that has provided the foundation for more discussions around the use of online training as a cost-effective measure to enhance performance abilities in staff. In its Strategic Plan for Human Resource Management, CSC states that there is a "recognized need for learning activities and [that] the demand from staff and bargaining agents exceeds the capacity of current CSC resources and structures for such activities" (CSC, 2007, p. 20).

Administrator 21: I'll also mention that another major area for us is emergency response team training. It impacts on our resources heavily because we have a lot of trainers that do the training. We have team leaders who get specialized training and we have a male team and we have a female team for female inmates, so from a management perspective it's a major challenge to fit that all in and get it done, be in compliance, and not spend a lot of money doing it.

Administrator 22: However, we also have to make commitments around budgets as well. Everyone is having fiscal problems, but we have made a decision to continue at all costs with the training. The first thing that sometimes is cut in this type of budget exercise is around training—do we really have to do the training now or can we put it off? If we put it off, it is our experience that it never is done. Therefore, we are encouraging the managers to incorporate the training plans right into the yearly budgets.

Administrator 23: Right now, for example, because of budget cutbacks the people at region who train our staff members up to deliver programs to offenders, they are not there. So our ability to deliver those programs, our ability to be trained in those programs, are diminishing. They are not there because of budget cuts—they have been reallocated out to the institutions.

Administrator 24: It's difficult. When you take away the vacation time, when you take away the two weeks at Christmas, the March break time. I have an assistant warden who is also a trainer at Cornwall. He's gone next week. All that impacts on getting work done at the institution. I guess the only way to describe it is you have to exercise self-discipline. You have to recognize the benefits of the training, realizing that you are not going to see the effects maybe for some time. But we've bitten the bullet and we sit down and we try to balance the operational side of things against the reality that people won't grow, managers won't grow, unless we send them off to undertake training.

The comments from Administrators 18 through 24 identify a number of challenges to meeting the training standards set by the CSC. Can you find some common themes between the challenges mentioned by various administrators?

Can you think of any innovative ways training might be done which would minimize these challenges?

Innovative Training Approaches

Many of the interviewees discussed a variety of innovative training approaches that are being explored to overcome the obstacles that prevent further management training.

Mentoring

Though it has not been implemented yet, mentoring programs for line staff coming right out of training into the institutional environment are currently being considered. Mentoring would be a peer support program to assist new staff with day-to-day issues they may be struggling with.

Self-Sufficient Training

A number of institutions have developed the capacity to conduct some training on site, reducing some of the costs. Some institutions are equipped with their own firing ranges and smoke houses. Others have trained staff who can conduct training in programs such as CPR.

Training Online

A number of positions in the CSC are career managed positions and an employee can go on the Internet and do self-study. Computer-based information and learning are more common and more available through the Service. The focus of most computer-based courses is on career advancement, so if someone coming up for a position in leadership or management wanted to know about roster management, he or she would be able to find a module on the topic online. At the same time, employees can also use computer-based training to increase their knowledge in a self-directed manner. Following the Arbour Inquiry, the CSC developed computer-based training that allows employees to test themselves on their knowledge. Interviewees, however, felt that many staff do not participate in online training because they feel that they are already overworked and do not have time.

Training: Measuring Effectiveness

As we have seen, the Correctional Service of Canada allocates time, money, and energy to training. But how does it know that its training is effective? Surprisingly, not much attention has been paid to formal evaluation of the training. Instead, its effectiveness seems to be evaluated through the day-to-day performance of staff duties:

Administrator 25: There are national training standards. Some standards are out of our control, like breathing apparatus. Canadian Standards Association and various acts impacting on that—*National Fire Safety Act* and various statutes and so on. We have to meet those standards in terms of equipment, the duration of the training, what the trainee has to show proficiency in. So do firearms. We would fall under the same scrutiny that a local police force, that the RCMP, that fisheries officers and conservation officers in terms of safe use of firearms.

So we are locked into a number of national training standards. How do we measure the results? Well, since I've been Warden nobody has been injured with a firearm, so our safety practices are effective. Use of force—there is a number of standards being measured. Did staff use the least amount of force? Were chemical agents properly deployed and utilized and so on? Every use of force is reviewed by the coordinator of operations, the deputy warden, the warden, Regional Headquarters, National Headquarters and the Office of the Correctional Investigator does sampling. So we have a lot of people reviewing our work, and if we see deficiencies then normally the approach is to correct those deficiencies through training or retraining. That's normally how we operate. I can't say that we have a formalized process in place for evaluation but that communication feedback link is there. That's one element of our training.

Administrator 26: In terms of how effectiveness is measured, there has been some discussion inside of CSC as to how to do such evaluations. I'm an advocate of evaluation myself and have suggested it in the past, but generally it doesn't happen. That is, we deliver the training, and based on the individuals' participation and completion of the training, we issue a certificate that says they have successfully completed the program. Of course, the degree of success differs from individual to individual, and some individuals will complete that training and be outstanding in their field and others will complete it and will definitely need to go back a second and third time and will struggle even after that. The problem is that we don't have a system in place that measures that at the time of the training. The proof I guess comes out later, when people actually report to their jobs, start performing their duties, and then we find out later that there are performance issues and so that's the, I would say, measurement process. The effectiveness of our training is in the performance of the duties. Now I should be careful, because in the COTP I am sure they do have tests and people have to pass at a certain level in order to qualify. They have to pass the firearms, self-defence, and they have to pass a number of other elements in order to become a correctional officer. Few people fail, but it happens. They have to pass some fitness requirements as well. But that's probably the only area where we have a built in assessment at the time of the training. All the other training is considered successful if the individual attends and completes all course requirements.

Although the importance of formal testing is discussed in these interviews, the importance of performance or application of newly learned skills is seen as another important measure of evaluating training programs. These measurements can be obtained through a formal performance evaluation done by management or by researchers, but it can also be done through self-directed performance evaluations. All of these methods have advantages and disadvantages.

Administrator 27: We do not do a lot of evaluations either at the national, regional, or even at the local level. We really don't. There is a small amount of it but.... The system actually begs for it at one level. If the manager is sending people away for the good and proper reasons that the course is for as opposed to a perk or time-out or that kind of thing, all of which have value—it is the degree of value that I'm talking about.

The other system that we have is through the appraisal process, where let's say an issue is identified—a weakness or a skill set that is required that we can then identify clearly and then have someone go on. If you do that properly, you would then evaluate at your next performance appraisal as to its effectiveness.

Administrator 28: I would say that each course probably has its own evaluation. I will use my self as an example. When I took crisis management, there is a test at the end; you have to reach a certain percentage to pass. So some of those have that in it but it depends on the type of course. So there may be some that are just knowledge and information, non-CO orientation, its orientation to the service, you evaluate the course content, the deliverers, that sort of thing. You are not going to see a test at the end to see if you know enough. So each, depending on the type of training you are going on, will have its own evaluation.

As a service accountable to the public, we certainly have a number of mechanisms in place to ensure that we are measuring our own performance on a number of issues. We compile statistics on several things. Some of the training is compulsory training for fire regulations or occupational health and safety regulations, or other policies that are outside of CSC but just within the public service or Canadian requirements like the Labour Code. So training does change when training needs to change. Certainly, with the introduction of the new Labour Code mainly about two years ago that became a huge purpose to make sure that we are at one hundred percent compliance in that mandatory training element. So there are different evaluation formats a lot of the times, depending on what the purpose of the training is for.

Administrator 29: As far as the measuring of the effectiveness of our training or programs, I think they have used people in research and how that works, for example, is a training may have been offered in 2001, and in 2002 or 2003 these research people may come around with a questionnaire and ask how the training has been effective in your area, etc. So for example, if you train in Cornwall, it will be that College who will do the follow-up and see how the skills you have learned have been effective. For example, in the firearms training staff are trained in the use of force, and if this is effective then our results will be better in our use of force reviews. Also, by debriefing you get some feedback from students and also, from the line staff, who are out there dealing with the inmates, provide excellent feedback as well, because the staff here at region are not the experts in the field any more—we are somewhat removed. Therefore, myself and the wardens will meet with all of the IERT and negotiator leaders on a quarterly basis and that gives them the opportunity to provide input into how effective the training has been and what types of skills the various teams require.

As indicated by the above comments from administrators, a formalized evaluation approach does not really exist within the CSC to evaluate the effectiveness of their training. Can you think of key elements that should be included in a comprehensive evaluation of the training offered within the CSC?

Retaining Staff

Organizational experts believe that staff commitment is an important ingredient to organizational success. Research has found that highly committed staff possess a variety of desirable characteristics that enhance the organization's ability to achieve its goals. For instance, highly committed staff are high performers, more involved in their jobs, and less likely to want to leave their organizations for new jobs. They also have less absenteeism, a high motivation to perform well at their work, and high job satisfaction. In 2000, Ole Ingstrup stated that most importantly, we need to encourage our staff. Encourage is a wonderful word that comes from the French *coeur*, which means heart, *en* which means put into. Put our hearts into it. Find staff doing things right, celebrate success, set a good example, encourage. Set the mission, build character. (Ole Ingstrup, *Making Ethics Work*)

The 1996 CSC All Staff Survey found a link between aspiration and staff commitment. Commitment was defined as the strength of an individual's identification with his or her work organization (Robinson, Simourd, and Porporino, 1991). Research also shows that opportunities to work in a variety of settings maintain employees' motivation and investment in their jobs (Riley and Wilder, 2002). The 1992 CSC Staff Commitment Survey found that the CSC's workforce was eager to be exposed to different types of work within the organization and wanted to have more opportunity to act in a variety of positions.

We know that job satisfaction is a major factor in retaining staff, and the 1994 and 1996 CSC all-staff surveys had some interesting findings:

A result that was highly consistent across the two survey periods concerns the dissatisfaction of correctional officers relative to other employees. In contrast, the next largest front-line group, case management officers, were relatively positive on most organizational domains and showed approval for the major objectives of the Service. However, on the vast majority of survey targets, correctional officers express the greatest degree of unhappiness and often only a slim majority expressed views that were supportive of the corporate objectives of the Service. For example, on attitudinal dimensions related to reintegration activities, correctional officers exhibit a need to develop greater appreciation for the importance of rehabilitation and empathy for offenders. Again, the relative differences between correctional officers and other occupational groups was a major finding of the first survey conducted in 1994. (*Making Ethics Work*)

In the 2005 Public Service Employee Survey, 92% of CSC staff surveyed stated that they were strongly committed to making their organization successful, but only 65% felt that the organization treats them with respect. In addition, 63% of CSC staff felt their organization was a good place to work, compared with 84% of staff in other organizations and agencies.

The 2005 Public Service Employee Survey identified three major areas of concern for CSC: harassment, employee grievances, and respect, trust, and accountability. To respond to these areas of concern, CSC co-developed an action plan with its six bargaining agents. Numerous actions are suggested in the plan, including increased training and awareness, clarifying roles and responsibilities, monitoring processes and trends, and improving communications across all levels. It is hoped that these actions will create a better work environment within CSC (CSC, 2007). Overall, the correctional administrators expressed fairly high job satisfaction.

Administrator 30: To the greatest degree, I have high job satisfaction. I love what I do and wouldn't want to do anything else. I've been doing this particular job for many years now and I will retire doing this unless they ask me to move on. But I love my job in programming, because I believe that even more than case management, programming is the heart of corrections. Case management doesn't change people—it's the process which manages change. It's programming, correctional interventions, relationships, and role modelling that changes people, and part of that comes from case management, from chaplaincy, from Aboriginal spirituality, from management, from inmate committees, from correctional officers and their day to day interactions with inmates. Nevertheless, the greatest tool, the most significant agent of change, is a program intervention. Why would I want to be involved in anything else? It is at the core of corrections and it is exciting because it is dynamic—growing, changing, improving, we succeed, we fail, we alter.

There are, however, instances where I get frustrated, overwhelmed, or extremely tired because there is so much to do. The longer you work at this job and the more experienced you become, you cannot help but see how very much more there is still left to do ... things you could be doing, but you don't do because you have a whole pile of other things you need to do first. That's what I mean about being frustrated, because you sit here and talk to your team about all of the things you would like to do and you realize you probably won't get to it in your career because sometimes it's hard enough to manage the day-to-day stuff. I think that's partly a resource issue—we don't have sufficient people and yet others may say we are too "rich." However, there aren't enough people to do all of the things that we could be doing. We don't even have sufficient people to deliver all of the programs we need to deliver to offenders. Offenders are being held up on their release date, which is not the end of the world, but they are being held up in part because we do not have enough programming resources.

Certainly the work load is incredible. I can work seven or eight sixty-hour weeks in a row, and at the end of it be no further ahead than when I went in to it. Or I can work weekend after weekend, and feel exhausted at the end of that, and then realize that I have the same eight projects on my desk that I had several weeks ago. Lots of time it's hard to get things done in this organization; there is a lot of bureaucracy and so on. But having said all of that, at the heart of my work I have a tremendous sense that what I am doing makes a difference and that I love what I do. I just don't love doing as much of it as I do, in such a short time frame, with so much pressure and such limited resources.

I think if you were to ask most people who are still in corrections and have been here for more than a year or two, for the most part they will tell you they are here because to a large degree they believe it is a good field to be in and they think it makes a difference, especially on the reintegration side of the house—maybe not so much in security, although I am not sure. They may also tell you that as much as they might see it in a very positive light, there are lots of things they would like to change such as the workload, stress, pressures, the time frames, etc. But there are also many rewards. Our recidivism rates are the lowest in the world, programs are really working, and offenders are changing. We are not foolish nor arrogant enough to believe that everyone who makes changes and becomes a law abiding citizen does so simply because of our programs—we provide effective interventions but there are many other factors to be taken into consideration. So programming might be the primary change factor or it might be the least influential one.

Once in a while policies may come out and you shake your head and wonder where the organization is going, why is it doing that, but you also know that some of it is driven by political issues or media attention or public reaction; sometimes it is driven by finances or even sometimes, by a lack of insight. Bureaucracy is an issue; sometimes it takes a long time to get something done. I have to admit that having worked at region now for around nineteen years, I enjoy the "regional" experience over the institutional experience. As much as working in the institutions or out in the community working with the offender are at the root of corrections, I always found it frustrating because your degree of impact or your capacity to impact on the operation is very minimal because you are so caught up in the day-to-day expectations. At RHQ I feel that I have accomplished considerably more than what I would have accomplished over this period of time in the institutions—almost every day here, you accomplish something which makes a difference. At the sites, sometimes you can go for weeks feeling like all you are doing is putting out fires, and although that is accomplishing something, it isn't really moving the agenda forward—it's really only keeping it stable. So, I myself have high job satisfaction in this role, but at times it is tempered by all of these things I have mentioned.

There has been an abundance of research done about the value of job satisfaction in relation to job performance. Organizations like CSC need to respond creatively to market force. For example, the whole issue related to succession planning and the aging out of the current leadership level means that for many organizations, organizational knowledge may vanish or become weakened. Another issue to be concerned about is employee drop out, seen in organizations that do not provide competitive rates and benefits, but more importantly do not provide a comfortable and positive work environment. One of the ways to enhance job satisfaction is to create an atmosphere where employees are motivated to come up with new and better ways of working and have a willingness to voice and discuss innovative ideas. Motivation and willingness are associated with both job satisfaction and morale, thereby enhancing cultural cohesiveness and somewhat ensuring the continuity of the organization itself.

Administrator 31: I have professed to a lot of people for a number of years that I like my job, but if I won the million dollars tomorrow, or half a million dollars tomorrow, would I work? I don't think so, but it doesn't have so much to do with job satisfaction as the fact that I would like to do something with my life. I've been doing this for a long time. On any given day I'm thankful that I've got the job that I've got. I like it. I like the fact that I can influence things, I like what I do, I like generally who I do it with throughout the system from here to Ottawa. So for me, I would have to say high level of satisfaction. I find meaning in what I do, I find it requires more intelligence than I have, more energy than I have. I mean, I could work twenty-four hours a day, seven days a week—there are so many things to do. I am lucky because I get out and about. I get to engage people. So I feel very fortunate. I mean, it has its frustrations, but I tend to take myself too seriously and the job too seriously. I would say overall in the course of a day I can go the full gamut, but generally I am happy that I have this job.

Administrator 32: I have high job satisfaction and again, I honestly believe that we are doing the right thing by slow and gradual reintegration. That's not to say that some offenders should never be released; I'm also a believer in that because there are some that will reoffend in the worst possible manner. They will kill again. I've seen corrections evolve too and it's an ever evolving thing, so maybe in ten years we will have something different and better, I don't know. But we are achieving what we should be achieving, and to me, you have to maintain some hope in everybody. I've been a Pollyanna all my life! My cup is half full and I have to reinforce that with the staff and the women here—that there is a better life for them out there and they have to make choices, and we are hoping that they will be making the choices that will be law abiding, and to provide them with the tools and the assistance and the encouragement to want to have both feet outside.

Administrator 33: Very high job satisfaction. I think we are going in the right direction. I think some of the things that CSC is doing is making a difference in making sure that the public is safe and that the inmates that we have under our care do return in. So I believe in that, so my job satisfaction is very high.

Administrator 34: I have high job satisfaction. At my level, there is lots of ability to do things using my expertise with a certain level of autonomy and some accountability. I have some freedom in decision-making within reasonable limits. My length of employment probably has something to do with my ability to fit into this position as well. The downside of my job is that, for example, technology, i.e., e-mail has just overwhelmed the current workload and consumed a great deal of time. In other words, there is a technology jam. We can't do what we want to because it's impossible to sift through and prioritize information without it becoming very time consuming. This also leads to a breakdown in the ability to communicate with one another and to problem solve. Sometimes it ends up being an exercise of "passing the buck."

Administrator 35: I love my job even though it is incredibly busy. I'm learning something every day and I think that's what makes it exciting in this business. We have compassion for what we do—we work with very difficult people, but they are people. And they are people who are going to be, potentially, living next door to me, so I can either ignore that or work with it. I think the amount of information that we have at our fingertips to evolve in that portfolio is just amazing.

Administrator 36: I have high job satisfaction and I am the type of person who would never stay in a job if I did not like it. I like this job. I get the chance to mentor and train young people, to espouse some of my values, and to have a part in the overall guidance of the system, so I have a passion for what I do. In this kind of environment right now, corporately, it seems to be in some ways going back to more of ministerial concerns, public sentiment, etc., and that seems to be swaying things a bit. We need to have people who are going to be able to keep corrections in the middle. So I like my job, I have a belief in the system, and I think that we have the best system in the world and people are coming from all over the world to look at it.

As mentioned above, the 1994 and 1996 CSC All Staff Surveys and the 2002 and 2005 Public Employee Surveys found that the correctional officers express the greatest degree of unhappiness and often only a slim majority expressed views that were supportive of the corporate objectives of the Service. How does this finding differ from the level of job satisfaction expressed by the administrators in the above comments? Can you think of some factors or influences that might offer some explanation as to the difference in job satisfaction between correctional officers and administrators?

Succession Planning

As we read earlier, more than 40% of CSC's staff could leave within the next 3-year period, the majority coming from the senior management levels (CSC Review Panel, 2007). This potential for a mass exodus will not end anytime soon in CSC, as 46.1% of all employees are currently 45+ years old and 30% are 50+ (CSC, 2007). To address this increase in departures, CSC has implemented succession planning programs across the organization. They identify individuals in the Service who are seen as future leaders and mentor them, with current management able to give them hands-on training while the experienced manager is still available to answer questions and teach. In theory, succession planning makes a lot of sense. However, the correctional administrators interviewed felt that in practice, succession planning in the CSC is falling short of its mark.

Administrator 37: We've tried to develop succession planning programs where we identify individuals as future leaders and we've had some success. One of the problems is when the finances get tight, you end up going back to the basics and only the things that you have to do. If succession planning is to be successful, we have to believe that—we have to put our money where our mouth is and we have to say, "okay, so and so you see as developing into a good deputy warden." Once they go through a certain level of training and pass a certain level of competencies in certain areas, then succession planning is very simple. If we want succession planning to be successful, particularly at the positions of the warden and deputy warden and assistant warden, we have to put resources in and say that for the next year, if you have been identified as a potential deputy warden, that you work with the deputy warden for a year and live and breath and do all the other stuff and learn in an apprenticeship style. That's how you do it. It's not complicated. We think it is going to happen through osmosis.

Administrator 38: The other one is our human resource practices. If we look at our region, there is quite a few of the managers that are in my age group and there is so much opportunity here now with the technology and those type of things. We have a lot of young people. There is going to be a gap there in getting the people that have the historical information. People are more mobile. In our region, I did all my career within a twenty mile radius, so I bring a historical agenda that is sometimes helpful, and sometimes people would say that it limits my vision, but you can't buy that. The managers coming in, some of them would have extremely good managerial skills but wouldn't have the experience that goes with that. So I think CSC has to put some effort into managing and ensuring that the people who are coming into those managerial positions get the appropriate training and succession opportunities. So you need to try and identify your younger staff who are interested in careers in a specific area and you use a mentoring system.

We have some extremely good people, but in times of restraint and those types of things it makes it very difficult for me to have someone to follow me for five or six months so that I am able to mentor. It doesn't have to be coexistence. You could identify a couple of senior managers that those people could call or approach when they are experiencing difficulty doing their job. I could from here, say, identify someone in another part of the region and weekly or monthly conference call with the person anytime that he or she is faced with an issue and consult. When we started doing that with some of the wardens, I think it works because you feel alone. When I came here I felt alone. I had quite a few years in parole so I knew that topic quite a bit but at my level I am the only one—the expert—so you look around and where are you going to get some advice?

Succession planning is an important step in ensuring that high potential candidates have the training and development that gives them skills and competencies needed for successful CSC operations. Such planning does not exist in isolation and must reflect CSC's strategic objective and goals. In addition to this, succession planning must involve senior management and should involve an overall organizational commitment rather than being labelled as just a human resources exercise.

Administrator 39: We are doing an analysis of certain employee groups—feeder groups, etc. Who is leaving and what does that mean for hiring strategies—external /internal postings. Mentoring an issue—very difficult to formalize and it is much easier when relationships develop between the staff. We supply an orientation checklist to each staff to foster rapport building and clarification through stating what the objectives of the function are, the basis for performance appraisals, housekeeping, etc. However, we are faced with a loss of history through the "greying of the Public Service." And the losing of this history forces people to ask the questions again and to view the answers.

Administrator 40: One of the areas I am watching, because of my age—being on the younger side—is the generation gap between our managers and those out in the field, and how we are going to manage that in the next few years because of the different philosophies of how we approach work and being in the workplace. The whole commitment of healthy work environment and what the Generation Xers perceive as being important in their lives versus what some historical generations have demanded in their work environment.

The concept of succession planning holds a lot of merit, particularly with the large percentage of CSC staff eligible to retire in the near future. Several barriers to successfully implementing succession planning are identified above by administrators. How could the CSC make succession planning more feasible and achievable?

Conclusion

This chapter has examined human resource management in the Correctional Service of Canada. Human resource management begins with recruiting the right staff with the "right stuff." Good recruiting lays the foundation for a workforce that will implement the mission statement and core values of the CSC, and training fosters and develops their skills, attitudes, and values. There are many challenges that slow or stop the implementation of all the training programs that have been developed by the CSC, the most common being budgetary constraints and time. Surprisingly, not much focus has been placed on formal evaluation of the training. Instead, its effectiveness seems to be evaluated through the day-to-day performance of staff. Once staff have been recruited and trained, retaining them is key to maintaining a strong and effective workforce. Without a focus on staff retention, all the efforts that have gone into recruiting and training are wasted. Staff who express high job satisfaction are more likely to remain with CSC and have a positive impact on the work environment. Finally, since a large percentage of the current workforce will retire in the near future, succession planning is becoming increasingly important to ensure the continued focus on the mission of the Correctional Service of Canada.

Human resource management in the Correctional Service of Canada is a time consuming and daunting task. However, in recognizing the key function that staff play in implementing the mission statement and core values of the CSC in practice, human resource management remains an area in need of great attention and focus.

Study Questions

1. Why is succession planning so important in the Correctional Service of Canada? Design a succession planning program for the Correctional Service of Canada which would be inexpensive to implement.
2. Pick a position in the Correctional Service of Canada. Discuss the characteristics and core competencies required by someone in this position.
3. You are responsible for training within the Correctional Service of Canada. Design an evaluation framework to assess the effectiveness of your training program.

Bibliography

*Items with asterisks are also suggested readings for this chapter.

Correctional Service of Canada (2002). *Performance Report for the Correctional Service* of Canada (CSC) for the period ending March 31, 2002. http://www.csc-scc.gc.ca/text/pblct/dpr/2002/section_2_departmental_performance_e.shtml

Correctional Service of Canada (2002). *Report of the Task Force on Security.* http://www.csc-scc.gc.ca/text/pblct/security/toce_e.shtml

*Correctional Service of Canada (2006). *Departmental Performance Report for the* Correctional Service of Canada (CSC) for the period ending March 31, 2006. http://www.tbs-sct.gc.ca/dpr-rmr/0506/CSC-SCC/csc-scc04_e.asp#_3_2

Correctional Service of Canada (2007). *2007–2008 Estimates: Report on Plans and* Priorities. http://www.tbs-sct.gc.ca/rpp/0708/csc-scc/csc-scc_e.pdf

Correctional Service of Canada (2007b). Strategic Plan for Human Resources.http://www.csc-scc.gc.ca/text/pblct/sphrm07_10/StrPlaHRMn_e.pdf

CSC Review Panel (2007). A Roadmap to Strengthening Public Safety. http://www.ps-sp.gc.ca/csc-scc/report-rapport/table_of_contents-eng.aspx

Instrup, O. (2000). *Making Ethics Work*. Remarks at the American Correctional Association Meeting. San Antonio, Texas. http://www.csc-scc.gc.ca/text/media/spchscommis/2000/00-08-15-eng.shtml

*Johnson, T. (1995). Stressing the value of targeted recruitment in corrections. *Corrections Today*, 57(3), 96–100.

*Lariviere, M. (2002). Antecedents and outcomes of correctional officers' attitudes towards federal inmates: An exploration of person-organization fit. *Forum*, 14(1), 19–23.

*Riley III, F. E. and Wilder, B. A. (2002). Hiring correctional staff with the right stuff. *Corrections Today*, 64(3), 88–92.

Robinson, D., Lefaive, P., and Muirhead, M. (1997). *Results of the 1996 CSC Staff Survey: A Synopsis*. Research Branch Correctional Service of Canada. http://www.csc-scc/gc/ca/text/rsrch/briefs/b17/b17e-eng.shtml

Robinson, D., Simourd, L., and Porporino, F. (1992). *Staff Commitment in the Correctional Service of Canada*. Ottawa: Research and Statistics Branch, Correctional Service of Canada. http://www.csc-scc.gc.ca/text/rsrch/reports/r21/r21e_e.shtml

*Robinson, D., Simourd, L., and Porporino, F. (1991). *Background to Staff Commitment_Research project*. Ottawa: Research and Statistics Branch, Correctional Service of Canada.

Treasury Board of Canada Employment Equity Division (2000). Employment Equity Division Homepage.http://www.hrma-agrh.gc.ca/ee/index_e.asp

8 Financial Resource Management in Corrections

In Chapter 4 we discussed how the Correctional Service of Canada has been influenced by current management and organizational theories and how the changes made have led to a system that is more open and participatory. The cost of this kind of management system is generally justified by the argument that the allocation of resources supports the goals and mission of the organization. Since the Correctional Service of Canada is a public service organization, it is accountable for its spending to the Canadian public and must be able to show that it both allocates its budget in a way that follows the mission of the CSC and recognizes the political and social realities in which it operates.

In this chapter we will first examine two different approaches to budgeting—line item budgeting and budgeting by objective—to consider which approach best fits with the management of the CSC. Then we will explore the budget in relation to the CSC's corporate objectives and related strategic outcomes and explore budget allocation and accountability within the CSC. Finally, we will look at how budgeting affects programming and planning from the point of view of correctional administrators.

Approaches to Budgeting

Ekstedt and Jackson (1996) define budget systems as "programs organized in order to access and monitor the resources needed to do the work. Budgets essentially do two things: (1) they are used to acquire resources; and (2) they are used to administer resources" (p. 162). Budgets are also used as planning documents and can be viewed as the blueprint for the allocation of funds (Jefferson, 1995). There are basically two ways of budgeting: line item budgeting and budgeting by objective.

Line item budgeting is the traditional and authoritarian approach; in it, "various elements of the operation are organized into individual categories (lines) of expenditures (sometimes called codes). In budgeting by line item, there is nothing detailed about any of the categories with regard to specific programs" (Ekstedt and Jackson, 1996, p. 163). For example, for the line of care and custody, the codes could include security, accommodation, health care, etc. Monies are either added to or subtracted from the previous year's budget lines, with little explanation of the reason for the existence of each line except that it had been funded the year before (Anderson, 1998). This method has been criticized because it gives no details about the services being provided, the policies in place, or the performance expectations for the coming year, and it merely maintains the status quo (Spicer, as cited in Jefferson, 1995).

On the other hand, budgeting by objective, using either a zero-based or planned program budgeting system, is intended to promote change (Ekstedt and Jackson, 1996). In zero-based budgeting, administrators build their budget from scratch each year, reviewing each area of the budget to justify costs or make changes. This yearly exercise "enables one to evaluate and allocate resources effectively and efficiently as well as providing one with the capability to identify, evaluate and communicate activities being pursued and alternatives under construction" (Jefferson, 1995, p. 2). Critics of zero-based budgeting stress the time it takes and note that it ignores the reality of political influence on budgets (Anderson, 1998). Planned program budgeting system is similar to zero-based budgeting, except that it assumes that there are certain elements in the budget that do not change from year to year and therefore do not need to be reviewed. However, like zero-based budgeting, planned program budgeting is a planning tool to address inputs and outputs, unlike line item budgeting, which is merely an accounting tool (Jefferson, 1995).

McKenzie (as quoted in Jefferson, 1995) argues that to develop an accurate budget, three sets of information bases are needed:

1. Information that allows the impact of policies to be monitored and evaluated;
2. Information that assist [national] goals and broad accountability requirements to be met; and
3. Information about [correctional] indicators used. (p. 33)

These information bases would be part of budgeting by objectives, but they would not be necessary for line item budgeting. Using such information bases fits better with the theory of organizational development and the management style now being used by the Correctional Service of Canada. Under a more participatory system, resource allocation is based on the goals and mission of the organization.

Several correctional administrators commented on CSC's shift from line budgeting to planned program budgeting:

Administrator 1: Well right now, half of our budget is applied against historical data. We are in the process of identifying resource indicators. Once we have resource indicators that have been approved, which would be based on inmate needs, once you identify a need in sex offenders you would apply the resource indicator against that and you would be getting your resources through that. In some of the fields we have that. We went to Treasury Board and got some money based on resource indicators. In Education, as an example, we don't have resource indicators so we look at previous years' expenditures, with the cost of living adjustment for contracts and those types of things, and the budget is adjusted accordingly. But the long term plan would be to have resource indicators for all the line programs that we are responsible for. So if your population needs vary, your budget allocation—your need—would shift, so your budget allocation would shift.

Budgets are allocated on a yearly basis by program. So I have a package for each operational unit and a package for each program. So in substance abuse I have my substance abuse budget—a sheet which shows how much I keep here, how much goes to each operational unit. I look at an operational unit, how much there is for substance abuse, sex offender—so I've got it both ways and I review that. It is not going to vary much because substance abuse—we know about seventy percent of the offenders have, need, some type of intervention, whether it is high intensity intervention, moderate, or low once we determine that. So it is pretty set and it is not going to vary much. All of a sudden if there is a quick shift, say more sex offenders, then we will be budget for it.

Administrator 2: In recent years, we have been resourced through what are called financial indicators. That process attempts to say that if you have a hundred inmates being admitted each month, you should have so many alcohol and drug officers, so many reception officers, and so forth. That process is about ninety-five percent accurate. Because we assess inmates at intake, we've captured over the years what their programming needs are. So we can fairly accurately say we need so many substance abuse programs seats, we need so many anger management seats, we need so many sex offender seats, so many violent offender seats, and that's how we get resourced.

It's also created an environment that there is little discretionary spending. We have a food services menu that says we should be able to feed inmates for four dollars, ten cents per person per day. So if you have a hundred inmates, you are resourced accordingly. There is no discretion for me to add or deplete from that, to take away from that budget. All our budgets are kind of set up in that way now. So they are distinct depending on what area.

In addition to the lack of discretionary spending due to resourcing through financial indicators, Administrator 3 suggests some other challenges with this type of budgeting:

Administrator 3: CSC has moved to, over the last couple of years, to what they call an A-base distribution of resources. "A-base" means going basically to ground zero and saying we need to perform this particular function—what are the staffing requirements, what are the operational requirements, equipment requirements, etc.? And building the budget basically from the ground up, this is sometimes referred to as zero-based budgeting. We did this using what we call resourcing indicators meaning that in order, for example, for an RHQ programs division to exist, what positions do you need to have, what people do you need to have, to carry out the functions related to programming? Well, it was determined that we need an RACP, we need clerical positions and we need someone to manage these specialized program functions—e.g., the substance abuse—and so source indicators are developed based on a functional analysis. That's been done in each of the areas, i.e., health care, security, case management, and so on. Then salary dollars are attached to those positions, as well as operating and maintenance dollars are also attached to those FTE's (full time equivalent). Ultimately, a total budget is arrived at for each functional area. Ottawa distributes money to the regions as the money comes from Treasury Board using resourcing formulas, and it's an attempt at creating an even playing field. It's an attempt at equitable resourcing inasmuch as, if every region needs an RACP, and needs four managers to manage these particular programs, and needs a program officer for every thirty inmates, then everyone will be funded, proportionately.

The bigger regions will get more money because they have more offenders requiring more delivery staff, while the smaller regions will get fewer. There are also, of course, economies of scale associated with manager positions. You don't get two extra managers just because your population is three times larger than someone else's region—you probably work a bit harder, but you get the same, single manager to manage that portfolio because the issues are the same everywhere; you are just dealing with more people, which does not necessarily imply the need for an extra position. We are technically supposed to be resourced regionally on a fairly equitable basis, and to the largest degree, I suppose that is true. When you do a detailed analysis you do find there are some unusual discrepancies, i.e., one region is getting twice the funding for violent offender programming than they should but only one-half of what they should be getting for substance abuse programming, while the other region is getting more in substance abuse and only half of what it should be getting for violent offender programming. When it's all averaged out it is much closer, but in particular areas there are sometimes anomalies, which make you raise your eyebrows wondering how they decided on those numbers. There are ongoing efforts nationally and regionally to identify those anomalies and to provide solutions to them by providing more stable resourcing indicators and levels. I think CSC is working hard to develop a fair budget distribution system, but we are not there yet.

Clearly, the Correctional Service of Canada is shifting its budgetary approach from line item to budgeting by objectives, but has not yet fully completed the transition. A number of anomalies still exist that impact CSC's ability to fully budget by objectives. How do you think Administrators 1 to 3 would respond to the question of whether line item budgeting or budgeting by objectives is a better fit for the CSC? Can you find examples in their comments which would support these responses?

The Correctional Service of Canada's Budget

In 2004, the average annual cost of incarcerating an inmate in a federal institution was $110,223 for men (maximum security), $71,640 for men (medium security), $74,431 for men (minimum security), and $150,867 for women (multi-level security). The cost of incarcerating women is much higher because there are fewer of them while there is also a legal requirement to provide service and program equity (Correctional Service of Canada, 2005). To supervise offenders on parole or statutory release, the average annual cost is approximately $19,755 per offender.

In 2005–2006, the budget for the Correctional Service of Canada was $1.597 billion. This funding supports a workforce of almost 15,500 staff and contractors at more than 200 sites across Canada, 365 days a year. At the end of fiscal 2005–2006, CSC was responsible for:

approximately 12,700 federally incarcerated offenders (excluding 1,200 offenders temporarily detained while on conditional release to the community) and 6,800 offenders actively supervised in the community. Over the course of the year, including all admissions and releases, CSC managed a flow-through of 25,500 different offenders. (Correctional Service of Canada, 2007)

According to the Correctional Service of Canada's Departmental Performance Report, in 2005–2006, Parliament approved the CSC budget of $1,597,238,000 in the Main Estimates (CSC Departmental Performance Report, 2006). The budget can be divided up in a number of different ways:

Table 8.1. Correctional Service of Canada—Budget by Main Elements

Main Elements	$M	%
Salaries	808.0	50.6
Employee Benefits Plan	162.6	10.2
Operating	488.4	30.6
Capital	138.2	8.6
TOTAL	1,597.2	

Source: CSC Departmental Performance Report, 2006

Table 8.2. Correctional Service of Canada—Budget by Planning Element

Planning Element	$M	%
Security	565.2	35.4
Health Care	117.4	7.3
Institutional Services	108.0	6.8
Accommodation Services	362.7	22.7
Case Management	254.6	15.9
Program Development	162.4	10.2
Inmate Pay	26.9	1.7
TOTAL	1,597.2	

Source: CSC Departmental Performance Report, 2006

Table 8.3. Correctional Service of Canada—Budget by Program Activity

Program Activity	$M	%
Care and Custody	1,153.3	72.2
Rehabilitation and Case Management	443.9	27.8
TOTAL	1,597.2	

Source: CSC Departmental Performance Report, 2006

According to the 2005–2006 Departmental Performance Report, the Correctional Service of Canada is facing a number of financial challenges, most of which are out of their control, including:

- Salary costs have increased from 54–65% over the past 11 years as a result of inflation and new collective agreements with key operational staff.
- 90% of CSC's expenditures are non-discretionary (e.g., salaries, utilities, food, medical services) and are driven by factors beyond CSC's direct control (e.g., inflation, price fluctuations, new employee contracts). This leaves very limited flexibility for policy and program modifications, or investments that could yield longer-term results.
- The basic maintenance requirements of CSC's institutions—CSC's nearly 200 sites have facilities dating from the early 1800s up to the present, with the majority being over 40 years old. In order to manage shortfalls in capital and operations, CSC has had to routinely delay basic maintenance in recent years. As a result, what were once routine maintenance items are now emergency maintenance issues.
- Many older facilities require updated security equipment to continue to ensure the safety and security of staff, the public, and offenders.

In 2005, five priorities were established in response to the changing offender profile, the focus on public safety, and the new Government's emphasis on crime prevention:

- Safe transition of eligible offenders into the community;
- Safety and security for staff and offenders in our institutions;
- Enhanced capacities to provide effective interventions for First Nations, Métis, and Inuit offenders;
- Improved capacities to address mental health needs of offenders; and
- Strengthened management practices. (Correctional Service of Canada, 2006)

Table 8.4 from CSC's Performance Report (March 2006) aligns the above strategic priorities to the program activities and provides financial resources information by program activity.

Table 8.4. Correctional Service of Canada Strategic Priorities

STRATEGIC OUTCOME: Offenders are safely and effectively accommodated and reintegrated into Canadian communities with due regard to public safety					
PAA Program Activity Expected Results	**Type**	**Departmental Priority**	**CSC Budget Base ($ Millions)**		
			2007-08	2008-09	2009-10
Care and Custody Expected Result: Reasonable, safe secure and humane custody	Ongoing	**Safety and Security in Institutions** Safety and security for staff and offenders in our institutions **Community Transition** Safe transition of eligible offenders into the community **Mental Health** Improved capacities to address mental health needs of offenders	1256.7	1288.2	1321.1
Rehabilitation and Case Management Expected Result: Safe reintegration to the community consistent with the law	Ongoing	**Community Transition** Safe transition of eligible offenders into the community **Aboriginal Offenders** Enhanced capacities to provide effective interventions for First Nations, Métis, and Inuit offenders	452.2	443.3	444.5
CORCAN Expected Result: Assisting in the safe reintegration of offenders by providing employment and employability skills	Ongoing	**Community Transition** Safe transition of eligible offenders into the community	0.0*	0.0*	0.0*
Corporate Services Expected Result: Direction and support so that offenders are safely and effectively accommodated and reintegrated into the community	Ongoing	**Management** Strengthened Management Practices	161.1	163.2	163.8
		TOTAL	1,870.0	1,894.7	1,929.4

Note: CORCAN operates as a revolving fund. The expenses of $77.5M are offset by the revenues of $77.5M and, as a consequence, the net impact on financial resources is nil. Source: CSC Departmental Performance Report, 2006

In addition to budgeting by strategic objectives, costs for corrections are also divided between capital costs and operational costs. Capital costs are "one time only" expenditures for specific items, such as building repair, upgrades, or replacement, whereas operational costs are ongoing costs for the continuing operation—such things as personnel, programs, hydro, and training. CSC reported that in 2005–2006, the total expenditures for CSC was $1,597.2 million, with $162.6M spent on contributions to the employee benefits plan, $138.2M on capital expenditures, and $1,296.4M on operating costs. Dividing the budget in this way gives a basis for evaluating how resource allocation impacts the purpose of CSC, either positively or negatively.

Budget Allocation

Once the Correctional Service of Canada receives approval for its budget through the estimates process, it is allocated regionally using financial indicators. This process is not without its flaws, as outlined by various correctional administrators:

Administrator 4: Our budgets are allocated on what happened last year. How much you spent or how much you didn't spend is one way we do it. We also do it according to workload formulas. Then we have the mother of all things called the financial review, which put together some—I mean depending on where you are, you would defend this or be aggressive about this—either aggressively defend it or aggressively tear it down. There were too many arbitrary allotments in it. This is something that they did once, and try as we might, we can't get them to undo. It was done from the perspective, from my view—though they had a lot of us in, and consulted with us and all this kind of stuff, and in the end they just went "we will do it this way"—and it was done by financial people and financial people can crunch the numbers. At their level it makes sense; what they are doing makes sense but they don't allow for sick leave, they don't allow for vacations, they don't allow for human factors, like some days I'm more energetic than other days. Some days, of course, the staff are more energetic than other days. And it doesn't allow for that kind of thing. There is not enough of a safety valve within it, so that you are constantly behind. We are constantly trying to figure out, what the hell am I going to do? How am I going to do this? Because it is literally an impossible task to do. So any of the nice things or the things even that we should be doing, we are not doing. I can't afford to hold a management meeting, a face-to-face management meeting, right now ... and there is reasons for this. There is cultural reasons, reasons of mismanagement, there is reasons of mismanagement at a number of different levels, either by omission or commission, throughout the system that have resulted in this kind of thing. Treasury Board has altered its rules that have resulted in us now trying to balance our budgets with tools that won't do the job on one level. At another level, they will do the job if we just apply them.

Administrator 5: The budget is allocated by the region based on financial indicators and our Regional Management Committee, which is the DC's monthly meeting with the wardens and the district directors; we talk about budgets at every meeting. We are in the process now where we will be discussing budgets and reallocations and the fine tuning. But the major distribution is done through financial indicators and it is purely mathematical—press the button.

[Note: the Regional Management Committee has been changed to the Regional Executive Committee since the 2007 reorganization.]

Unfortunately, the financial indicators don't capture all the realities. I'll give you an example. Correctional officers as federal employees accrue sick leave. When a correctional officer is absent, they are replaced. So, if a correctional officer becomes ill and is off for two hundred days, I have to replace that person, and we are not resourced to replace that person for that period of time. Return to work programs—very topical in 2003—we have a return to work program. In return to work programs you tailor it to the individual and you come up with meaningful work that allows a person to return. We are not resourced for that. We don't dump a person into another job that is resourced. If the return to work program is to be properly resourced, we need to get an x number of jobs that could be used as return to work. I have return to work cases, so I have to take from Peter to finance that program.

Administrator 6: I do have some play in how the money for case management is distributed out there. Our budget for case management is based on offender caseload ratio of one parole officer to twenty-five offenders. We base our resourcing strategy around that. It's not written in stone, but this is the framework for allocating money. However, there is sometimes some give and take in this process. And we provide clerical support for every four parole officers in the institutions. In the community it is based on a funding formula according to their workload, and their workload is driven by the number of reports they are completing, their frequency of contact to help with offenders, and that type of thing, so it is a little bit different. That's reviewed by Finance, I believe twice every year, to determine if there needs to be adjustments made.

As demonstrated in the above comments, financial indicators do not always make the best sense when applied to the practical realities of the day-to-day operations within the CSC. Based on the comments from Administrators 1 through 6, can you identify some of the strengths and weaknesses of using financial indicators to allocate budgets in the CSC?

At Regional Headquarters, some correctional administrators have very small budgets with little or no discretionary spending:

> **Administrator 7:** CSC is facing a serious financial situation overall. RAP budget is strictly to run my shop—i.e., the provision of cell phones, pagers, supplies, local travel—internally for the unit/staff. The budget is not for training, programming, etc., which comes from other budgets.

> **Administrator 8:** We don't carry a budget in the similar fashion that the regional administrator of corrections programming would. The budget I carry is basically for the salaries of my staff with some money for travel or minor expenditures.

Budget Accountability

The Correctional Service of Canada has put various mechanisms in place to attempt to be accountable for its spending and to minimize waste. Accountability within the CSC is an ongoing issue, as explained by the following correctional administrators:

> **Administrator 9:** Over the years there have been horrific wastes. If you look at my office, it is extremely well appointed. I worked in a non-profit organization and I know people who still work in those systems, and they suffer because they don't have the things that they need to do the job. We do—it's the level that we are talking about. The level of doing it, the level of training, the convenience of training. For example, we train in hotel rooms with coffee and donuts. It's horrific. We don't need to do that, but that's the way we were doing it, and staff members who have seen that expect that. Cell phones in the government. I mean, I've seen the most senior of managers to the line staff member use a cell phone in a room when there is a land line there. It just drives me to distraction. So there are those kinds of things that are still going on that we have to get control of. Overtime in

institutions is a horrific problem, and trying to get control of those kinds of things will redirect those funds to where it is not as questionable as it is right now.

From the time we see a problem—see it as an organization, not as an individual—but see it as an organization and then mobilize to do something about the problem, a lot of sins occur. A lot of harm occurs, and that's the problem of being so big. That's the problem of not having a local manager be truly accountable for the budgets and what we spend it on.

We have accountabilities but they are not really accountabilities, although the system is introducing more and more. If I overspend, they give me more money. One time I lost here, I lost sleep, I stood on my head to try and balance budgets. I evoked the wrath of many of the staff members because I wasn't doing certain things that they thought I should be doing to try and meet that budget. I came in on budget, I was able to do it. A colleague down the road had meetings, did this, did that, used cell phones ... we all get the same salary. It doesn't matter how hard you work, we all get the same salary.

Administrator 9 suggests some areas where a redirection of funds could occur and also how in the past there has been no recognition for CSC managers who were accountable for their budget and stayed on budget. Administrator 9 then goes on to discuss one way that CSC has tried to change but that this attempt has also been problematic:

Now though, they have introduced, for example, at-risk pay for certain senior levels. The chatter is, whether it happens or not I don't know, if you do not reach your budget, your at-risk pay is at risk. People like me who don't have at-risk pay say, "talk to me in a language I understand." You either give me the money to do the job and then hold me accountable for how I spend it, do that. And the rest will look after itself.

When I go over [budget], ... I've had to hire in extra staff because I've had someone out on long-term sick leave. Someone on long-term sick leave, they don't fund you. Well, I still have the work to do, so your choice is do I do the work or do I meet the budget. I'm going to assume you want me to do the work so I'm going to bring somebody in. Well, that will result in me not meeting my budget. That will result in me being short by these numbers of dollars and that's the reason I'm short. It's not because I'm out having training sessions at the hotel, paying for coffee and donuts, and paying two hundred dollars for the room for the day.

It's the way we do the accounting and the way we hold people accountable that's of issue for me. What the system does, the system keeps bailing everybody out. I'm allocated a budget but I'm part of a regional operation. And within these things there is frozen things, there are some that are to be used for this but they come unthawed, and you can use it over here ... it just goes on and on.

Administrator 10: I have to balance the budget. I have to pick an area where I think it will have the least impact, and what you do is you go back to your corporate objectives, mission statement, whatever, and of course, first and foremost is the protection of the public. The standard for us is to have two motorized patrols. I could say we are only going to use one and save that money, but am I prepared to risk manage at that level?

Administrators 9 and 10 discuss the issue of being accountable for balancing their budgets. Can you identify specific instances of how they decide how to balance their budget and how each interprets the importance of this process? In other words, can you identify consistencies or inconsistencies between each of the interviews and the policy of the CSC to balance the budget? Is that need for accountability to balance the budget demonstrated in the administrators' interviews?

One way CSC has tried to develop some control over how budgets are spent is through functional control of budgets. As detailed in Chapter 3, each Regional Headquarters has sectors that oversee a specific area. These areas allocate budgets to the institutions or offices for a specific purpose. For example, the regional administrator for correctional programming would allocate a certain sum of money to each institution or office to be used only for programming. This manner of accountability was described by an interviewee:

Administrator 11: The other kind of thing is that we are under functional control of the budget. What that means is each of the sectors within our organization ... I talked about two arms—institution and community. Well, we also have sectors—security, programming, integration, personnel, finance, policy, planning, etc., etc. As we go around the circle, we have all these sectors. These are functional to line managers such as me. They are there to try and help me do the job, or they are also there to make sure that I am accountable for the things that I do, like we have accountability and performance assurance as a sector.

Now, these sectors give us money to do their job. Programs get funded nationally, it comes into programs, and then programs allocate it out to community operations. That's on a regional basis. They give me the money and that's based upon what we did last year and what we are projecting to do this year.

The way the budget is set up, it takes away the temptation for me to take resources from programming because programming is the primary area that does reduce risk. It has been shown to reduce risk. If you don't do any programming and all you do is incarcerate, risk reduction is minimal. Actually, there is some studies that show it going up.

However, functional control over budgets is not without its flaws, as the same interviewee explains:

However, they only fund you at the level of eighty percent in doing it because the system hasn't taken into consideration idiosyncrasies. Or they fund you at seven-eighths of a PY—a person year. So, inevitably you are going to be short one-eighth. So, the sector gives you that. Now if you don't do what you are supposed to do with that, the sector is supposed to sanction that in some form or another. They don't. So, managers learn that very quickly, and they didn't do what they were getting money for to offset where they weren't getting the money. What that resulted in was, nationally, the amount of money spent on programs—twenty million dollars, which was earmarked for programs—didn't get spent on programs because it got spent on other kinds of things. So, now the system comes along and says "look, Treasury Board won't give us any money for women but because we are not spending all the money on programs that we should, programs now have to find the money within their allocations for women." So, us that were spending the money as we should—and we are still getting less twenty percent—now, we've got another problem. That's the kind of system I work in.

Those that were not spending the money where they should, they don't have a problem. They can now spend it in programs and say, "look how good I am." It's all there; it's where the people apply it and to what degree they apply it. It should have been sanctioned, it should have been acquired, reports should have been done, but for a bunch of reasons they are not. There is a lot of reasons why that happens. The rewards and punishments are not as directly proportionate to the productivity as they should be. And besides, in all our organizations, you go along to get along. There's that, which is an element of the culture. Now, we are trying to become more corporate, more business-like, so we are trying to change some of these kinds of things, but you can get a manager, either the functional or the line kind, that can develop ... we've got a lot of intelligent people so you get a lot of rationalization. We don't have the ability to hire and fire that the system demands as the ultimate reward and sanction. We don't have as a system the tools to do it. We have words and soft measures ... things like "your at-risk pay is at risk". I don't make an at-risk pay. So what are you going to do to me? You are not going to give me the money, so okay, you tell me how you would decide this. How would you decide how you are going to spend when you don't have enough money to spend it on? And when we have been writing for three years that the system for funding is not as accurate as it should be given the ramifications. So everybody knows that, so everybody is trying—part of another reason why there is a lack of accountability. Everybody knows that the system is less than perfect so they are all trying to help each other make up for that. To get the job done overall. So, have we done the job overall? Yes, there is going to be winners and losers. Some people are going to get away with doing less, other people are going to have to do more. But *c'est la vie*. That's the way it is so you've got to make up your own mind how to deal with these things. It's always a bit of a frustration.

Again, the goal of financial accountability by using tools such as functional control over budgets does not always take into account the day-to-day realities of the CSC. Based on Administrator 11's comments, can you identify the benefits and weaknesses of using a functional control system of budget allocation in the CSC?

Budget for Programs and Planning

As we have read in previous chapters, programming, training, development, and planning are all critical factors in CSC's drive to achieve its mission statement. These areas, therefore, warrant a closer look to see how they are affected by financial decision-making. The impact of budgets on training was discussed in Chapter 7. However, the correctional administrators interviewed were also asked to comment on how budget allocation affects resource allocation for programming and planning:

Administrator 12: There isn't much room to move money between different programs during the budget year. It is pretty tight. Like any other organization, there are budget crunches to manage, but before asking for money—let's say I run short in substance abuse—before asking, I would look at all the other budgets to see if there—because our program officers are cross-trained. So I might train you in substance abuse. If you are with us for any length of time I will train you in family violence, I'll train you in living skills, so once the person is cross-trained, I am able to move resources around to be able to do that. Any change in that I would like to be appraised of. I am in the process of doing the need now for next year. Our year goes April to March 31st. If there is any shift I like to be appraised because you might have—I look at the regional picture, you look at the site picture—so you might want to move but I might have more important needs at some other site. But usually it is a joint thing. We have access to the same database. Plus, I have regional meetings on a quarterly basis, sometimes more often, to look at those issues also with the assistant wardens and program managers in the community. Just like anybody else, we take the fiscal situation quite seriously. Like anything else, we are always able to do better and it is good that we review, which we do regularly. At this stage of the game, if there was more money we could do more, but I think we are in the situation to still maintain the capability of offering programs based on offender needs in our region. I wish that we had more money—I would have more staff here, but the service provided to the inmates is still pretty good.

Administrator 13: Part of the community corrections' problem is that it is a small sector of CSC. It actually has approximately the same number of offenders, but there is an old cultural way of looking at the community as if the community was going to take care of the offenders when they come back. Well, they haven't. It works well for people to believe that we should, but they don't, and more and more as dollars have shrunk within the society, community agencies are more and more discriminating as to who they help, and they see federal offenders, for example, as under the envelope of federal monies. But most of our federal monies go to institutions and running National Headquarters and regional offices, and there is just small amounts left over for community. What is left over, ninety percent of it goes to staff salaries. So the amount of money you get to manage is ten percent maybe, that need to cover your paper, your telephone, your gas, it's rental of room, it's training, travel expenses for staff members that go to training or go to a meeting, those kinds of things.

The other things, accommodations, for example—halfway houses—that is a funded thing. You have a budget and there is no restriction on that budget. You spend more or less—that's the way it goes. Other kinds of tools that we have, like urinalysis, there is restrictions. They are saying, "look, you are spending too much money. You've got to bring it down." We are saying, "we are going to spend that money directly proportionate to our perception of the risk." So, I am attaching it to principles of case management as opposed to principles of meeting the budget. So, in those things I don't bother; as long as it is considered good case management, we will spend the money on it. As long as the item is being managed, we will spend money and the budget will end up being what the budget is and if I am short, I'm short. *C'est la vie.* It's not because of mismanagement. It's because there is not sufficient dollars in there to do the job in terms of good corrections.

Administrator 14: Budgeting is always one of those important variables, but we've been very fortunate in being able to manage the mental health and physical health budgeting from our facility for the whole region, and so we've been able to ensure that the monies that are allocated by Treasury Board for the purposes of interventions and our training in fact stay in that envelope. And so at least in our region we've been very lucky in being able to ensure that we can carry through with the programming that we are expected to provide.

Administrator 15: We are a small department and have a smaller budget … In terms of planning, we went through an exercise this year where we didn't get a lot of our budgets up front, and so it was difficult to plan because we didn't know what kind of allocation we were going to get for this year. Therefore, the first quarter of the year was problematic, for example, because my budget came quite a bit later than some of the other peoples did. In other words, my budget did not come at the beginning of the fiscal year. I had to run short in my department, so I was not able to staff one of my vacancies and so we ran a little bit behind this year. The thing about my budget, though, is that it is primarily for my own travel, the maintenance of my department and the only training it affects is really the IERT budget. In addition, I am responsible for purchasing the IERT equipment, etc. if it needs to be replaced or is damaged. Therefore, I do not really have a lot of budget allocation.

In many large organizations like CSC, budgeting is the most essential piece to successful and ongoing operations. A freeze on budgets or a delay in resource allocation can have a profound effect on institutional operations. Budget deficits are often cumulative from one year to the next, eventually leading to less than a 100% budget to address operational needs. One of the areas strongly affected by budgeting decisions is programming. Some administrators believe that there are ways to overcome some of the consequences of budgeting decisions. For example, instead of offering a specific program on multiple sites, that program could be offered at one site and inmates would attend programming at that site. Another suggestion is to use local program developers instead of using corporate or other outside expertise.

Administrator 16: With the budget allocation for our shop, we do look after things like programming and some training—most of the training development side of course, is on the corporate side of the house—but the budget allocations so far have not affected our ability to program. What we need to look at is how we are going to work with our money smarter. So instead of having a certain program in every institution, say in a medium institution, what we might do is have the family violence program at one institution, have the moderate sex offender program at another institution, and perhaps the anger management program at another, and if the guys need those programs they will have to go from one to the other. This would be an alternative to have three of these programs running at every institution, and this would free up resources for us to utilize other programs in other places as well. Therefore, for the guys in the medium-level institutions, we would have to move them around so they could take the different programs. The minimum institutions primarily have relapse programs because offenders have already done the programs. Therefore, if a guy had to go to the one institution, for example, for an intensive family violence program, they can go from wherever they are, because it is a multi-level facility. Then when they are finished, they would be expected to go back to one of the other institutions.

We have in the past been providing duplicate programs because we had it at every site, and these days it is just not cost effective to do that. So we need to look at how we can do this better, and the only way we can do this is to move the offender and that has worked well so far, as long as they are motivated to do programs. Moreover, those who do not want to do programming will be in a special spot anyway, so they would not be moving anywhere. Most of the offenders don't mind it—many of them are receiving very short-term sentences. In other words, they are getting four- or five-year sentences or under that, which means they are out in three years. This means they have to really focus and work through their programming if they have any hope of getting out prior to Warrant Expiry, so most of them are quite cooperative in doing those kinds of things.

Programming always has to be very creative in trying to meet the needs here. We have a Program Board that for the year, sets out to have a regional committee that discusses programs—what the programs are going to be about, how many programs we will have to offer, and which institutions they will be in—and this gives us some idea of what we are looking at. This gives the case managers, for example, the ability to look at a particular case file of someone who needs this particular program and is medium security, so they might make the decision to put them into a particular program in their current institution. Alternatively, perhaps they cannot put this offender in the program being offered at the institution they are in, so the case manager will need to look at a "seat" elsewhere in another institution.

Administrator 17: The bottom line is, if you're asking me are the resources we get in programming adequate enough to meet the program needs at the regional level, the answer is no. That is an unfortunate reality, because what happens is that every year you get slightly behind in terms of your programming response. For example, if you are three percent out this year, then next year you have a hundred and three percent to program for, and if you are two percent out that year, then it is a hundred and five percent the following year, and so on. The backlog becomes larger, and what happens is that the first ten percent of your resource allocation goes towards cleaning up the backlog, and when it comes time to address your hundred percent needs, you only have ninety percent worth of resources left to do it. It becomes a vicious circle because every time you fall behind it becomes cumulative and it creates situations such as, in this region, the reality of having a fairly significant number of offenders incarcerated beyond their day and full parole eligibility dates, and to some degree, at least, that is due to our inability to program for all offenders in a timely fashion because we don't have the resources to do it. Certainly, programming resources and resources in most areas is a concern for most managers.

Our budget has been increasing consistently since the early 90s because CSC has moved more and more each year towards a programming agenda, and we've introduced more new programs, requested more money from the Treasury Board for new programs, and so on. Of course, because the cost of doing business increases—i.e., contracts with our staff have gone up and a program officer who was earning forty thousand dollars three years ago is now earning fifty thousand dollars type of thing … so … so, yes, your budget goes up, but that doesn't mean that we can necessarily do more. It simply means that it is going up because of related costs and it goes up proportionately to those costs. In some cases we have received extra money, which allows us to do extra things, but by and large, we have not grown in size over the last number of years.

The development and planning of programs to the largest degree takes place at the national level, and they have a budget specifically for program development, research, etc. We do some program development regionally, and we do a lot of program planning regionally, and that is just built into our function such that we do not get extra resources for that. You could never say that we cannot plan because we do not have the resources—we plan within the resources that we have, and without this planning the money would be wasted. Therefore, that is an area that we definitely invest in. In terms of program development, this region probably more than any other is very active in program development, and we have some great people here at Regional that have great reputations as program developers and have been instrumental in a number of CSC programs. So a lot of programming has been developed locally and no money is ever allocated for that, as it comes out of our existing resources. National core programs are developed at the national level, generally, and are funded there, with dollars allocated from Treasury Board or from special initiatives.

The administrators above generally agree that more money for programming and planning would benefit the system and those in it. For the most part, they also feel that CSC is providing a pretty good service to inmates on the current budget. However, several comments were made on how to better spend the money currently allocated to programming and planning. Can you identify what these suggestions are?

Many correctional administrators currently working in the system have pointed out that resource allocation has a profound impact on the ability of CSC to "contribute to the protection of society by actively encouraging and assisting offenders to become law-abiding citizens, while exercising reasonable, safe, secure, and humane control." Research has also shown that programming is a critical factor in an offender's ability to successfully reintegrate into the community. Therefore, by investing resources in programming now, CSC will realize cost savings in the future.

Conclusion

The Correctional Service of Canada is a billion dollar enterprise. The importance of spending this money in a focused and directed manner that strives toward the mission of the CSC is essential for a number of reasons. First, CSC is publicly funded. "Undirected spending violates a fundamental rule for public administration. The public service has no right to spend more money than necessary to meet its objectives. Therefore, the public service has an obligation to consider the appropriateness of its spending" (Ingstrup, 1995, p. 16). Second, how

CSC chooses to allocate its funds has a direct impact on the ability to successfully reintegrate offenders into the community. Though the Correctional Service of Canada has implemented some processes and procedures to make it more financially efficient, effective, and accountable, it still has a considerable amount of work to do in perfecting its financial management and creating the best possible opportunity to meet its organizational goals and objectives successfully.

Study Questions

1. What approach does the Correctional Service of Canada use to allocate its budget? Why do you think CSC has chosen this approach?
2. How would a reduction in resources affect the ability of the Correctional Service of Canada to fulfill its mission?
3. Discuss the measures the Correctional Service of Canada has taken to become financially accountable. In what other ways could CSC improve its financial accountability?

Bibliography

*Items with asterisks are also suggested readings for this chapter.

Anderson, J. (1998). Techniques for governance. *Social Science Journal*, 35(4), 493–497.
*Correctional Service of Canada (2002). *Performance Report for the Correctional Service of Canada (CSC) for the period ending March 31, 2002.* http://www.csc-scc.gc.ca/text/pblct/dpr/2002/section_2_departmental_performance_e.shtml.
Correctional Service of Canada (2005). *Basic Facts About the Correctional Service of* Canada. http://www.csc-scc.gc.ca/text/pblct/basicfacts/BasicFacts_e.shtml
*Correctional Service of Canada (2006). *Departmental Performance Report for the* Correctional Service of Canada (CSC) for the period ending March 31, 2006. http://www.tbs-sct.gc.ca/dpr-rmr/0506/CSC-SCC/csc-scc04_e.asp#_3_2
Correctional Service of Canada (2007). *2007–2008 Estimates: Report on Plans and Priorities*. http://www.tbs-sct.gc.ca/rpp/0708/csc-scc/csc-scc_e.pdf
*Ekstedt, J. W. and Jackson, M. A. (1996). Administrative Programs by Type and Objective. In, *The Keepers and the Kept: Introduction to Corrections in Canada*. (pp. 240–255). Toronto: ITP Nelson.
*Ingstrup, O. (1995). *Only Those Who Believe Can Stay the Course in Turbulent Times*. Ottawa: Canadian Centre for Management Development.
Jefferson, A. (1995). Decentralizing budgeting: Getting the most out of disbursements of funds. *Education Canada*, 35(4), 33–35.

9 Women in Federal Prison

This chapter considers topics related to women in federal prisons. The topic of female offenders has been much discussed in the last few decades. Much of this discussion has centred on calls for the closure of the first federal penitentiary for women, the Prison for Women, or P4W as it was commonly known. Now that its closure has been achieved, attention is being paid to other issues that face federally sentenced women (FSW).

This chapter first presents a brief history of the incarceration of federally sentenced women, followed by a profile of these women. Next the topic of mothers in prison is examined, taking a closer look at the mother-child programs that exist in Canada and how they compare to the ways other countries deal with this unique population.

The Incarceration of Federally Sentenced Women

The first record of female offenders being placed in a prison in Canada comes from 1835, when three women were placed in the infirmary of Kingston Penitentiary. A separate ward for women was established in 1853 (Vachon, 1994). In 1934, the first federal penitentiary for women, Prison for Women, opened in Kingston, Ontario. Four years later, the Archambault Commission called for its closure. Since then, almost a dozen reports from government commissions and task forces have recommended its closure. The three major reasons for this recommendation were:

- the incarceration of women far away from their families
- the quality of rehabilitation programs available to women in the institution

- the incarceration of women offenders in a facility with a higher security level than required (Auditor General of Canada, 2003, 4.12)

Though all reports recommended closing the Prison for Women, they differed on what should replace it. The options proposed included creating federal-provincial joint initiatives, building new federal facilities in regions of the country, and transferring full responsibility for women to the provinces.

One of the major criticisms of the Prison for Women was its isolation. The centralized location of the single federal prison for women placed extreme restrictions on the contact federally sentenced women had with their families. Women who were not from southern Ontario, often lost contact with their children and families because their families could not afford the costs of traveling to visit or making long distance phone calls.

To help alleviate this situation, in 1973 the Correctional Service of Canada negotiated Exchange of Service agreements with the provinces, whereby federally sentenced inmates, male and female, could apply to serve their time in a provincial institution closer to home (Task Force on Federally Sentenced Women, 1990). Though this agreement allowed some women to be closer to families, it created problems of a different nature, the main one being the lack of programming in provincial institutions for long term offenders. In 1982, Québec negotiated the Tanguay Agreement, which ensured that all federally sentenced females from Québec would serve their time in provincial custody (Task Force on Federally Sentenced Women, 1990).

In the early 1980s, after the Canadian Human Rights Commission ruled that because women had less access to rehabilitation and training programs than men, female offenders were being discriminated against (Vachon, 1994), the programs and services for women in the Prison for Women began to improve. However, it also created an even bigger gap in access to programs between federally sentenced women serving time in provincial institutions and those in the federal Prison for Women (Task Force on Federally Sentenced Women, 1990). At the same time, the number of transfers, which had been steadily rising, stabilized after most provinces, with the exception of Québec (which was bound by the Tanguay Agreement to take all transfers), began to set eligibility criteria for transfer. Consequently, "federally sentenced women must, first, be eligible for transfer and, second, make the choice between serving their sentences in their home provinces or accessing the more extensive programs and services which were developed to reflect longer term needs" (Task Force on Federally Sentenced Women, 1990).

In 1988, British Columbia negotiated the first agreement (Burnaby Agreement) that "reflects a holistic approach to program needs as well as formal recognition in the terms of the agreement that program development and delivery is a dynamic process" (Task Force on Federally Sentenced Women, 1990). One interviewee comments:

> **Administrator 1:** Mixing federally sentenced and provincially sentenced women together, of course, has happened all the time. The benefits for the federal women, the federal women have always been entitled to the programs that we offer to all federal offenders, and because of the federal/provincial mix, the latter group had always been able to access those federal programs.

Also in 1988, the then commissioner of the Correctional Service of Canada, Ole Ingstrup, established a Task Force to review the situation of federally sentenced women. He made a commitment to address the needs of these women based on the findings and report of the Task Force, whose mandate

> required members to examine the correctional management of federally sentenced women from the commencement of sentence to the date of warrant expiry, and to develop a policy and a plan which would guide and direct this process in a manner that is responsive to the unique and special needs of this group. (Task Force on Federally Sentenced Women, 1990)

In April 1990, the Task Force tabled its report, *Creating Choices: The Report of the Task Force on Federally Sentenced Women.* The Task Force concluded that:

> The ability of CSC to meet its responsibility for federally sentenced women has been eroded by trying to fit a small, diverse, relatively low-risk group of women with multi-faceted needs into a system designed for a large, more homogenous and higher-risk population. In the process, inequality and insensitivity to the needs of federally sentenced women have become unanticipated consequences of our current system.

Creating Choices proposed that the Prison for Women be closed and replaced with a healing lodge for Aboriginal women and five regional facilities. The report also recommended the development of women-centred correctional programs and a comprehensive community release strategy. This report became the foundation on which a new approach to serving federally sentenced women was built.

In July 1992, the Construction Policy and Services/National Implementation Committee submitted its report, *Regional Facilities for Federally Sentenced Women Operational Plan,* which outlined the operational model for the proposed regional facilities. Also in 1992, the federal government proclaimed the *Corrections and Conditional Release Act,* which included a specific commitment in Section 77 of the Act to provide programs specifically for women. The section states that the CSC shall "provide programs designed particularly to address the needs of female offenders." In July 1994, CSC published the *Correctional Program Strategy for Federally Sentenced Women.* This document both set out the framework for FSW program design and delivery and defined the core programs. Its purpose was to ensure program consistency in the new regional facilities for federally sentenced women.

However, before the new facilities could be opened, a series of incidents occurred in April, 1994 at the Prison for Women in Kingston, Ontario that attracted national and international coverage. It began when inmates and correctional staff were involved in a violent confrontation resulting in the inmates being placed in the segregation unit. A few days later, an all-male Institutional Emergency Response Team from Kingston Penitentiary was called in to conduct a cell extraction and strip search eight women, six of whom had been involved in the violent incident on April 22. As per CSC policy, the actions of the IERT were videotaped. On May 6th, five inmates were transferred to the male psychiatric treatment facility in Kingston Penitentiary. They were not returned to the Prison for Women until mid-July, where they remained in segregation until December. On February 14, 1995, the solicitor general received a special report from the correctional investigator regarding these incidents. One week later, this report was tabled in the House of Commons and the solicitor general announced that an independent inquiry would be established. That evening, the CBC program *Fifth Estate* aired substantial pieces of the video taken during the IERT cell extraction and strip search of the six inmates.

On April 10, 1995, the governor general in Council appointed the Honourable Louise Arbour, justice of the Court of Appeal of Ontario, to head the independent inquiry. Its mandate was to

> investigate and report on the state and management of that part of the business of the Correctional Service of Canada that pertains to the incidents which occurred at the Prison for Women in Kingston, Ontario, beginning on April 22, 1994 and further, to make recommendations to the policies and practices of the Correctional Service of Canada in relation to the incidents. (Arbour Commission, 1996)

In April 1996, the solicitor general released the report prepared by Madam Justice Arbour. This exhaustive report, *Commission of Inquiry into Certain Events at the Prison for Women in Kingston*, contained copious recommendations in many areas including cross-gender staffing, use of force and IERT's, Aboriginal women and the healing lodge, general correctional issues, segregation, accountability in operations, complaints and grievances, outside agencies, and the creation of a deputy commissioner for women. The report again underscored the need to close the Prison for Women and open regional facilities.

Between 1995 and 2001, the Correctional Service of Canada opened six new regional facilities for federally sentenced women. The facilities were opened as detailed in Table 9.1.

Table 9.1. Regional Facilities for Women

Name	Location	Opening Date	Capacity as of March 31, 2005	Population as of March 12, 2006
Fraser Valley Institution	Abbotsford, British Columbia	Mar. 2004	52 -44 med/min -8 structured living environment **In 2006 a ten-bed secure unit was scheduled to open	46
Edmonton Institution for Women	Edmonton, Alberta	Nov. 1995	110 -87 med/min -8 structured living environment -15 secure unit (max)	99
Okimaw Ohci Healing Lodge	Maple Creek, Saskatchewan	Aug. 1995	28 -28 min/med	21
Grand Valley Institution	Kitchener, Ontario	Jan. 1997	103 -80 med/min -8 structured living environment -15 secure unit (max)	91
Isabel McNeil House	Kingston, Ontario	1990	10 -10 min	5

Name	Location	Opening Date	Capacity as of March 31, 2005	Population as of March 12, 2006
Joliette Institution	Joliette, Québec	Jan. 1997	**99** -81 med/min -8 structured living environment -10 secure unit (max)	75
Nova Institution	Truro, Nova Scotia	October 1995	**70** -52 med/min -8 structured living environment -10 secure unit (max)	49

Population is as of March 12, 2006 from Offender Management System and does not include those who are temporarily detained. There are also 12 women offenders incarcerated in the women's unit at Regional Psychiatric Centre (Prairies) and three on remand. Source: Correctional Service of Canada, 2006

In 1996, the Correctional Service of Canada ran into some difficulties with a small number of the women in the regional facilities:

> In 1996, shortly after the opening of the first new regional facilities for women offenders, it became evident that a small portion of the population (approximately 15%) was unable to function in a community-style living environment. As an interim measure, CSC transferred maximum security women requiring a greater degree of structure and control to three units co-located within existing men's facilities in Saskatchewan, Québec and Nova Scotia. These units are physically separate from the remainder of the facility. Minimum and medium security women requiring long-term intensive mental health treatment were transferred to mental health units at the Regional Psychiatric Centre in Saskatchewan and the Prison for Women in Ontario. (Correctional Service of Canada, 2000)

In September 1999, the Intensive Intervention Strategy was announced by the solicitor general. It called for the creation of secure units and structured living environment houses at the four regional women's facilities for women classified as maximum security and for those with serious mental health needs. It set a target date for full implementation as of September 2001 (Watson, 2000). The first phase of the Intensive Intervention Strategy was the closure of the Prison for Women on July 6, 2000. By December 2001, the regional facilities were operating the Structured Living Environment Houses. In January 2003, the first of five secure units opened at the Nova Institution in Truro, Nova Scotia.

This opening was followed by the secure unit at the Edmonton Institution in February 2003, the secure unit at the Joliette Institution in Québec in April, 2003, and the secure unit at the Grand Valley Institution in Ontario in October 2004. A ten-bed maximum secure unit at the Fraser Valley Institution in British Columbia was scheduled to open in 2006.

During the development of regional facilities for women, federally sentenced women in British Columbia continued to be housed at the provincial Correctional Centre for Women in Burnaby under the Exchange of Services Agreement with the Province of British Columbia. In 2002, the BC Government announced its plan to close this facility. In September 2002, CSC announced its plan to convert the Sumas Community Correctional Centre in Abbotsford to a multi-level security facility for federal women in the Pacific region, including those currently at the Correctional Centre for Women (CSC News Release, April 2003). The new women's facility became operational in March 2004 and is called the Fraser Valley Institution.

As mentioned, the lack of programming, specifically women-centred programming, emerged as an issue in numerous reports and criticisms of the federal women's correctional system. The establishment of the regional facilities and the program development work conducted since the *Creating Choices* report has resulted in some progress. However, the 2003 Report of the Auditor General (4.3) made the following criticisms regarding programming and services for federally sentenced women:

There are gaps in the delivery of programs and services both in the institutions and in the community:

- Correctional Service does not consistently deliver rehabilitation programs on time for incarcerated women offenders. These programs are a critical factor in preparing offenders for a National Parole Board review at their parole eligibility dates;
- Correctional Service needs to implement a comprehensive, more gender-specific model for treating substance abuse, a much-needed program for the rehabilitation of women offenders;
- women offenders have little access to meaningful work opportunities and employment programs while they are incarcerated. Gaining work skills is considered an important factor in their successful reintegration into the community;
- Correctional Service Canada has difficulty meeting the program and service needs of women offenders in the community. Lack of substance abuse programs and inadequate mental health services are critical areas for improvement (Auditor General of Canada, 2003).

Correctional administrators also commented on programming for women in general and the differences and similarities between male and female offenders. Though there is recognition that there are more programs for women today than there were 20 years ago, and that gender- and culturally-based programs are highly successful, gaps still exist in some areas because of the challenge of implementing programs when the numbers of women in the institutions are so small. Differing opinions exist on whether programming should be reinvented from scratch or if it can be adapted from an existing male program:

Administrator 2: I guess in terms of programming for federally sentenced women. I understand and agree with the concept of creating choices and the issue that women, for the large part, are victims because of their gender. But at the same time, and I guess it goes back to the same issue, if we allow inmates to hide behind the victim issue—"I am a victim and it is not my fault, it is someone else's fault"—then we will never move forward.

I see, whether it be interest groups or advocacy groups or whether it be the public, I think what works in male corrections can be adapted to work in female corrections, and if it has been working in male corrections and it has been positive, not to use it or not to adapt it simply because it was designed for men I think is wrong. You take a program that works, and if the person has a handicap you adapt it to meet their needs and so that they can take advantage of it.

So, female corrections—I think one of my jobs is to kind of temper that temptation that everything has to be reinvented for women. It has to be adapted, it has to be applied, and you have to use the gender test and so on and so forth, same as you do for mental health groups and so on, or challenge groups. And that has worked here. Not from a programming perspective, but from a behavioural management program. We've been successful in managing very disruptive inmates at this institution—female inmates. We have some of the worst of the worst. They've taken hostages at other institutions, they send them to us. And what is done is we've gone right back to basics. We present a very controlled environment. They are moved in handcuffs and it is a very simple process and they understand that. It is very controlled, very humane. Staff are protected but the inmate understands that to gain more freedoms they have to behave. And it has worked. Maybe only for a day—there are all kinds of relapses—but the plan just keeps cycling over and over. We had one particular case where a very, very difficult inmate involving three hostage-takings in less than a year, harmed other inmates, attempted to harm staff with weapons, and so on. Spent all kinds of time in segregation. We actually got that person out of segregation and into the general population. We got her moved to medium security. Now she's had a relapse but that's eight months since us. You've got to build on those successes. So that was a very simple program that worked for the male population. They understand that and it works for the female population. We adapted it in terms of use of force and sensitivity to gender and so on, but that's the big challenge of female corrections is the management of human behaviour.

Administrator 2 emphasizes some similarities between male and female offenders and cautions against always thinking that everything has to be re-invented for women, whereas Administrator 3 articulates the differences be-tween the two groups:

Administrator 3: I think with women's corrections in general what hap-pens a lot—we in many ways are often at the end of the road. So they've knocked on many doors through the health care profession, perhaps through juvenile or straight to provincial corrections, mental health agen-cies. They've knocked on those doors and many of those doors have been shut behind them. They come to federal corrections down that pathway and there becomes the expectation that the feds are going to fix everything that's taken a long time to break. So by the time that she does enter the federal system, you go back knocking on those doors and those doors aren't open anymore. So we are going to have to continue to target, to create, new relationships. It's not for CSC to invent them. A lot of those services and relationships are out there. We have to become part of that network. They are still there, so that's where we don't necessarily have to lead; we have to get connected and try and forge new partnerships and services for what we have here.

There are real and true differences between male and—I don't even like the term men and women offenders. We have to educate within the service of what those differences are while I had some experience with men. I knew they were different, but it was very hard to articulate what the differences are. After the last few years I can articulate them and how the needs are certainly different. I can walk into a male institution and you walk into the visiting area and it is full. You are booking your table one or two weeks before to make sure you have a table. Here it is just the opposite. We have two offenders a week get a visitor—that's it. So you are not only a bad per-son, a bad mother, and a bad citizen because you've been caught. You go and do your time and when you are done, you come back out. So the men maintain their girlfriends and their relationships while in prison. I would say of ninety-nine percent of the women who had a relationship on the street when they came in, the relationship ends. The greater majority are mothers, so either by choice they don't want their children to see them in prison, so they don't come to visit them, or the guardians of the children don't want the children to see them in prison. So we have more usage of our private family visiting area, which is at least the most home-like surrounding, that they can, at least for the next couple of days, try to live the way they lived before they came in. But the visiting, you won't see it like you do in the male institutions. For me that was the biggest shock, to not have any—I had never thought of that difference.

Societal values have not changed a lot towards women in prison from a reintegration perspective because they have better results, they have better successes, and I'll often challenge parole board members and other personnel—"when was the last time you picked up a paper and read some sensational story about a woman on the front page?" So is risk assumable? For a lot of them it is. And they are going to go back—these women will go back and be with their families, be with their children. Now there are— another realization for me is part of the survivors of abuse. I'm not going to marginalize or generalize in this, but a lot of women were the product of single mothers or broken homes and part of the survivors, and who raised them in many ways were their own mothers. These women have children and they participate in survivors of abuse and trauma, and they go back to the trauma that they experienced as a child and all that. What many of them come to realize is the abusers in their lives were their moms, and who is raising their children? And you or I may think, 'well, we're going to say it was their father or their stepfather'—we're going to jump to that. In many, many, many cases it wasn't the male model, it was the female.

If you think that men and women are exactly the same on the street, then you can believe that male offenders are exactly the same as women. But are you the same as your wife or husband? Again, I don't want to stereotype, but women like to talk! If there is something going down, women are going to tell you—whether you want to hear it or not, they are going to tell you. So if you say, "we don't want to listen," no, women want to talk, so you listen. Male institutions, you don't necessarily know what is going on. You know something might be happening, but here we are going to get a heads up. So I say on my epitaph please put "puter-outer of the sparks," because that is what it comes down to. When they are telling us, act on it. Put the spark out. If you don't it will turn into a fire. It is as simple as that. And that is dynamic security. Listen, listen, listen. Something comes up, negotiate, negotiate, negotiate. If you can't, if you are done negotiating, then it is time to negotiate a little bit more. Women will talk it through. We don't react in a physical way, we react in an emotional way, in a verbal way. I think as a service we can take a page out of women corrections.

Administrator 4: Although we can still talk about lack of programs, etc., the fact is that we have a one hundred percent more now than we did ten years ago. I think that when we are talking about a lack of programs for federally sentenced women, it is because they are such small numbers and such small groupings it is very difficult to provide some of the large scale employability training programs that the women would like to have—in other words, they miss out because of their numbers, I think. Therefore, they have to do it on a much more individual and smaller scale, which works well for some but not for others. The gender specific programming that is coming is quite good now—I think we are getting some very good programming and there is always more to be done. The Aboriginal women's programs are extremely good, which are culturally based. The women are expected to work into the program and to work based on the cultural values, so they have to learn two things there.

We still have many programs that were originally designed for men and have been adapted, and some of them I do not think are that bad. However, we have to be careful. We start to get into a bit of a diatribe and we start to ghettoize people. For example, with Aboriginal programming, if you are an Aboriginal offender and you want to have Aboriginal program-ming, then you go over here. If you are a woman offender and you want to have programming, you should go over here. I agree that there are some programs that are very specific for each of these groups—they should have these, and they should probably be designed by women or by the Elders for the Aboriginals. Nevertheless, I think there are still some skills that are common to all groups, where we have to learn to live and work together. For example, one of the things I find, especially with the women, is that the women-centred training is very good. However, the mistake we made, when everybody was on a real high roll with the Federally Sentenced Women's Task Force about how women had been victimized all of their lives, etc., which was all true, was that this doesn't take away from the fact that, they can be very nasty and they do bad things. We forgot about that, and they sometimes do bad things more often than the men do, because the women have even less control over emotional aspects of some of their stuff. It is because of many of those issues that happened to them and it all bears on that. The women experience different issues than the men in many cases. In addition, the issues that are similar are different because the reactions are different, and the way a woman may react to things is different from how a man may react to the same issue. Therefore, when you talk about sexual abuse or familial types of abuse, neglect, and isolation, a woman will react very differently to that in some ways than a man will. That is where we have to get the programming into place, and they are starting to get these into place.

How do the above comments from administrators fit with the criticisms from the 2003 Report of the Auditor General regarding programming and services for women? There are several instances in the interviews where administrators speak about the differences and similarities between male and female offenders and how these differences and similarities should or shouldn't influence programming. Can you identify some of these instances?

Between April 2003 and January 2004, independent agencies issued three reports on federal corrections for women: the Office of the Auditor General, the Standing Committee on Public Accounts, and the Canadian Human Rights Commission. The reports acknowledged the progress by CSC to improve the institutional accommodation and programs offered to women in federal corrections. Each report also put forth a number of recommendations to improve existing practices, particularly in the areas of security classification, case management and programs.

In the *32nd Annual Report of the Correctional Investigator, 2004–2005*, a recommendation was made that

> in May of 2006 the Minister appoint an Expert Committee to publicly report on the progress detailed in the Service's response on the advancement of human rights, fairness and equity issues since Madame Justice Arbour's report of 1996—the Committee's report to be provided to the Minister by October 2006.

The correctional investigator also raised a number of issues relating to women offenders. Table 9.2 outlines the current status of the issues raised by the correctional investigator:

Table 9.2. CSC's response to issues raised by the Correctional Investigator, 2004–2005

ISSUE	UPDATE/RESULT
Over-classification of Women	• 5% initially classified at the maximum security level; • 44% and 51% initially classified at the medium and minimum levels, respectively.
Gender Responsive Tools	• Proposals for development of Initial Classification Tool received in July, 2005, with completion of tool anticipated in 2008. • Security Reclassification Scale for Women Offenders (SRSW) implemented on June 1, 2005: • recommends more placement of women at minimum security, and fewer at medium and maximum security; • significantly more predictive of institutional misconduct than the structured clinical assessment; • valid for Aboriginal women.
Segregation (from 2003–04 to 2004–05)	**Voluntary** • significant decrease in admission, from 40 to 26; • significant decrease in number of women that spend 10 days or less, from 39 to 20; • slight increase in the number of women that spend between 11 to 31 days, from 1 to 6 **Involuntary** • slight reduction in admissions, from 258 to 249; • slight decrease in the number of women who spend 30 days or less, from 239 to 233; • slight decrease in the number of women who spend between 31 and 275 days, from 19 to 16. • Introduced pilot of biannual reviews of cases of 30 consecutive or 60 cumulative days in a year spent in segregation to identify preventive strategies and best practices; • Opening of the women's unit at Institut Philippe Pinel de Montréal (IPPM) in May 2004 has assisted in alleviating the long-term segregation situation.
Re-offending Rates	• 2003–04: the revocation rate for women offenders was: 0.56% (3 out of 534) for violent re-offending, and 4.68% (25 out of 534) for non-violent re-offending; • 2004–05: the revocation rate for women offenders was: 0.39% (2 out of 519) for violent re-offending and 4.43% (23 out of 519) for non-violent re-offending.

ISSUE	UPDATE/RESULT
Access to Gender-Specific Programs	• Programs specific to women, based on advances in knowledge about women offenders, now include, among others: • Women Offender Substance Abuse Program; • Survivors of Abuse and Trauma; • Circles of Change; • Spirit of a Warrior (two programs specifically developed for Aboriginal women); • Mother-Child program; • Peer Support program; • Pawsitive Directions; • Mentoring programs; • Dialectical Behaviour Therapy (DBT) (offered in Structured Living Environments and Secure Units) ; and • Psycho-social Rehabilitation (PSR) (offered in Secure Units) • Some programs have been modified to allow for continuous entry; • CSC is closely monitoring waiting lists.
Meaningful Employment and Employability Programming	• *Employment and Employability Skills Program* was developed in conjunction with the Conference Board of Canada and piloted at two institutions. • training will be provided to trainers in the fall of 2005; • program will be offered at all sites in 2005/06. • In 2004–2005, 8% increase in the number of women assigned employment from previous FY, from 487 to 525 women.
Training in Women-Centred Approaches	• The Women-Centred Training Program is mandatory for all staff working with women and is part of the National Training Standards; • sensitizes staff to issues of sexism, racism, disability, sexual orientation, physical and or sexual abuse, self-injurious and suicidal behaviour, addictions, mental health issues, and Aboriginal traditions and spirituality with a focus on women; • Refresher training will be implemented in 2007.

Source: Correctional Service of Canada Response to the 32nd Annual Report of the Correctional Investigator, 2005–2005. http://www.csc-scc.gc.ca/text/pblct/ci04-05/toc-eng.shtml

Ten-Year Status Report on Women's Corrections

In response to the correctional investigator's recommendation and to coincide with the 10 year anniversary of the Honourable Louise Arbour's report, *Commission of Inquiry into Certain Events at Prison for Women in Kingston*, in 2006 the Correctional Service of Canada issued the *Ten Year Status Report on*

Women's Corrections. The Committee reviewed what changes CSC had implemented to address the recommendations from major reviews, what accomplishments had been made, what challenges were faced in doing so, and what the next steps were. In reviewing the recommendations that had been made in major reports over the last ten years, the following theme areas emerged:

- Human rights
- Cross-gender staffing issues
- Aboriginal women offenders
- Security classification
- Management of security incidents
- Segregation
- Programs and community transition

It was noted that although mental health was not a key area for review, due to the increasing numbers of offenders with mental health problems, this is an area that CSC would be focusing on in the future.

The Profile of Federally Sentenced Women

Chapter 3 gave some basic facts about the female federal inmate population. Apart from the figures, however, there are a number of other significant differences between female and male offenders. The following fact sheet compiled by the Elizabeth Fry Society presents a succinct snapshot of female offenders:

> While more than 80% of women have progressed beyond Grade 9, for women prisoners the figure is closer to 50%. In 1996, 80% of the women serving time in a federal facility were unemployed at the time of admission compared to 54% of men.

> Women in prison experience great limitations in terms of access to university level education, as well as vocational programs aimed at the development of marketable job skills.

> More than half of all charges for which federally sentenced women are convicted are non-violent, property and drug offences. One reason why women only account for 5% of admissions to federal penitentiaries is because they are far less likely than men to commit or to be convicted of serious crimes of violence which result in sentences in excess of two years.

Women account for less than 5% of all individuals serving sentences of 2 years or more and the vast majority of women prisoners are first time prisoners. In 2001, 82% of federally sentenced women were serving their first federal sentence.

The fastest growing prison population worldwide is women, and in particular, racialized, young poor women and women with mental and cognitive disabilities. The increasing numbers of women in prison is clearly linked to the evisceration of health, education, and social services.

The Canadian Human Rights Commission found correctional practices violate the human rights of women prisoners and a profound discriminatory impact was recognized since women are more deeply affected by segregation than are men. Women tend to experience segregation as rejection, abandonment, invisibility and denial of their existence. Segregation does not further women's rehabilitation and it often jeopardizes a woman's safety and mental health.

Women who are classified as maximum security tend to be so designated because they are labelled as having difficulty adapting to the prison (i.e., institutional adjustment), rather than because they pose a risk to public safety.

In 2001–2002, more than four of ten priority complaints and grievances (those considered to have a significant impact on a prisoner's rights and freedoms) were *not* processed within established time frames.

Two-thirds of federally sentenced women are mothers and they are more likely than men to have primary childcare responsibilities.

Separation from their children and the inability to deal with problems concerning them are major anxieties for women in prison.

Relative to men, women pose a far lower risk to the safety of the community upon release and lower rates of recidivism.

The recidivism rate for federally sentenced women is approximately 22%, as compared to 59% for men. Only 1–2% of federally sentenced women are returned to prison as the result of the commission of new crimes. The overwhelming majority represent women who have their parole revoked as a result of administrative breaches of conditions of community release. The re-offending recidivism rate of women released from the Okimaw Ohci Healing Lodge is even lower.

Eighty-two percent of all federally sentenced women report having been physically and/or sexually abused. This percentage rises to 90% for Aboriginal women.

The context in which federally sentenced women are charged with causing death is important in understanding the risk they pose to society. In many cases, the actions were defensive or otherwise re-active to violence directed at them, their children or another third party. (Elizabeth Fry, 2005)

The Mother-Child Program

In addition to the facts listed above, one significant characteristic of federally sentenced women is that "the majority of women who come in conflict with the law are mothers. Most of them were the sole supporters of their families at the time they were incarcerated" (Pate, 2000, p. 10). In fact, to draw attention to the importance and reality of this issue, the Elizabeth Fry Society ends their National Elizabeth Fry Week on Mother's Day.

Historically, the ability of a mother placed in a federal institution to maintain contact with her children was extremely limited. As noted earlier, before the closure of the Prison for Women, isolation from families was a major criticism of the women's correctional system. Women who applied under Exchange of Service Agreements with their home provinces in order to be closer to their families often sacrificed access to programs and services. The Task Force on Federally Sentenced Women (1990) articulated the plight of these mothers to maintain contact with their children while incarcerated and offered some recommendations:

Two out of three federally sentenced women are mothers, who said they had primary responsibility for their children. Many of these women spoke of the intense pain and anxiety caused by the separation from their children and of their sense of powerlessness when their children are placed in foster homes. Federally sentenced women who chose to remain in their home provinces under Exchange of Service Agreements, told researchers they did so primarily to maintain regular contact with their children.

Currently, visiting policies differ from prison to prison. The cost of transportation, the willingness of foster parents to facilitate visits, the cost of telephone calls, are all factors that, despite written policy, greatly affect women's ability to maintain contact. With respect to infants, only two provinces enable women to keep their infants during the critical bonding stage.

The Task Force discussed the issue of mothers and children at length. Following its review of the available literature, the Task Force concluded this complex issue could not be amply dealt with in the time available and that there is no one simple answer or formula. The Task Force recognized that the issue involves others besides the mother, the child and the Correctional Service of Canada. The extended family and child welfare agencies also have a role to play.

The Task Force further agreed that the environment at most of the current facilities for women in Canada is not appropriate for children.

Although the Task Force concluded that this issue deserves further study, it was decided that:

- new facilities must provide a home-like environment and sufficient flexibility to enable a child or children to live with their mother;
- decisions should be made on an individual basis;
- the Correctional Service of Canada should be the facilitator in the decision-making process, assisting and supporting the sentenced mother in her negotiations with the applicable child welfare agency.

The Task Force further decided that where a live-in arrangement is not possible, the Correctional Service of Canada must provide the necessary resources to enable regular and close contact between mothers and children. (Task Force on Federally Sentenced Women, 1990)

So, when the opportunity presented itself with the plan to close the Prison for Women and open regional facilities, the Correctional Service of Canada began to explore how to implement a mother-child program within its new regional facilities.

In July 1992, the Construction Policy and Services/National Implementation Committee submitted its report, *Regional Facilities for Federally Sentenced Women Operational Plan.* In it, the committee discussed the mothers and children program:

> One of the major concerns identified in the Task Force was the separation of women from their children and families. This was particularly critical given the number of women who have children. Clearly, the notion of providing more contact within the family unit is important.
>
> The goal of the mothers and children initiative is to foster positive relationships between mothers and their children, with the well being of the child being the priority. Various residency, visiting and program options will be available based on the unique relationships and needs of both the child and the mother. Case-by-case eligibility for participation will be assessed and each woman will be given the opportunity to choose whether or not she will assume an active parenting role. Participation for all parties will be voluntary.
>
> The components of the Mother-Child Program are intended to be integrated and should be seen as a holistic approach to promoting mother-child interactions. The program will be flexible but will include the following options:
>
> - visiting through open visits
> - visiting through the private family visiting program
> - visiting on and off site between the mother and child while the child resides in a local foster care or alternative placement
> - occasional on-site residency of the child with the mother
> - part-time (weekends and holidays) on-site residency of the child with the mother
> - full-time on-site residency of the child with the mother
> - parenting programs
> - on-site day care
> - after-school programs
>
> One of the difficulties in establishing children's programs is that the laws regarding children are under provincial jurisdiction. Coordination with and consent from the respective provincial authorities are

required. It is expected that on-going costs directly related to children (e.g., food, clothing, toys), will be covered by private sources or provincial welfare. Health care will be under the auspices of the provincial health authorities. (Correctional Service of Canada, 1992)

In "It's about time: the legal context of policy changes for female offenders" (1994), Maria Vachon took up the issue of inmate children and prison reform:

Creating Choices highlighted the difficulties faced by women unable to have their children with them and, in many cases, geographically isolated from them.

In response, the Correctional Service of Canada has agreed that women with children should have a variety of on-site residential and visiting options when the new facilities are open. Where it is in the best interest of the child, a mother will even be able to care for her child in the institution until the child is of school age.

In the interim, the Prison for Women has dealt with nine pregnant inmates since 1990; Saskatchewan Penitentiary, with one. In most cases, the child was born during the mother's conditional release. A few babies spent their first days in the institution, however, before being transferred with their mother to a provincial facility.

Recently, one mother was (with the consent of the commissioner) allowed to care for her child at the minimum-security institution in Kingston. The efforts made to accommodate expectant mothers over the past few years seem to demonstrate the Service's acceptance of the task force recommendations. (Vachon, 1994)

In July 1994, CSC published the *Correctional Program Strategy for Federally Sentenced Women*, the document that set out both the framework for FSW program design and delivery and defined the core programs. Programs for mothers came under the category of living skills in the core programs and were described as follows:

The 1990 survey found that two-thirds of FSW had children. Many of these women had tremendous concern over lost custody of one or more of their children and reported that contact with their children, regardless of their age, was essential to personal well-being. The majority of the Prison for Women population and 40% of the provincial population indicated an interest in programs about children. Programs addressing issues surrounding coping with parenting in prison and parenting from a distance are required, as well as early childhood development for those women who will participate in the residential programs for children that will be part of the facilities.

The *Parenting Program* is very important to the women. The existing program will be reviewed and enhanced so that it also deals with issues specific to FSW. It will be mandatory for those women whose children are in residence and should serve as a type of prerequisite to more in-depth early childhood development courses. (Correctional Service of Canada, 1994)

In 1995, a study was undertaken by Labrecque to explore certain issues regarding the mother-child program in greater depth. In particular, the points requiring further clarification included: the critical stages of the development of the child; the essential conditions for the child's well-being; the impact of the child's circumstances on his or her development; suggestions and solutions regarding these circumstances; the relevance of setting up parenting skills acquisition programs for clients; and the relevance of staff training. The resulting document, *Study of the Mother-Child Program (1995)*, examined these issues as well as "situated the mother-child program in the context of the development and operation of FSW facilities" (p. 1). The document examined the stages of development of the child, fundamental needs of the child, a description of the proposed mother-child program and problems involved with the plan, prevention, and suggestions for making the program more effective.

The impact of this study and the next steps taken were described in a document produced by the CSC National Headquarters, Federally Sentenced Women Program, in December 1995: *Overviews: Correctional Service of Canada Regional Facilities for Federally Sentenced Women:*

Creating Choices recommended that the facilities have a residential mother-child program which would run the gamut from full-time residency to part-time residency to occasional residency to regular or enhanced visiting (e.g., everyday after school).

A contract was awarded and a literature review was done to assess the feasibility of such a program within the design and management model of the new facilities to ensure that the program would be in the best interests of the child.

A draft policy developed on the basis of all available information was sent out for consultation in September 1995 to FSW, facility advisory committees and CAEFS, CCJC, and NWAC. Consultation input has been collated and problem areas requiring further work have been identified. It is anticipated that the draft policy will be submitted to ExCom for final approval in February/March 1996. As was done with the draft, the final policy will then be submitted to the Solicitor General. In accordance with a previous ExCom decision, all facilities currently have a number of rooms reserved for children.

A review of the mother-infant programs described in the November 1995 Corrections Compendium indicates that the CSC draft policy is consistent with existing programs, including the one at Bedford Hills [located in New York]. All programs have an assessment component, including such factors as general behaviour of the inmate and ability to care for the child and a program plan. Most programs focus on infants with the maximum stay being around 18 months. The extensive use of volunteers in the Mother-Infant Program at Bedford Hills is a model which CSC hopes to emulate. (p. 49)

In October 1995, the Okimaw Ohci Healing Lodge opened in Cypress Hills, Saskatchewan. In this 30-bed healing lodge for federally sentenced Aboriginal women, the Mother-Child Program began as a pilot part-time program only in July 1996 and became a full-time program in August 1997. Norma Green (2002) describes the program:

The children live with their mothers and go to the Day Care Centre during the day, while the mother participates in programs. Children are an important part of the lives of Aboriginal and First Nations people. Children are considered close to the "Creator", and are special to Aboriginal families and communities. Therefore, having their children on site is important for offenders and staff. The children bring joy, hope and anticipation to everyone. (p. 49)

According to the Correctional Service of Canada, in September 1997, an interim policy was put in place that allowed mothers who gave birth while incarcerated to keep their children with them. The eligibility requirements

were those outlined in the draft Commissioner's Directive being developed for
the Mother-Child Program at the time. During this period, the approval for
all participation came from the deputy commissioner for women. In January
2001, the Commissioner's Directive #768 was published. Since then, women
have been able to bring their children in from the community (that is, they
don't have to give birth in prison).

When the women's institutions were first opened the number of spaces allocated in the Mother-Child Program was:

- Nova–4
- Joliette–5
- Grand Valley Institution for Women–8
- Edmonton Institution for Women–3
- Okimaw Ohci Healing Lodge–8

However, inmate accommodation is always the priority. The fire codes require that the housing units in the regional institutions have a maximum of
ten persons, and a child counts as one (it does not matter if children sleep in
their mothers' rooms). In some institutions, the Mother-Child Program has
not been really implemented because of the size of inmate population accommodation.

Since the promulgation of the official program in 2001, 19 different women
and 22 children have participated (as of November 2003). A few women's requests have been refused, either because they did not meet the eligibility criteria
or participation was not deemed in the best interest of the child. In November
2003 there were three participants, two full-time and one part-time. A program
evaluation has taken place, but it was not yet available at date of publication
for this book.

Some correctional administrators commented on the Mother-Child Program in the following way:

Administrator 5: The Mother-Child Program is huge, and I have never
seen such change in some women. One of the biggest problems that we
always face with the women, even though their numbers were relatively
small compared to men, was that, well, you could go into any men's jail
on any Saturday afternoon when visiting is on and you will see moms
and kids, wives and sweeties, and all of that, in visiting the guys. Do the
same thing in a women's prison during visiting hours and you will very
rarely see a significant other, you may see a mom with children or a foster
family, but with women, their relationships often do not last when they

go to jail. Therefore, they lose out on two things: they lose out on the fact that they do not have a spouse—many of them have not had any kind of a spouse anyway, before they went in. Most of them have children and most of these are in-care somewhere, either with Social Services or with a family member, etc....

On the other hand, the men seem to have relationships that last for some reason or they develop more relationships while they are in jail, but they always have girlfriends or there is a wife or someone. Kids are not as big an issue to men but to the women they are. Women have usually lost control of their kids but the men have not—the men always have somebody who is looking out for their kids. Therefore, for a woman, her whole focus is that she is going to get her kids. First, she is feeling all sorts of guilt because she has not parented her kids, most of them have no idea how to parent their kids, and they have not been parented properly themselves. Therefore, they drug themselves up and that is it. Therefore, when they get out of jail, they either get their kids and then they cannot handle it and end up back into substance abuse and all other kinds of stuff. Alternatively, they do not get their kids, and they cannot that handle that and they do the same thing. Therefore, it is important for us in the Mother-Child Program to be able to teach the parenting skills portion of that.

Because of the paramount role that children play in the lives of mothers, the Mother-Child Program is available in federal institutions for women. Administrator 5 goes on to explain how the program works:

They are able to have the child or children with them if they can meet certain criteria; for example, they cannot have the child or children with them if they have ever been involved in a crime that involves children. If they meet the criteria and apply, then the team—including Social Services, who are part of that team—makes the decision. For example, if they are pregnant when they come to us and going to have a baby, they would have to be with us for a certain period of time, and we would be looking at their behaviour, because they would have to earn their way for this. As well, they would have to take a parenting course, so they are assessed to see what parenting skills they possess and they have to provide for this child. What this means is that while the offender is in prison, the money that she makes goes toward the upkeep of that child, i.e., diapers. CSC puts in a percentage and they provide a percentage. Our responsibility is to make sure the mother and the child are healthy and are kept healthy. Therefore, if the child gets sick, the child goes outside the institution for their health care needs—we do not provide that here for the children. Of course, if it were something like the child fell and cut their lip, we would deal with that here. So they have to meet the criteria, they would live in a house with other women who met the criteria even though they may not have children themselves but they also been affected perhaps by being in an abusive relationship or having children, and they are favourable to having other women and their children join the house. The child can stay with them up to the age of four years, full-time.

These women also have to be solely committed to their corrections plan and they have to be committed to working with Social Services in terms of determining what is in the best interest of the child's welfare. At the age of four years, they have to have a placement for that child if they are not out by then. They had to have arranged with Social Services for a family and they would then meet that family or choose a family member of their own. The child could be brought on weekends and holidays to visit—they can also apply to have their children over the age of four years come to visit them in the family unit on weekends and stay with them. Nevertheless, it is very well structured and it does teach them a lot about the day-to-day responsibilities. For example, if you and I have children, we are living in a house together, and I have an anger management program from one o'clock to three o'clock this afternoon, I have to arrange with you or with someone else in the house to babysit my child while I am gone. Then I have to be reciprocal, so when you are having your program or a visit or something, I will help. Therefore, in the real world sense, you need to be able to get up in the morning at seven to get your child ready for the outside daycare because you have an eight o'clock job that starts. Most of these women have never experienced this on the outside, do not know the proper nutritional needs or meals for children, and they learn how to do all of that stuff on about twenty dollars per week. Most of these women will go out and be living on some type of assistance for a period of time and they have to know how to exist.

The Mother-Child Program can benefit both young moms with newborn babies and those with older children. Administrator 5 explains the origins of the program and potential for its growth:

This program exists across regions in all of the women's facilities, if they have children who meet the criteria. We can go for a period where there is no Mother-Child Program, as there are no mothers there who either have children or wants to have them. Most of them are happy to have their children come and visit in the private family trailer once every three to four weeks, and some women do not want their children to see them in jail. Nevertheless, for the young mom who is having a baby and does not have a lot of experience, this program is ideal. In terms of being able to study the impact of this program, most of the children who came in to the program were young and the mothers have left with them. We have had a couple of mothers who had to make placements for their children and that is always painful, but they were able to place their children with family. Therefore, the child in this program has a good start in bonding with the mother.

One of the big factors for these women when they get out is that they have often lost contact with their children, even though they have written letters, etc., but that is not the same. When you come back into a mother role and want your children to live with you, you may have an eight- or ten-year-old boy who does not want to listen to you anymore or alternatively, a fourteen-year-old or a teenager who has maybe grown up with the grandmother. So these facilities have only been open about seven years now and we are just starting to get the data on this program, but it has worked well. We took this concept from the Americans, who have had mother-child programs running very successfully for years. For example, there is a model in the Bedford Stuyvesant area of New York running quite successfully in the Bedford Hills Correctional Facility for Women, which had its origins on that nation's first nursery prison concept that evolved more than one hundred years ago. And what is most interesting about that program is the involvement of the fathers; the facility has a daycare and the fathers can drop the children off at the daycare inside, or whoever else it is that is looking after these women's children on the outside. Therefore, they have different kinds of programs in the States and in Europe. Therefore, what I can see coming down the road will be our ability to respond to a few of the men/fathers who would like to take parenting classes and programs as well.

Administrator 6: We have a family program but we haven't had any children—we have a capacity to have them—but we haven't had any children here for ten years. When the original facility was built, the two houses were both our mother-child homes. So, on the main floors there are connecting bedrooms so the women can have her child or children with her. So they would be in regular housing units in one of the two houses that can accommodate children. The CD on mother-child was prorogated or deferred last year. We currently have a request for part-time mother-child, so it's in the assessment stage and that too is always in the best interests of the child so we are at the Children's Aid assessment level. They will be making that determination. So the children are both school age. The mother is asking for them to come in part-time over March break and summer time so there is more frequent access. That's where we are at right now. We don't have any women right now that are pregnant. Any request for under the age of either four or six—I can't remember—we haven't had any requests since I've been here—they can live with them full-time. Once they reach school age, at either six or seven, then they become part-time. Otherwise, families can participate in the private family visiting but not under the Mother-Child.

There is certainly debate about whether or not infants, toddlers, or other children should be in prisons. Some argue that prisons are inappropriate places for children and that under no circumstance should children be placed in them. Others believe that a woman who breaks the law forfeits her right to be a mother or that it makes her an inappropriate person to raise children. Based on the comments above, how might Administrator 5 or 6 respond to these arguments?

Others argue that separating a mother and child is much more harmful to the emotional and social development of the child than being in a prison. At least by keeping the mother and child together in a supportive environment, programs and services can be implemented and monitored to support that mother in developing the skills and knowledge she needs to raise a child. As the profile of female offenders shows, many of these women came from very troubled pasts. Most research in the crime prevention field indicates that social development is the most effective form of crime prevention. As Matusicky (1998) stated:

> both research and experience into antisocial behaviour indicate that the roots of crime and victimization lie, in large part, within the social and economic environment of the child. Put in its simplest terms, to reduce crime and victimization, we must support families and provide opportunities for children from the very beginning of their lives. (p. 1)

Given that 56% of women in federal penitentiaries are between the ages of 20 and 34, 82% are serving federal time for the first time and 63% are serving a sentence under six years, it seems logical to conclude that most will be returning to the community and becoming the sole parent and provider for their children again.

Internationally, there seems to be agreement that arrangements should be made for pregnant inmates to deliver their babies in public hospitals and not in the prison. The major reasons given for this decision are ensuring professional obstetric assistance and avoiding the stigma of having prison as the place of birth on the child's birth certificate (APCCA, 2000). However, little consensus seems to exist internationally about whether or not a woman should be allowed to keep her baby with her in prison and, if so, for how long. The following table illustrates this diversity among countries.

Table 9.2. International Mothers in Prison Programs

Australia	**Queensland:** to 2 years in Brisbane Women's Prison or up to 5 years in Helana Jones Community Corrections Unit **Adelaide:** to 2½ years if born in prison **Sydney:** to 5 years in two open centres
Belgium	To age 2
Denmark	Men and women prisoners can have children with them if they are to be released before the child turns 3; in practice, rarely in prison
Finland	To age 2, can be extended, particularly in open unit
France	To 18 months
Germany	To age 6: six closed prisons to age 3 and two open prisons to age 6
Greece	To age 2
Hong Kong	To 3 years. In practice very few children are in prison
Hungary	If born during custody period, until they are 6 months but can be extended to 12 months if release date is near
Iceland	Very young babies for breastfeeding/special care needs
Indonesia	To age 2
Ireland	To age 3
Italy	To age 3
Japan	Up to one year of age

Kiribati	While mother is lactating
Korea	Up to 18 months
Luxembourg	To age 2
Malaysia	Up to age 4
Malta	To 1 year but only two women have taken advantage of this when the alternative was for the children to be in care.
Netherlands	Five closed prisons to 9 months ; Ter Peel prison, to age 4
New Zealand	Up to six months while child care arrangements are organized
Portugal	To age 3
Singapore	To age 3
Spain	To age 6
Sweden	Up to one year of age; average stay 3 months (rarely in prison), open prison of Vangdalen allows children under age 2
Switzerland	To age 3
Thailand	To age 3
United Kingdom	Depends on prison: Holloway (largest all-female prison) and New Hall until 9 months; Askham Grange (open prison) and Styal until 18 months. There are three open prisons in England but only AG has baby facilities
United States	**New York:** Bedford Hills and Taconic Correction Centre: up to 12 months with possible extension if mother will be released by the time the child is 18 months **Nebraska:** a unit for pregnant women who are within 18 months of their release date
Vietnam	To age 2

Source: International Centre for Prison Studies, 2000; Caddle, 1998; APCCA, 2000

Other countries have a very different approach, as was discussed at the 20th Asian and Pacific Conference of Correctional Administrators in 2000:

> New Zealand, as a matter of policy, does provide facilities for babies to stay with their mothers in prison. As an alternative, early release or temporary release may be granted to prisoner mothers, but if this is not practicable, arrangements are made for daily visits to the prison

by the baby for breast-feeding in an appropriate setting. Arrangements will also be made where necessary for mothers to express their milk for delivery to the baby located elsewhere.

Similarly, in the Peoples Republic of China, the Prison Law provides that convicted female criminals who are pregnant or breast-feeding their children may not be taken into custody, and the Criminal Prosecution Law provides that such female offenders may serve their terms outside prison. Also, in Mongolia women prisoners who give birth are allowed home for 18 months to care for their babies and then return to prison. (APCCA, 2000)

So, perhaps the choice is not as simple as either having children in prisons with their mothers or separating mother and child. Perhaps a third option exists: altering the way the justice system deals with mothers. There is no systematic evaluation in the area of mother-child programs, but there appears to be some data that indicate well-structured programs can produce a preventive effect (Labrecque, 1995).

Conclusion

The situation of federally sentenced women has garnered a lot of attention in recent years. The Prison for Women, a target of controversy and criticism since the day it opened, has finally been closed. The new regional facilities across the country, including an Aboriginal healing lodge, strive to alleviate some of the additional hardships women serving time in the Prison for Women endured by trying to bring these women closer to their families. New programs, such as the Mother-Child Program, have also been designed specifically to meet the needs of women. In the area of federally sentenced women, the Correctional Service of Canada has made significant progress in endeavouring to ensure that its mission and core values apply to female, as well as male, inmates.

Yet, Correctional Service of Canada's work in this area is far from over. Program needs and significant gaps still exist in delivering services and programs in both the community and the institutions. Correctional Service of Canada must also continue to evaluate the programs they are delivering to ensure they are meeting the needs of federally sentenced women.

Study Questions

1. Discuss some of the issues that face federally sentenced women but not federally sentenced men.
2. Should mother-child programs exist in federal institutions?

3. You have been hired to evaluate the Mother-Child Program. Discuss how you will design your program evaluation.

Bibliography

*Items with asterisks are also suggested readings for this chapter.

APCCA (2000). *Women Prisoners. Record of the Twentieth Asian and Pacific Conference of Correctional Administrators.* Sydney, Australia. http://www.apcca. org/News&Events/record_of_20th_appca.htm

*Arbour, L. (1996). *Commission of Inquiry into certain events at the Prison for Women in Kingston.* Ottawa: Public Works and Government Services Canada. http:// ww2.psepc-sppcc.gc.ca/publications/corrections/199681_e.asp

Caddle, D. (1998). *Age limits for babies in prison: Some lessons from Abroad.* Home Office Research, Development and Statistics Directorate. Study No. 80. London: Home Office.

Correctional Service of Canada (1994). Correctional Program Strategy for Federally Sentenced Women.

Correctional Service of Canada (2002). *Regional Facilities for Federally Sentenced Women Operational Plan.* Office of the Deputy Commissioner for Women National Headquarters. http://www.csc-scc.gc.ca/text/prgrm/fsw/fsw12/region_women_facilit_fsw12-eng.shtml

Correctional Service of Canada (2000). *The Transformation of Federal Corrections for* Women. http://www.csc-scc.gc.ca/text/pblct/choix/index_eng.shtml

Correctional Service of Canada (2005). *Response from the Correctional Service of Canada to the 32nd Annual Report of the Correctional Investigator 2004–2005.* http://www.csc-scc.gc.ca/text/pblct/cio4-05/toc-eng.shtml

Correctional Service of Canada (2006). *Ten Year Status Report on Women's Corrections.* http://www.csc-scc.gc.ca/text/prgrm/fsw/wos24/index-eng.shtml

Elizabeth Fry Society (2005). *Fact Sheet on Women in Prison.* http://www.elizabethfry.ca/eweek06/factsht.htm

Green, N. (2000). Okimaw Ohci Healing Lodge: A federally sentenced women's initiative. *Forum on Corrections Research,* 12(1).

International Centre for Prison Studies (2000). *Council of Europe Annual Penal Statistics* 2000. http://www.eurochips.org/

Labrecque, R. (1995). *Study of the Mother-Child Program.* Correctional Service of Canada—Federally Sentenced Women Program. http://www.csc-scc.gc.ca/text/ prgrm/fsw/fsw24/toce-eng.shtml

Matusicky, C. (1998). Preventing Crime by Investing in Families. *Family Connections* Winter. British Columbia: BC Council for Families. http://www.bccf.bc.ca/ catalogue/index.php?cPath=34&osCsid=970b7e9e7800c24ee7e1f9499f97fda8

Office of the Auditor General of Canada (2003). *Chapter Four: Correctional Service of Canada: Reintegration of Women Offenders.* Ottawa. http://www.oag-bvg. gc.ca/domino/reports.nsf/html/20030404ce.html

Pate, K. (2000). *Women In Corrections: The Context, the Challenges.* Paper presented at the Women in Corrections: Staff and Clients Conference convened by the Australian Institute of Criminology in conjunction with the Department for Correctional Services SA and held in Adelaide, 31 October–1 November, 2000. http://www.aic.gov.au/conferences/womencorrections/pate.pdf

Shaw, M. (1989). *Survey of Federally Sentenced Women.* Ottawa, Canada.

*Task Force on Federally Sentenced Women (1990). *Creating Choices: The Report of the Task Force on Federally Sentenced Women.* Ottawa: Correctional Service of Canada. http://www.csc-scc.gc.ca/text/prgrm/fsw/choices/toce-eng.shtml

Vachon, M. M. (1994). It's about time: The legal context of policy changes for female offenders. *Forum on Corrections Research* 6(1). http://www.csc-scc.gc.ca/text/ pblct/forum/e061/e061ind-eng.shtml

Watson, L. (2000). The Intensive Intervention Strategy for Women Offenders. *Let's Talk* 1(8).

Suggested Readings

Bonta, J., Pang, B., and Wallace-Capretta, S. (1995). Predictors of recidivism among incarcerated female offenders. *The Prison Journal,* 75(3), 227–294.

Correctional Service of Canada (2003). *Commissioner's Directive—Institutional Mother-Child Program.*http://www.csc-scc.gc.ca/text/plcy/cdshtm/768cd-eng. shtml

10 Unique Prison Populations

This chapter presents a brief discussion of a number of special populations issues identified by the CSC interviewees, including *older and elderly offender populations, ethno-cultural offenders, and offenders with Fetal Alcohol Spectrum Disorders.*

The "Greying" of Canadian Offenders

There are several reasons for considering older offenders as a special group within the overall penitentiary population. As they age, their health needs increase and their ability to participate in meaningful programming as part of their release plan seems to decline. Just as we tend to expect the older adult in the general population to require more specialized health services and sometimes "institutionalized" care—for example, in a continuing care or assisted living facility—this level of care may also be required by older offenders in federal correctional institutions. Such specialization of services is very expensive. In the U.S., for instance, the annual cost of incarcerating an offender is $23,000 U.S., whereas the cost of incarcerating an elderly offender is $69,000 U.S.

According to Dr. Julius Uzoaba (1998), researcher for the Correctional Service of Canada, older offenders are generally considered to be those between 50 and 64, while elderly offenders are 65 or older. Those offenders who are 70 or older are often referred to as geriatric offenders. For our purposes, the term "older" will be used in a general way to refer to all offenders over 50.

In the U.S. one out of every 23 inmates in prison is 55+ years, an 85% increase since 1995. Part of this is due to an 83% increase in the number of prisoners serving a life sentence from 1992 to the present. Of those, one-quarter will not qualify for parole. The average time to be served by newly convicted lifers in the U.S. was 21 years in 1991; by 1997, this increased to 29 years.

At any one time, older offenders constitute a small proportion of those incarcerated in Canadian penitentiaries, but as the general population ages, the population within the prisons will also age. Statistics Canada reported that 19.7% of the overall population in 1996 was 55 years or older. According to Griffiths and Cunningham (2003), older offenders—those ages 50 and up—make up around 10% of the offender population. Uzoaba (1998) noted that between 1993 and 1996, the population of older offenders grew rapidly. However, Griffiths and Cunningham (2003) suggest that it will eventually reach upwards of 20% (see Table 10.1).

Table 10.1. Institutional Population: 1993, 1996, and 2002

Age (years)	Number			% of Population		
	1993	1996	2002	1993	1996	2002
Under 50	12,021	13,448	10,945	91.6	90.7	86.1
50-54	524	632	786	4.0	4.3	6.2
55-59	264	377	504	2.0	2.5	4.0
60-64	200	200	255	1.5	1.3	2.0
65 and up	116	170	217	0.9	1.1	1.7
Total ages 50 and over	1,104	1,379	1,762	8.4	9.2	13.9

Source: Uzoaba, 1998, p. 12. Reproduced with the permission of the Minister of Public Works and Government Services Canada, 2009.

The majority of older offenders are more likely to be serving sentences for sex crimes or other violent crimes. They also generally have needs that are substantially different from younger offenders. For example, they often have special needs and therefore require special attention and treatment. Some of the characteristics of this population that may distinguish them from the younger offenders are that they are more likely to have witnessed spousal abuse during childhood, have a poor relationship with their siblings, and they are often sexually dissatisfied in their marital relationships. Likewise, their history of alcohol use often differs from that of younger offenders in that they have an earlier onset age of drinking, a pattern of regular drinking, or a history of drinking binges, excessive usage during drinking events, and drinking to relieve stress. As well, unlike their younger counterparts, older offenders are less likely to attend substance abuse treatment and even more unlikely to have completed such treatment. Dr. Uzoaba's (1998) study resulted in the emergence of three distinct categories of older offenders:

1. Offenders incarcerated while young who grew old in prison in the course of a lengthy incarceration or life imprisonment. These offenders are most likely serving their first incarceration and tend to be model inmates. For example, a review of 309 homicide offenders incarcerated in the Pacific Region revealed that 33% of the sentences being served were more than 20 years in length, with one offender serving 34 years on an indeterminate sentence. For 78% of these homicide offenders, this was their first federal incarceration (Mumford, 2001). In 1996, of the population of offenders 50 years or older, they made up around 10% of the group;

2. Multiple or serial re-incarcerations—that is, offenders with a criminal career over time. These are often the "old cons", or chronic offenders who frequently recidivate. Such offenders are considered to be low risk and see themselves as career criminals, mostly committing property offences. In 1996, 17% of the older offender population made up this group of offenders; and

3. Offenders serving their first incarceration late in life, and for most of their life were law abiding citizens. This group experiences the most difficulty adjusting to institutional life, such as that which exists in penitentiaries. Approximately 73% of the older offender population are represented by this group. (p. 5)

Table 10.2. Categories of Older Offender Population by Region (1996)

Category	Atlantic	Québec	Ontario	Prairies	Pacific	National
Incarcerated	1,393	3,753	3,743	3,396	1,922	14,207
On register	1,474	4,011	3,995	3,565	2,059	15,104
Under 50	1,302	3,665	3,544	3,243	1,821	13,575
Age 50-54	66	178	208	142	90	684
Age 55-59	50	97	118	82	68	415
Age 60-69	42	59	101	86	63	351
Age 70+	14	12	24	12	17	79
50 and Over	172	346	451	322	238	1,529

Source: Uzoaba, 1998, p. 15. Reproduced with the permission of the Minister of Public Works and Government Services Canada, 2009.

In 1996, Ontario had the largest older offender population, and Québec had the largest population of offenders under 50 (see Table 10.2). Interestingly, compared to younger offenders, older offenders are more than twice as likely to be serving time for violent crimes of passion, such as the murder of a spouse, neighbour, or relative (Mumford, 2001; Uzoaba, 1998). Compared to the arrests of persons of all ages, a high proportion of arrests of older citizens are for crimes of violence and sexual offences (see Table 10.3). According to one CSC administrator:

Administrator 1: We could develop our peer support—that would be like an attendant care type program—and there is other options too depending on the type of illness or the type of level of requirement that the person would need, but we haven't crossed that bridge yet, but it is certainly something we are trying to plan for in the future.

Right now we have a very young population. I haven't seen that in the male institutions where I have worked, and more specifically related to sex offenders. Male sex offenders that have committed crimes way, way back, whose victims have come forward now, certainly are a way larger increase right now, anyways, to over age fifty and serving a long sentence.

In one institution, peer support is available. In a February 2008 speech given by the correctional investigator of Canada (CIC), the needs and challenges of working with aging offenders were highlighted. In doing so, the CIC noted that CSC failed to live up to its own recommendations made in 2000–2001. The exception was Pacific/RTC Institution, which implemented a Peer Care Assistant Program to work with aging offenders with health issues, and in particular those in palliative care (The Correctional Investigator Canada, Feb. 4, 2008).

In general, older offenders often led conforming lives and were "model" citizens prior to their incarceration, with a higher social status, positive attitudes toward life, and affirmative religious attitudes (Uzoaba, 1998). As a result of some of these factors, such offenders often find it difficult to adjust to the deculturalization characteristic of prison socialization.

Table 10.3. Distribution of Age Categories of Older Offender by Offence Category

Offence	50-54	55-59	60-64	65-69	70+	Total
Homicide	185	106	54	15	15	375
Robbery	123	49	21	7	1	201

Offence	50-54	55-59	60-64	65-69	70+	Total
Sexual	216	159	109	60	43	587
Drug	88	41	10	12	0	151
Other	119	64	20	17	8	228
National	731	419	214	111	67	1,542

Source: Uzoaba 1998, p. 17. Reproduced with the permission of the Minister of Public Works and Government Services Canada, 2009.

As a consequence of growing older in prison while serving a lengthy sentence, older offenders have different problems than the rest of the offender population (Uzoaba 1998) (see Table 10.4). According to Uzoaba, some of these relate to:

- medical care needs
- problems adjusting to imprisonment
- programming needs
- peer relationships in prison
- family relationships
- parole considerations (p. 60)

Table 10.4. A Comparison of Older and Younger Offenders' Perceived Stressors

Stress type	Younger offenders (%)	Older offenders (%)
Offence & sentence issues		
Getting parole	57	57
Getting transferred	39	35
My offence	47	54
Length of sentence	59	64
How soon until I will be released	63	64
Personal stressors		
Family issues	64	68
Physical health	47	54
Mental health	39	31

Stress type	Younger offenders (%)	Older offenders (%)
Relationship with inmates	40	35
Relationship with staff	40	33
Physical safety	33	33
Institutional stressors		
Drug/alcohol problem	20	7
Financial problems	32	21
School or work	29	18
Double bunking	59	55
Getting enough tobacco	37	24
Percentage scoring as stressed	37	30

Source: Gal, (2002). http://www.csc-scc.gc.ca/text/pblct/forum/e142/e142d-eng.shtm. Reproduced with the permission of the Minister of Public Works and Government Services Canada, 2009.

Some of the factors that exacerbate mental health problems are stress and depression. The strain of incarceration accelerates the physical and mental health status of the older offender. The two most significant stressors according to Gal (2002) were being locked up and abrasive interactions with other offenders.

Adjustment to Imprisonment

Some researchers believe that untreated psychological and emotional issues affect the adjustment of older offenders in prison, although they generally suffer fewer adjustment problems than the younger offenders, according to Uzoaba (1998). This is especially the case for older offenders incarcerated at an earlier age who have served a lengthy sentence. Older offenders who have been able to maintain contact with their families are better adjusted than those who have not. Of course, the length of time an older offender has to serve is a crucial variable in keeping or breaking social contacts with family or the "free" community. For example, the longer the length of incarceration, the more the offender's social roles and attachments outside of the penitentiaries will decrease. This fact inevitably leads to emotional trauma and isolation, and usually results in a growing dependency on the institution itself. Exchanging "outside reference groups for inmate reference groups and conventional roles for roles assured in the prison subculture" is often characteristic of institutional dependency

(Uzoaba, 1998. p.67). Aging inside these institutions is different from aging in the community primarily because prison environments are abnormal. Such offenders often demand more of staff's time and energy, and they are more likely to have chronic complaints. According to Uzoaba,

> ... older offenders are traditionally characterized by poor adjustment, depression and unhappiness, intellectual ineffectiveness, negative self image, feelings of personal insignificance and impotency—view of self as old and unable to compete or face problems—docile, submissive with a low range of interests and activities. (p. 67)

Programming

Are older offenders proper candidates for treatment programs? Most programs are focused on rehabilitating offenders to prepare them for their eventual release back into the community and often focus on educational upgrades, employment skills development, substance abuse, anger management, family violence, and so on. Although some older offenders may express an interest in such programs, they are overlooked for various reasons: reduced funding that forces correctional administrators to choose younger offenders who may be more likely to benefit from treatment/programming over older offenders; the belief on the part of some staff that "you can't teach an old dog new tricks," they are past their prime; the complication of diminished physical, intellectual, and emotional states, sometimes brought on by old age and long confinement; and the lack of motivation. This lack of motivation may be based on the belief that their ability to participate in specific programs is vastly hampered in some way or that such programming is irrelevant.

As a result, some correctional administrators may tend to ignore these offenders and this may result in offenders feeling further isolated. Most correctional programs do not, for the most part, meet their needs. Programs for this group should be integrated, comprehensive, and structured to promote life-satisfaction and successful reintegration into the community. While some researchers argue that this group of offenders should be placed in a special unit, others believe that the distribution of older offenders throughout the prison environment has a stabilizing effect and that older offenders should be placed in correctional environments most suited to their needs. One CSC administrator pointed out:

Administrator 2: One of the issues we anticipated is that we would need a lot more programming for elderly offenders. To date we have not seen as many as we anticipated, which is good. But notwithstanding, we certainly do need to have the capacity to work with offenders who are reaching old age and/or those who are just acutely sick.

Existing programs also need to be modified for the older offender, who, for example may be unable to sit for two to three hours per day, for a three-month program period. Wellness programs such as low-impact exercise, ceramics, walking, gardening, woodworking, etc., should also be developed for older offenders.

Peer Relationships in Prison

According to Uzoaba (1998), research on this offender groups' relationships with peers is mixed. On the one hand, such relationships are seen as critical because friendships in prison offer the older offender an important means of daily support and provide opportunities for shared, intimate conversations on a variety of subjects. However, such friendships are not often based on trust, and in many cases are viewed as a reflection of personal weakness and potential danger. On the other hand, older offenders are also characterized as loners who frequently do not join groups. When friendship networks do form, they are most often based on ethnicity rather than age.

Family Relationships

Lengthy incarceration may have devastating effects on relationships with significant others, and the cutting of ties with families and/or friends may result in the offenders withdrawing into themselves or seeking emotional support from within the correctional setting. Often it leads to institutional dependency or institutional neurosis. Uzoaba (1998) has stated that offenders who have cut or lost all ties to the outside and who have lived long periods of time within the correctional facility are more concerned or anxious about reintegration into society, and are therefore less willing to attempt it. This severing or withering away of outside ties can be the result of several factors, such as:

- the crime involved a family member, especially in the case of a sexual offence;
- the offender is illiterate, so written communication is practically impossible;
- the spouse or other family member(s) is too old, too far away, or disabled and are unable to travel to the correctional institution;
- the correctional institution itself may create special situations or problems for family members impacting, their ability to visit the older offender.

The family plays a vital role in the lives of offenders, providing some "natural" protection and sometimes serving to reduce tension and hostility. It is important to recognize that there is a positive relationship between family visitations and positive parole outcomes. The question is whether this positive correlation also applies to older offenders.

Parole Consideration

Lack of motivation, particularly that associated with attending and completing programs, often reduces the older offenders' chances for parole. In fact, these offenders are often viewed as being uninvolved in correctional institution organizations, having no support systems, having no place to live, having health problems, and being unemployable. Most of these factors are taken into consideration by the parole board, which often puts the older offender at a great disadvantage. Parole is also considered to be a reward for good institutional adjustment, which is partially demonstrated by participation in programming. Since the majority of older offenders do not participate in programming, they are not in a position to show any positive changes to the parole boards. The lack of appropriate programming for the older offender, combined with the staff's lack of insight into the dynamics of aging makes the older parolees' chances for reintegration into the community very poor. This situation underscores the older offenders' reluctance to apply for parole, although as a group they are better parole candidates than younger offenders.

Medical Issues

According to Uzoaba (1998), some researchers believe that offenders in prison age faster than the normal population because of their lifestyle, and they typically cite a ten year differential between the overall health of the prison population and that of the general population. For older offenders this means a much earlier onset of health concerns that combine with the gradual decline and deterioration that aging may bring about. For example, among the elderly and geriatric offenders, Uzoaba (1998) noted a high incidence of multiple chronic health problems such as severe heart problems, diabetes, hypertension, stroke, cancer, Alzheimer's disease, Parkinson's disease, ulcers, emphysema, diminished hearing and eyesight, loss of memory, and so on (see Table 10.5). And along with the fear of growing old in prison, there is the fear of dying there, especially for those with many more years left to serve. Likewise, the stigma of dying in prison often has significant consequences for family members and/or descendants.

Table 10.5. Health-related Concerns of Male Inmates at Intake by Age, 2002

Need Domain	Age (years)		
	<50	50-64	65+
Special needs	13.1%	17.8%	32.8%
Health concerns—immediate attention	12.0%	16.1%	27.2%
Taking medication	26.5%	35.3%	56.0%

Source: Canadian Journal of Public Health, 2004, p. S20

Among this population, prevalence rates for alcohol abuse (58%), anxiety (45%), and depression (35%) were relatively high. Approximately 19% of older offenders compared to 25% of younger offenders scored higher on depression scales, and although older offenders constituted approximately 8.5% of overall offender populations (1991/92 to 1996/97), they made up 10% of the offender population who committed suicide (Gal, 2002).

According to a CSC interviewee:

Administrator 3: Just briefly on the elderly and geriatric ... we do have the capacity to accommodate disabled offenders. All the houses that are constructed below are all accessible. The row houses on the top are not new and were not built for that purpose. The institution itself is fully accessible. For geriatric ... geriatric in our definition is fifty plus a day, so anyone fifty years of age and over. Considering that many offenders who are with us over the age of fifty, they have been with us for a number of years, and physically they tend to be about ten years older than their biological age, so fifty is what is used. I only have two women here that are of that age. [This institution] does not have its own twenty-four-hour health care unit, so concerns that come up with the women—"if I was to get gravely ill, what would happen to me?"—all of the external requirements for medical needs—the women are escorted outside the institution, and that was part of our own physical location with being only a kilometre away from the regional hospital. We do blood work and we have clinics for general practitioners to come in, OB/GYN comes in, psychiatrist comes in, but we refer women to physiotherapy as an alternative to medication and that sort of thing, or eye doctors, or dentists, that sort of thing is outside the institution. So if a woman was to become seriously ill it may require transfer to another facility, but we do have—I shouldn't say construction is totally over for us either—we do have, we are in the architectural design phase of what we call the remaster or redevelopment plan of this main administrative building which includes health care and be able to expand our capacity and to have other options too.

Older offenders require a full range of health care services; some may require continuous care for their health problems, while others may need constant monitoring. Incarceration may cause many of the crucial health needs of older offenders to be inadequately met. In addition to special medical needs, there is the added problem associated with daily delivery of medications and possibly routine sick call services to the less mobile older offenders. This situation, in turn, creates a greater burden on both the medical and CSC staff. It therefore raises the important point that such a population of offenders may require the services of professional staff familiar with the physical components of the aging process and the patience and training to deal with them (Uzoaba, 1998). Can current correctional facilities meet the needs of such offenders, including the need for convalescent treatment?

Another area of health that poses great challenges for the older offender and CSC is mental health. Depression is a major medical problem among older offenders—this group has the highest suicide rate. Some of the changes that have been observed among older and geriatric offenders serving lengthy senten-ces include: "depression; anxiety; introversion; neuroticism and emotionality; apathy; dependency on staff and [lack of] routine" (Uzoaba, 1998, p. 63).

Moreover, as mentioned earlier, excessive regular drinking by this popula-tion has often led to alcoholism, which creates significant medical and social problems among older offenders. Aside from enforced abstinence, alcoholism often goes untreated in correctional institutions. The health of an older offender is perhaps the most important factor to him or her because it determines not only his or her level of program participation, but also the type of adjustment he or she makes. As a CSC interviewee said:

Administrator 4: Given the troubling stats around diseases like AIDS, as well as general diseases that people get, like cancer or anything else, etc., we have been pushing for a number of years to get palliative care.... We now have a wonderful doctor on contract who specializes in palliative care and takes over the medical management of offenders when we reach the point where that kind of intervention is necessary to return that person to the most stable/comfortable state of health as is possible.... This would involve the Chaplain, and/or the Native Elders, case managers and the medical staff, i.e., nurses, sometimes on a team basis. Wherever possible we get them out and into the community, and again that is one of the interesting aspects of the CCRA, which is the requirement of the Parole Board to examine the cases of those offenders who are terminally ill with a view to releasing the offender even if they would not normally be released.

Again, this is a very unique and humane clause, which again, I don't think exists in any other law. The only offenders who are not subject to that opportunity are those offenders who are in the early years of a life sentence. But in other cases, anybody who is eligible but has been perceived to be too risky and/or has not met the necessary program requirements to normally be released into the community have to be looked at almost from a reverse onus perspective in terms of trying to get them into a palliative care facility or even back to their home or families so that they can die at home We just recently managed to transfer a guy a couple of days before he died, back to his home in the eastern part of the province, and it was wonderful that he could die a dignified death together with his own family rather than here in jail. But for those we cannot achieve that for, the families come in to be with their loved ones. And in the new hospital that we just built we have the capacity to have them stay overnight and that kind of thing. And again, it's to treat individuals with dignity, particularly at a time, when they are facing their ultimate challenge of dying, and hopefully they can to it with grace and with caring and with love. And again, this reflects back to the point I made earlier, and that is that our primary responsibility is to incarnate values of humanity and caring, and that to me is what this business is all about. No matter if it involves managing offenders from a perspective of security—we can still do that in a dignified and caring way and explain why you are doing what you are doing and ensure that people do not do anything more in terms of controls unless it is absolutely necessary.

Other Considerations

The majority of offenders in federal institutions are between 20 and 30 years of age, and institutions are therefore designed to accommodate this general age category, not older offenders. "Accommodation" includes the physical layout, conditions, structures, and social realities of the institutions, which often do not meet the needs of older offenders. In addition, certain institutional design aspects create barriers for some older offenders. Also, they are often victimized or fear victimization, which may present challenges for correctional administrators trying to provide protection for a vulnerable group of offenders. For example, in terms of accommodation requirements, should older offenders be integrated with other offenders of all ages or should they be separate, and if the latter, at what age should that separation occur?

Older populations do not face a constant threat of victimization outside of correctional facilities. Some suggest that violence in penitentiaries is the result of overcrowding, ethnic differences, inadequately trained staff, perceived injustices within the system, double-bunking, and short-sighted correctional administrators (Uzoaba, 1998). However, the discussion of integrating versus not integrating older offenders continues and includes some of the additional points noted in Table 10.6.

Table 10.6. Integrating versus Not Integrating Older Offenders into General Prison Population

Integrating	Not Integrating
Views older offenders as those with prestige and deference within the institutional status hierarchy	Views older offenders as a vulnerable population prone to violence/victimization and who also have special needs
Holders of wisdom regarding institutional operations	Helps to facilitate implementation of special programs
Provides "seniority," experience in prison ways, initiating norms and occupying leadership roles	Contributes to positive mental health and social adjustment
Helps to prepare others in the informal social structure for "life in the yard"	Prevents "old cons" from sharing too much knowledge with younger, inexperienced offenders
Older offenders perform a vital function of maintaining order in the prison population, aiding custodial and institutional control—stabilization	May be quieter and less troublesome
Senior inmates assign a subordinate status to newly admitted prisoners and monitor or oversee the acceptance of the norms of the culture	Promotes better adjustment and adaptation
	Recreation/work opportunities may be limited in this setting
	Prevents older offenders from interacting with younger offenders, when they prefer not to be with those of their same age

According to Dr. Uzoaba (1998), both types of housing raise questions in respect to the concerns of older inmates; however, accommodating such offenders can happen in any of the following ways:

1.   They can place older offenders with other adult offenders and provide them with special accommodations that would include specific housing areas, special diets and job assignments;
2.   They can segregate older offenders by placing them in special facilities well equipped to handle their needs and problems. This could be one minimum facility in each region, where the number warrants;
3.   They can release on parole non-violent elderly offenders over 65; and
4.   They can release non-violent geriatric offenders of 70 years and over and place them in institutions for seniors in the community. (p. 75)

In terms of housing such offenders, one CSC interviewee commented:

Administrator 5: Again, that is something unique in Canadian law, where you can only hold people at a level of control that is required for that individual and that it is against the law to provide any controls that are not required in terms of a particular risk for a particular individual. This is something that is very, very unique to Canada, because in most jurisdictions they keep people anywhere that they want, for as long as they want, and in any security level that they want, i.e., if they want to put them into maximum security, and then they just go ahead and do it. We are not allowed to do that; unless the case is reviewed and we have to provide very clear evidence that the person requires that level of structure and control otherwise we are mandated by law to move them to lower security. And I think that is a wonderful component of our law. But again, this supports our mission of treating people with dignity and also trying to return people to the community with the necessary supports whenever feasible. As well, this also applies to how we might want to deal with our older offender population in the future, in terms of housing them at lower security levels.

As Administrator 5 reminds us, the CSC mission statement emphasizes the importance of treating people with dignity and respect and returning them to the community wherever that makes the best sense. Administrator 4 also discusses a unique clause in the CCRA, which requires the parole board to examine the cases of offenders who are terminally ill with a view to the need to treat such offenders in the most humane manner possibly. This often involves the potential release of such an offender prior to their eligibility release date. Given the discussion in this chapter on elderly offenders, what are your views on applying some special considerations to those older offenders who have spent some time in prisons so they can be released early on compassionate grounds?

One reason the segregated versus integrated issue remains an ongoing debate is that there is little research on how older offenders are affected by their prison environments. Whether the choice is segregation or integration, it is important that these facilities meet the special needs of such offenders for humanitarian as well as legitimate human rights reasons. In the words of Dr. Uzoaba (1998), "all demographic indicators point to the inevitable fact that our society is growing old. Corrections, like the rest of other social institutions, must be prepared to deal with the outcome of the 'greying of Canada' in prisons" (p. 87).

Ethno-Cultural Offenders

Although there is limited research in the area of ethno-cultural offenders or multicultural offenders with respect to the correctional system in Canada, this section presents a brief discussion on two issues related to this population: *racism* and *challenges in providing services* to this population of offenders.

Racism

> A Negro or Chinaman may say 'your God shall be my God,' but they can not say 'your people shall be my people.' (Fisher, 1911, p. 2 as quoted in Mosher, 1996, p. 424)

Racism exists in the general population, and therefore it likely exists in our institutions, including federal penitentiaries. Racism affects the institution as a whole, offenders and staff persons alike. However, according to Wortley (1996), with the exception of studies focusing on various aspects of the lives of Aboriginal peoples, there has been very little research done on other minorities within the Canadian criminal justice system. Some argue that this lack of research may reflect our country's lack of concern or interest about the issue. Others also argue that with Canada's "acceptance" of its official policy on multiculturalism and the lack of a long history of slavery, such as was seen in the United States, citizens are not interested in debates about the existence or consequences of racism within institutions like federal corrections. But certain new trends in immigration and extensive media coverage focusing on crimes committed by minorities may be bringing the issues of race and discrimination to the forefront.

In 1994, Gabor suggested that a lack of interest or agreement around collecting criminal justice statistics that include "ethnicity" stimulates negative stereotyping because there is a lack of dialogue about the issues. He pointed out that in nearly all societies there are differences in the criminal involvement among groups and that such differences are significant enough that they should be addressed.

For several decades, immigrants have represented approximately 16% of Canada's population. Statistics Canada estimates that by 2017 the immigrant population will represent 22.2% of the Canadian population. The birthplace of immigrants has also changed in recent years, with an increasing proportion being Asian-born. Since 1961, the proportion of European-born immigrants arriving in Canada has been declining steadily. The majority of the recent immigrant groups have come from Asia, Latin-America, Africa, and the Caribbean. This influx has highlighted cultural, religious, and linguistic distinctiveness from the dominant population groups in Canada.

Although there is a lack statistical information available on the ethno-cultural breakdown of offenders in Canada's federal penitentiaries, some evidence suggests that, apart from Caucasians, who make up the largest percentage of CSC offenders, First Nations and Métis are the next two largest distinct groups. However, Blacks, Asians, and Southeast Asians seem to be becoming the next largest groups of offenders, particularly in the Pacific region (Table 10.7). According to Griffiths and Cunningham (2003),

> ... although they [Blacks] account for only .02 percent of Canada's population and .03 of Ontario's, Black males make up 5 percent of federal institution populations and 11 percent of Ontario's institution population. Black females compose 7 percent and 9 percent of these respective populations. (p. 226)

Table 10.7. Ethnicity of Federal Inmates by Region (%)

Race	Pacific	Prairie	Ontario	Québec	Atlantic	Total
Caucasian	70	52	73	89	86	73
Aboriginal	22	41	9	6	7	18
Black	1	3	13	5	7	6
Asiatic	2	.4	2	.1	.2	.8
Japanese	0	.1	0	0	0	0

Race	Pacific	Prairie	Ontario	Québec	Atlantic	Total
Korean	.1	.1	0	0	0	0
Chinese	1	.4	.2	0	0	.3
S. Asian	.8	.6	.7	0	0	.4
E. Indian	.6	.2	.5	0	0	.3
Filipino	.2	.5	.1	0	0	.2
Hispanic	.3	.1	.3	.1	0	.2
Arab/W. Asian	.9	.6	.6	.6	.2	.6
S.E. Asian	1	.8	.9	.2	0	.7

Source: Canadian Journal of Public Health, 2004

Other research has shown that racially hostile environments, racial segrega-tion among and within institutions, and failure to accommodate the service and program needs of Black and other racialized groups have existed in some of Ontario's prisons (Mosher, 1996; Chow, 1996). For instance, according to Mosher (1996), in Ontario in 1995 "the incarceration rate for Black adult males was five times the rate for white adults and the admission rate for Black women was almost seven times that of white women" (p. 416).

Since October 1994, CSC has had a policy aimed at determining the needs and specific cultural characteristics of minority offenders. The policy stipulates, among other things, that racial harassment and discriminatory behaviour will not be tolerated. Placement of offenders will be determined solely on the basis of risk and the individual's needs, not on the basis of race, culture, language, and/or religion. It also emphasizes the contributions ethno-cultural communities make (Correctional Service of Canada, Commissioner's Directive 767).

Providing Services to an Ethno-Cultural Population of Offenders

The CSC Commissioner's Directive 767 states that ethno-cultural programs must be created to help offenders reintegrate into society, and they must offer the chance for change, address key issues such as crime, cultural awareness, spirituality, and employment, and must be provided with adequate resources and funding to facilitate implementation. Dr. Emerson Douyon (as quoted by Amella, 2005) stated that,

> CSC programs are void of culture—a hidden aspect of the personal-ity ... behind the criminal acts, there are attitudes, beliefs and values

that are shaped by culture ... each program should, therefore, have a specific cultural component depending on the ethnic groups ... this pluralist ethno-cultural approach would help with the effective management of diversity in prisons. (p. 10)

One of the important considerations that is often overlooked by CSC and other public institutions (for example health care/treatment centres) is the importance of diet. Dietary requirements are often consistent with various ethnic traditions and religious standards. Likewise, the importance of maintaining contact with family members on a frequent basis is also important to various ethnic groups. Another important factor is the existence of some prejudices among staff and members of different cultural groups. Staff may use labelling to convey disrespectful connotations toward different offenders and display negative attitudes that are detrimental to intercultural harmony. Prejudice can arise among various cultural groups whose past experiences have been in socio-political systems where there are anti-police and anti-prison traditions and cultures.

According to the CSC interviewees on the issue of ethno-cultural offenders:

Administrator 6: Ethno-cultural—we have, as I've said in this region, we have a higher proportion of African-Canadian offenders than Native, and that's been the profile here. So are there specific needs? I think we always have to stay within the mark and encourage that. We have a regional advisory committee for women, which is representative, again, of the population, so sometimes there is different events that come up, different needs. At this point I think the Service itself has identified a need for programs—specific programs, but at least in this region, we are working on that as well. We are not diversified other than that. It is not a lot of different cultures coming together here.

Administrator 7: Looking at the report we have printed off here from RADAR, which is a type of population profile based on race, this gives us a sense at least of the myriad of ethno-cultural groups that are represented within the institutions, and it is broken down on this report by site. Caucasians are the largest group in all sites, but we also have a large Aboriginal population as well as the Métis group. What this report shows is that there is quite a significant variety of ethno-cultural groups within the institutions. I would have liked to look at a more regional report however, which this doesn't give us, and we can do that if we look for more detail through the use of the OMS (Offender Management System), and we could find out regionally, for example, what percentage of our population are Blacks, Indo Canadian, Chinese, and so on. This information may also be available on CSC's internet site, or it might be available from our National Headquarters Office, and so if you or students could tap into that internet site, it would be an opportunity to learn a fair bit about the diversity of our offender population, because that is normally maintained, I think, on our national site. The point that is being made though, I think, is that there is a tremendous blend of nationalities, ethnic groups, language groups in the prison environment now and it is getting more and more significant. Every year there is a rising percentage of the population that is represented by non-Caucasian offenders.

Administrator 8: We do address the needs of multicultural offenders in the area of religion, and to some degree in terms of their cultural practices. For example, our regional administrator of chaplaincy has entered into many contracts with Sikhs, rabbis, and other spiritual leaders from the community who come in and provide spiritual support and assistance in the same language that the offender speaks. We also honour their religions' celebrations, their holy days, and their diets ... those kinds of things are all recognized and supported to whatever degree is possible and sometimes at considerable cost to the Service as well. But those things are "easy to do" when compared to the programming issue. That will remain the final barrier, in my view, for this group in terms of their reintegration potential. This would be an excellent topic for further study—to come up with some possible solutions. Ultimately, the solution would be to one day come up with enough CSC staff who are fluent in the languages that these individuals speak, who can then observe and assess behaviour and translate that into English for the Parole Board and so on, and provide a true sense of where that individual is at. That, in my view, is some years away and may never be achievable. And even if we could get the staff, would we be prepared to translate all of the materials, study guides, pre-and post-tests, reading materials, exercises, role plays, etc. which is also a huge cost, into all of these different languages? And there could be ten to twenty of these for a relatively small number of offenders. So ESL (English as a second language) might ultimately be the answer—to raise the level of the offenders' English skills so that he can take our programs, which are, incidentally, designed around the sixth to eighth grade level. That might be quite a distance to come for people who have never spoken the language.

And of course this also brings up the whole issue of shorter sentences, meaning these offenders will be delayed right up until the last possible moment. It is almost as though these individuals are automatically sentenced to their full statutory sentence requirements when some of them would probably be very good candidates for early reintegration with the right intervention, if we had the capacity to assess their progress. And of course, some people might question why we would spend so much time on these people, who represent about three percent of the population; however, these same three percent might also represent fifteen percent of those who pose a risk to society. And really knowing how these people are thinking and what progress they've made, as we really have no sense as to where they are at with respect to the risk they pose to society. So can we afford not to program for these people who do not speak English yet and without programming are inevitably coming back into prison?

Administrator 9: The language ... that too is something we are trying to increase. At this point it is all based on service to the public because we don't have the minimum five percent French-speaking offenders here, but that could change.

There are many challenges when working with a diverse population, particularly the population being served by CSC. For example, there may not be uniformity of culture within broad ethno-cultural groups, presenting even more of a challenge. There are some differences in patterns of offending that are related to ethno-cultural groups, and these may require the need to develop culturally appropriate programs rather than utilizing programs developed for the mainstream or dominant populations found in society.

Administrator 10: Canada is a bilingual country and certainly recognizes the language and culture of our francophone citizens in terms of requiring bilingual signage and things like that in certain locations, and of course the government of Canada honours the notion of Canada having two official languages, and all of its forms and all of its correspondence are done in both official languages. That is enshrined in law, in terms of the statutes of this country. Beyond that, there is no legislation that requires Canada or any government office to recognize or respond to the specific language or other needs of other ethnic groups—that is, there is no legal requirement. However, there is a Commissioner's Directive that states that CSC, to the greatest degree possible, should respect the cultural and spiritual differences of all groups, and that we should attempt to respond in a sensitive fashion and a meaningful fashion to their needs and customs. This whole area, in my view, also represents another ethical dilemma for CSC, because in fact we have a policy that states that we should be providing culturally sensitive programming and so on, but it is next to impossible to achieve. Why I say this is because there is such a variety of languages. For example, there are several languages just within the Asian culture so that one person is speaking a language and the other person won't understand it. So in an institution the size of [this institution], you could have ten or twelve different language groups who could conceivably all require programming in their own unique language. The costs of that and the logistics of that are just enormous and absolutely impractical.

The fact is that we can never respond as we might want to, or as our policy might suggest that we should, to the needs of these various groups. And in particular, where it becomes a very difficult issue is around the area of programming. On the one hand we have a National Parole Board and we have the Correctional Services of Canada that believe firmly in the utility of programming to prepare offenders for release. On the other hand, we have a population of offenders who can't access those programs because their language doesn't allow them to. As a result, they are most definitely disadvantaged in terms of their release potential. Of course, society is also disadvantaged in terms of whether these offenders get a little bit of programming, or in fact any programming, before being released back into communities, and these offenders may benefit less from this programming and ultimately will be returned to society less changed or less convinced of the need to change. Ultimately, that represents a higher risk to society.

This also extends to the problems with being able to communicate with all levels of staff. And it opens up the whole area of different learning styles. For example, every culture has a different learning style and we know this to be particularly true, for instance, with Aboriginal people. They certainly need to have their programs delivered in a different fashion than the mainstream programming. They learn with much more hands on and experiential things as opposed to, say, lectures and so on. However, our programs now, for the most part, are geared toward the mainstream population. That is not to say that we haven't learned and subsequently adapted our programs for the Aboriginal offender population. There is, of course, some expectation for that group as well, within policy and law. Beyond that, there is not a lot of motivation for CSC to move toward specialized programming for the ethno-cultural population.

The reasons for that are, of course, the complexities, the logistics of it, the costs associated with it, the fact that the numbers are very small, and that makes it difficult to provide these services in a group-based fashion. If you had insufficient numbers of offenders with similar language needs and culture needs in any particular institution, you could try to amalgamate or consolidate all of these individuals into one site so that you could get a group of ten. But that is very difficult because of incompatibles, because of security levels, because of the location of families and community support, and all sorts of other things that need to be taken into consideration.

One of the most frustrating things for me as a programmer is that almost every month we get a letter from the field saying we have an offender, he's Asian, and he speaks Mandarin—he's extremely motivated but he can't understand English and he can't take our programs. What are we going to do for him? The answer is that basically we can't do anything for him in the way of correctional programming. Our only response at this point is ESL, academic upgrading, and working with him in a very intense fashion, perhaps with other Mandarin-speaking offenders who also speak English and can act as interpreters, tutors, and work with the individual on a day-to-day basis—work with teachers, work with tapes, and so on. The goal is to try to help them develop sufficient English skills in order that they may participate in the English or mainstream programs. Of course, this might be questionable in terms of specificity and responsivity to the individuals' learning styles. Without question, this is an area that CSC has to explore, and I am not sure what the answers are because from a cost perspective, it would seem to me to be prohibitive to adapt and translate all of our programs into all of these different languages.

Of course, not only do you have to adapt and translate the programs, but you also have to have staff who speak those languages to deliver them, and these staff are difficult to recruit, even though we do recruit within those visible minority groups. It is very difficult to find the right people to fill the right jobs to deliver a translated program to a large enough group of offenders. So it is an area that needs some attention. Similarly, for offenders with fetal alcohol syndrome or fetal alcohol effects—people with marginal mental capacities—our programs are not adapted at this point for those groups either—not specialized. They are not reduced in their complexity to the point where those groups can absorb them. This is also a similar problem faced by school districts with the influx of children from other cultures. We have looked at using interpreters, because the immediate reaction is 'let's put this guy into a regular class and let's put him in there with, say, another Mandarin-speaking offender who also speaks English and have the other offender interpret the program.' The problem of course is you have no idea of how the other person is interpreting, what he is saying, whether the language is an exact translation.

Likewise, there is all sorts of fear around how much the other individual understands, the comprehension may or may not be there—we can't assess his regurgitation of the skills, his demonstration of the skills—so an interpreter isn't the answer. Even getting a community volunteer translator or a paid translator, you can't be sure if the interpretation is exactly what the program is stating and therefore it makes it next to impossible to assess risk. If I am going to say that this person has now gained that much information and is now a manageable risk in the community, I want to make sure that what I am saying is accurate. I cannot be sure of this if I do not understand or cannot communicate myself. Going through a translator is good from an assistance perspective for ESL, for tutoring, or to bring language skills up, because then you can assess the degree to which the offender has captured English-speaking skills. But in programming this is a very different thing.

The importance of recognizing the difficulty for people raised in two different cultures cannot be overstated. For example, although mainstream populations may be encouraged to open up and share personal experiences as a sign of progress or atonement, other less predominant cultures may experience strong cultural controls that promote a sense of shame for wrongdoing and therefore elicit reservations around sharing personal issues.

Administrator 11: You have reminded me of another very important point, and that is that some of these cultures look at people in jail as failures and as blemishes on the reputation or image of their own race or culture. Therefore, there is a strong resistance to having anything to do with offenders while they are incarcerated. In other words, he's doing his time, paying his debt to society, and when he comes and has paid that debt, then we will work with him—why would we come into prison and work with him when he doesn't deserve it? Historically, there was some of this with the Aboriginal population and we've overcome that to a large degree, I think, through a lot of outreach, working with the Reserves, Bands, and leaders in the Aboriginal communities. We are there now with these ethno-cultural groups in some of the cases and there is not always a lot of sympathy or empathy or willingness on the part of community citizens to come into the institutions and to work with offenders. Many of them don't see working for corrections as a particularly grand career plan. It is not an easy task to recruit and not always easy to convince the community to come in and work with offenders. So recruitment could be hampered, for example, by the country of origin of potential applicants and how they view various authorities, for example, the police, the prison system, the government, and the fear they might have around those bodies of authority.

The administrators raise a lot of interesting points in their discussion around culturally unique offenders, including their educational, programming, language, and religious needs, and the reintegration of these offenders into cultural milieu's, which may reject the individual on the basis that they offended in the first place. Another issue that was raised earlier in this chapter was the issue of cultural practices including special diets. In order to minister to the needs of this unique population increased cost and logistical challenges need to be recognized and acted upon. Administrator 8 questions the validity of spending the dollars on a population who make up around three percent of the population. What might some of the pros and cons be of spending additional dollars to meet the needs of this unique offender population? Are there partnership opportunities with members of the community that CSC could encourage in order to more fully meet the needs of culturally distinct offenders?

Within the system as a whole there has been very little research done on these unique populations other than on Aboriginal peoples. Studies of the over-representation of some ethno-cultural groups could perhaps help to identify if and where discriminatory practices were occurring within the criminal justice system and encourage the development of remedies. Likewise, having an understanding of the complex mixture of ethnicities, cultures, religions and so on will help Correctional Services of Canada to better prepare themselves to meet the needs of these unique offender populations.

Adult Offenders with Fetal Alcohol Spectrum Disorder

Administrator 12: FAS/FAE (Fetal Alcohol Syndrome/Fetal Alcohol Effects) is something the Service in general is recognizing more. We have had some training, individual training, because the women, again—the type of women that we have received, many with reliance and drug addiction and in fact, women seem to be suffering with the long term effects of FAS/FAE. We have developed some better tools to make the diagnosis. It is not something we tested for before but there is certainly more of an awareness and there is more of an acknowledgement that the needs are different and more so higher risk in Aboriginal communities. Some of that has been identified.

Somewhere between philosophical debate and scientific inquiry lies the real truth about the effects of Fetal Alcohol Syndrome and Fetal Alcohol Effects on the innocent victims of these disorders, their families, and society in general. Fetal Alcohol Effect is not a milder form of FAS, and "... people with FAE have the same risk of developmental and behavioural disabilities as those with FAS" (Conry and Fast, 2000, p. 2). Fetal alcohol spectrum disorders (FASD), which is not a diagnosis in and of itself, is a term that describes the population with alcohol-related disorders. Fetal alcohol spectrum disorders and other alcohol- and drug-related birth defects are 100% preventable, but there are no known cures because these individuals suffer from permanent brain damage. Researchers and scientists have known for a long time that alcohol is one of the most toxic substances that humans can consume and they have been able to study the development of the fetus exposed to alcohol, following this development through to childhood and adolescence. In fact, British Columbia and Washington State have been research leaders in such areas as the diagnosis, prevention and management of fetal alcohol spectrum disorders in children and adolescents (Dr. K. Asante and Dr. J. Conry personal communications, February 18, 2003). What researchers have concluded is that FAS is the leading cause of mental disabilities and birth defects in North America, and the lifetime education and health costs for each individual affected with FAS/FAE exceeds two million dollars (Dr. K. Asante and Dr. J. Conry personal communications, Feb. 18, 2003).

Because FAS was recognized as a syndrome only in 1973 and because only a few doctors have been able to make the diagnosis, there are probably many undiagnosed youth and adults with this syndrome. Also, because of changing features and growth, the diagnosis is often more difficult to make in adolescence and adulthood (B.C. Fetal Alcohol Syndrome Resource Society, 1998). The Asante Centre in Maple Ridge, British Columbia is one of only nine facilities in Canada that provides diagnosis and assessments for FAS, processing 40 to 50 such cases annually. And although in British Columbia both the Asante Centre and the Sunnyhill Substance Exposure Resource Team have the capability to do such assessments, there are not yet proper and standardized diagnosis and assessment tools, reliable diagnostic procedures, or even a common terminology with respect to FASD. In addition, the only facility with the capability and expertise to engage in formal FAS diagnosis for adults is the Asante Centre; however, there are no funds currently available for these services. To further complicate the issue, there is no standardized FAS training available in British Columbia for physicians, psychologists, speech and language pathologists, family support workers, or nurses. Finally, there are limited databases containing FAS/FAE data available for research purposes.

Development of FAS/FAE and Prevalence within the Population

Alcohol disrupts the fetal development because it effortlessly crosses the placenta and enters the fetus of a pregnant woman who drinks. It takes approximately twice as long for the fetus' body to metabolize and eliminate alcohol as it does the pregnant woman's. Addictions practitioners and other professionals have long said that every drink the mother takes is comparable to the fetus having four such drinks. That said, there are no identified safe levels of alcohol consumption during pregnancy. Rather, there is a continuum of alcohol effects that depend on how much alcohol the pregnant woman consumes as well as other maternal factors such as genetic makeup and the response of the fetus to the alcohol. However, some evidence suggests that most infants diagnosed with FAS—the most severe end of the continuum of effects from alcohol consumption—have been born to women who are described as heavy drinkers in terms of both frequency and amount (Boland, Burrill, Duwyn, and Karp, 1998; Conry, 1990, and Streissguth and Randels, 1988). For example, according to the Institute of Medicine, "… maternal exposure is characterized by substantial regular intake or heavy episodic drinking" (Conry and Fast, 2000, p. 11).

World estimates show that there are between 1.3 and 1.9 cases of FAS per 1000; however, as of 1998 there was no national data for Canada (Boland *et al.*, 1998; Stratton, Howe, and Battaglia, 1996 as cited in Conry and Fast, 2000). It does appear that among certain Aboriginal groups the incidence of FAS is much higher and estimates vary. Furthermore, women who have already had a child born with FAS have a "very high reoccurrence rate with an incidence estimate of 771 out of 1,000 births" (Boland *et al.*, 1998).

Estimates of the incidence for full FAS in British Columbia range from one in 500 births to one in 3000 births, with the rate for other alcohol-related effects estimated at five to ten times higher. Prevalence of FAS and other alcohol related effects in *high risk populations* may be as high as one in five (from B.C. data, 1981, 1987, and 1993, as reported in Streissguth and Randels, 1988; and Conry and Fast, 2000). These figures translate into 96 children with full FAS syndrome out of approximately 48,000 births each year in B.C.

Characteristics of FAS/FAE

An essential piece of an assessment for FAS/FAE is the mother's history, and because this is often excluded in assessments done by psychologists and/or neurologists in the criminal justice realm, it also means they may overlook a potential FAS diagnosis in adults. In addition, facial features do not affect the brain functioning, so a diagnosis relying on facial anomalies alone does not necessarily mean individuals will be affected in the same way. FAS requires the identification of three criteria, including (a) prenatal and/or postnatal growth delay, (b)

characteristic cranio-facial anomalies, and (c) central nervous system impair-
ments. FAE often has two but not all three of the formal features of FAS, plus
maternal alcohol consumption. However, the damage is permanent in both cases.

Challenges Faced by FAS/FAE Offenders and the Criminal Justice System

High rates of criminality have been repeatedly described in FAS populations
and it is estimated that a large number of prison inmates in Canada are victims
of FAS (Rouleau, Leichek, and Gideon, 2003), although Gideon stated at the
2002 FACE Conference that there was no substantial data to prove that this was
the case (Canadian Center on Substance Abuse). Nonetheless, as a result of the
level of impulsivity and poor judgement displayed by individuals with FASD,
they often find themselves in contact with the criminal justice system as both
perpetrators and victims. The role of drugs and alcohol should not be ignored
as a likely predisposing or reinforcing factor in terms of such individuals acting
out their impulsive behaviours, often in a criminal manner. In fact, in a study
done by the Motherisk Program in Toronto, which involved 173 problem drinking and drug abusing mothers or expectant mothers suspected of having FAS
who also had maternal histories of problem drinking, the results indicated that
such women were six times more likely than the general population to commit
crimes (Rouleau *et al.*, 2003).

There is also evidence that some affected individuals are limited in their
ability to experience remorse or guilt, not because they are malicious, but because they cannot make the connection between their actions and the effects
or consequences of their actions on others (Dr. Art Gordon, Clinical Director
of CSC Regional Health Center and Chairperson of the Regional FAS/FAE
Committee, personal communication, April 9, 2003; Conry and Fast, 2000).
Although criminal behaviour is largely impulsive rather than premeditated
among this population, according to Streissguth *et al.*, (1991), the most reported
crimes committed by those with FAS/FAE were theft and shoplifting, although
that does not preclude the commission of other types of offences. For example,
Andrew Boyd (Westcoast Genesis House Society, personal communication,
April 10, 2003) and Dr. Art Gordon mentioned that many FAS/FAE offenders
whom they come in contact with have offended sexually. Streissguth *et al.*, (1991)
further stated that the maladaptive behaviours and cognitive deficits associated with FAS/FAE frequently lead these individuals into trouble with the law.
These problems are often heightened by substance abuse and the development
of a substance dependency or addiction. And although there is a good deal of
evidence of the "link between FAS/FAE and criminality ..." (see, for example,
Boland *et al.*, 1998), there is very little research that focuses on FAS/FAE in the
criminal justice system. A further complication suggested by some research-

ers (Conry and Fast, 2000; Streissguth *et al.*, 1991) is that individuals with FAE rather than FAS may be more often involved with the criminal justice system. However, because they are more difficult to recognize because their symptoms are less apparent and less pronounced, they are more likely to go undetected in the prison system and therefore not receive the help they need.

Since so little is known about this adult population in terms of program and treatment needs and so many of these individuals seem to be involved with the criminal justice system, it is vital that CSC develop a method of screening and assessing or otherwise identifying these individuals early on in the incarceration process or during a pre-sentence investigative process. Such a process is in the very early stages of conceptualization (Boland *et al.*, 1998). According to Dr. Art Gordon (2003), Correctional Service of Canada could do a better job at identifying such offenders; however, he admits that there is no reliable diagnostic process for adults, although some of the neurological research is looking promising. Furthermore, Dr. Gordon suggests that rather than focusing on diagnostic labels such as ADHD, FAS/FAE, solvent abusers, and so on, which are all representative of a group defined as brain damaged offenders, it might make better sense to focus on the behavioural indicators.

Dr. Gordon (2003) suggested that the 25-item structured learning assessment currently done on all offenders entering the correctional system could be adapted. This could be used to look at specific areas of learning for each offender and this information could help illustrate differences, and in turn it might suggest some useful strategies for assisting unique populations, such as those with brain damage. Conversely, this process could be done with some tweaking of the current Offender Intake Assessment, done on all offenders coming into the system, to identify some markers specific to this population, which would help to distinguish them from the "normal" offender population. This latter suggestion could result in an approach whereby all offenders who experience problems, and in particular, problems associated with brain damage, would have access to services or programs linked to identified learning needs rather than to their respective diagnoses. Some of these needs are already identified in part through the use of the CLAI, the Computerized Lifestyle Assessment Inventory used by CSC. Modifications to it could assist researchers in collecting data and other important information related to this and other unique offender populations (Gordon, 2003; Boland *et al.*, 1998). In addition to these suggestion, less of a diagnostic approach could also be achieved through the use of such instruments as the Vineland Adaptive/Maladaptive Behaviour Scale, the Fetal Alcohol Behaviour Scale, the Symptom Checklist and the Life History Interview (Streissguth and Randels, 1988; Boland *et al.*, 1998), again, with more of the process focused on the offenders' specific learning problems.

Programming for FAS/FAE Offenders

According to Streissguth *et al.*, (1991), such offenders work best in an environment that has little stimulation, is uncluttered and has order, structure, and predicable routines (see also Conry and Fast, 2000; Boland *et al.*, 1998). Providing such an environment requires a great deal of support and supervision with positive feedback because such individuals tend to get into trouble within the prison system as well as outside. Part of the reason for this may be that there are too many distractions in the environment and these individuals have a tendency to become overwhelmed in social situations, partly because they have an overly trusting nature and belief in others, including other offenders. Dr. Gordon (2003) stresses the fact that it is common knowledge that such offenders are quick to pick up additional or enhanced criminal behaviours from the higher functioning offenders who share the prison environment. He therefore believes that it is important to transform their ability to acquire skills to the process of learning healthy survival skills. Dr. Gordon questions whether these FAS/FAE offenders are demonstrating an inability to learn or simply the inability to learn what we want them to learn. Secondly, there is no evidence as to whether such offenders would do better if they were housed in separate, specialized facilities and did their skills-based training together or whether they do better in a "mixed" group. For example, 50% of the group in the Northstar Program for lower functioning sexual offenders come from the brain damaged group. In other words, which environment helps the individual to get better control over their environment? Dr. Gordon suggests the answers to these questions are probably three to ten years away.

In addition to the problems associated with FAS/FAE already mentioned, such individuals have high rates of depression, substance abuse, and suicide attempts, and they are possibly overrepresented within the offender population. In addition, sexually inappropriate behaviours and psychiatric problems are common among them. Therefore, these needs must also be identified and attended to in designing treatment that targets maladaptive behaviour and decreases the secondary disabilities so that the highest possible level of functioning can be attained.

Streissguth *et al.*, (1991) and other researchers have concluded, however, that although this population is only now being identified, research on children with FAS/FAE suggests that programs must be structured and use simple concrete instructions. The programs should include basic life skills, such as communication, healthy socialization, money and time management, healthy recreational activities, as well as anger management skills. Although such programs already exist in CSC, they are offered at a level that may not be useful for FAS/FAE offenders, who require ample time for practice and repetition. Also, group size is important because of the potential problem of distractibility and over stimulation that may arise in large groups. Examples of such specialized programs do exist outside of the prison surroundings in B.C. (e.g., Westcoast Genesis House Society and Phoenix Drug and Alcohol Recovery and Education Society).

According to Andrew Boyd, executive director of Genesis House and a former CSC employee (personal communication, April 2003), sometime around 1997 the commissioner of CSC decided that programs to meet the unmet needs of four unique offender populations—aboriginal, aging, mentally disordered, and female—would be better delivered in the community. As a result, in the fall of 2000 Genesis House, a 20-bed facility, was established with funding from the federal government as a residential or halfway house for FAS/FAE offenders as well as mainstream offenders. Genesis House offers an intensive, highly structured setting to provide a smoother transition back into the community. Mr. Boyd used the recommendations in the Boland report to develop the framework for his program, relying on what he describes as the external brain model. In other words, because FAS/FAE offenders experience cognitive deficits, cognitive skills programs—the backbone of the majority of CSC programs—simply will not work. Instead, there is a focus on developing interdependence skills based on a model of support, repetition, and structure.

Of the 20 beds, six are reserved for FAS/FAE offenders because (through a process of trial and error) the staff at Genesis House recognized that six was a stable number to work with. The staff complement is eight or nine at all times of the day, and each staff member buddies up with an offender and assumes responsibility for skills-based training, for example, daily chores. In other words, the process operates as high-intensity supervised case work, so healthy relationships are built between the staff and offenders, and between volunteers and offenders as well. The use of both staff and volunteers provides an avenue for continuous monitoring, which is necessary for this group of offenders, especially with their heightened risk of gravitating toward continued use of various substances. Mr. Boyd believes that, nationally, close to 80% of all offenders have been identified as having a low to moderate level of substance use, and this population is especially vulnerable to such problems.

There is no specific duration of the program at Genesis House, which does not offer "treatment" because they believe there is no treatment for individuals with permanent brain damage. In other words, they operate on a management model that focuses on skills required for daily, non-offending functioning. Their clientele are identified as the lowest-functioning FAS/FAE individuals, highly vulnerable and unstable, who frequently breach their parole because of technical violations. Success is difficult to measure, but some benchmarks include the ability of the offender to spend greater periods of time in the community in a healthier and functioning manner, decreased number of house violations, decreased number of technical violations, and the ability to develop interdependence skills. As of the end of 2003, some 60 offenders have enjoyed the benefits of the atmosphere, relationships, and structured model of daily living offered by Genesis House. Similarly, Michael Wilson, executive director of Phoenix Drug and Alcohol Recovery and Education Society states that the Society also provides up to 20 beds for offenders released from federal penitentiaries. It includes offenders characterized by FASD, a population that appears to be growing in terms of requiring supportive beds and skills-based programs post-release (personal communication, June 2003).

The Correctional Service of Canada, in cooperation with the University of Manitoba embarked on a research project involving FASD in offenders who resided at Stony Mountain Institution. According to Dan Kunic, a researcher for the CSC Addictions Research Centre, Drs. Albert Chudley, Patricia Mac-Pherson, and Brian Grant conducted the research study over a one year period. According to these researchers, "the most critical information is evidence of being exposed to alcohol before birth (maternal drinking history). Therefore, the study was designed to maximize the likelihood of obtaining that information for each participant" (personal communication, June 2003). Prior to 1972, hospitals and doctors did not ask about maternal drinking during pregnancy. Each participant will undergo medical examinations and tests to determine the incidence rate of FASD among the offender population, which is one of the goals of the project. As mentioned previously in this chapter, estimates vary widely in terms of what percentage of offenders have FASD. However, in late 2004 CSC developed a tool to assess FASD among offenders and this tool is currently being piloted in one of the institutions.

As Conry and Fast (2000) noted, people with FAS/FAE have had a considerable impact on the criminal justice system, from enforcement to the provision of legal services to special programs in the correctional facilities. Of course, the answer to effectively working with offenders with FASD lies in our ability to provide education and prevention, early diagnosis, and interventions, both to the women who are vulnerable and their offspring. And certainly that is where the greatest emphasis and most funding are directed. And while we might want to look for such unique offenders among the disadvantaged population groups, the fact is that FAS/FAE can be found in all segments of society. FAS/FAE is a lifelong disorder and some people with this disorder may require 24-hour supervision to protect both them and the public. We know this population is disproportionately represented in our prisons. Whether they remain criminals may depend on how the criminal justice system responds to their situation— that is, whether their handicap is recognized and accommodated or whether the victimization and misunderstanding continues. The bottom line is that changing the living environment for people with FAS/FAE is more feasible than changing the person, although the Regional Treatment Centre in B.C. does have a row in an entire unit that deals with offenders who have cognitive deficits such as from FASD.

Individuals afflicted with FASD have organic brain damage—a birth defect caused by a substance. In this case, the substance is legally sold in Canada. FASD is 100% preventable. People with FASD are not just one ministry's problem, and perhaps the reluctance to acknowledge the enormity of the problem comes down to money, but society inevitably pays now or pays later. Jailing people is expensive.

Conclusion

This chapter has discussed several issues of importance to correctional practice. For example, the issue of identifying the needs of offenders with fetal alcohol spectrum disorders, which to date has not been a widely researched topic—at least not with respect to adults with FASD and in particular, adult offenders. Furthermore, ethno-cultural offenders also present some unique challenges, with respect to cultural practices and language differences, for example. As CSC tries to honour its mandate and prepare these offenders for reintegration into the community, challenges seems to culminate in a dilemma described as "funding versus principles." Lastly, the whole notion of aging offenders – those who are incarcerated at an advanced age already and those who have spent many years within the institutional setting and thus evolved into the aged and/ or geriatric offender—all pose special challenges as well.

CSC has taken some steps to address the needs of these unique populations. Plans are underway to obtain approval and funding to implement a research project aimed at determining the prevalence of FASD offenders within the general adult offender population. In addition to this, it is the hope of CSC to develop a comprehensive screening tool to assist in identifying offenders at intake who might be characterized as having FASD. Also, CSC has entered into many discussions and planning regarding the best options for housing and programming needs for aging and geriatric offenders. In any event, it is the desire of CSC to treat these unique offender populations with dignity and to try to return people to the community with the necessary supports wherever it is feasible to do so.

Study Questions

1. Pick one of the unique population groups discussed in this chapter and discuss some of the challenges to providing programs to meet their needs.

2. Using information from this chapter, discuss some of the characteristics that differentiate the older population from the younger population of offenders.

3. Discuss and describe Dr. Uzoaba's three distinct categories of older offenders.

4. What are some of the pros and cons of integration versus segregation of older offenders? Which position do you support and why?

5. What are some of the challenges faced by CSC administrators and staff in terms of complying with Commissioner's Directive 767?

6. Dr. Art Gordon of the CSC believes that the focus should not be on diagnostic labels, such as FASD, but on the behavioural indicators. Discuss the pros and cons of using either focus.

Bibliography

*Items with asterisks are also suggested readings for this chapter.

Older and Geriatric Offenders

A Health Care Needs Assessment of Federal Inmates in Canada (March/April 2004). *Canadian Journal of Public Health,* 95(1).

Correctional Investigator Canada. (February 4, 2008). *Speaking Notes for Mr. Howard Sapers, Correctional Investigator. Appearance before the Special Senate Committee on Aging.* http://www.oci-bec.gc.ca/newsroom/speeches/20080204_e.asp

Erger, J. and Beger, R. (Dec. 2002). Geriatric nursing in prisons is a growing concern. *Corrections Today,* 64(7), 122–128.

Gal, M. (May 2002). The physical and mental health of older offenders – Table 3. *Forum on Corrections Research,* 14(2). http://www.csc-scc.gc.ca/text/pblct/forum/e142/e142d-eng.shtml. Reproduced with the permission of the Minister of Public Works and Government Services Canada, 2009.

Griffiths, C.T. and Cunningham, A.H. (2003). *Canadian Criminal Justice: A Primer* (2nd edition). (p. 226). Toronto: Thomson Nelson.

Morton, J. B. (Jan.2001). Implications for Corrections of an aging prison population.*Corrections Management Quarterly,* 5(1), 78–89.

Mumford, S.A. (2001). *Double down—It's all in the Cards: Pre-Offence, Offence and Post Release Use of Alcohol and Other Drugs by Homicide Offenders.* Burnaby BC: School of Criminology, Simon Fraser University.

*Uzoaba, J. (1998). *Managing Older Offenders: Where do We Stand?* Research-Branch, Correctional Services of Canada. 13(2) Tables 4, 7, 10. Reproduced with the permission of the Minister of Public Works and Government Services Canada, 2009.

Ethno-cultural or Multicultural Offenders

A Health Care Needs Assessment of Federal Inmates in Canada (March/April 2004). *Canadian Journal of Public Health,* 95(1).

Amellal, D. (2005). A Diversified Correctional Approach. *Let's Talk,* 30(2).

Chow, H. (1996). The Chinese community leaders' perceptions of the criminal justice system. *Canadian Journal of Criminology,* 38(4), 477–484.

Correctional Service of Canada. Commissioner's Directive 767 on Ethnocultural Programs Performance and Compliance Indicators. http://csc-scc.gc.ca/text/pblct/ethno/perform-cd767/perform-767-eng.shtml

Do you speak English? (Dec. 2000). *Corrections Today,* 62(7), 164–167.

Gabor, T. (1994). The suppression of crime statistics on race and ethnicity: The price of political correctness. *Canadian Journal of Criminology,* 36(2), 153–164.

Griffiths, C.T. and Cunningham, A.H. (2003). *Canadian Criminal Justice: A Primer* (2nd edition). (p. 226). Toronto: Thomson Nelson.

Hatt, K. (1994). Reservations about race and crime statistics. *Canadian Journal of Criminology,* 36(2), 164–166.

Heilman, K. and Lawson, K. (Dec. 2000). Facilitating communication with limited and non-English speaking offenders. *Corrections Today,* 62(7), 84–88.

Johnston, J. P. (1994). Academic approaches to race-crime statistics do not justify their collection. *Canadian Journal of Criminology,* 36(2), 166–174.

*Mosher, C. (1996). Racism and Criminal Justice: Minorities and misdemeanours: The treatment of black public order offenders in Ontario's criminal justice system —1892–1930. *Canadian Journal of Criminology,* 38(4), 413–438

Proulx, N. (1999). International working group on cultural diversity. *Let's Talk,* 24(5).

Statistics Canada. http://www42.statcan.ca/smr08/smr08_053_e.htm

*Wortley, S. (1996). Justice for all? Race and perceptions of bias in the Ontario criminal justice system—A Toronto survey. *Canadian Journal of Criminology,* 38(4), 439–468.

Offenders with Fetal Alcohol Spectrum Disorders

Best Practices: Fetal Alcohol Syndrome/Fetal Alcohol Effects and the Effects of Other Substance Use During Pregnancy. (2000). Prepared by Gary Roberts and Jo Nanson for Canada's Drug Strategy Division, Health Canada.

Boland, F., Burrill, R., Duwyn, M. and Karp, J. (1998). *Fetal Alcohol Syndrome: Implications for Correctional Service.* http://www.csc-scc.gc.ca/text/rsrch/reports/r71/r71e_e.shtml

Boyd, S. C. (1999). *Mothers and Illicit Drugs: Transcending the Myths.* Toronto: University of Toronto Press.

British Columbia Fetal Alcohol Syndrome Resource Society. (1998). *Fetal Alcohol Syndrome Community Action Guide: Working together for the prevention of Fetal Alcohol Syndrome.*

Canadian Centre on Substance Abuse. *B.C. Ministry for Children and Family Development. 3rd Annual Fetal Alcohol Canadian Expertise (FACE) Research Roundtable.* (September 10, 2002). Webcast: "Interventions" presented by Dr. Gideon Koren, Director, Motherisk Program, Hospital for Sick Children in Toronto.

*Conry, J. and Fast, D. (2000). *Fetal Alcohol Syndrome and the Criminal Justice System.* Vancouver, BC: Law Foundation of British Columbia.

Conry, J. (1990). Neuropsychological deficits in Fetal Alcohol Syndrome and Fetal Alcohol Effects. *Alcoholism: Clinical and Experimental Research,* 14, 650–655.

*Fast, D., Conry, J. and Loock, C. (1998). Identifying Fetal Alcohol Syndrome among youth in the criminal justice system. *Journal of Developmental Behaviours Pediatrics,* 20, 370–372.

Legge, C., Roberts, G. and Butler, M. (2000). *Situational Analysis: Fetal Alcohol Syndrome/Fetal Alcohol Effects and the Effects of Other Substance Use During Pregnancy.* Canada's Drug Strategy, Health Canada.

MacPherson, P., and A. E. Chudley. 2007. *Fetal Alcohol Spectrum Disorder (FASD): Screening and estimating incidence in an adult correctional population.* Presented at the 2nd International Conference on Fetal Alcohol Spectrum Disorder: Research, Policy, and Practice Around the World, Victoria, British Columbia.

Nechi Training, Research & Health Promotions Institute. *Visions.* Website to promote education and awareness with respect to Fetal Alcohol Spectrum Disorders http://www.visions.ab.ca/

Peele, S. and Brodsky, A. (1991). What JAMA study on genes and alcoholism tell us. In, Stanton Peele and Archie Brodsky, *The Truth About Addiction and Recovery.* (pp. 383–386). New York: Simon and Schuster.

*Rouleau, M., Levichek, Z., and Koren, G. (2003). Are mothers who drink heavily in pregnancy victims of FAS? *Journal of FAS International,* 1(4), 4–11.

*Streissguth, A.P., Aase, J.M., Clarren, S.K., Randels, S.P., LaDue, R.A., and Smith D.F. (1991). Fetal Alcohol Syndrome in adolescents and adults. *JAMA,* 1961–1967.

Streissguth, A.P. and Randels, S. (1988). Long term effects of Fetal Alcohol Syndrome. In G.C. Robinson and R.W. Armstrong (Eds.), *Alcohol and Child/Family Health.* (p. 135–150). Vancouver: University of British Columbia.

Werner, L., Morse, B.A, and Garrido, P. (1989). FS/FAE: Focusing prevention on women at risk. *International Journal of the Addictions,* 24, 385–395.

11   Prison Health Care Issues

There has been a brief discussion of some health-related issues in previous chapters, such as in Chapter 10 *overview of elderly and geriatric offenders* and Chapter 2's discussion *ethical issues around harm reduction.* This chapter will focus primarily on three significant areas related to health concerns for CSC offenders, as identified by CSC administrators: *addictions and communicable diseases* and *mental health; behavioural disorders and brain injuries;* and *concurrent disorders.* Although it would be impossible to discuss any one of these issues in depth at this time, some brief information will be presented to address these topic areas.

Inmates, like all Canadian citizens, are entitled to essential health care and reasonable access to non-essential health care. As CSC faces increasing budgetary pressure to maintain quality health care for inmates, costs have increased by almost 60% over the past ten years with little opportunity for cost-saving measures in the delivery of these services. CSC lists the following as some of the reasons for the increase in costs: *higher rates of mental health problems and substance abuse problems, higher prevalence of HIV/AIDS and hepatitis B and C, an aging inmate population, higher cost of drugs (increases 15% per year),* and *CSC must cover 100% of the costs associated with outside hospitalization and for 24-hour escorts* (CSC Speakers Binder).

The offender population is often from a socioeconomic environment that is not conducive to adequate, age-appropriate health care, and in most cases the health care provided during incarceration is all that is available to them. There are a significantly greater number of occurrences of infectious diseases and mental health disorders among incarcerated populations, many going undetected and untreated. In addition, the rapid turnover of some offender populations makes the identification, prevention, and medical management of offender populations extremely risky and difficult. Furthermore, nowhere has the issue of providing treatment in a correctional facility become such a contentious issue as is the case surrounding the treatment of addictions. The presence of drugs is of great concern to CSC, as it is often related to the commission of crimes, the transmission of infectious diseases, and violence in institutions. The ongoing dialogue has raised ethical issues around the provision of methadone maintenance treatment and safety issues around the provision of needle exchanges inside the walls of correctional institutions. Time and time again, research has shown strong links between crime and drugs/drug use, and CSC's drug strategy aims to eliminate drug use in correctional facilities by reducing both the supply and the demand for drugs among offenders. However, while there is some general agreement around the punishment fitting the crime, there is much less agreement around the treatment for those convicted who also have addictions.

Addictions and Issues Related to Communicable Diseases

According to the CSC Performance Report (2002), the offenders entering the system today are presenting with more complex issues and challenges than they did in the past. For example, CSC estimates that "… 80 percent of offenders are poor at problem-solving; 72 percent are unable to generate choices and 78 percent are considered impulsive. Prior to their admission, 79 percent of offenders abused alcohol and/or drugs" (p. 11). The overall health of offenders is much worse than it is within the general public, primarily because of the severe substance abuse practiced by those who are incarcerated. It affects their ability to successfully reintegrate into communities and also greatly increases the cost of medical care within CSC.

Substance Abuse and Addictions

According to a recent report done by Motiuk and Vuong (June 2006), as of December 31, 2005, there were 5,588 identified drug offenders under federal jurisdiction, or one quarter of the total offender population (those in institutions, as well as those on parole and, other conditional releases). Of the 2,654 drug offenders held within institutions, representing approximately 23% of the overall institutional population, about 664 were held in maximum security institutions while about 1,327 populated medium security facilities. Motiuk and Vuong further state that the institutional drug offender population has increased by just over 5% in the 10-year period from 1995 to 2005. Furthermore, it is estimated that 80% of offenders at some point abused alcohol and/or drugs, and between 38–44% were considered to be dependent on one or more of the substances they were using (Thomas, May 2005). Moreover, it is estimated that one third to one half of offenders have used or do use substances while incarcerated.

In a study done by MacPherson and Fraser (June 2006), the results of random urinalysis demonstrated that the type of drugs offenders use have not changed significantly since 1996. For example, of the positive urine screens, THC is the most common substance used (82%), with opiates (15%), benzodiazepines (6%), cocaine (1%), and amphetamines <1% following distantly behind. In terms of drug types found in urine screens, the following Table illustrates gender differences:

Table 11.1. Gender differences in drug types found through random analysis

Drug Type	Men (%)	Women (%)
THC	81	9
Opiates	12	26
Benzodiazepine	7	62
Cocaine	2	3
Amphetamines	<1	1
Other drugs *	4	13

* Other drugs include methylphenidate, Prozac, LSD, PCP, alcohol and pentazocine (synthetically prepared narcotic drug used to treat mild to moderately severe pain i.e. Talwin). Among women, 11% of samples in the "other drugs" category were positive for Prozac. Source: MacPherson and Fraser, June, 2006. Reproduced with the permission of the Minister of Public Works and Government Services Canada, 2009.

The results illustrated in Table 11.1 suggest that men most likely test positive for THC while women more often test positive for benzodiazepines in random urine samples.

Before determining which program is suitable for offenders with serious alcohol and/or other drug problems, it is necessary to assess whether they have characteristics associated with such problems. CSC has developed a new assessment tool to help provide better answers and better treatment-matching capabilities. Prior to 2003, CSC relied on the CLAI (Computerized Lifestyle Assessment Inventory), a 600-item inventory launched in 1989–1990 (Kunic, 2003). As technology began to age and change, the CLAI started to fail and CSC had no succession to replace it.

In addition, an accreditation panel review of program delivery and assessment expressed concerns about the continued use of this tool and the fact that it duplicated some of the factors on the offender intake assessment. The panel recommended using something specific to substance use and those in the field wanted a tool that was shorter than the CLAI, with no duplication of factors being assessed elsewhere. They also wanted something that was simpler to use and capable of linking substance use and abuse to criminal behaviour and assessing motivation for change. What evolved was the development of the CASA (Computerised Assessment of Substance Abuse), a 315 item cognitive behaviourally-based tool. Men must have a grade five reading level and be able to use a computer to use CASA. It also has a unique mouse-over capability, so that if certain text is highlighted the offender can ask the computer to read out that portion for clarity purposes. It can also provide immediate translation between English and French. This tool is currently being used with men only, since CSC researchers and administration agree that in its current form it does not fit the specific needs of female offenders.

In trying to match both the severity of offender substance use and offender profiles including static and dynamic risk factors with the appropriate level of substance use treatment required (low, moderate, high), the CASA has become an invaluable tool. For example, according to Kunic (June 2006), offenders who were rated by the CASA as having more severe substance abuse problems were also more likely to have higher need ratings and criminal risk ratings on the OIA (Offender Intake Assessment) and on the SIR-R1 (Revised Statistical Information on Recidivism Scale). These offenders would require a more in-tensive, highly structured treatment program to reduce the risk of reoffending upon release.

To provide some comparisons, we will take a brief look at substance abuse among the offender population in New Zealand with respect to substance abuse and addictions. New Zealand has a population of four million people and one national corrections system. Approximately 83% of the inmates within the New Zealand correctional system (compared to 32% of the general pub-lic) have experienced problems with alcohol or drugs at some period in their lives (Morris, 2001). Within the New Zealand correctional system, alcohol and drugs are viewed as medical problems, as part of the offence cycle, and in terms of overall prison safety—a source of concern with respect to contraband and antisocial behaviour. Currently, there has been an increase in the use of amphetamines, methamphetamines, and "party" or "rave" drugs such as GHB. Part of the reason for this is that it is easier to smuggle these drugs into pris-ons and they are harder to detect. Since drug and alcohol abuse is seen as a core criminogenic problem, it is dealt with in a number of ways. Psychologists sometimes treat offenders at high risk of reoffending and with a high need for substance abuse treatment; however, they may receive interventions from one of three other options:

- brief harm reduction involving group treatment (approximate cost in Canadian dollars is $80 per intervention);
- group treatment plus some individual therapy (approximate cost in Canadian dollars is $550 per intervention);
- intensive treatment in a 182 day residential program, with 400 people per year accessing this program (approximate cost in Canadian dollars is $15,748 per intervention). (Morris, 2001, p. 19)

The expected benefits of treating these offenders is estimated to be 19 New Zealand dollars (or approximately $15 Canadian) saved for every New Zealand dollar spent. In Canada, for every dollar spent on providing addictions treatment, Canadians save $11 in health-related costs. In addition, New Zealand provides a number of drug-free units "… where inmates receive additional privileges for adapting a drug-free lifestyle" (Morris, 2001, p. 19). According to Morris, three distinct subgroups are incorporated into the overall offender populations and these groups typically access alcohol and drug interventions in ways shown in Table 11.2.

Table 11.2. New Zealand's Unique Prison Population and Alcohol/Drug Interventions

Prison subgroup	Alcohol and drug intervention
Maori—New Zealand's indigenous population. They make up 50% of the prison population but only 12% of the general population	Culturally-based program such as the *Te Wairua o nga Targata* [the Spirit of the People]. Seven modules consisting of 70–80 hours of programming, delivered to those Maori serving community-based sentences. Within prison exists four Maori units focusing on cultural values to address offending and aid in rehabilitation
Women—make up 5% of the prison population and 24% of those are serving community-based sentences. They are over-represented among the alcohol and drug abuse stats, especially with respect to the use of hard drugs	Can access a drug-free unit once they have completed an intensive drug and alcohol treatment program
Community based offenders—they make up approximately 21,000 offenders serving a variety of community-based sentences	Although treatment programs are generally run by local providers, they are generic and not necessarily designed for a correctional context. These programs are being phased out in favour of dedicated programs to address criminogenic needs

Source: Morris, "Alcohol and drugs: A perspective from New Zealand." Reproduced with the permission of the Minister of Public Works and Government Services Canada, 2009.

Based on offender intake data as of 2005, CSC described substance use among offenders as follows: 61% abused alcohol alone, 69% abused drugs, and 47% abused both alcohol and drugs. Within the offender population, 44% were described as polydrug users, meaning that they used more than one drug, often at the same time. Only 24% of federal offenders did not have a problem with either substance. Similar to the statistics previously identified in the New Zealand study, an estimated 80% of federal offenders identified substance use as a serious issue for them. In fact, according Roy (2001), approximately 56% were intoxicated when they committed their most current offence. This figure is consistent with a study done by Mumford (2001) on convicted homicide offenders in British Columbia, which identified 57% as either being under the influence of or withdrawing from alcohol or drugs at the time of their offences. Further research done by CSC concluded that as the severity of the alcohol and drug problem intensified, so did the probability that a crime would be committed. For example, 50% of those with low severity substance use problems used substances during the commission of their crimes; whereas, 90% of those with high severity substance use problems used substances during the commission of their offences (Roy, 2001). Like their New Zealand counterparts, CSC believed that substance use and abuse was part of the profile of *criminogenic factors* to be taken into consideration when assessing the offender.

Another concern is drug use within correctional institutions; a small percentage of offenders first use drugs while serving their sentences—especially hardcore drugs. Approximately 6,000 random drug tests are conducted each year, with close to 75% resulting in negative findings. Enhanced security measures have also resulted in an increase in the seizure or confiscation of drugs, as Table 11.3 indicates:

Table 11.3. Institutional Seizures of Alcohol and Other Drugs

Substance	1999/00	2000/01	2001/02	2002/03	2003/04	2004/05
Miscellaneous pills (#)	1894	2979	3769	4788	3999	4955
Cocaine (grams)	159	355	180	159	128	272
Opiates (grams)	164	245	208	226	92	310
Alcohol & brew (litres)	8918	8245	9576	8731	12358	8707
THC (grams)	5444	8014	7481	9358	9984	8400
Opiates (pills)	509	482	1011	1570	2267	2237

Source: CSC DPR 2.1.1 Security Sub Activity, April 10, 2005

In Canada, CSC has introduced a methadone maintenance program, which was discussed in more detail in Chapter 2. Methadone is a synthetic drug that acts on the same opiate receptors as heroin does, and therefore reduces the withdrawal symptoms that heroin users frequently experience when trying to discontinue use. The effectiveness or duration of the effects of methadone is about 24 to 36 hours compared to four to six hours with heroin. However, methadone does not produce euphoria or sedation that often accompanies heroin use. As a result, there is an added benefit to having individuals on the Methadone Maintenance Treatment Program (MMTP) because they are often able to lead more normal and productive lives. The goals of the program are to achieve a decrease in intravenous drug use, needle sharing and other HIV risk behaviours, a decrease in criminal activity associated with such use, as well as increased productivity and an increased likelihood that the offender will continue in MMTP after release.

Addressing the impact of the use of injection drugs and opiates in general, a CSC administrator commented:

Administrator 1: Harm reduction I think is a hugely important area within corrections. The introduction of methadone as a way of allowing guys to get away from their day-to-day addictions has been very, very useful to us and of course to the offenders themselves, as it has gotten them out of the day-to-day rat race, i.e., figuring out how they are going to get their drugs from day-to-day and how they are going to pay for them—are they going to have to extort someone or commit some other crime and those sorts of things that are associated with heroin use or any other chemical usage. It helps them to get down to the business of addressing their criminogenic needs, once they are on the methadone, and I have talked to a number of inmates, and once they are on the methadone they are able to start reorganizing their lives and to think about what brought them to the place that they are in. As long as they are trying to meet their addictions needs they simply do not have any capacity to participate in any programming, and again it is absolutely crucial for them to have meaningful support systems. And again I had occasion to talk to a prominent politician on that issue and he feels very much the same way and he thinks we need to strengthen the methadone capacity in the community because if you want these people to live reasonably successful lives in the community, they can't do this if they are fighting their addiction on a day-to-day basis.

Many people are concerned because they view this as replacing one addiction by another and this creates a lot of concern among the politicians, for example, who are very anti-methadone programming. The transition to methadone changes the lifestyle and personal lives of offenders, and if they want to take the step to reduce their use of methadone, this is a choice that some of them can make, whereas for them to lose their addiction directly is virtually a hopeless exercise. Therefore, it is absolutely crucial to us to have the methadone program as well as other programs, such as the one involving distribution of clean needles, etc., in helping to prevent the transmission of diseases.

While it does seem to acknowledge the existence of drugs within facilities, the reality is that drugs do exist and will continue to exist within facilities. And the more we can reduce the appetite for drugs within our facilities through programs like the methadone program, this will have a direct impact for example, on our ability to curtail the level of violence within institutions because people will not have to be chasing and engaging in behaviours associated with obtaining drugs on a day-to-day basis. And it also has a positive effect on the families of offenders, because it tends to be the poor wife of the offender or some other wife of an offender who is extorted into bringing in the drugs, and so when you can stop that chain of behaviour it allows for relationships to improve, it allows women to come in because they are not as terrified in terms of pressure to bring in drugs, and so it creates a much safer and much healthier environment for everybody.

As mentioned at the beginning of this chapter, ongoing debates have highlighted the views both supporting and opposing addictions treatment within correctional institutions, and nowhere is this more noticeable than around treatment strategies that are associated with harm reduction. Clearly this has presented a dilemma for many administrators, although Administrator 1 supports the use of methadone as a harm reduction strategy to help combat heroin and other opiate use among inmates. What are your views around the use of methadone as a method of treating such drug addiction, and how might you respond to Administrator 1's views?

As of December 2004 there were 512 offenders on the MMTP with another 42 undergoing assessment for initiation of treatment. In the 2004–2005 time period, CSC introduced a Methadone Maintenance Treatment Program database designed to allow for the ongoing collection, management, and analysis of MMTP participant information. As shown in Figure 11.1, the majority of participants are located in the Pacific region, and numbers of offenders involved in the program have increased both regionally and nationally.

Figure 11.1 MMTP participants by region

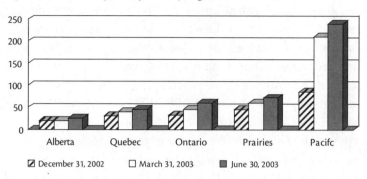

Source: CSC OMS, 2003

MMTP is cost effective and known to reduce the transmission of blood borne diseases such as HIV or Hepatitis C among injection drug users. According to CSC, the cost of treating an offender with HIV is approximately $30,000 annually versus $11,695 annually, which is the cost of putting an offender on the MMTP. Cost comparisons are shown in Table 11.4:

Table 11.4. Cost Comparisons for MMTP

Indicator	Annual cost (CND) per person (2002)
Untreated opiate addict	49,000 (societal costs, i.e., health costs, productivity losses, victimization, criminal justice costs)
HIV treatment	20,000
Hepatitis C treatment	25,000
Hepatitis C monitoring	1,200
Incarceration male/female	66,381/110,473
MMTP	11,695

Source: Report on the Evaluation of CSC's Methadone Maintenance Program, 2003

Earlier in this chapter, research was presented that identified substance use among offenders. Generally, research results have supported the belief that as much as 80% of offenders are substance users. In addition to this, the association between crime and substance use is well documented. As a result, CSC developed a series of national substance abuse programs for those offenders experiencing addictions as a way to not only promote healthier, alcohol and drug-free lifestyles, but also to reduce crime. It is critical for security and public safety that those offenders whose substance abuse is directly related to their criminal activities are provided with alternative skills and strategies to modify this pattern in order to decrease their rates of recidivism. Some of these substance use programs were offered within the institutions, while others were community-based programs. All of these programs have been accredited by an international panel of substance abuse experts.

Some of the earlier programs, such as OSAPP/ALTO (a moderate intensity program) and CHOICES (low intensity community-based program), were developed to meet the needs of offenders. During the evaluation of these programs it was determined that there were some shortfalls. One of these was in the provision of *maintenance*, a set of skills that provides the offender with ways to stay substance-free and to avoid relapsing. This was not consistently provided in the programming offered. In addition, according to Long (June 2006), those offenders with the most serious substance use problem were the ones most likely to drop out and therefore not benefit from the programming. Furthermore, evaluation done on the programs revealed the following:

> To maximize safety and security, early admission of offenders into the substance abuse programs was necessary. In the absence of this, the Service was relying primarily on interdiction measures while offenders continued their drug seeking and using behaviours without the intervention necessary to help them stop. Gaps in the ability to provide appropriately matched services, with an increasing number of offenders requiring high intensity intervention, had an impact in the areas of management and reintegration. (Long, June 2006, p. 39)

As mentioned previously, it was clear that the existing programs did not meet the needs of the more severely addicted offenders, who, according to Eno, Long, Blanchet, Hansen, and Dine (2001), make up as much as 37% of the offender population and who are described in the opening summary as:

- being in the highest need category;
- being more likely to have used alcohol and drugs on the day of the crime;
- having the highest rates of previous convictions;
- having the highest rates of unsuccessful attempts at cutting down;
- being more likely to need help to stop or control their drinking;
- having the highest rate of drinking and drug use;
- recidivating at higher rates than those with lesser substance abuse problems.

For these reasons, CSC developed HISAP (High Intensity Substance Abuse Program), which was based somewhat on a combination of the OSAPP and CHOICES programs. It was intended to help offenders deal with their substance abuse problems over longer periods of time. HISAP, although better adapted to meet the needs of 70% of the offenders who have identified substance use as a serious problem for them, was also found lacking in its ability to reach those offenders most affected by substance abuse, in particular during the post-release phase. Table 11.5 provides a comparison between OSAPP, CHOICES, ALTO, HISAP in terms of program structure—that is, number of hours, duration, and so forth, and a profile of the typical offender who might benefit from such programs.

Table 11.5. Comparison of OSAPP, CHOICES, ALTO, and HISAP

Program Name	Structure	Offender Characteristics
OSAPP *	Offers 26 3-hour sessions and three individual sessions with the program facilitator.	Offenders with moderate to high severity. Targets offenders who are within 6 months of probable release.
ALTO	Offers 26 3-hour sessions and three individual sessions with the program facilitator. This program is specifically designed for the francophone population.	Offenders with moderate to high severity. Targets offenders who are within 6 months of probable release.
CHOICES	Offers two phases: Intensive phase delivered over a 1-week full day or a 2-week half-day period. Maintenance phase, once a week for 12 weeks. Only offenders who successfully complete Phase One can attend the maintenance phase.	Directed at those offenders who have been released to the community, and is therefore offered in the community. Acts as a relapse prevention program.
HISAP	Offers 100 2-hour sessions with about eight sessions per week. The overall program length is 4–5 months.	Namely for offenders with severe, chronic, long-term addictions.

* Interestingly, according to Roy (2001), although most offenders choose abstinence, "… of those offenders who completed OSAPP with the goal of moderating their use of alcohol and other drugs [they] were reconvicted at a significantly lower rate than those who were attempting to abstain completely from all intoxicants" (p. 6). Source: Eno *et al.,* (2001), Delnef (2001). Reproduced with the permission of the Minister of Public Works and Government Services Canada, 2009.

In 2004–05 CSC implemented a new model for the treatment of substance abuse—NSAP or the National Substance Abuse Program. According to CSC, NSAP is founded on an integrated theoretical model which posits that patterns of substance abuse have multiple determinants and can be explained, in part, by learning principles. Substance abuse is a maladaptive response to ongoing problems in living. Behaviour is initiated and maintained by past learning experiences, including peer modeling, reinforcement contingencies, cognitive expectations or beliefs, and biological influences. Therefore, if substance abusing behaviours are learned, then the same processes can be used to assist the individual to develop more adaptive cognitive and behavioural coping responses. The model is able to provide a variety of programming in terms of intensity (high, moderate, and low) and design in order to fit the needs of individual offenders (see Figure 11.2).

Figure 11.2 Offender Program Participation

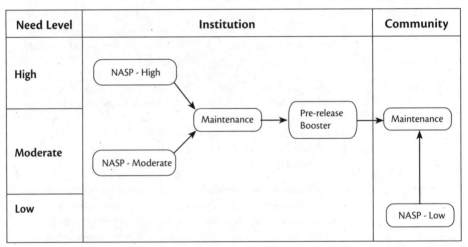

Source: Correctional Service of Canada. Substance Abuse Program

In order to participate in NSAP, the offenders' substance abuse must be identified as a criminogenic factor. This would mean that almost half of the male institutional offenders in the population are candidates for NSAP (Long, June 2006). However, not all offenders have the same severity level when it comes to substance use issues. In order to address the varying severity/needs levels, NSAP has developed high intensity 89-session, moderate intensity 26-session and low intensity ten-session programs. Four key life areas are the focus of these programs, including creating better relationships, feeling good, establishing a more satisfying life, and building personal control and freedom. A maintenance piece is built into these programs and there is a continuous intake for both the institutional and community-based settings. In addition to this, offenders who attend the institutional programming must also attend the pre-release booster no more than three months before their release into the community. This helps to mitigate potential relapse and to provide better community reintegration for these offenders.

The emphasis of the NSAP on substance abuse and criminality is necessary to assist offenders in analyzing their patterns of behaviour. The intent of this is to reduce both relapse and recidivism. Furthermore, the provision of these programs begins as early in the offender's sentence as possible and avoids the previous system of stacking programs of varying intensity to achieve the identified goals and address the varying levels of severity of substance use. Programs are less educational and more experiential, focusing on skills development and practice. Offenders are therefore provided with the ongoing structure and support for skills acquisition and rehearsal through the program and ongoing maintenance in the institution and community, as required (Long, June 2006; Correctional Service of Canada, Substance Abuse Program).

More than 200 CSC staff have been trained and certified to deliver these programs in institutions and community. According to CSC, more than 3,000 offenders per year attend NSAP, while more than 5,000 offenders participate in some type of substance abuse intervention each year. For those who attended NSAP, preliminary results have shown that there is a 19% reduction in recidivism and a 50% reduction in new convictions when compared to a matched sample (Correctional Service of Canada, Substance Abuse Program; Correctional Service of Canada, Substance Abuse Programs for Federal Offenders).

In addition to offering the NSAP to men, CSC developed the Women Offender Substance Abuse Programming (WOSAP) in 2003 to address the substance abuse needs of all women offenders. This program was launched as a two-year pilot ending May 2005. WOSAP offers formal interventions in addition to focusing on building a supportive institutional community for the development of healthy, functional relationships. Three modules form the core of the program and include:

1. Engagement and Education (E&E)—offered to all women in the institution regardless of identified substance abuse problem;
2. Intensive Therapeutic Treatment (ITT)—for offenders with moderate to high substance abuse needs; and
3. Relapse Prevention and Maintenance (RPM)—offered in both the institution and the community to address problematic behaviours related to crime, including substance abuse.

WOSAP is holistic and multi-dimensional and it reflects the unique experiences of women. Its key themes include gender responsiveness, community involvement, empowerment of the women, and it focuses on strengths versus disabilities (see Appendix D).

In a 2003 presentation, Lucy Hume of the CSC Addictions Research Centre described the population of female offenders with substance abuse problems:

- 813 offenders, with 44% in custody and 56% in the community;
- comprise less than 4% of overall offender population;
- average sentence is 3.4 years;
- 50% have less than grade 10 education;
- most suffer from some form of trauma, which may be generational;
- often these women are marginalized;
- most became criminally involved through their various relationships;
- younger group who engage in criminal behaviour at an earlier age;
- more than 70% were involved in drugs or alcohol at the time of the offence;
- often use alcohol and/or other drugs to self medicate or to cope;
- 52% were under the influence of alcohol and/or other drugs at time of their offence.

The first national training session for WOSAP was held in May 2003 with subsequent implementation in four women's federal institutions as well as Burnaby Correctional Centre for Women and Okimaw Ohci Healing Lodge. Since 2003, WOSAP has been introduced to 22 community sites, with two additional national training sessions. Feedback collected from program participants and facilitators informed two sets of revisions to both the program manual and implementation guidelines, resulting in a standardized yet dynamic program responsive to the unique needs of each site.

More women offenders have a problem with drugs (80%) rather than alcohol (50%), and in terms of problematic substance use, women reported that cocaine (68%), opiates (56%), crack (51%), and heroin (46%) were the most addictive and the hardest to quit. Although marijuana use was very common, only 16% indicated that it had reached the problematic stage of use. Although the E&E component of the WOSAP is offered to all women with substance use problems, approximately three quarters were assessed as having a moderate to severe substance use problem, whereas 95% of those attending the ITT module had a moderate to severe substance use problem (Furlong and Grant, June 2006).

Much of the literature supports a strong connection between traumatic experiences and the onset of substance use, often leading to problematic use for women. Substance use becomes a maladaptive coping strategy for dealing with these traumatic experiences, and the majority of women who participated in the ITT module of WOSAP admitted to engaging in these behaviours because of past trauma. WOSAP responds to traumatic experiences by addressing the first stage of trauma recovery, although many of these women would require more intensive trauma work not found within WOSAP. Additionally, substance use is a significant criminogenic factor. Almost all women offenders (91%) stated they were under the influence of drugs and/or alcohol at the time of their most recent offence. Interestingly, more women reported that drug use, rather than alcohol use, had more of an impact on their criminal behaviour.

Results have shown that WOSAP has had a beneficial impact on women who have attended the programming. For example, relationships with significant others have shown some improvement with respect to women defining and identifying healthy, supportive relationships in their lives and being able to maintain such relationships. Given that one quarter of the women had intimate partners who were substance users and more than two thirds had at least one family member who also used substances, improvement in the area of relationships could have a significant impact on relapse and recidivism. These findings are consistent with current feminist theory, which explains substance abuse within the context of women's relationships. Relational theory posits that women develop a sense of identity and achieve psychological health through mutually supportive relationships and through a sense of connection with others. A lack of such relationships may translate into increased vulnerability to substance use. Women may also use substances as a means of connecting to substance-abusing partners (Furlong and Grant, June 2006).

In addition to the development of NSAP and WOSAP, CSC also identified the need to develop programs to meet the needs of Aboriginal offenders experiencing problematic substance use. Although already over-represented in the federal offender population, demographic trends, including a relatively young population and increasing urbanization, suggest that the number of Aboriginal admissions to federal institutions will continue to increase over the next few decades. As has been discussed previously, substance abuse is linked to increased rates of criminal offences, incarceration, and recidivism in the general public, and this association holds true among Aboriginal peoples as well, where more than 90% of federally sentenced Aboriginal offenders have an identified substance abuse problem (Varis, McGowan and Mullins, June 2006).

According to Varis *et al.*, (June 2006) in recognition of the needs of the Aboriginal offender population CSC developed the 16-week AOSAP (Aboriginal Offender Substance Abuse Program) pilot or demonstration project in 2004. This is a culturally sensitive program that seeks to reduce the risk of relapse and recidivism in part by improving the program completion rates for Aboriginal participants through the incorporation of both contemporary approaches as well as traditional Aboriginal teachings. The services of Ancestral Visions of Tyendinaga Mohawk Territory in Ontario, with support from the Aboriginal Initiatives Branch and the Reintegration Programs Branch (Aboriginal Programs unit) of CSC, were involved in the designing of this specialized program. Five demonstration sites offered the initial program and the second phase included three more sites. In September 2004, five Aboriginal correctional program officers and five institutional Elders, one from each region, participated in program training for the demonstration phase of this project. Training continues as changes are made to the manual and as new facilitators and Elders join the demonstration project.

The AOSAP responds to the needs of Aboriginal men (First Nations, Métis, and Inuit) by taking a holistic approach, ensuring that the impact of addiction is examined through physical, mental, emotional, and spiritual dimensions. Currently, the needs of Aboriginal women offenders in relation to substance abuse treatment are under review, and research on the AOSAP will be highly instructive as to future directions for the Aboriginal women offender population. The specific objectives of the program are as follows:

- Awareness: develop awareness of linkages between substance abuse and criminal offending;
- Motivation: develop opportunities to engage and motivate participants in a positive change process;
- Skill enhancement: develop skill base to promote an alcohol-and-other-drug-free lifestyle (physical, mental, emotional, and spiritual); and
- Spiritual connection: introduce cultural activities as a means of healing. (Varis *et al.*, June 2006)

Lastly, CSC has developed Intensive Support Units, or ISUs, which complement existing substance abuse programs. These units are intended to provide safe housing and support for those offenders who are assigned to them and who have chosen to live a drug-free lifestyle. The environment is structured and the units offer "an array of inducements, sanctions, lifestyles and support" to the offenders (Grant, Varis, and Lefebvre, 2005, p. 4). Grant, Varis, and Lefebvre (2005) described the benefits of the ISUs by stating they provide the offender with supportive units using specially trained personnel. This has reduced the presence of drugs and alcohol through increased searching and drug testing beyond what is specific under Canadian law. Also, one in five of the occupants of ISUs chose to live there to reduce their exposure to drugs even though they are not substance users themselves. ISU residency offers no special programs or privileges according to Varis, Lefebvre, and Grant (June 2006). Typically, the occupants of ISUs are younger, serving shorter sentences for non-violent offences, and are rated as lower risk on static factors. Although Aboriginal offenders represent 16% of the total offender population, they represent close to 12% of ISU residents and are therefore under-represented in this population. Currently, there is at least one ISU in nearly all of the CSC facilities, which translates into 1,100 beds at 43 sites (CSC Performance Report 2002).

Recently, a study was conducted to assess the impact of ISUs across several factors, including institutional behaviour, the presence of alcohol and drugs on units, and perceptions of staff and offenders (Varis, Lefebvre, and Grant, June 2006). Some results of the study demonstrate that although there were more searches in the ISUs, there was a lower rate of substances and substance-related contraband found in cells and on the offenders. Offenders in ISUs also had a lower rate of positive urine screen test results, which translated into a lower rate of misconducts on the units and in the general corrections setting. Varis *et al.*, (June 2006) calculated that a "potential cost savings of $8,000 per ISU participant was realized due to decreased incarceration time resulting from earlier release (via discretionary release) and the reduced likelihood of readmission" (p. 32).

CSC is committed to helping offenders become more aware of the dangers of substance use issues and the spread of infectious diseases. It committed $17.1 million over 3 years ending with the 2003–04 period toward treatment, prevention, and security initiatives directed at substance abuse and the spread of infectious diseases. In addition, CSC opened the Addictions Research Division facility in Montague, PEI in 2001. According to the 2002 CSC Performance Report, "this facility is designed to be the cornerstone of all CSC drug and alcohol research, as well as a forum for provincial, national and international research partnerships."

Communicable and Infectious Diseases

Offenders often have a history of high-risk behaviours, including injection drug use, working in the sex trade, having unprotected sex more frequently with high risk partners, and so on. As a result, they may have acquired infectious or blood-borne and sexually transmitted diseases prior to their incarceration, although infection can also occur afterwards. The transmission of other diseases such as tuberculosis has also been documented within penitentiaries. As mentioned elsewhere in this text, prison drug use and the related harms, including the potential for the spread of communicable diseases are a major worldwide public health concern. All prisoners will eventually be released back into communities, and if left undetected and untreated, have an increased likelihood of passing these diseases on to the general public (Thomas, June 2005).

The number of reported cases of HIV/AIDS in the federal correctional system in Canada rose from 14 in January 1989 to 159 in March 1996 to 233 in December 2001 (Thomas, June 2005). According to CSC's Performance Report (2002), the prevalence of such infectious diseases is higher in the offender population than in the wider population. In fact, the Report states that

> ... in the 2000 and 2001 calendar years, HIV infection rates among offenders were 1.6 percent and 1.7 percent respectively, compared to 0.13 percent of the general Canadian population. The rate of infection for Hepatitis C during the same period rose from 19.3 percent to 22.3 percent, compared to 0.8 percent in the general population. Thirty-three percent of HIV infected people also have Hepatitis C.

In addition to this, it has been noted that HIV and overall Hep C rates are especially high for federal female inmates (Thomas, June 2005). For example, in 2001, a greater prevalence of HIV cases was discovered among female offenders than among males—4.7% versus 1.7%. For women, this is a lower rate than that of 2000, while the rate for men remained comparable.

One of the correctional administrators said:

> **Administrator 2:** Just in our region alone we have around five hundred people with Hepatitis C and as well a number of people with AIDS,... so it is very important to us to stop the transmission of diseases within the institutions. So while some may argue that this type of program supports criminality,... it is done for their protection and for the protection of others who may be in custody and who might get involved in that kind of danger-ous behaviour, whether it is sexually transmitted or transmitted through the use of needles or whatever. And so from a harm reduction perspective it is crucial for us to be involved in a big way. So we need the support and understanding of politicians and also to show them how crucial it is to the safety of their communities and that [harm reduction] it is a tool just like any other health promotion, health prevention tool. It is not much different from what we are trying to do now with the SARs outbreak—we are trying to prevent others from becoming contaminated, and so harm reduction strategies prevent that from happening and that is the rationale for using that kind of strategy.

Table 11.6 shows there was a 3% increase in the percentage of HCV (Hepatitis C) cases reported in CSC from 2001–2004 (23.5% or 2,993 cases compared to 26.65% or 3,303 cases). In the general Canadian population the infection rate was much lower—0.8%. According to Prithwish (2002), new cases of HCV were much more likely to be found among the existing population of offenders than in new admissions. One explanation may be that advancements in testing over the past few years have made it possible for CSC to identify existing cases more accurately. As in the case of HIV infections, women were more likely than men to have the virus for Hepatitis C. For example, 41.2% of female offenders compared to 23.2% of male offenders had tested positive for Hepatitis C at the end of 2001.

Other infectious diseases, including sexually transmitted infections (STIs), also contribute to the burden of disease within the CSC environment. Diseases such as Hepatitis B and STIs are often identified through their symptoms rather than screening. Although Prithwish (2002) indicated that the number of Hepatitis B cases declined between 2000–2004 within CSC offender populations, (0.3% to .13%), this rate was still much lower than the rate of the decline of cases in the general Canadian population, which was estimated to be between 0.5% and 1.0% in 2000. Increases were also noted in some of the STIs within the CSC population between 2000–2004, while the number of cases in the general Canadian population was lower. Data released in 2005 by CSC indicates the prevalence of a variety of infectious diseases among CSC offenders as shown in Table 11.6.

Table 11.6. Prevalence of Infectious Diseases Among CSC Offenders

Disease	Dec 2001		Dec 2002		Dec 2003		Dec 2004	
HIV/AIDS	223	(1.8%)	251	(2.04%)	227	(1.86%)	182	(1.47%)
Hepatitis B	43	(0.3%)	30	(0.24%)	17	(0.14%)	16	(0.13%)
Hepatitis C	2993	(23.6%)	3173	(25.81%)	3111	(25.54%)	3303	(26.65%)

Sexually Transmitted Infections (STIs)

STI	Dec 2001		Dec 2002		Dec 2003		Dec 2004	
Chlamydia	23	(0.18%)	53	(0.43%)	58	(0.48%)	53	(0.43%)
Gonorrhoea	13	(0.10%)	20	(0.16%)	7	(0.06%)	11	(0.09%)
Syphilis	0	(0.00%)	3	(0.02%)	4	(0.03%)	10	(0.08%)
Other STIs	35	(0.27%)	53	(0.43%)	85	(0.70%)	91	(0.73%)
Latent TB Infection	2658	(21.20%)	2219	(18.80%)	N/Av		N/Av	

Source: CSC DPR 2.1.2 Health Care Services Sub Activity, April 10, 2005

CSC must find innovative and effective ways to curtail the transmission of these diseases among the offender populations in light of the tremendous burden such diseases impose in terms of both financial and human costs. There are several things we know about the CSC population of offenders:

- high rates of substance abuse among inmates;
- high rates of injection drug use by inmates prior to and during incarceration;
- high rates of risky behaviours related to tattooing and piercing;
- high rates of infection with HCV and HIV;
- high prevalence of risk factors for developing active TB disease;
- low rates of testing uptake for blood borne viruses and STIs. (*Canadian Journal of Public Health*, S35).

Some of the ways CSC has addressed these issues of transmission involve the adoption of some harm reduction techniques as well as education for both staff and offenders. Some of the strategies include:

- the provision of education materials and programs for offenders and staff;
- the availability of condoms, dental dams, water-based lubricants, and bleach in all institutions;
- the promotion of immunization for Hepatitis A and B;
- the provision of treatment for Hepatitis C in institutions;
- the provision of a methadone maintenance program for opioid addicted offenders;
- consideration for expanding the harm reduction initiatives, including safe tattooing and needle exchange;
- pharmacological remedies such as naltrexone or antabuse;
- in-reach by groups such as the Vancouver Persons With Aids (PWA) Society.

In addition to this, CSC uses drug dogs to locate drugs in institutions, as well as ion scanners, which detect different microscopic particles discharged by items such as drugs, or particles which may cling to or be absorbed by skin or clothing.

Many inmates are vulnerable to blood-borne pathogens due to high-risk lifestyles before they arrive in prison and while incarcerated. Some of these risk behaviours include injecting drugs, sharing needles, body piercing, tattooing, and unprotected sexual relations. According to Thomas (May 2005), the single most important risk factor in the transmission of HCV in Canada is through injection drug use, and the sharing of drug injection equipment is a statistically significant predictor of infection rates. Although it is difficult to assess the precise prevalence of injection drug use, some researchers suggest it is important to address the transmission of these diseases through the implementation of prison-based needle exchanges.

Harm Reduction

Chapter 2 provides further discussion on the issues surrounding the adoption of harm reduction, most of which are viewed through a moral or ethical lens. Nowhere is this issue more contentious than when discussing interventions and strategies for dealing with the transmission of communicable diseases in Canada's prisons and penitentiaries. In examining high-risk lifestyles among inmates, Thomas (May 2005) noted that out of 7,105 male inmates, (1995–97) and 4,285 male inmates surveyed in 1995, he found the following results: 18.3% injected prior to incarceration; 38.7% shared injection equipment; 11% injected while incarcerated; 41% shared injection equipment; 45% acquired tattoos while incarcerated; 17% acquired piercing; 25% could not be sure their equipment was clean; 6% MSM in prison; and 61% did not use condoms. As mentioned previously, it is difficult to get an exact number of individuals injecting drugs, but one thing is clear: these high risk activities have resulted in the huge increase in the spread of communicable diseases.

In order to address some of these behaviours and the resulting health issues, Thomas (May 2005) further argued for a number of harm reduction measures to be implemented in the criminal justice settings in Canada. They include: removal of abstinence as a condition of participation in drug or alcohol treatment while in prison or on parole; disregarding positive results for cannabis use in parolee urinalysis unless the drug use is directly connected to the offender's criminality, (cannabis has a relatively low harm potential and there is a need to differentiate substances according to the health and social harms they generate); providing bleach to inmates for sterilizing injection equipment (as of September 2002, all CSC institutions provided bleach to inmates explicitly as a harm reduction measure); providing methadone maintenance therapy to opiate-dependent inmates and parolees, (as of 2002, most correctional jurisdictions in Canada had methadone treatment available to prisoners). More controversially for some, Thomas also advised that sterile injection equipment (syringes) be provided in jail/prison, though, several organizations and reports (including the Correctional Investigators 2004 Report) have recommended the establishment of these prison-based needle exchange programs, (pp. 4–6).

Discussions are continuing among researchers (like the Canadian Centre on Substance Abuse) and CSC about the viability of having a needle exchange program inside institutions. Such a program will likely be effective in reducing the spread of infectious diseases and should be used in combination with con-dom dispensing and other safe sex practices to increase the success of program objectives. There are many hurdles to cross, however, before this can become a reality.

Mental Health Issues

A dilemma exists within the justice system when administrators are faced with incarcerating offenders who suffer from mental health problems, includ-ing those who are suicidal. These individuals often fall through the gaps in the social safety net—a net that seems to be devoid of community-based services to intervene in a timely manner. According to Daigle (2007), these offenders are often "more vulnerable to arrest because of their behaviour and they are more likely to cyclically encounter both the mental health and criminal justice system" (p. 63). Governmental bodies and non-profit agencies are faced with a similar dilemma as overall political goals change and affect the resources and funding needed to run community-based programs. In British Columbia, for example, a decision was made to close a large residential facility that typically housed individuals with mental health problems, who struggled to survive in mainstream society, and this led to the return of such individuals to various communities.

These communities are also often not equipped to handle these individuals, and thus the cycle of "offending" and "criminalizing" begins. The criminal justice system has not been set up to offer the level of treatment and reinte-gration these individuals require. Some would argue that the needs of these offenders would be better served in a wider community setting dedicated to those with severe mental health problems rather than a criminal justice setting. And preferably with intervention prior to any involvement with the law. But, Daigle suggests that the likelihood of recidivism exists as a result of a weakened and under-resourced community mental health system and an unresponsive criminal justice system. However, as a consequence of formal reviews, CSC is building a more responsive system that will provide a full-spectrum response to the mental health needs of offenders from intake assessment to release in the community.

Studies done by CSC in 2001 have indicated that apart from substance use disorders, 43% of offenders could be diagnosed with Axis 1 disorders and of those, approximately 12% suffer from serious and persistent mental illness re-quiring immediate interventions (Daigle, 2007). More recently, other studies have indicated that in Québec, for example, the percentage of offenders with serious and persistent mental illness was close to 30% and CSC reports an increase (as much as 61%) in newly arrived inmates being diagnosed with a mental health issue. In addition to the presence of mental health problems, there is the issue of suicidality among offenders. According to Daigle, although the suicide rate in prisons is much higher than that of the general public, it is not a common event. While males commit suicide more often than females, females more often than males engage in suicide attempts and other self-harming behaviours such as self-mutilations. Psychological and "environmental autopsies" performed by CSC on 66 suicides committed in Canadian penitentiaries have identified some important common factors: individuals who committed suicide were most likely to be male Caucasian, under the age of 39, serving a sentence of 2–5 years. They were also likely to be single and housed in medium security facilities. In addition to this, they were also more likely to be incarcerated for robbery or murder, have lengthy involvement with the criminal justice system, and be involved in a serious incident within the institution (Daigle, 2007).

This chapter next briefly discusses mental illness, behavioural disorders, brain injuries, and concurrent disorders. It is important to remember that within the field these four descriptors are applied differently and they often overlap in both research and discussion.

Mentally Ill Offenders

According to Boe and Vuong (2002), a study done by CSC in 1988 identified the "lifetime prevalence rate of psychotic disorders among federal male inmates to be 10.4%" (p. 6). Although many researchers in the U.S. argue that the offender population within American prisons has not been well studied, some estimates suggest that between 16 and 30% of inmates in jails or prisons have a diagnosable mental illness (Faust, 2003; Taylor, 2001). Following the 1998 CSC study, an effort was made to collect statistics on a regular, ongoing basis in order to track the prevalence rates of mental health problems among the general offender population. Among the eight indicators that were selected for this purpose were:

- current and previous diagnosis as disordered;
- current and previous prescribing of medications;
- current and previous hospitalization for mental health issues;
- receiving outpatient services prior to admission.

Table 11.7 (next page) shows the results of this tracking for the years 1997 to 2001.

Table 11.7. Federal Admission Trends/Number and Percentage of Admissions with a Mental Health Indicator

Calendar year	1997		1998		1999		2000		2001	
	n	%	n	%	n	%	n	%	n	%
Diagnosed current	265	(6.2)	280	(6.4)	292	(7.0)	289	(6.9)	355	(8.5)
Prescribed current	443	(10.3)	495	(11.2)	564	(13.4)	605	(14.3)	751	(17.9)
Hospitalized current	80	(1.8)	81	(1.8)	73	(1.7)	77	(1.8)	89	(2.1)
Outpatient current	211	(4.9)	206	(4.7)	235	(5.6)	263	(6.2)	287	(6.8)
Diagnosed past	418	(9.8)	439	(10.0)	480	(11.4)	509	(12.2)	555	(13.4)
Prescribed past	962	(22.5)	1,039	(23.8)	1,139	(27.3)	1,207	(29.0)	1,351	(32.6)
Hospitalized past	687	(16.0)	678	(15.4)	713	(17.0)	719	(17.2)	789	(19.0)
Outpatient past	724	(17.0)	677	(15.5)	791	(18.9)	910	(21.8)	885	(21.4)
Estimated valid assessments	4,338		4,448		4,237		4,243		4,231	
Federal admissions	4,491		↑ 4,590		↓ 4,319		↓ 4,309		↓ 4,298	

Source: Boe and Vuong, 2002, p. 6–7. Reproduced with the permission of the Minister of Public Works and Government Services Canada, 2009.

As this table demonstrates, although overall federal admissions increased from 1997 to 1998, there was a steady decline in 1999, 2000, and 2001. However, over the same five-year period the numbers and percentages across the eight mental health problem indicators have increased, in some cases quite substantially. For example, according to Boe and Vuong (2002), since 1997 the number of admissions with a current diagnosis at intake increased by 37%, from 265 to 355 cases.

Boe and Vuong (2002) have concluded the following:

- six out of every one hundred new federal admissions arriving from the court in 1997 were "diagnosed as disordered currently." By 2001, this proportion had increased to 8.5 per 100, an increase of nearly 40% from five years earlier, or 90 more diagnosed inmates during a period where there had been an overall decline of 90 admissions during the same period.

- on December 31, 1997, nearly eight out of every hundred federal inmates had a positive OIA assessment as "diagnosed as disordered currently." By December 2001, this proportion had increased to nearly 10 per 100, an increase in the proportion by 24% from five years earlier. Among those with an OIA (Offender Intake Assessment) the number increased from 615 to 953 or an increase of nearly 340 cases. (p. 8)

Once entering a federal correctional institution inmates are assessed to determine where they should be placed. If at this time or at any other time during incarceration it is determined that the individual requires intense mental/psychiatric care, they are referred to a CSC treatment centre (such as the Regional Treatment Centre, the multi-level assessment and treatment center) or, in the case of women offenders, to a Structured Living Environment (SLE) house. SLE houses are designed to provide a treatment option for minimum and medium security women with cognitive limitations or significant mental health concerns who require more intensive supervision.

Offenders with mental disorders often experience difficulty adjusting to prison life. While in custody, they have a higher risk of committing suicide or injuring themselves than offenders without mental illness. Furthermore, they may require more assistance in the reintegration process, particularly to secure required support services such as counseling and appropriate housing. There are limited community supports for these offenders, a reality that may affect their eligibility for conditional release and, ultimately, their safe reintegration into the community.

As has been mentioned earlier, many mentally ill offenders, especially those characterized as having a serious and persistent mental illness, often will not comply with treatment or medication, which affects their ability to recognize that they are ill. They are a small but growing population of individuals who encounter the criminal justice system and, as is the case with other mentally ill offenders, treatment for this population must involve both the criminal justice system and community treatment alternatives. Although CSC offers treatment for mentally ill offenders in specialized centres such as those in Ontario, the Prairies, and the Pacific, treatment must continue once the offender is released into the community, and that is where the link is the weakest—the continuum of care. As one CSC administrator stated:

> **Administrator 3:** That of course is a huge challenge for our mentally ill guys as well ... the lack of community resources to continue the treatment regime for released offenders ... so that's another major area that I've been pretty excited about. We've (CSC) worked very hard in the last few years to try and develop community resources. We have been able to take a quite a number of our seriously mentally ill guys and return them into our communities in a structured way. We've been doing a lot of follow up and using my staff to work with the parole officers and we've even had our psychiatrists going into the communities to work with some of these guys to make sure that they have the necessary follow up.

With respect to the Mental Health Strategy, according to the 2002 CSC Performance Report:

> offenders suffering from mental disorders often require specialized care. Male offenders requiring inpatient treatment beds may be transferred to regional treatment/psychiatric centres. Some offenders are housed in regular institutions but with additional supports available to them. Women offenders with significant health needs are housed in separate units in each of four women's facilities. The Prairies Regional Psychiatric Centre also has a unit dedicated to the intensive treatment of women offenders.

Provision of even minimal treatment for offender populations with mental illnesses can be a vexing and extremely costly problem. In many cases, the availability of mental health services in the community has decreased and prisons and penitentiaries have been used as an adjunct to the mental health system. This becomes a huge challenge because although the numbers of admissions to CSC of mentally ill offenders has decreased, of those who are diagnosed with mental illness, their disorders are more complex and they have a much lengthier history of the existence of mental illness. For example, according to CSC approximately 19% of the inmate population suffers from mental disorders that may require specialized interventions. CSC provides a range of treatment services to address these needs.

- **Intensive (acute) care** is provided for acutely mentally disordered offenders (e.g., psychotics and schizophrenics) primarily through beds in the regional treatment/psychiatric centres.

- **Intermediate care** is given to offenders with chronic mental disorders as well as to those who require crisis intervention and transitional care.
- **Ambulatory care** is provided to offenders who require some mental health support during a personal crisis. Care is provided on an out-patient basis through the services of psychologists and mental health nurses. (CSC 2002 Performance Report)

According to Motiuk (2004) the increasing costs of providing mental health care, the demands on community mental health resources, the limited capacity for clinical mental health assessment at intake, the limited intermediate care options, the physical condition of some treatment centres, and the difficulty in attracting professionals to work in a prison environment all pose additional challenges for CSC to optimize quality mental health care and ensure that these individuals' needs are addressed continuously while incarcerated and when released to the community.

Behaviourally Disordered and Brain-Injured Offenders

Generally speaking, offenders who are not "true mental health" cases are sometimes loosely grouped within a category that includes behaviourally disordered and brain- injured offenders. Offenders considered to be behaviourally disordered often include those with a DSM Axis II diagnosis. Others may be low functioning or mentally retarded. Researchers Nichols, Bench, Moriok, and Liston (2003) distinguished between those with mental illnesses and those who are low functioning by describing the former as individuals who are often treatable with the use of medications and the latter as those who need learning skills and coping mechanisms that allow them to lead a more normal life. Nichols *et al.*, (2003) also described the need to supervise these offenders apart from the general offender population because they concluded that such offenders are much slower to adjust to prison life than the general offender population. The process is much more difficult for them and although they are capable of learning job skills or life skills, it takes them a much longer period to acquire them. Likewise, because they have difficulty with communication skills, they are frequently aggressive or violent and may present a threat to correctional staff. In addition, researchers such as Nichols *et al.*, (2003) also believe that because some of these offenders are lower functioning, they are often the target of more sophisticated "criminals" who may teach their skills to such a group, and victimize them both physically and sexually.

CSC administrators' comments about behaviourally disordered offenders included the following:

Administrator 4: Another area that we are going to be focusing on, and perhaps the most challenging area, is for the behaviourally disordered offender. They do not seem to have the internal impulse controls and tend to be quite [reactive]. And we have been working with a number of individuals this year where we have had some wonderful success with offenders who have been involved with some fairly violent kinds of behaviours. A number of these guys would have been diagnosed as personality disorders deemed untreatable, and we are having some reasonably good success with a combination of medication and intensive structured programs. We've been able to take an individual right out of the special handling unit and in a period of eight months, starting from the point where he continually broke up his cell for the first two weeks to the point where he is now reading books and working on such skills as exercising self-control. For example, I am amazed with the results of one case where the individual was locked up at a very early age for many years in maximum institutions and special handling units and was continually in segregation. We were able to work with this individual by providing a lot of special attention and a lot of structure. However, we have only had one incident over the last eight months. And we are fortunate to have a neuro-psychiatrist as well as a neuro-psychologist working with us in this program. We've been able to put together some well-structured plans for these people and it seems to be working really, really well. So building structure, skill building around healthy controls, and using a narrative therapy approach, and perhaps some use of medications underlies the belief that all people can change.

Administrator 5: In our new facility we are targeting a full range that will house sixteen behaviourally disordered offenders, who are guys we will be pulling from segregation pops, and that type of thing—in other words, guys who just can't seem to live in any type of normal population setting even in maximum security, and hopefully help them to develop the skills to rehabilitate. This would be through both the application of pharmacological remedies and intensive behavioural management strategies. And this an exciting prospect and something that we believe we can do. So this an up and coming challenge for CSC because we never manage to develop a good capacity to change these guy's behaviour patterns, and so they tend to get out and recycle rather quickly and also tend to get involved in some rather violent activities on the street. And some have been in custody from very young ages because of the nature of their behaviour, and so some have been in custody from the time of their teens and have been in prison for many years.

We have been achieving a lot of success through a combination of caring and kindness in combination with a lot of structure and control. And by that I mean "control" in the positive sense, by helping them to develop self-control and to make decisions in new ways and teaching them that they are accountable and that they have to write themselves a new story—a narrative therapy approach to writing your new history and creating yourself a new history. And this whole approach stems from the strong belief in a person's capacity to change no matter how difficult their past has been. I think that this is absolutely our philosophy and this is something we try to inculcate in all who are involved—that with their support and with the belief that guys can make good decisions, by assisting them with controlling impulsivity, that perhaps guys can start over again and create a new story where tomorrow they are in control of their behaviour. So that's one of our new challenges.

The challenges in working with this population have been noted earlier in this chapter, and include the fact that much more time is needed to work with offenders who suffer from these disorders in order for them to learn or relearn coping and life skills. Although there are more resources now to treat those offenders who are diagnosed as having "true" mental health disorders, individuals who are brain-injured or have an Axis II diagnosis, typically personality disorders generally do not benefit from the increased resources.

Administrator 6: Here we are in the process of redevelopment, moving from a population of one hundred sixty offenders to a population of around four hundred offenders, and in the new facility which we have been working on for some six to seven years, we are going to be doing a lot of new and innovative programs. One of the biggest changes is that we are going to initiate an approach to dealing with offenders in what is described as a rehabilitation unit where we are going to have ninety-six offenders who are not true mental health cases, but who have fairly serious brain problems of various kinds, some of which I have already alluded to. We are going to try for the first time to develop a lot of programs that are unique in the sense that people do not have to have literacy skills in order to gain from the mainstream programs. While CSC has done a wonderful job in the offering of many programs, such as those based on cognitive skills, substance abuse, etc., they are not really well designed for people who do not have reading skills, have marginal intelligence, and so this is one of our major goals. We are hoping that five or ten years from now we are going to have programs for these kinds of people that are hopefully as effective as our intensive sex offender and violent offender programs are today. These essentially evolved the same way—that is to say, they started out in the treatment centres and then incorporated some standardized treatment that is used across the country and around the world.

[Note: As mentioned previously in this chapter, some institutions have areas set aside for the housing and treatment of offenders with significant cognitive disorders not due entirely to mental illness.]

Concurrent Disordered Offenders

In Canada, individuals who have both addictions and mental health issues are known as "concurrent disordered individuals"; however, elsewhere this disorder is also referred to as "dual diagnosis disorder" or "co-occurring disorder." One of the problems facing individuals with concurrent disorders is stigmatization. Both mental illness and addictions are subject to moral beliefs that suggest that individuals with one or both disorders have control over the acquisition of these disorders, or somehow choose to become mentally ill or addicted. At times such views may also be reflected among mental health and addictions workers, as well as some corrections staff.

Research suggests that the presence of psychiatric illness increases the likelihood of a substance use disorder by 2.7 times, and the presence of substance use disorders increase the likelihood of psychiatric disorders, 2.3 times if the substance used is alcohol and 4.5 times if it is other drugs which are used (Skinner, 2000).

Health Authorities in British Columbia have stated that their mental health clinics serving the general public often count as many as 70% of their clientele as having concurrent disorders—that is, both an Axis 1 diagnosis and a substance use disorder. Similarly, in the alcohol and drug clinics and programs, the population identified as having concurrent disorders ranges between 30 and 50% of the overall clientele, with a variety of DSM diagnoses. Some of the characteristics of concurrent disordered clients are summarized in Table 11.8.

Table 11.8. Characteristics and Risk Factors Found in Concurrent Disordered Populations

Characteristics:	At higher risk for:
Have a poorer prognosis than those with single disorders	Violence, both as a victim and a perpetrator
Experience high unemployment	Higher use of acute inpatient days in both psychiatric and medical facilities

Characteristics:	At higher risk for:
Experience loss of family connections	Homelessness
Often unable to follow available treatment	Physical health problems are exacerbated by their impaired ability to follow through on treatment
Frequently experience physical health problems	High usage of emergency services, i.e., higher rates of hospitalization
Engage in behaviours that create serious risk of homelessness, criminal charges, suicide, and becoming infected with communicable diseases	Suicide and early death, i.e., higher rates of suicidal behaviour
Display greater symptom severity	Incarceration
Are often treatment non-compliant, i.e., poor medication compliance	Life-long income assistance and support

In addition to this, such individuals were more likely to have experienced a more rapid progression from initial substance use to a stage of drug dependency and also more likely to have rapid recurrence of symptoms following release from treatment.

According to the Mental Health Evaluation and Community Consultation Unit at the University of British Columbia, in a study of 546 clients in a New York site (MHECCU December 2001, Bulletin 2),

- women with co-occurring disorders were four times more likely to use emergency room services in the previous four months;
- men with co-occurring disorders were five times more likely to have been victims of violent crime;
- people with co-occurring disorders were 1.7 times more likely to use psychiatric inpatient services.

Very little Canadian research is available on the population with concurrent disorders within federal or provincial correctional institutions. However, in the U.S. the topic has been considered for some time, and several unique programs have been piloted that address issues specific to this offender population. Our discussion of the characteristics of this population leads us to assume that we can also expect to find concurrent disordered individuals among the offender population in Canada, and that they would present some interesting and complex challenges. In the U.S., for example, Lamberti, Weisman,

Schwarzkopf, Price, Ashton, and Trompeter (2001) have estimated that 700 persons per 100,000 reside in jails and prisons and that within this offender population "... the current prevalence of severe mental illness ranges between six and 15%" (p. 64). Furthermore, according to Lamberti *et al.*, (2001) this population is over-represented in the offender population (estimates are that 2.8% of the general population have severe mental illness). They are typically incarcerated for misdemeanours, such as, drunkenness, minor theft, public nuisance, and so on, and they are often held in jail for longer periods than the general offender population who commit the same offences. Many of these offenders have substance use disorders, are homeless, and are typically treatment non-compliant, characteristics similar to those already presented.

In findings similar to those of Lamberti *et al.*, (2001), Godley, Finch, Dougan, McDonnell, McDermeit, and Carey (2000) estimated that in the U.S. five percent of jail detainees and 13% of the prison population have severe psychiatric and substance abuse disorders. Similarly, according to Godley *et al.*, other researchers have found a significant percentage of such individuals within specific prison populations, as shown in Table 11.9.

Table 11.9. Estimated Percentage of Concurrent Disordered Offenders within Prison Populations

Researcher(s) (U.S.)	Sample Description	Concurrent Disorders	Source
Teplin (1994)	728 offenders	35% had MH disorders and 29.1% had substance use disorders	Godley et al., 2000, p. 137
Teplin, Abram, and McClelland (1996)	1,272 female offenders	80% meet DSM criteria for one or more lifetime psychiatric disorders; 60% were either substance abusing or substance dependent	Godley et al., 2000, p. 137
Chiles, Van Cleve, Jemelka, and Trupin (1990)	General offender population	84% of those with mental illness also had co-occurring diagnosis of alcohol or other drug use or dependency	Godley et al., 2000, p. 137
Edens, Peters, and Hills (1997)	General offender population	3–11% of prison population have co-occurring disorders (Axis 1 and substance use disorders)	Edens et al., 1997, p. 439

Godley *et al.,* (2000) also suggested that in the U.S. the arrest rates of individuals with mental health problems were 0.76 to 1.96 times higher than those for the general population. Many of these individuals would not be accepted by treatment programs designed for "pure types" (p. 138). In other words, those individuals with no mental illness could go to substance abuse treatment programs and those with no substance abuse issues could attend mental health treatment programs, a common theme in the general treatment community in both Canada and the U.S.

Perhaps, as some have argued, the explanation for such high incarceration rates among this population is the result of deinstitutionalization in the U.S. and Canada, which has been described as the criminalization of the mentally ill. Jails, prisons, and penitentiaries have been evolving into a type of "surrogate" mental hospital.

There are three general goals when trying to address concurrent disorders:

- exploration of substance use behaviours and problems;
- determining mental health issues and symptoms;
- understanding the relationship between substance abuse/dependence and psychiatric symptoms.

Traditionally there have also been three approaches when dealing with concurrent disordered clients:

- sequential approach—first deal with the addictions, then the mental health issues;
- parallel approach—treat problems separately but at the same time;
- integrated approach—treat both problem areas in a single treatment program.

The integrated approach is now generally accepted as the best approach for treating concurrent disordered clients, and as Edens *et al.,* (1997) noted, such approaches should include:

- use of multidisciplinary staff with a blend of mental health and substance abuse training;
- consideration of both disorders as primary, although a simultaneous focus is not always necessarily provided within each intervention;
- a focus on individualized assessment of skill deficits and symptom severity;
- utilization and integration of psychopharmacological interventions;

- provision of long-term treatment focus, with an emphasis on phases of intervention;
- recognition that the need for treatment extends beyond the institution and into the community;
- acknowledgment of the integral role of self-help efforts.

Such an approach involves a liaison between the criminal justice system and the health care system, particularly with respect to treatment modalities for concurrent disordered individuals both during the period of incarceration and in the post-release period. As Godley *et al.,* (2000) stated, these individuals often get stuck in the criminal justice system because they are unable to complete regular probation or parole requirements and because they are prone to recidivism. Finally, from a cost/benefit perspective, pre-treatment would impose a lower cost on society than incarceration after the fact. In terms of trying to provide ongoing treatment and support for offenders with mental health issues, one correctional administrator commented:

Administrator 7: The other thing which we started to do, which I think is a wonderful thing to do, is that the CCRA has a unique section that allows people to return to custody voluntarily and this allows guys when they are starting to decompensate or struggling while they are in the community to return to the safety of the hospital. And we've had a number of guys who have come back for periods of time just to reorganize or recalibrate their medications and to re-plan for when they start to struggle on the street. One of the unfortunate realities is that we have a lot of guys who have been in the hospital for a dozen years plus, and so it becomes a safe place, it becomes home, and our big challenge is to get them to move along. And so what we've tried to do and what my philosophy has been is that in many respects it's like kids leaving home. It is okay to leave for few days and then we take them back and ask them how it went and then try it again and then let them go out, and if they go out for awhile you tell them they are always welcome to come home, and whether that's even going out to transfer to another institution they can always come back when they need some safety and when they need to recharge their battery. It allows us to progressively reinforce their skills to live in a semi-independent way, and obviously that's where our occupational therapists and our specialists of that kind have a great role to play in helping to teach them the necessary skills to live in a semi-independent way.

We've been doing that with a community house that is at our Centre for a number of years, where guys have been released to live in a semi-independent way in the old facility. Now the community correctional centre is closing and we will be working more with other facilities to ensure that this capacity continues. We will also be doing some of that internally by using some of our older private family visiting units, which will not be required when we get our new facility. Guys can stay there for a few days and we can teach them how to take care of themselves as a transition to the community. This is because transitioning for these guys is obviously the challenge. For a lot of these guys it's the issue of skills. We aren't expecting a lot of these guys to be employable, etc., but we don't want them to end up back in our facility or in another facility. I just had an occasion recently to spend some time with the minister of state for mental health when he toured our facility. We talked about how we have to collectively ensure that these guys don't recycle between the provincially-run psychiatric facilities, provincial corrections, and our facility ... so we need to take a much more collaborative approach and form partnerships so that together we can provide the structures and support to give these guys some chance to survive on the outside.

[Note: the use of older private family visiting units did not work out—the buildings were deemed unfit and consequently destroyed.]

Figure 11.3 Recycling of offenders through three governmental institutions

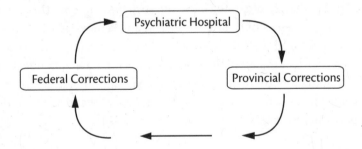

Administrator 7 (cont.): A lot of these guys don't offend because they are criminals. They offend because they don't make good decisions because of their mental illnesses, or because of their lack of skills. It's not rehabilitation for a lot of them, it's habilitation or it's socialization compared to resocialization, so we have to provide the support structures for them to succeed. In a similar way with our treatment of violent and sex offenders, it is not really that we ultimately treat them so that their deviance is gone. What we are trying to do is to provide them with the skills so that they can see when they are starting to get into trouble, when they are starting to lapse, so as to prevent a relapse. It is not really treatment so that the end is that the problem is gone. It's so that the end is that they develop enough skills and we have enough knowledge of them so that both through our own supervision and through their own capacity to monitor their behaviour they develop those skills to assist them as they start getting back into their cycle. So those are some of the issues that we are currently struggling with.

Deinstitutionalization has reduced the amount of available in-patient care required by these individuals. As the opportunity for treatment in community facilities decreases, the number of offenders with concurrent disorders continues to rise, and some may argue that a parallel system for the treatment of such issues has now evolved within the walls of correctional settings. Correctional administrators continue to be faced with the dilemma of providing treatment to offenders with concurrent disorders and determining the cost/benefit of such treatment. However, as this section on concurrent disorders has illustrated, providing such treatment often reduces the potential risk of violence for both staff and other offenders. Ultimately providing effective health care will reduce recidivism upon release and optimize community safety.

Do you think it is likely that, given the policy described by Administrator 7 of allowing offenders to go out for a few days and returning to the safety of the hospital voluntarily, coupled with the fact that community-based mental health services are shrinking, more offenders are likely to remain somewhat institutionalized rather than reintegrated back into society? How does this fit with the mission of CSC in terms of the rehabilitation and reintegration of offenders?

CSC has recognized that they have an additional role, one that assumes the responsibility for looking after the needs of the vulnerable offenders and the strategies to address both mental health problems and suicide are interwoven. As ironic as it may seem, as Daigle (2007) has said, perhaps incarceration is a good opportunity to at least start the healing process.

Conclusion

Like the previous two chapters, this one discussed certain special topics. It has focused on health care issues as they pertain to addictions and communicable diseases, mental health issues, behavioural disorders and brain injuries, and concurrent disordered offenders.

Many of these offenders will impose a heavy cost burden associated with the specialized medical care and other treatment they need. They did not often receive appropriate health care prior to being incarcerated, which poses additional challenges for health care professionals, both in the area of costs and in the need to have more specialized staff to work with these offenders. Nonetheless, it has been a goal of CSC to improve the overall health of all offenders who suffer from health issues. Although the provision of such medical and other treatment services within CSC is challenging, it is at the post-release phase where the continuum of care seems to be the weakest, that is, at the community level. Perhaps this is where the greatest challenge lies for CSC, the offender and society—the development of community resources to provide ongoing services.

Study Questions

1. Describe the differences between the CLAI and the CASA.
2. Discuss the benefits and drawbacks of having a methadone maintenance program for offenders inside a prison or penitentiary.
3. CSC has developed several programs to deal with the issue of alcohol and drug abuse and addictions within the offender population. Do you believe these programs can adequately deal with this problem? What else, if anything, could CSC be doing in order to deal with this issue?
4. Some professionals have suggested that in order to deal with communicable disease CSC should establish needle exchanges within the institutions. Do you support this? Why or why not?
5. In reference to Table 5.1, Chapter 5, how might the current political climate impact any attempts to implement a needle exchange program inside CSC institutions?
6. What are some of the challenges facing CSC in trying to provide treatment and programming for offenders with mental health issues?
7. Describe what is meant by the "sequential approach", "parallel approach," and "integrated approach" when dealing with concurrent disordered offenders. What approach would you suggest and why?

Bibliography

*Items with asterisks are also suggested readings for this chapter.

Substance Abuse and Addictions

Canada's Drug Strategy (2005). *Substance Abuse Programs for Federal Offenders.* http://www.hc-sc.gc.ca/ahc-asc/pubs/drugs-drogues/fs-fi/substance-toxicomanie_e.html

Canadian Journal of Public Health (Mar/April 2004), 95(1).

Correctional Service Canada (2002). *Performance Report for the Period Ending March 31, 2002.* http://www.csc-scc.gc.ca/text/pblct/dpr/2002/toc_e.shtml

Correctional Service Canada. *Speakers Binder.* http://www.csc-scc.gc.ca/text/pblct/ guideorateur/toc_e.shtml

Correctional Service of Canada. *Substance Abuse Program.* http://www.csc-scc. gc.ca/text/prgrm/correctional/sub_e.shtml

Delnef, C. (Jan 2001). Correctional Service of Canada Substance Abuse Programs: OSAPP, ALTO and Choices. *Forum on Corrections Research,* 13(3), 35–40.

Eno, J., Long, C., Blanchet, S., Hansen, E., and Dine, S. (Jan. 2001). High Intensity Substance Abuse Programming for offenders. *Forum on Correctional Research,* 13(3), 45–46. http://www.csc-scc.gc.ca/text/pblct/forum/e133/r33m_e.pdf. Reproduced with the permission of the Minister of Public Works and Government Services Canada, 2009.

Furlong, A. and Grant, B. (June 2006). Women Offender Substance Abuse Programming Interim Results. *Forum on Corrections Research,* 18(1).

Grant, B., Varis, D., and Lefebvre, D. (Mar 2005). *Intensive Support Units (ISU) for Federal Offenders with Substance Abuse Problems: An Impact Analysis.*

Hume, L. (2003). *Innovative Approaches for Addictions Assessment, Programming and Research in Correctional Service Canada—Addictions Research Centre, PEI.* Paper presented at the 29th Canadian Congress on Criminal Justice, Vancouver, BC.

Kunic, D. (2003). *Innovative Approaches for Addictions Assessment, Programming and Research in Correctional Service Canada—Addictions Research Centre, PEI.* Paper presented at the 29th Canadian Congress on Criminal Justice, Vancouver, BC.

Kunic, D. (June 2006). The Computerized Assessment of Substance Abuse (CASA). *Forum on Corrections Research,* 18(1).

Lightfoot, L.O. (1989). *The Offender Substance Abuse Pre-release Program.* Correctional Service Canada.

Lightfoot, L.O. and Boland, F.J. (1992) *CHOICES: A Community Correctional Brief Treatment, Relapse Prevention and Maintenance Program.* Correctional Services Canada.

Long, C. (June 2006). Developing national substance abuse programs in Canadian federal corrections. *Forum on Corrections Research,* 18(1).

MacPherson, P. and Fraser, C. (June 2006). Random urinalysis testing in federal corrections. *Forum on Corrections Research,* 18(1), p. 4, Table 2. http://www.cdc-scc.gc.ca/text/pblct/forum/index-engl.shtml. Reproduced with the permission of the Minister of Public Works and Government Services Canada, 2009.

Morris, R. (Jan 2001). Alcohol and drugs: A perspective from New Zealand. *Forum on Corrections Research,* 13(3), 18–19. http://www.csc-scc.gc.ca/text/pblct/forum/ e133/133g_e.pdf. Reproduced with the permission of the Minister of Public Works and Government Services Canada, 2009.

Motiuk, L. (2004) *The Changing Federal Offender Population—Meeting the Challenge. Canadian Criminal Justice Association, 2004 Justice Report,* 19(3)

Motiuk, O. and Vuong, B. (June 2006). Re-profiling the drug offender population in Canadian federal corrections. *Forum on Corrections Research,* 18(1).

Mumford, S.A. (2001). *Double down—It's all in the Cards: Pre-Offence, Offence and Post Release Use of Alcohol and Other Drugs by Homicide Offenders.* Burnaby BC: School of Criminology, Simon Fraser University.

Report on the Evaluation of CSCs Methadone Maintenance Program (394–2–024). Performance Assurance Sector, August 2003.

Roy, M. (Jan 2001). The national drug strategy for the Correctional Service of Canada. *Forum on Corrections Research,* 13(3), 5–6.

Varis, D., Lefebvre, D. and Grant, B. (June 2006) Intensive Support Units for federal offenders with substance abuse problems: An impact analysis. *Forum on Corrections Research,* 18(1).

Varis, D., McGowan, V., and Mullins, P. (June 2006). Development of an Aboriginal Offender Substance Abuse Program. *Forum on Corrections Research,* 18(1).

Communicable and Infectious Diseases

Correctional Service of Canada. DRP 2004-2005. Section 2 Analysis of Program Activities. http://www.tbs-sct.gc.ca/rma/dpr1/04-05/CSC-SCC/CSC-SCCd4502_e.asp#_ftnref22

Prithwish, D. (May 2002). Infectious diseases in Canadian Federal Penitentiaries 2000-2001. *Forum on Corrections Research,* 14(2), 24–27.

Thomas, G. (May 2005). *Harm reduction policies and programs for persons involved in the criminal justice system.* Ottawa, Ont.: Canadian Center on Substance Abuse.

Thomas, G. (December 2005). *Assessing the Need for Prison-based needle Exchange Programs in Canada: A Situational analysis.* Canadian Centre on Substance Abuse.

Mental Health Issues

Boe, R. and Vuong, B. (2002). Mental health trends among federal inmates. *Forum on Corrections Research,* 14(2), 6–7, Tables 2, 3. http://www.csc-scc.gc.ca/text/pblct/forum/e142/142b_e.pdf. Reproduced with the permission of the Minister of Public Works and Government Services Canada, 2009.

Daigle, M. (2007). Mental health and suicide prevention services for Canadian prisoners. *International Journal of Prisoner Health,* 3(2). 163–171.

Edens, J., Peters, R. and Hills, D.(1997). Treating prison inmates with co-occurring disorders: An integrative review of existing programs. *Behavioral Sciences and the Law,* 15, 439–457.

Faust, T. (2003). Shift the responsibility of untreated mental illness out of the criminal justice system. *Corrections Today,* 65(2), 6–8.

Godley, S., Finch, M., Dougan, L., McDonnell, M., McDermeit, M., and Carey, A. (2000). Case management for dually diagnosed individuals involved in the criminal justice system. *Journal of Substance Abuse Treatment,* 18, 137–148.

*Lamberti, S., Weisman, R., Schwarzkopf, S., Price, N. Ashton, R., and Trompeter, J. (2001). The mentally ill in jails and prisons: Towards an integrated model of prevention. *Psychiatric Quarterly,* 72(10), 63–77.

Mental Health Evaluation and Community Consultation Unit. Bulletin No. 2: *Concurrent Disorders: Substance Use Disorder and other Mental Health Disorders—Dimensions of Policy and Practice.* December 2001. http://www.mheccu. ubc.ca/publications/

Nichols, M., Bench, L., Moriok, E., and Liston, K. (April 2003) Analysis of mentally retarded and lower-functioning offender Correctional programs. *Corrections Today,* 65(2), 199–122.

Skinner W.F. (2000). *Concurrent Disordered Clients.* A presentation at a Mental Health Conference, Victoria BC.

Taylor, E.R. (2001). Using algorithms and protocols in diagnosing and treating offenders with mental health disorders. *Corrections Today,* 63(4), 80–84.

Suggested Readings

Beyrer, C., Jittiwutikarn, J., Teokul, W., Razak, M.H., Suriyanon, V., Srirak, N., Vongchuk, T., Tovanabutra, S., Sripaipan, T., and Celentano, D. (June 2003). Drug use, increasing incarceration rates, and prison associated HIV risks in Thailand. *AIDS and Behaviour,* 7(2), 153–161.

Broner, N., Huy, N., Swern, A., and Goldfinger, S. (2003). Adapting a substance abuse court diversion model for felony offenders with co-occurring disorders: Initial implementation. *Psychiatric Quarterly,* 74(4), 361–385.

Burke, K. (Aug 2001). Psychiatric aspects of Hepatitis C treatment in prison. *Corrections Today,* 63(4), 75–78.

Dolan, L., Kolthoff, K., Schreck, M., Smilanich, P., and Todd, R. (2003). Gender-specific treatment for clients with co-occurring disorders. *Corrections Today,* 65(6), 100–108.

Hume, L. (June 2004). A gender-specific substance abuse program for federally-sentenced women. *Forum on Correctional Research,* 16(1).

Jones, R. (Oct. 2003). Hepatitis C. *Corrections Today,* 65(6), 78–85.

Langner, N., Barton, J., McDonagh, D., Noël, C., and Bouchard, F. (May 2002). Rates of prescribed medication use by women in prison. *Forum on Corrections Research,* 14(2).

Mental health care in Correctional settings in European countries: France, Switzerland and Scandinavian countries. (1990). *Forum on Corrections Research,* 2(3).

Taylor, E. R. (2001). Using algorithms and protocols in diagnosing and treating offenders with mental health disorders. *Corrections Today,* 63(4), 80–84.

Varis, D. D. (Jan 2001). Intensive support units for federal inmates: A descriptive review. *Forum on Corrections Research,* 13(3), 41–43.

Xie, L. (2000). Gender difference in mentally ill offenders: A nationwide Japanese study. *International Journal of Offender Therapy and Comparative Criminology,* 44(6), 714–724.

12 The Future of Canadian Corrections

Throughout the presentation of material in previous chapters there has been an opportunity to examine issues currently facing corrections in Canada, primarily through the eyes of CSC administrators. Although there are many important topics that could be discussed, this chapter will focus on presenting issues, concerns, and successes with respect to what the future holds for Canadian corrections as raised by the CSC interviewees. In order to do this, an examination of the following topics is presented: *political/international influences; public perceptions; financial pressures; assessments; correctional facilities; technology; privatization; training issues; the issue of harm reduction.*

Political and International Influences

In previous chapters we have often mentioned correctional practices in the United States and whether or not they influence practices here in Canada. The U.S. moved from a practice of rehabilitation throughout much of the early 20th century to one of retribution and crime control driven by political pressure and public fear around potential victimization and rising crime rates. Similar to an emerging debate in Canada, the ongoing discussion in the U.S. centres on policies of incapacitation and deterrence versus rehabilitation. In Canada there appears to be a focus on community-based corrections, programming, rehabilitation, and restorative justice, while at the same time there is a call for harsher penalties, for example, for adolescent offenders and for offences involving violent crimes. In other words, the emphasis seems to be shifting in some arenas to one of *crime control* through the increased control over the offender, a trend that is also prevalent in the U.S. This shift can be illustrated in the ongoing discussions around the elimination of the provision of "early release" for offenders as well as the elimination of parole. In other words, while there is some general agreement around the need to change offenders, this is often couched in debates around the best way to achieve such an outcome.

In the U.S., themes around incapacitation and deterrence often include "three strikes and you are out," truth sentencing, mandatory sentences, indeterminate sentences, the war on drugs mentality and the use of supermax prisons. According to McKenzie (2001), indeterminate sentencing is based on the medical model; in other words, offenders were given sentences with a wide range of minimum and maximum lengths during which they were expected to become rehabilitated or "treated." Whether they achieved this or not was determined by correctional officials who exercised a great deal of discretion when tailoring programs to the needs of the offender. Likewise, incarceration had as its purpose the application of deserved punishment—nothing more, nothing less.

Rehabilitation, however, recognizes that change is possible through treatment and programming, although the current belief has shifted from the need for voluntary participation to the use of coercion of offenders in terms of treatment participation. This is done by using drug courts or probation and parole, for example—systems that are used in Canada to achieve similar results. However, there is also recognition in the U.S. that programs offered during the rehabilitation era of the early 20th century often failed because they were underfunded and poorly implemented. Current models in both the U.S. and Canada focus on smaller unit correctional institutions, which provide flexibility and the opportunity for "community-oriented treatment; upgrading of education and vocational training; modern correctional industries aimed at rehabilitation; and an expansion of graduated release and furlough programs" (McKenzie, 2001, p. 301). However, for the future there is some suggestion that the focus in the U.S. will be directed at more of a risk assessment and management approach, one that no longer considers the individual needs of the offender or their future and one that is politically supported. As McKenzie states, "the fear is that such a philosophy will set up a 'we versus them' mentality that manages offenders but fails to view them as part of the community" (p. 309). Will this also be the direction that Canada takes? Let us turn now to what some of the CSC administrators have to say:

> **Administrator 1:** I am afraid. I am afraid that it is going to go more conservative. I am afraid that the right wing people are going to get us. And I think it is partly my fault because we weren't able to deliver what we said were going to deliver in the '60s and '70s or early '80s. We didn't deliver. I've always felt in corrections if we had just a little more time and a little bit more money we could get there. But we are a system that is never going

to have that. It is only as of late that I have come to that realization, so for a long time I have been really frustrated. You see it there but you can't get it. But how could they? How could the government pour the resources in here in order for us to be really good? How could they do that, because that would say to a lot of marginal people who aren't in our system, just hanging on, come in here man, life would be better for you. Because in order for us to do it better, we have to make life better. We have to have the accommodations, we have to have the trained staff, we have to have the programs, we have to have the research—that's the only way we can do it. I'm not talking about a television in every room, and a stereo in every room, I'm not talking about those kinds of things.

Administrator 2: What we have I believe we can defend because it works, and I think that we perhaps will have to vocalize that more. What I find interesting is the Americans are looking more and more towards us and we have many, many other international interests in the way that we do corrections. Our commissioner and myself will both equally state, I believe, we have one of the best correctional systems in the world. Can we improve? I think with more tools at our disposal—women as an example, there is so few. Are many of our tools the best tools we can have? No, because we don't have the base of women to validate some of them or takes a long time to validate. We have certainly started to identify the differences, not only with women but with other cultural groups, and making those specifications that we differentiate. We need to differentiate who our offenders are. The American culture is the melting pot, but we still allow for multicultural differences and all the rest, so I just hope we maintain our own identity, but the reality is that there is some political influences there. A change in political power will certainly change our system.

Administrator 3: That's a tough question to answer. There is certainly public pressure out there to tighten up on corrections in terms of releasing offenders into the community. There are some disbelievers in parole and whether or not it works. There is of course the American model, which is much tougher on crime, but we also have to balance that out with the research, which tells us that what we are doing is making a difference. I would not like to see us moving to the American model of "tightening up." I would like to see us improve on the interventions we have available, which supports offenders rather than to abolish what we do or change what we do. There are some European countries—Amsterdam, the Netherlands, certainly—whose models are very similar to ours. In Australia the model is also similar to what Canada does. Ours is a model that a lot of third world countries are starting to pick up, which is very interesting. We had two or three staff members who actually went and did training courses in Namibia and the experience that they brought back was incredible. They are trying to adopt what we do in a structure that, for example, doesn't have the necessary funding to back it—they are trying to model the philosophy but the infrastructure is not there.

Administrator 4: For the most part, the people that we get in—and I'm talking fifty to sixty percent of them—and I'm not talking about the mentally ill or the mentally perverted, which would fall into the category of mentally ill. I'm talking about fifty percent who are cognitively distorted, who saw their father and their uncle tell them that it is okay—they like it. Even when they say no, they like it. People grow up with that cognition. People grow up thinking it is okay to use aggression, and the degree of aggression is to the degree that you are supposed to win. And men are taught to win. From very early stages, men are taught to win—football, hockey, baseball, scouts, and it goes on and on and on and on. So, we should be asking ourselves why are these people doing what they are doing because they actually think it's okay to do it? They have come to that rationalization, they've allowed themselves to do that, and why not? Everybody else is doing it, they are just not getting caught. Or if they get caught they've got enough money for lawyers that they can get away with it. So what we catch are the "inadequates" and then we beat the bejezus out of them. We don't catch the people in Enron, the biggies. And when we do, we allow perversions.

Just how far can corrections in Canada go in attempting to improve the services and at what cost? Will current political powers, both in the U.S. and Canada, be more conservative or liberal in their views, and how will that affect the way the public views crime? There is also some suggestion that what we see in our Canadian prisons are the marginalized and often disadvantaged individuals who play a lesser role in criminal activity. Are we catching the "right" criminals?

Administrator 5: What I've seen is that politicians are less or not as individualized and opinionated in their own regard. They are more politically attuned to what's going on, on CTV or the *Globe and Mail*. I mean, you take a politician like Tommy Douglas, who was a convicted individual. Public opinion didn't sway him a heck of a lot. He had his beliefs, he had a vision, and so on and so forth. I see the newer politicians as being more self-serving and wanting to become re-elected, more like the American system.

Administrator 6: Well, I certainly think that it is more on the political forefront than it has ever been in its history. There are opposing viewpoints, certainly from a political standpoint, and the other parties that are not currently in power have made it more Americanized in terms of making it a political platform. So it draws more attention and the media plays a role in that too because of the reports. I don't think we can underestimate that reality that Canadians will be influenced by our politicians and the politicians are influenced by Canadians. I hope that we will maintain our own identity. I hope that we will continue to avoid the pressures to become more like our U.S. counterparts.

Administrator 7: In terms of, for example, the abolitionists view that all prisons should be abolished.... Our biggest pressure right now is the U.S.—for example, if you look just at the contentious issue of decriminalizing or legalizing marijuana and look at the pressure we are getting on that issue alone—this would be an indication that I don't see us moving in that direction. My opinion is that I don't think we are going to see any drastic changes to the way we manage corrections in Canada. I certainly see us becoming more structured in the way we manage corrections. We are into the issue of focusing on a concept called regimes. So unless they change the CCRA we will still have maximum, medium, and minimum classifications, but we will have regimes within those security levels. So this is designed to deal with specific intervention groups within that security level—intensity of interventions or high needs identification.

[Note: the concept of having regimes within the various security levels did not manifest themselves once Commissioner Lucie McClung left CSC in 2005.]

This will certainly bring much more structure to, for example, categorizing offenders into manageable groups, but with the key goal, of course, of preparing them for release still. So if we know we have pockets of offenders that are difficult to deal with, then let's group them together and provide the proper intervention techniques for that group. So, for example, if we have a group of highly disruptive offenders within a maximum security setting, let's group them together and basically apply the suitable intervention, i.e., perhaps removing their televisions with the premise that they must earn that back by changing their behaviours as a possible intervention. It actually enhances our ability to work with that group and to bring them to where we need them, to actually be acceptable into society.

So basically we are swinging from a position of, say, the *Charter*, that states offenders will basically have this and that even though they are incarcerated inmates, and the public pressure over here, saying that this doesn't make sense. So how do we show them discipline and all those other types of issues? So we certainly aren't moving in the other direction; we are moving to a more structured corrections in terms of clearly identifying the groups of offenders who need specific interventions and then developing those interventions. I believe that's a healthier approach and a healthy shift, but at the same time we aren't changing our mandate. We are still providing the interventions and techniques to successfully reintegrate them, but we are doing it in a way that puts a healthier spin on the balancing incarceration.

Public Perception

There was a belief among some of the CSC administrators that public perception of corrections was not always favourable and there were concerns raised about the role of CSC in providing a more positive and healthy image of itself. However, it was acknowledged that the mass media and political influences, largely through the presentation of misinformation (in addition to the lack of transparency on the part of CSC), have painted a rather skewed and damaged portrait of CSC policies and practices. This often translates into a reduction in funding and programming, particularly programming identified as "leisure" in nature. But, the consensus was that CSC could do more to promote the good work that is done, and this is reflected in the following comments:

> **Administrator 8:** Public opinion is good to a point, but public opinion isn't necessarily the right thing. An example of that from my perspective is capital punishment. Fortunately, the politicians are not swayed by that public opinion because public opinion would have capital punishment reinstated in Canada. But the politicians fortunately see both sides of the story. It doesn't protect anyone. The research is strong there.

> **Administrator 9:** I do think public opinion is shifting a little bit again in terms of corrections—perhaps more so than in the past. Certain politicians are making huge cases related to correctional operations and issues—largely very uninformed cases—but they are doing damage to perceptions in general. This in combination with some of the media responses has not

always presented corrections in a favourable light. Therefore, I think recent incidents, like the social that happened in the Prairies and another one in Ontario where the inmates were reportedly drunk, potentially lead the public to become slowly disenchanted with corrections. Unfortunately, these are incidents that should have never happened. These are not incidents that we support as an organization, they're mistakes made by people who are in positions of responsibility. They come back to reflect very badly on us and it does not matter that we discipline the people and so on—it just leaves a bad taste in people's mouths. If enough pressure mounts up and enough pressure gets directed, there may be pressures to cut back on programming, to reduce expenses, to treat offenders a bit differently— take away privileges—no more arts and crafts, or temporary absences or sports activities or the use of weights in the workout room. Forget about the fact that these may be fitness activities or lifestyle enhancements that in many ways helps offenders to develop a more positive self-image, which they may not have had and which might have been part of their overall life problems. Some of these guys have gone on to be umpires in local community softball teams, referees in soccer leagues, and some have gone on to open their own stores for making moccasins or selling their carvings. It is not as though we do not have success stories, but what you hear about are often the failures.

Political ideology and international trends in penology aside, the question that requires more discussion and consideration is how is CSC promoting its own organization—that is, what is the message given to the public? What steps have been taken to educate the public on the goals of CSC with respect to offender reintegration? Although CSC administrators believe they are doing a good job in "delivering the goods," they have done a less than stellar job of relaying that message to the public. Perhaps the debate of public or citizen involvement in an advisory capacity in terms of CSC operations is now, more than ever, well worth some consideration.

Administrator 10: I am a little worried that if we are not careful and CSC does not do a better job of promoting its own positive image and successes, we may end up being forced into a position where we may have to pull back a little on our reintegration agenda. For example, the decision to put all lifers in maximum security for the first two years in my view is a questionable decision; you should always assess on a case-by-case basis. But to make a blanket statement or policy is inconsistent with our individualized treatment approach. It will be interesting to see what comes of this in a couple of years—maybe it won't change at all. We always seem to go through the ups and downs in terms of public perception, and some years seem to be more favourable than others. However, currently I feel we are in a bit of a downward trend and it all depends if we come out of this or it gets worse, in which case we may see some changes.

Administrator 11: CSC has not been a good communicator in being able to sell our product. It is a hard product to sell. If I go to you in the community and say that I am going to release ten lifers or ten rapists and they are not going to hurt you, it is a hard product to sell. In the past I think we were secretive, we weren't sharing as much as we wanted to. I think we have to open our book; we need to speak more, get our partners involved a little bit more in helping us communicate and things like that, because ninety-seven to ninety-eight percent of the offenders are going to return at some point in time. I would rather that they return knowing that they are not going to hurt your grandmother, my grandmother, your kids or my kids, and those sorts of things. We have got to empower the public to believe that we are good at what we are doing. We know that we are good at what we are doing and now we've got to get the public.

Only a few years ago the federal correctional system in Canada seemed hesitant to disclose information about its operation and this has now changed so that openness and accessibility are actively promoted. It is time to move further, for there is a need for an active effort to disseminate information to the public about actual practices in the entire criminal justice system.

Financial Pressures

One area of great concern to the interviewees was based on the pressure for CSC to provide programming and other services to offenders, particularly to offenders characterized as highly marginalized, criminally entrenched, and often cognitively impaired, while trying to adjust to budget cuts. Many of the administrators believed that the future would also invite further reductions to funding, which posed a dilemma—how to continue to provide "good" corrections, consistent with the legal mandate of CSC, while operating on a shrinking budget. Here is what they had to say:

Administrator 12: I see some clouds on the horizon and it involves finances. The system, the Canadian system that has been built—multifaceted, multidisciplinary—for example, we have nine psychologists working at our institution. The neighbouring counties, their education system, have two psychologists. We are an expensive operation. If you are going to address criminal behaviour, criminal behaviour of thirty-year-olds, who have that kind of history, and you are dealing with violence, you are dealing with sex offending, you are dealing with high intensity substance abuse programming, you are dealing with high intensity family violence issues—you don't do that with five and ten cent Band-Aids. It's expensive. You need well-trained staff. Our high-risk programs pair together a program officer and a psychologist. That's an expensive program. Addictions—the whole issue of harm reduction, the whole issue over infectious diseases—that's expensive to take care of many of those cases. So you contrast that—what that tells me is that costs are going up.

This isn't the time to be trying to save money. So costs are going up, it's expensive, and yet the Canadian public—because of the way the media has portrayed criminals and corrections in Canada as being soft places—the Canadian public does not appreciate the problem, the complexity of the problem, and the cost to take care of that problem. It's unfortunate, but I think the future is going to be that we are going to have to make tough decisions in terms of where are we going to put our dollars. Up to this point in time we've cut out the fat, we've been innovative and done more with less, but it is still a very expensive way to manage four hundred inmates.

Administrator 13: I was coming in today and on the radio—Céline Dion is worth three hundred five million dollars. I don't know what that means. Why as a society would we allow that kind of stuff? At the same time that we are allowing that, we are going to stand on the neck of somebody who is cognitively distorted, who, because of their educational ability and their social environment, have not had the ability to get out—not all of them but some just can't. They need extra help that they didn't get. At one time in corrections we were able to take marginal cases, get them out on parole, get them to work as a dishwasher, maybe they got married and had a couple of kids, and maybe they had a beat up old car, but they were living the life. Today those same offenders are now working for the biker gangs and the other gangs in this city because they can get women, they can get status, and they can get money. So they have to do time every now and then, that's the price. Whose fault is that? It is easy for the capitalist to blame the individual. Well, it's not all the individual; they are only part to blame. But anyway, a lot of things to do.

Administrator 14: I think it is going to get worse before it gets better. We are already planning for that. We know that next year we are going to have approximately five to six million less in this region than we had last year. We just came from a two-day meeting. There were about forty people from across the region from institutions and communities identifying areas of where we could cut that amount of money for the next fiscal. It is my understanding that there are a couple of issues that play into why we are getting less money. Corrections has funded a couple of major issues from their existing budget. The Methadone program … [was] taken from our existing budget. That's one reason, but the other part is the—I think it's all of the different departments are going to have to come up with—they are taking a reduction in their budgets next year. Again, it is my understanding that those monies will be going to the army. The CSC's part of that budget is one hundred million dollars but I'm not sure if it is actually going to the army. All I know is that CSC is getting a hundred million less next year.

So the financial aspect is not going to get better and we've been cutting and cutting and cutting. We've had a couple of major exercises this year where it's where can we cut, where can we cut? Doing things differently as opposed to the same way we have been doing it. I don't see it getting better.

The point that it is at now is—and there is even an assessment going on nationally—what are we legally required to do and what are we doing that's good corrections? And they are two totally separate issues. We are doing a lot of the good corrections stuff but we are not funded for it so we can't do all that good corrections stuff.

Administrator 15: I think we are sort of at a point from a financial management point of view we have to lose some stuff. Certainly, if we have a minister who sees the good corrections aspect of it, they will try to continue to fund that kind of stuff, but I think it's out of their hands as well.

Assessment

Although the financial pressures were of concern to many of the CSC administrators, a few of them also believed that there was a need to learn to do better work with respect to the assessment of needs of the offenders. This would provide better treatment/program matching to the specific needs of the offenders as well as ways to evaluate the outcomes and improve upon the results. However, there was a belief that CSC was already moving in the direction of improvements in these areas:

Administrator 16: In the direction we are going now, I see us as getting better at identifying the needs. What I would like to do in the program section, and I'm just talking from the area that I'm working in, is to get a little bit better at assessing. Developing tools that are more accurate in assessing the needs. In substance abuse, in sex offending, I think we are getting there. In the living skills component I think our tool could be improved. So having a little bit more research around that area in identifying ... we will never have—it's not like a test where you take two plus two and you come up with four, two plus two and you come up with six, but I would like to get as close to as accurate an answer as that in assessing offender needs. I think we have the programming to treat but the some of the tools in some of the programs should be better at measuring the gain. So if we concentrate a little bit better in that I think we would be in a good position.

Administrator 17: Now we know generally that some of the programs we do offer are good, but if offenders take a program, I know that two-thirds of those, their chances of staying in the community have been increased but I don't know which one yet. We could get better at that, so if we could say that offenders, because of certain things they did, that would be the pinnacle of good corrections. But we know that two-thirds of people that we put in do better upon release than those that don't take programming. Now it is getting better at when we shoot, hitting the target.

Correctional Facilities

There was some mention made previously in this chapter around the move to build smaller correctional units, or housing units, with minimum and medium security ratings that are more conducive to community programming, post release. These correctional units would also be supportive of ongoing correctional staff and offender interactions, reflective of the use of a dynamic security model, which is currently in place in most places. This "university campus-like" atmosphere promotes "good" corrections and serves to break down the barriers between offender and staff. Grouping of offenders would be much smaller and perhaps rely more on behavioural characteristics in terms of forming these groups, which may be more practical for programming purposes. Although some of the literature suggests that the U.S. is following a similar path, there is also some indication that they are building many more supermax institutions, with higher levels of security and control and an atmosphere characterized by isolation and de-personalization. This is not the direction that CSC sees itself going.

Administrator 18: I think that the road we have paved for ourselves in the future, although it may change and progress, is to remain a leader, globally, in correctional practice. There have been some rumours going around re-privatization, that this could happen some day, and some talk about maybe doing it in one of the provinces, first. We are constantly building new facilities, and we are redeveloping RHC [Regional Health Centre] right now—there are plans I believe to redevelop Mission Institution and Kent Institution. And in this whole development/redevelopment phase we are changing the whole focus of corrections. We are getting away from the old secure prison environment that has many barriers and lots of gates and officers working control posts in the big kiosks and big bubbles and moving to a more open environment where there is more interaction between staff and inmates.

In addition, like I mentioned earlier, this is the kind of stuff that promotes good corrections and it is breaking down the barriers, with the new institutions, new facilities and new open environments, open concepts. Moreover, even though they may resemble, somewhat, university campuses, they are still correctional facilities with the capability of instilling a sense of pride in those who work there, and is probably better for the inmates too, and I think this is a positive thing. There will still be those out there who believe in the old model or version of correctional institutions or who believe that the inmates have it too soft but that is not for me to say.

Administrator 19: I do not see a lot of privatization, but I do see us building new facilities and they will look different. Some of them already are, and that has caused some controversy. We have definitely moved into the era where these buildings are no longer those great big dome-like penitentiaries, but are now housing units. We find the offenders come to us, we look after them hand and foot and body and soul for twelve years— wash their linens, cook their meals, and they do not have a clue when they get out how to live in a family kind of environment. So you have six to eight men working and living together in a housing unit, they have to feed themselves, do their own laundry, keep the house up, they have to budget, they have to know what they are doing, and they have to live together as a small group. When you live in a small group, you get to experience all of the idiosyncrasies that you do in regular family life. For example, some guy is driving you crazy right now, and what are you going to do about it? You are not going to be able to just go out and slam the range door. You will have to sit down with him and negotiate these things. I think we will see more of these small groups, where they can also practice the skills that they learned through programming, etc.

Perhaps, as some administrators have suggested, it is not the emphasis on the building of more new prisons that is important, but rather the configuration and utilization of the current structures. Such configurations would stress a model that is more community oriented, with smaller, more concentrated groups of people and a staffing model that compliments this structure.

Administrator 20: There has been an almost zero expansion of Correctional Services of Canada in the last few years. I think the last facility to be built was the one for federally sentenced women at least three or four years ago. The current construction at RHC (Regional Health Centre) is an expansion more than it is a new facility. I think that in the future you will see more of that—expansion and renovations. Building a new building is extremely expensive and it is difficult to find good, appropriate locations. Expansions, refinements, enhancements, renovations, retrofitting, upgrading security systems, etc., will be what occurs in the future. I do not think you will see new prisons being built for a good many years. There is good capacity in most sites.

Double-bunking is an issue, there is no question about it, and I do not think it is the right strategy for managing offenders. Many of the incidents in jail have something to do with double-bunking. It is an issue for offenders and a stressor for staff. It is not a very dignified way to live, sharing a room with an open toilet, etc. It is not the end of the world, but it is not great and it is difficult to control who is responsible for what, i.e., assaults, or if you find drugs, whose are they … so there are all sorts of legal issues around that. It is not a direction the Service wants to continue in, and they are making every effort to deal with this. Therefore, as the population grows and declines and continues this cycle, what you will see is more expansions somewhere, which is exactly what the construction at RHC is designed to offset—the rather slow increase in the inmate population.

Administrator 21: I also think we are moving away from seeing huge ranges or huge units of people, with say a hundred and twenty people on a unit and trying to manage that, we are going to be looking at behavioural groupings a bit more. Get smaller groups of guys together. Say, for example, the guys that are unmanageable and in every institution you probably only really have eight, nine or ten individuals that are really, really the bad boys. How would we manage them differently if we could physically put them into a unit together and what would we do with them? What would the rest of the environment and the rest of the institution be like if these ten guys are moved elsewhere, where the rest of the population does not have to interact with them? What kind of program do we have in place for that type of behavioural group and what would they have to do to get out of that particular unit in order to live in the larger population?

I think we are moving more into looking at managing behavioural groups and smaller groupings rather than these huge a-hundred-and-twenty bed units and stuff, because they are very unmanageable. I am not aware of any other country that has this type of units or groupings, although there may have been a few bits-and-pieces around dealing mostly with specific populations. We have had, going into our third year, Intensive Support Units for inmates who want to live drug free. So these are small groupings, the same kind of thing that I spoke to earlier, i.e., here are the rules for you coming in and here are the rules for you going out, and these are some of the things you are going to do while you are here. We have units for Aboriginal offenders where they do special cultural programs, and so we do have smatterings of that here and there. I think there will be a more concerted effort at looking at these models.

A *community regime* is also something that we have been talking about— what do we do with those guys who are sitting in a maximum or a medium institution because of behaviour or whatever, but they are going to come out into the community in six to eight months but they are not going to live in a minimum institution. What kind of community regime would we have? We have to teach them many skills—some of them have never seen a bank machine in their life—so how do you connect them back into the community? Some of these guys do not even have family any more. Therefore, it is much easier to work with guys in a small grouping because they are all working on the same goals than to have a guy working individually with a parole officer to try to get all of that stuff.

Administrator 22: Technology is ever increasing, especially in security, and the new security technology is just incredible. It helps us to do our jobs better, helps us to be more accountable, and it makes inmates more accountable because they know they cannot get away with things if they know they are being monitored. I just think we have an exciting future and it's on the right path. However, unfortunately we are always concerned with budget cuts and may be facing a two to three percent cut for the next fiscal '04–'05 year, so you wonder where the future is going to take us. We have the right track, we have the right ideas, and we all have the will to make it work, but there is some talk, even here, of doing some downsizing. If you had been here four years ago, we had only seventy staff and we are up to one hundred and forty now. So I think they are probably going to downsize the regions a bit and perhaps at National Headquarters, but we will also be putting more accountability back into the institutions. And it is a cycle, and we have gone through these cycles before. There are some people at Regional Headquarters that worked here in the 1980s for example, when this place got cut down to a staffing level of about twenty people. In addition, over the years since then it has just continued to grow. Therefore, I can see us being cut down again, not to twenty people of course. It is because of the changes to the law of course, the focus on compliance, and we have put more programs in place, all designed to meet our objectives and our goals.

Technology

In addition to the new reality in prison construction and design discussed previously, is the need for more sophisticated technology, which will affect all realms of correctional practice, from the administrative level to the movement of offenders throughout the institutions. The Offender Management System, for example, is currently undergoing an upgrade to the OMSR (Offender Management Systems Renewal), which will enhance its capability to share data across other systems within corrections and perhaps other parts of the criminal justice system. Another area where technology will advance will be in the area of security and offender control; however, there seems to be some suggestion that the focus will mainly be on outside perimeters and on maximum security institutions. But, the concept of technology could also be applied to areas such as DNA testing, drug testing, pharmacological treatment of offenders, and so on. In that regard, the U.S. seems to be much further ahead in its sanctioning of various forms of technologies to control and monitor offenders, which seems to raise some ethical issues as well.

Administrator 23: We have been tremendously affected by technology. Our OMS, for example, has gone through a number of enhancements. For the last few years, we have been on an email system that is quite unique. I am sure we are moving toward the day of electronic filing, where everything will be done electronically and you will not have paper files anymore. We are moving more toward teleconferencing or video conferencing and away from traveling because travel is too expensive. You cannot keep giving people thirty-five hundred dollars to travel to Ottawa and you cannot keep asking people to travel over Saturdays and give up their weekends because the rates are lower and they can get a six hundred dollar flight instead.

Administrator 24: Detection of drugs is an important issue of course. We use ion scanners and drug dogs and I am sure that will continue. There are new personal portable alarms being developed that use a GPS, which gives off signals, and you know exactly where the person is within two feet when their alarm goes off so you know precisely how and where to respond. There are new cameras being developed, new lights being developed, new security perimeter detection systems being developed as well. It is a very active technology market out there for corrections—some magazines are devoted entirely to this stuff. Plus detection of weapons, knives, and different search techniques and things like that—SCBA and ERT equipment, etc.

Administrator 25: We have a lot of technology and I think we may see more of that on the perimeters—I hope we don't see more of that inside—however, maybe we will see that more in the maximum institutions, where things are controlled more by technology. When you have that, though, you lose the dynamic security aspect, and that is something we are really working toward, dynamic security. The Pacific Institution has opened up and along with RHC are both on the same campus within the same fenced area. Therefore, this is really an innovative way of looking at corrections, because you have a huge psychiatric and medical hospital in the same fenced yard as the multi-level institution. So how are they going to utilize this model? Well, that is why the intensive programming is at Pacific, because they have the psychological and psychiatric things there. I think we may see a lot more marrying of different types of concepts and models.

Administrator 26: I think we will continue to be affected by technology, but in the end corrections is a people field—it's all about human interaction, modelling, encouraging, helping offenders on that road to change and to a place where they can at least see what options there are out there.

Privatization

According to the April 2007 issue of the *National Post*, the current Conservative government is looking at the privatization of Canadian penitentiaries. Part of the rationale for this is the anticipated explosion in the penitentiary population by requiring minimum jail terms for those convicted of drug-related offences. In addition to this, automatic jail terms would be handed out to those convicted of gun-related crimes. This is reflective of the 2007 government's law and order perspective. Although Ontario had the first privatized jail in Canada, operated by a U.S. corporation, after the expiration of the five-year contract no renewal agreement was initiated.

Administrator 27: Privatization of prisons is interesting—a significant number of American prisons are privatized and there are no federal prisons in Canada that are privatized, although there may be some provincial ones, for example, the Ontario provincial system has at least two now, I believe ... and the latest being a very large prison. There are of course interesting pros and cons about that approach ... some people feel that it is more cost effective—certainly you would not have the same overtime bills that you have in our system. At the same time, there probably isn't the same level of programming or perhaps not the same sophistication in programming. They certainly do have school, and might have life skills programs, or substance abuse programs and things like that. But I doubt they would get into things like sexual deviance, anger and emotion management, family violence, and other issues that are dealt with in our system. Privatized prisons do offer something, but I am not convinced that they represent the best intervention model.

Administrator 28: I think there is some potential for a pilot project, but probably not for a few years. For example, in Ontario and in some of the prisons of the U.S. some have been successful and some haven't, and they are looking at what went wrong in the ones which weren't successful and what worked in those which were, i.e., best practices and so on. If there is enough success out there with privatized prisons I think there is potential for a pilot within some of federal corrections. I think it would be very much designed around the current model. In other words, there would still be very much a reintegration model; a very high level of emphasis on program interventions; very much emphasis on dynamic security; very high level of communication between staff and offenders; and nowhere in the institution would be off-grounds for staff. There would still be very much community involvement and interaction and the use of temporary absences and visitation. High levels of connection with community agencies, partnerships, circles of support. But it would just be managed by a private company, and they would probably get more money than some of the other private companies that run prisons because the expectations would be high, but it would be interesting to see if they could do it slightly more effectively, for example, with overtime issues/costs; perhaps slightly lower wage or reduced costs because the benefits package would be less or different—the federal government benefit package is around twenty percent—etc.

There might also be other economies of scale that they might be able to achieve through creative design, the use of multi-level institutions or creative integration of departments and that sort of thing. I think it would be utterly fascinating to be part of something like that and perhaps come back after retirement and work in that type of environment, trying to make a go of it. However, I would not want to see a private prison run much differently than we run our current prisons, because I think we are doing the job now the right way. You could have a private enterprise run the system, but the model or design would have to remain the same as it is now.

Perhaps the concept of privatization versus publicly funded corrections is more closely related to the underlying mission or agenda promoted by various corrections systems. As some administrators have stated elsewhere, privatization may be more closely associated with control and containment of large populations of offenders, many of whom are serving lengthy sentences, a model frequently seen in the U.S. In addition to this, some of the opinions expressed suggest that a private-for-profit system of corrections would be less likely to pay inmates a decent wage for work done and be even less likely to offer job training that requires higher level, competitive skills for the job market.

Administrator 29: The numbers of offenders who are incarcerated in the U.S. are dramatically greater per thousand than is the case in Canada. I read somewhere recently that one in every thirty-two Americans in the next ten years, will be incarcerated, which works out to about three and a third percent of the entire American population or six to seven million people that will spend some time in a correctional facility, and that really is amazing. What this says to me is that whatever we are doing in Canada, is keeping those numbers down. Our federal corrections population has not grown dramatically over the last several years and we do not anticipate huge growth over the next several years. In the American system they have been building jails at a rapid rate and they cannot even keep up with the demands. U.S. jails are overflowing and every year there are more people incarcerated, so something is not working down there and is working up here. I believe it is the focus on reintegration and pro-social intervention.

Administrator 30: Several states still differ in their opinion of what a correctional system should be. The privatization of the institutes down in the States has not been beneficial either. California built two large, private jails that they have never been able to open. When you have fee for service or a profit-making organization there is going to be a profit made somewhere and it will not really be to the benefit of society, I think, in many cases. So we are still watching the one in Ontario to see what's happening with that. However, we are starting to see the same kind of pattern there—very little programming. On the other hand, we have a prison industry here where the offender is actually taught skills and they actually have transferable skills when they go out into the community, and they are paid a decent wage according to what we pay for a decent day's job. Many of our offenders do not have either work ethics or skills and they have to learn these. Moreover, you do not get these by sweeping a range for four or five years.

Training

Much has already been said in Chapter 7 on the topic of training; however, there were some concerns around the current financial commitment to provide training, as expressed by some CSC administrators. In turn, this results in training becoming somewhat of a "perk" rather than a requirement for skill building in support of the application of more effective correctional practices. Furthermore, once mandatory training requirements were met, further training was almost impossible to obtain. There was not much optimism that this would change in the future:

Administrator 31: One thing I would like to see, and I am hoping we will move in this direction, is a much-enhanced training and development program within CSC. It's one of the weakest areas in corrections and we invest a very small amount of money in training. Many organizations spend a significant amount of their corporate budget on training—CSC spends very little. In addition, it shows. You get people who do not know much about programming and this leads to bad referrals, or you get people who do not know how to write reports effectively, prepare a case to the Board, or deal with a detention hearing or a judicial review. The turnover is fairly dramatic, and every time you get a new staff there is more training involved. I do not think we invest the kind of energy in training in this organization that we need to.

I would like to believe the organization would see this as a weakness. I have spoken to the auditor general and I hope other people did as well. Then perhaps CSC will see that and may decide to increase the funding allocations for training. It would not take a lot to see a difference. This could increase staff morale and satisfaction, because we do lose people. They find themselves overwhelmed—they get thrust into positions they are not ready for and feel like they are going to fail or not succeed. No one wants to work in a job where they feel they are behind all of the time, or that they are failing, or that they will make a mistake one day that will come back and embarrass them or get somebody killed. Those are the kinds of pressures people feel and this is an important issue for CSC, and this is an issue that I would like to see them focus on.

Administrator 32: One of the reasons that training is not a huge area of expense for CSC is exactly what I have just said. If the dollars for program delivery are tight, then we are going to invest the majority of those dollars in the delivery function because public safety depends more on that than on staff training. Staff training then becomes a nice thing to have rather than an essential thing to have. Having said that, though, there are some training requirements in the organization that are essential, such as fire-arms and first aid training, for example, so some things remain mandatory and you do those regardless of what they cost. However, once you get past the mandatory training, training drops off dramatically because of the financial implications.

Harm Reduction

The debate over how far CSC should go in the development and implemen-tation of harm reduction measures is one that is not easily resolved. As one administrator has stated:

Administrator 33: Harm reduction presents a moral and ethical dilemma and is a contentious issue in society generally, but within the corrections system, with offenders, probably even more so. We have chosen to adopt our own version of harm reduction based on what will be palatable in terms of public reaction, politicians' reactions, the House of Commons, and so on. In my view, this is an issue that CSC has to address.

The evidence is quite clear that an increasing number of offenders entering the criminal justice system have problematic substance use problems and that the spread of communicable diseases is on the rise. Many of these diseases are the result of sharing injection drug use equipment—needles. Although CSC has instituted some harm reduction measures—for example, bleach kits, MMTP, distribution of condoms—it has not addressed the issue of injection drug use in prison. Thomas (Dec. 2005) has argued that the establishment of prison-based needle exchanges is the right thing to do. He cites evidence that dispels the myth that prisoners use syringes as weapons against other prisoners or staff. Other benefits include a reduction in abscesses, reduction of overdose incidents and deaths, increase in referrals to drug treatment programs, reduction of tension among prisoners and staff, and an increased awareness about disease transmission and risk behaviours. Thomas justifies the establishment of prison-based needle exchanges in Canadian prisons on the following grounds:

- Legal/constitutional rationales—there exists a number of international laws and charters that are relevant to the issue of prisoner health. In addition to this is the issue of Human Rights, which has the status of customary international law and is therefore binding on all states.
- Moral/ethical rationales—the United Nations Commission on Human Rights reiterates the moral and ethical obligations of governments for preventing the spread of infectious diseases among prisoners. By entering prisons, prisoners are condemned to imprisonment for their crimes—they should not be condemned to HIV and AIDS.

Prison-based needle exchange programs are not new phenomena—they have existed in prisons around the world for many years. Although the subject initiates heated debate by both those who support and those who oppose such programs, Thomas (2005) believes that CSC will need to "weigh the evidence and rationales offered in favour of implementation of needle exchanges in prison against the political and economic constraints" (p. 14). These final words were offered by one administrator:

Administrator 34: If we support a harm reduction model, we should embrace it totally in the same manner that the community does or we shouldn't be in the business of harm reduction at all because I am not sure that we should distinguish between levels of harm reduction.

Conclusion

Where is Canadian corrections headed in the future? There does seem to be an indication that the concept of evidence-based correctional practice, which focuses on the use of science as well as expertise related to best practices is a tool very much favoured by CSC to understand and answer questions about the practices, policies, and, more specifically, the programs being offered. Technological advances or expert systems aimed at improving information systems, which assist in the management and planning of corrections, are already being implemented, for example, in profiling high-risk offenders and for performing crime mapping, etc. Furthermore, such systems are capable of setting up simulations to help administrative efficiency by improving the capacity of correctional organizations to develop decision-making processes related to the effective processing of human beings in correctional settings, and their continued use in the future seems imminent. Furthermore, the use of smaller housing units seems to be the direction that CSC is moving in, as well as a reduction in the use of double-bunking of offenders. However, there is no doubt that many factors will influence crime in the future, such as trends in crime and the ability of CSC to respond to this. Other factors such as demographics, political influences, changes in family life, the emerging role of women, etc. will also determine the direction that CSC will take. Some final words by CSC administrators seem to suggest that the future may hold many promises:

> **Administrator 35:** Society must realize that the correctional system does not create criminals; society/families creates criminals and correction's task is to take the problems that society creates and try to correct them and to turn them back into people that society can utilise in an effective and beneficial way again. And oftentimes I think society gets mixed up and thinks that corrections is at fault for these people coming back into the community and sometimes committing more crimes. It is not our fault; sometimes we cannot be successful in the time we have or the person is so damaged they are beyond helping. To summarize, one of the directions that CSC has to go in is towards a much-enhanced image, and that means we have to respond to inaccurate stories by politicians and the media. We have to provide enough good news stories to the media and the public to sort of say, "yes we have some failures, but there are many positive things happening too." We have to brighten up our image, and CSC needs to invest in training and in P.R.

> **Administrator 36:** I think the Service is on the right track. The Service is becoming very knowledgeable about the business we are in. We are hiring, our hiring practices are good in that we hire people with the right skills and they are professional in their approach. It brings us in this century to being able to lead and show the world that in partnership with others we have a chance to bringing some of the cycles that have been going on for a long time to an end.

> **Administrator 37:** The future looks bright … it's too bad the future is going to be short for myself, only another five or six years. The young people coming in that want that type, have that type of philosophy, it's a good place to be.

Many of the regional administrators who were interviewed stated that the purpose of corrections is primarily the protection or safety of the public, and secondarily the rehabilitation and reintegration of the offender into the community. Canada, like other democratic countries, takes a zero tolerance stance with respect to the violation of human rights, especially the rights of the public. Respect for human rights is the bedrock upon which all correctional interventions should also be based. Humanizing the incarceration experience through a rights-oriented model promotes responsible behaviour that reinforces the safe and timely reintegration of offenders back into society. There is virtually no evidence to suggest, for example, that a harsher, more punitive correctional model is a better way of rehabilitating criminals, deterring crime, or reducing reoffending rates. Most Canadians want their governments to deal with root causes of crime as opposed to building more and more prisons and penitentiaries, perhaps supporting the belief held by some that incarceration alone does not necessarily lead to a safer, more humane, or more satisfying notion of criminal justice. However, there will always be a need for prisons. But such prisons should not be punishing places; rather, they should help prisoners rehabilitate themselves. Canadians generally, support the rehabilitative principle of corrections—in other words, the orderly, safe, and timely re-entry of offenders into society.

But others have argued that it is the experience of imprisonment as a response to crime that may be viewed as being criminogenic itself—it may produce and reproduce the very behaviour it seeks to control. Likewise, the experience of imprisonment may actually create disrespect for the very legal order in whose name it is invoked. Moreover, although it can be said that at one time it was the duty of the citizen to hate the criminal, nowadays this is considered reactionary and distasteful. Nevertheless, there remains an underlying emotional ambivalence that shapes our attitudes towards punishment and has so far prevented the civilizing effects of transformed sensibilities from being fully registered within the penal sphere. Certainly this has been demonstrated in Canada's shift in correctional practice from rehabilitation to punishment and back again to rehabilitation, which reflects its remarkable resiliency in spite of a continuous stream of criticism. The correctional system in Canada has been equally accommodating to shifting emphasis on the purpose of criminal sanctions, be they retribution, deterrence, reformation, or incapacitation.

Correctional institutions in Canada have become the repositories for those individuals that society has deemed deserving of imprisonment, and as Peter MacNaughton–Smith writes:

> Criminals are wicked (and we are rather good) but they are not really wicked, they're sick (so I suppose that we are not really good, we're just healthy) and in any case it doesn't matter which they are because the things they do are dangerous and inconvenient (and what everyone else does is always safer and more convenient) and we have to teach them a lesson, which they won't learn because they're incorrigible, and we have to integrate them back into the community, and also

> symbolize society's rejection of them. The young ones are the worst and we must spare them the shame of being treated like real criminals. Now some of these clichés may well be true, or may well not be, but they cannot all be true at once; we shall not believe anyone who asserts too many of them together. They are rather like proverbs: you can find whatever you want. Which ones the powerful members of the society believe are true will surely make a difference to what that society does; yet human society as a whole, over nearly all of its geography and history has done very similar things in the name of the law and has offered whichever reasons happen to be in fashion at the time. When the reasons change and the activity remains, the reasons begin to look like excuses.... In our own age (perhaps it is the age of mystification) the reasons are advanced almost proudly in self-contradictory pairs such as justice and rehabilitation. (As cited in Michael Jackson, 2002, p. 124)

Corrections in Canada is all about altering behaviours of those who must face the criminal sanctions pronounced by the court. The humanity, dignity, safety, security, and protection of both society and the offender are all linked to that single objective. There is no way for society to go back in time, to correct those events that brought the offender to the place of imprisonment. We can only correct the behaviour that got them there now and may inevitably get them there again in the future.

Study Questions

1. This chapter discusses concepts such as "crime control," a shift that is beginning to appear in Canada. Are there any similarities between this concept and the practice of "truth sentencing" in the U.S.? Provide examples to support your answer.
2. Debate the pros and cons of "voluntary" versus "coerced" participation by offenders in terms of treatment programs.
3. Do you support the use of institutions in Canada for the purpose of incarcerating offenders? Why or why not? Are there other models that might be more effective?
4. Why is it important to foster a positive image of correctional practice within the public sphere and the media?
5. What are some of the forms of technology currently utilized by CSC to make correctional practice safer, more effective and efficient? The U.S. uses various

forms of technology to control and monitor offenders, raising some ethical concerns. Would this be a concern for Canada as well? Why or why not?

Bibliography

Fabelo, T. (May 2000). *"Technocorrections": The promises, the uncertain threats.* Paper presented at Sentencing and Corrections Issues for the 21st Century.http://www.ojp.usdoj.gov/nij

Jackson, M. (2002). *Justice Behind the Walls: Human Rights in Canadian Prisons.* Vancouver: Douglas & McIntyre.

McKenzie, D. (Sept. 2001). Corrections and sentencing in the 21st Century: Evidence-based corrections and sentencing. *The Prison Journal,* 81(3), 299–312.

Public attitudes toward the criminal justice system in five countries: Canada, United States, Holland, Australia and Great Britain. (1990). *Forum on Corrections Research,* 2(1).

Epilogue – It Depends

As complex as the arguments about what constitutes "crime" or how an individual becomes identified as a "criminal" are, the arguments surrounding what it means to have *effective correctional practice* seem equally so. The application of correctional practice has evolved over time and is heavily influenced by prevailing ideologies. Many of these ideologies spring from values rooted in classical, positivistic, and critical criminology. The importance of professional ideology in shaping our current correctional practices and practitioners cannot be overstated. As we move forward through the 21st century, it is important to touch briefly on these concepts and understand how they have influenced Canadian correctional practice and to identify how they may also be reflected in the many administrator interviews, which are an integral part of this book.

In some ways, one might argue that Canadian corrections has come full circle. Influenced in its early developmental stage by models originating in the U.S. and the U.K., which focused on punishment as the goal, the Canadian correctional system finds itself once again resisting both influences from our neighbours to the south and some of our own political figures in addressing rising crime rates. Nonetheless, CSC has established a strong international reputation for cutting edge correctional practices, including a strong emphasis on human rights and the use of rehabilitation when dealing with offenders. However, nothing is static in the field of criminal justice debate, especially with respect to what works and what does not work, and we all use different lenses when considering these questions. Our favourite Canadian response is "it depends." Nonetheless, much of the ways in which we answer these questions are influenced by what Cullen and Gendreau (2001) refer to as "professional ideology" (p. 313). To be really effective the ideology must not be seen as an ideology, but as an agreed upon set of beliefs and "background assumptions" that are "obviously true." The questions, then, are these: does our current professional ideology lend itself to knowledge destruction? What doesn't work in corrections or knowledge construction? How can we best "correct" offenders? And how much of the prevailing professional ideology is supported by empirical evidence versus being conditioned by social experiences and values? Perhaps one thing we can all agree on is that penology is not an exact science.

The influence of early ideologies, bound by positivistic thinking, is still prominent in some correctional practices and settings today. The emphasis on science was critical and spawned the need for more evidence-based and rational correctional practice and policy. First and foremost was the belief that crime had definite causes which could be unearthed by systematic scientific enquiry. Punishment was ineffective and at best counterproductive in reforming offenders. And because causes of crime were unique to the offender, so too should the intervention be unique or individualized, and the correctional setting was the most appropriate place to deliver such interventions or treatment. However, for this approach to be effective, it was essential to thoroughly investigate the offender, both psychologically and physically, to flush out the "underlying and constant cause of crime" (Cullen and Gendreau, 2001, p. 316). Although some of those causes were thought to be unique to the individual, others examined the role of social or group relationships and the impact on the individual and criminal behaviour. Offshoots of this particular ideology include the emergence of behavioural science units with the ability to "diagnose" individual criminal cases, specialized treatment programs, and community-based treatment. But did it work?

Researchers argued that the effectiveness of strategies posited by positivistic thinking, i.e., rehabilitation, could be measured by a reduction in recidivism. However, a mounting wall of organized scepticism denounced rehabilitation as not effective, stating that recidivism rates were at an all time high or at the very least, remained unchanged. Accordingly, increasing professional ideology supported the "nothing works" notion when it came to correctional practice. Political unrest, distrust in the government, and epithets like, "welfare state" and more importantly, the "therapeutic state" plus the rejection of benevolent paternalism of which corrections was a part, all signalled a shift among several criminologists in terms of their beliefs about crime and crime reduction. Rehabilitation was viewed as an effort to adjust offenders to a society that was at its core unjust and criminogenic. The solution to crime was not fixing people but fixing social injustices. This emerging ideology included the rejection of science as the only means to building correctional knowledge. If anything, science demonstrated that nothing related to the correctional system reduced crime at all. However, in a parallel process, prevailing political ideologies once again ushered in a more punitive approach to crime and the handling of offenders. Intensive supervision, drug testing, electronic monitoring, and home confinement were considered to be part of this crime control agenda. In the meantime, criminologists sought ways to address increasing inequities and the growing "social malaise."

But, like the shifting sands of a desert, criminological ideology has once again shifted. This is partially the result of other ideological positions, such as that of Canadian psychologists, who were in a discipline outside of mainstream criminology and to a certain extent not swept up in the shifts of ideology. They believed that the evidence supported the "fact" that treatment effects are heterogeneous and when offered using the *principles of effective treatment*, did in fact reduce recidivism. It is at the juncture of these three prevailing professional ideologies that we once again find ourselves—first, the "nothing works" ideology supported by proponents of social justice, second, the "what works" supported by believers of scientific enquiry and evidence-based "treatment"; and a third emerging ideology that supports a more punitive/control agenda.

There will always be critics of ideologies who focus on a more punitive approach, or a treatment orientation supported by concepts of rehabilitation, or one that focuses on addressing issues of state control over individuals and the social injustices that result. Whatever approach is taken, there will be costs and benefits associated with it, and there will be both dangers and possibilities at the individual and the systems levels as a result. What we can hope for is the emergence of a new vision of professional ideology that is more diverse in the kinds of research and thinking that it will tolerate. This leads into the explanation as to why we've subtitled this epilogue as "It Depends." It would seem to us that no matter which of the professional ideologies prevail, our answers to the problem of criminals and how to deal with them, often *depends* on several factors. For example, dealing with a sex offender may differ from that of dealing with an adolescent who continues to engage in drug dealing. In some ways, this inconsistency seems to represent some of the prevailing "responses" to crime control that we see in the field of criminology and correctional practice.

We end this book with a challenge to the reader—one that is presented in the Preface. Examine that which is *said to be true* with the *application of truth in real life situations*. Venture forth and use the concepts captured in this book to help form your ideas and knowledge around the purpose and operations of corrections in Canada, and ask questions, challenge perceptions to form your own, new, professional ideology.

Appendix A
Definitions and Concepts

Term / Acronym	Definition
A-base distribution of resources	The process of starting from ground zero, identifying the functions to be performed, deciding what the staffing, operational, equipment requirements, etc. are, and basically building the budget from the ground up. Resourcing Indicators (guidelines) are established based on cost drivers, which identify anticipated/required expenditures.
ADCCO	Assistant deputy commissioner corrections operations.
Administrative Segregation	Administrative segregation is the separation for specific cause of certain inmates from the general inmate population. Inmates may be segregated involuntarily or voluntarily.
Arbour Commission	The Commission of Inquiry into Certain Events at the Prison for Women was appointed April 10, 1995. Its mandate was to "investigate and report on the state and management of that part of the business of the Correctional Service of Canada that pertains to the incidents which occurred at the Prison for Women in Kingston, Ontario, beginning on April 22, 1994 and further, to make recommendations to the policies and practices of the Correctional Service of Canada in relation to the incidents." A report was released on April 1996 with several recommendations. Further information can be found at the following website: Department of Solicitor General of Canada http://ww2.psepc-sppcc.gc.ca/publications/corrections/199681_e.asp

Term / Acronym	Definition
Axis I	According to the DSM IV, these are clinical disorders including: • Disorders usually first diagnosed in infancy, childhood, or adolescence • Delirium, dementia, amnesic, and other cognitive disorders • Mental disorders due to a general medical condition • Substance related disorders • Schizophrenia and other psychotic disorders • Mood disorders • Anxiety disorders • Somatoform disorders • Factitious disorders • Dissociative disorders • Sexual and gender identity disorders • Eating disorders • Sleep disorders • Impulse-control disorders not elsewhere classified • Adjustment disorders • Other disorders that may be a focus of clinical attention
Axis II	According to the DSM IV, these are personality disorders or mental retardation including: • Paranoid personality disorder • Schizoid personality disorder • Schizotypal personality disorder • Antisocial personality disorder • Borderline personality disorder • Histrionic personality disorder • Narcissistic personality disorder • Avoidant personality disorder • Dependent personality disorder • Obsessive-compulsive personality disorder • Personality disorder not otherwise specified • Mental retardation
CAEFS	Canadian Association of Elizabeth Fry Societies.
CBRF	Community-based residential facilities.
CCC	Community Correctional Centres.
CCJA	Canadian Criminal Justice Association.
CCMD	Canadian Centre for Management Development.

Term / Acronym	Definition
CCRA	*Corrections and Conditional Release Act* (1992). An Act respecting corrections and the conditional release and detention of offenders and to establish the Office of Correctional Investigator. Administered by CSC and accountable to solicitor general of Canada. Replaces the *Parole Act* and the *Penitentiary Act*.
CD	Commissioner's Directives. Subject to the provisions of the CCRA, the commissioner may make rules for the management of the Service and generally for carrying out the purposes and provisions of s.97 (CCRA) and the regulations. The commissioner may designate as Commissioners Directives any or all rules made under s.97 and the Commissioners Directives shall be accessible to offenders, staff members, and the public.
CMLC	Correctional Management Learning Centre—in Cornwall is a major source of training for management.
CORCAN	CORCAN is a key rehabilitation program of the Correctional Service of Canada. It is mandated to provide employment training and employability skills to offenders in federal correctional institutions in support of the social policy of the Government of Canada. CORCAN operates in 31 sites across Canada and has five business lines: agribusiness, textiles, manufacturing, construction, and maintenance and services (such as printing, scanning, and laundry).
Correctional Investigator	The Office of the Correctional Investigator was established under the CCRA. The correctional investigator is appointed by the governor in Council for a term not exceeding five years, though can be re-appointed for a further term at the end of the first term. Section 167(1) of the CCRA details the function of the correctional investigator: 167. (1) It is the function of the Correctional Investigator to conduct investigations into the problems of offenders related to decisions, recommendations, acts or omissions of the Commissioner or any person under the control and management of, or performing services for, or on behalf of, the Commissioner that affect offenders either individually or as a group.

Term / Acronym	Definition
Correctional Officer (CO)	This term has replaced "guard" to denote the professionalization of the position and to acknowledge the role in "correcting" or re-habilitating offenders. The change in names is representative of a historical shift in correctional philosophy, informed by a medical or rehabilitative model in provincial and federal corrections. This is the term formally used by the Correctional Service of Canada and the Union of Solicitor General Employees (The Union agency for correctional officers is now UCCO). Correctional officers are also known as CX1 or CSX (correctional officer 1) and CX2 (correctional officer 2). Correctional managers are now CX4.
Correctional Plan	Correctional planning is a process used by CSC to foster changes in behaviour. Specific needs are identified for each offender to address, and are linked to the program and/or treatment, which will assist the offender to adopt socially acceptable behaviour. This is recorded in a document called the Correctional Plan. It is expected that the offender will work towards changing his or her criminal behaviour throughout the sentence. The offender's progress in meeting the requirements of the correctional plan is monitored continually and is a primary consideration in any decision related to the offender.
COTP	Correctional Officer Training Program.
CPSIN	Canada Public Safety Information Network.
Creating Choices	Report of the Task Force on Federally Sentenced Women tabled April 1990. *Creating Choices* proposed that the Prison for Women be closed and replaced with a healing lodge for Aboriginal women and five regional facilities. The report also recommended the development of women-centred correctional programs and a comprehensive community release strategy. This report became the foundation upon which a new approach to serving federally sentenced women was built.
Daubney Report (1988)	A Report of the Standing Committee of Justice and Solicitor General on its Review of Sentencing, Conditional Release and Related Aspects of Corrections. According to Ekstedt and Jackson (1996) this report "sought to establish a philosophy of corrections management." The consultation process behind this extensive report which examined the goals and objectives of corrections, was broad and included "judges, lawyers, academics and other professionals, as well as members of the public" (p.41).

Term / Acronym	Definition
Day Parole	Means the authority granted to an offender by the Board or a provincial parole board to be at large during the offender's sentence in order to prepare the offender for full parole or statutory release, the conditions of which require the offender to return to a penitentiary, a community-based residential facility, or a provincial correctional facility each night unless otherwise authorized in writing.
Dynamic security	Security that is predicated on a model that sees offenders and staff interact more regularly than in static security.
ETA	Escorted Temporary Absence, granted by the warden or administrator. Section 746.1 of the *Criminal Code* stipulates that, except with the approval of the NPB, no absence with escort (other than for medical reasons or to attend judicial proceedings or a coroner's inquest) may be authorized for an offender sentenced to life minimum, where the offender has more than three years to serve before PED.
Ethno-cultural population	(see also CD 767—CSC Policy on Ethno-Cultural Offender Programs). Often refers to concepts such as the racial or linguistic ties, social and religious structures, intellectual and artistic manifestations that characterize a society.
Ethics	The application of moral values or principles to decisions in public or private life *or* a term used to describe certain specific types of behaviour, usually related to a profession, and these are often specified in a code of ethics *or* ethics as the study and analysis of what constitutes good or bad conduct or behaviour.
Ethical bind	According to Ekstedt and Jackson (1997), this refers to a "contradiction or an apparent conflict between values and options for behaviour" (p. 242).
Federally Sentenced Women	Refers to women who have been sentenced to terms of imprisonment of two years or more, and are therefore under the jurisdiction of federal correctional authorities. It cannot be used, however, when one refers to all incarcerated women in Canada, most of whom are serving a sentence of less than two years, or are on remand awaiting trial, in which cases they are incarcerated under provincial jurisdiction.
Full Parole	Means the authority granted to an offender by the federal Parole Board or a provincial parole board to be at large during the offender's sentence.
IERT	Institutional Emergency Response Team.

Term / Acronym	Definition
Inmate	Meaning incarcerated in a Correctional Service of Canada facility.
IPSO (SID)	Institutional preventative security officers, who are responsible for the maintenance of security within the institution. Since the reorganization of 2007, these positions are called security intelligence officers.
ISU	Intensive Support Units used to support and offer incentives to those offenders who have chosen to live a drug-free lifestyle within the institutional environment.
Line Item Budgeting	Line item budgeting is a traditional and authoritarian approach to budgeting where various elements of the operation are organized into individual categories (lines) of expenditures (sometimes called codes).
Morals	Refers to what is judged as good conduct or behaviour (and immorality as bad conduct) *or* the application of morality when discussing the total person or the sum of the person's private actions or behaviours in every sphere of life and often describe a person as being "moral" or "immoral."
Moral Contract	According to Ekstedt and Jackson (1997), the moral contract has to do with public expectations about the boundaries within which any governing agency must operate when carrying out its practices.
NWAC	Native Women's Association of Canada.
Offender	Meaning either operating out of the community on a day or full parole or statutory release or residing in a residential centre, which is more connected with the community than CSC itself.
OIA	Offender Intake Assessment.
OMS	Offender Management System.
PDP	Personal Development Plans.
Planned Program Budgeting	Planned program budgeting system is similar to zero based budgeting, with the exception that it assumes that there are certain elements in the budget that do not change from year to year and therefore do not need to be reviewed each year.
Post Orders	Orders or instructions which describe in greater detail how to apply the Commissioner's Directives (normally related to specific jobs or posts, i.e., much like a mini job description for that assignment).

Term / Acronym	Definition
PPA	Personal and Portable Alarms
RA	Regional Administrator such as RACP—Regional Administrator of Correctional Programming.
RADAR	Reports of Automated Data Applied to Reintegration.
RHQ	Regional Headquarters.
RRAC	Regional Reception and Assessment Centre.
RTC (RHC)	Regional Treatment Centre. In British Columbia, the RTC is co-located with the Pacific Institution, though they are two different entities. It was known previously as RHC—Regional Health Centre.
SCUBA	Mandatory training for the IERT that relates to the use of gas gear, tanks, masks, etc. in order to protect themselves. This gear is used when correctional officers are put in the position of dealing with inmate disruptions, i.e., riots, trashing ranges, taking hostages, lighting fires, and officers use gas or smoke bombs to deal with the situation (self-contained breathing apparatus).
Security Classification	The security classification of each offender is first established during the reception process, primarily using the Custody Rating Scale. The security classification is subsequently reviewed at key points throughout the sentence using the Security Reclassification Scale. The Custody Rating Scale is used for all offenders, while the Security Reclassification Scale is only used for male offenders, and the Security Reclassification Scale for Women is used only for female offenders. According to the *Corrections and Conditional Release Act and Regulations*, offenders are assigned the least restrictive security classification based on an assessment of factors related to public safety, escape risk, and institutional adjustment. Offenders are normally accommodated in an institution of a security level which offers a regime of control, supervision, programs, and services consistent with his or her assigned security classification.
Standing Order	A standing order is generally a standard procedural instruction outlining general routines and is constantly in force.
Statutory Release	Statutory release means release from imprisonment subject to supervision before the expiration of an offender's sentence, to which an offender is entitled under section 127 of the CCRA. This normally occurs when two-thirds of the sentence has been served.

Term / Acronym	Definition
Structured Living Environment (SLE)	Houses designed to provide a treatment option for minimum- and medium security women with cognitive limitations or significant mental health concerns who require more intensive supervision.
TBS	Treasury Board Secretariat.
Truth in Sentencing	*Public Act 217–218* of 1994 created Truth in Sentencing by eliminating disciplinary credits from the sentences for violent and assaultive crimes, by ending placement in residential program centers for all offenders and by adding "disciplinary time" to the sentences of those found guilty of breaking prison rules. (Michigan Document of Corrections, 1998 Annual Report)
UAL	Unlawfully at large.
UTA	Unescorted Temporary Absence. An unescorted temporary absence (UTA) may be granted after an offender has served one-sixth of the sentence or six months, whichever is greater or in the case of lifers etc., can be granted after 4/5 of the sentence prior to Full Parole eligibility has been served. Offenders classified as maximum security do not qualify for UTA's. Temporary absences are authorized by either the warden of the penitentiary or by the National Parole Board (NPB), depending on factors such as the type of release, and the offender's sentence and security classification.
Values	Have been described by some as referring to desirability, or worth or importance and as judgments of worth are often parallel to moral judgments of goodness and right.
Zero-Based Budgeting	In zero based budgeting, correctional administrators build their budget from scratch each year, reviewing each area of the budget to justify costs or make changes.

Appendix B
CSC Institutions by Region and Security Classification

Atlantic Region

Penitentiaries for Men

Atlantic Institution (Max.)
Renous, New Brunswick

Dorchester Penitentiary (Med.)
Dorchester, New Brunswick

Shepody Healing Centre (Multi)
Dorchester, New Brunswick

Springhill Institution (Med.)
Springhill, Nova Scotia

Westmorland Institution (Min.)
Dorchester, New Brunswick

Carlton Centre Annex (Min.)
Halifax, Nova Scotia

Carlton Community Correctional Centre
Halifax, Nova Scotia

Parrtown Community Correctional Centre
(Min.) Saint John, New Brunswick

Newfoundland and Labrador Community
Correctional Centre (Min.)
St. John's, Newfoundland

Institutions for Women

Nova Institution for Women (Multi.)
Truro, Nova Scotia

Québec Region

Penitentiaries for Men

Archambault Institution (Med.)
Sainte-Anne-des-Plaines

Cowansville Institution (Med.)
Cowansville

Donnacona Institution (Max.)
Donnacona

Drummond Institution (Med.)
Drummondville

Federal Training Centre (Min.)
City of Laval

La Macaza Institution (Med.)
La Macaza

Leclerc Institution (Med.)
City of Laval

Montée Saint-François Institution (Min.)
City of Laval

Port-Cartier Institution (Max.)
Port-Cartier

Regional Mental Health Centre (Multi)
Sainte-Anne-des-Plaines

Regional Reception Centre (Max.)
Sainte-Anne-des-Plaines

Sainte-Anne-des-Plaines Institution (Min.)
Sainte-Anne-des-Plaines

Hochelaga Community Correctional Centre
(Min.) Montréal

Laferrière Community Correctional Centre
(Min.) Saint-Jérôme

Institutions for Women

Joliette Institution (Multi.)
Joliette

Québec Region (cont.)

Penitentiaries for Men

Marcel Caron Community Correctional Centre, Québec Area (Min.) Québec, City

Martineau Community Correctional Centre (Min.) Montréal

Ogilvy Community Correctional Centre (Min.) Montréal

Sherbrooke Community Correctional Centre (Min.) Montréal

Institutions for Women

Ontario Region

Penitentiaries for Men

Bath Institution (Med.)
Bath

Beaver Creek Institution (Min.)
Gravenhurst

Collins Bay Institution (Med.)
Kingston

Fenbrook Institution (Med.)
Gravenhurst

Frontenac Institution (Min.)
Kingston

Joyceville Institution (Med.)
Kingston

Kingston Penitentiary (Max.)
Kingston

Millhaven Institution (Max.)
Bath

Pittsburgh Institution (Min.)
Kingston

Institutions for Women

Grand Valley Institution for Women (Multi.)
Kitchener

Isabel McNeil House (Min)
Kingston

Ontario Region (cont.)

Penitentiaries for Men

Regional Treatment Centre (Multi)
Kingston

Warkworth Institution (Med.)
Campbellford

Hamilton Community Correctional Centre
(Min.). Hamilton

Keele Community Correctional Centre
(Min.). Toronto

Portsmouth Community Correctional
Centre (Min.). Kingston

Institutions for Women

Prairies Region

Penitentiaries for Men

Bowden Institution (Med.)
Bowden Farm Annex (Min.)
Innisfail, Alberta

Drumheller Institution (Med.) (Min.)
Drumheller, Alberta

Edmonton Institution (Max.)
Edmonton, Alberta

Grande Cache Institution (Min.)
Grande Cache, Alberta

Grierson Centre (Min.)
Edmonton, Alberta

Pê Sâkâstêw Centre (Min.)
Hobbema, Alberta

Regional Psychiatric Centre (Prairies) (Multi.)
Saskatoon, Saskatchewan

Institutions for Women

Okimaw Ohci Healing Lodge (Min.)
Maple Creek, Saskatchewan

Edmonton Institution for Women (Multi.)
Edmonton, Alberta

Regional Psychiatric Centre (Prairies) (Multi.)
Saskatoon, Saskatchewan

Prairies Region (cont.)

Penitentiaries for Men

Institutions for Women

Riverbend Institution (Min.)
Prince Albert, Saskatchewan

Rockwood Institution (Min.)
Stony Mountain, Manitoba

Saskatchewan Penitentiary (Multi.)
Prince Albert, Saskatchewan

Stony Mountain Institution (Med.)
Winnipeg, Manitoba

Willow Cree Healing Lodge (Min.)
Duck Lake, Saskatchewan

Osborne Community Correctional Centre
(Min.), Winnipeg, Manitoba

Oskana Community Correctional Centre
(Min.), Regina, Saskatchewan

Pacific Region

Penitentiaries for Men

Institutions for Women

Ferndale Institution (Min.)
Mission, British Columbia

Fraser Valley Institution (Multi.)
Abbotsford, British Columbia

Kent Institution (Max.)
Agassiz, British Columbia

Kwìkwèxwelhp Healing Lodge (Min.)
Harrison Mills, British Columbia

Matsqui Institution (Med.)
Abbotsford, British Columbia

Mission Institution (Med.)
Mission, British Columbia

Mountain Institution (Med.)
Agassiz, British Columbia

Pacific Region (cont.)

Penitentiaries for Men

Institutions for Women

Pacific Institution (Multi.)
Abbotsford, British Columbia

Regional Treatment Centre (Multi.)
Abbotsford, British Columbia

William Head Institution (Min.)
Victoria, British Columbia

Chilliwack Community Correctional Centre
(Min.)
Chilliwack, British Columbia   Institutions for
Women

Fraser Valley Institution (Multi.)
Abbotsford, British Columbia

Appendix C
Historical Snapshot of Incarceration Rates, Internationally

# - How western nations compare	Nation	Incarceration rate per 100,000 (1985)	Incarceration rate per 100,000 (1995)	Percentage change
	Russia		690	
# 1.0	United States	313	600	+92
	Belarus		505	
	Ukraine		390	
	Latvia	640	375	-41
	Lithuania	405	360	-11
	Singapore		287	
	Moldova		275	
	Estonia	455	270	-41
	South Africa		265	
	Cook Islands		225	
	Hong Kong		207	
	Romania	260	200	-23
	Czech Republic	270	190	-30
	Thailand		181	
	Poland	270	170	-37

# - How western nations compare	Nation	Incarceration rate per 100,000 (1985)	Incarceration rate per 100,000 (1995)	Percentage change
	Slovakia	225	150	-33
	S. Korea		137	
	Kiribati		130	
# 4.7	New Zealand		127	
# 4.8	Portugal	90	125	+39
	Fiji		123	
	Hungary	220	120	-45
# 5.2	Canada		115	
# 5.2	Luxembourg		115	
	Brunei Darussalam		110	
	Bulgaria		110	
# 5.5	Scotland	100	110	+ 10
	Macau		107	
# 5.7	N. Ireland		105	
# 5.7	Spain	60	105	+75
	Malaysia		104	
	China		103	
# 6.0	England/Wales	90	100	+11
# 6.3	France	75	95	+27
# 7.1	Germany	90	85	-6
# 7.1	Austria	120	85	-29
# 7.1	Italy		85	
# 7.5	Switzerland		80	
	Turkey	90	80	-11

# - How western nations compare	Nation	Incarceration rate per 100,000 (1985)	Incarceration rate per 100,000 (1995)	Percentage change
# 8.0	Belgium	65	75	+15
# 9.2	Sweden	50	65	+30
# 9.2	Netherlands	35	65	+86
# 9.2	Denmark	65	65	
# 10.0	Finland	80	60	-25
# 10.9	Greece	35	55	+57
# 10.9	Ireland	55	55	
# 10.9	Norway	45	55	+ 22
	Croatia		55	
# 10.9	Malta		55	
	Solomon Islands		46	
# 15.0	Iceland		40	
	Bangladesh		37	
	Japan		37	
	Slovenia	7-	30	- 57
	Cyprus	30	30	
	Philippines		26	
	Cambodia		26	
	India		24	

The pound symbol, #, signifies a Western (long democratic traditions) nation, and the number of times higher the United States incarceration rate in 1995 was when compared to that nation's incarceration rate in 1995. U.S. incarceration rates in 1995 were five to 15 times higher than all other Western nations. Chart is in descending order according to incarceration rate for 1995. The overall incarceration rates combine prisons and jails in nations. The historical rates chart was created mainly by combining some charts found in the Sentencing Project report, "Americans Behind Bars: U.S. and International Rates of Incarceration, 1995."http://www.sentencingproject.org/pdfs/9030summary.pdf

Appendix D
Women Offender
Substance Abuse Programming

Admission ⟶ **Pre-release/Release/WED**

Initial Engagement	Substance Abuse Education	Substance Abuse Therapeutic Program Emotive/Cognitive		Relapse Prevention/ Maintenance (Institution)	Relapse Prevention/ Maintenance (Community)
Transition Pre-release – 4 sessions					
1- 2 Sessions (within first 72 hours)	8 sessions 4 (x) weekly or 2 half days	20 sessions 2 (x) weekly	20 sessions 2 (x) weekly	Ongoing weekly (20 week cycle)	

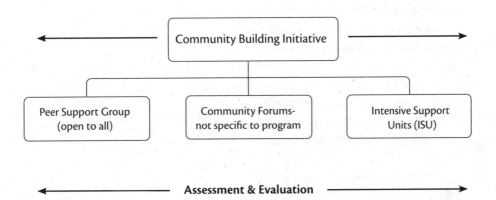

← Community Building Initiative →

Peer Support Group (open to all) | Community Forums- not specific to program | Intensive Support Units (ISU)

← **Assessment & Evaluation** →

This book's text is set in Warnock, a
contemporary typeface grounded in the
classic proportions of oldstyle Roman type.
The headings, figures, and tables are set in
Cronos, which derives its appearance from
the calligraphically inspired type of the
Italian Renaissance. Both typefaces
were designed by Robert Slimbach.

This book was printed by Hignell Book
Printing on Rolland 100 Print paper, which
is 100 percent post-consumer recycled. This
Ph neutral paper is processed chlorine free,
and is Forest Stewardship Council certified.